The ADMINISTRATIVE Professional

Technology and Procedures | FOURTH CANADIAN EDITION

DIANNE S. RANKIN
LLC

KELLIE A. SHUMACK
PHD

EVA TURCZYNIAK
MA

NELSON

NELSON

The Administrative Professional, Fourth Canadian Edition
by Dianne S. Rankin, Kellie A. Shumack, Eva Turczyniak

VP, Product Solutions:
Claudine O'Donnell

Publisher, Digital and Print Content:
Alexis Hood

Marketing Manager:
Jennifer Pau

Content Manager:
Rianna Genore

Photo and Permissions Researcher:
Carrie McGregor

Production Project Manager:
Shannon Martin

Production Service:
SPi-Global

Copy Editor:
Dawn Hunter

Proofreader:
SPi-Global

Indexer:
SPi-Global

Design Director:
Ken Phipps

**Post-secondary Design Project
Manager:** Pamela Johnston

Interior Design:
Liz Harasymczuk

Cover Design:
Liz Harasymczuk

Cover Image:
mapodile/Getty

Compositor:
SPi-Global

Library and Archives Canada Cataloguing in Publication

Rankin, Dianne S., author

The administrative professional : technology and procedures/Dianne S. Rankin, LLC, Kellie A. Shumack, PHD, Eva Turczyniak, MA. — Fourth Canadian edition.

Includes index.

First three Canadian editions written by Patsy Fulton-Calkins and Diane Blaney. First Canadian edition published under title: Office procedures for administrative professionals.

Issued also in print and electronic formats.

ISBN 978-0-17-683218-6 (softcover)
ISBN 978-0-17-686154-4 (PDF)

1. Office management—Handbooks, manuals, etc.
2. Administrative assistants.
3. Office management—Textbooks.
4. Textbooks. I. Shumack, Kellie Ann, 1967-, author II. Turczyniak, Eva, 1978-, author III. Title.

HF5547.R36 2019
651   C2018-905477-8
              C2018-905478-6

ISBN-13: 978-0-17-683218-6
ISBN-10: 0-17-683218-1

In loving memory of my mother, Barbara.
– Eva

Brief Contents

Contents

Preface

To the Administrative Professional

Congratulations on embarking on your academic journey to gain the skills and knowledge required to become a valued and respected administrative professional. As you progress through your studies and the chapters in this book, you will learn about the roles and responsibilities of administrative professionals, as well as how such factors as globalization, technology, and legislation affect your role. Each chapter in this textbook is designed to provide you with insight into the duties of an administrative professional and to provide you with opportunities to practise and acquire those skills so that you are prepared for employment.

As a graduate myself of an office administration program, the skills and knowledge I acquired during my studies allowed me to gain meaningful employment as an administrative professional. I continue to use those skills in my teaching and personal life. I encourage everyone to read the professional profiles of graduates, which will provide you with insight and inspiration on the career possibilities that await you.

I wish you the best of luck in your studies and in achieving your career and life goals.

Eva

New to This Edition

The textbook has been updated throughout to include the latest in technology, tools, and procedures to prepare you for success as administrative professionals. Many projects are new, updated, or expanded. Outlined below are the updates and changes made within each chapter.

Part 1: The Workplace Environment and You

- **Chapter 1: Entering the Workforce and Becoming a Professional**—In this chapter, updates have been made to *Employability Skills 2000+*, as well as the professional organizations and certifications administrative professionals can pursue. This chapter has expanded discussion of business organizations and the importance of social media and online professional profiles for networking. New topics include gender identity, health and safety awareness, and the importance of understanding the mission, vision, and values of an organization.
- **Chapter 2: Managing and Organizing Yourself, Your Time, and Your Workspace**—This chapter has updated discussions regarding the organization of files, paper, and email, as well as workspace organization. A new section has been included about streamlining repetitive tasks. The life management section has also been updated and has new images.
- **Chapter 3: Working Ethically**—Updates in this chapter include references to new legislation in Canada regarding mandatory retirement and disability accommodations. Updated and new examples regarding ethics have been included. New sections in this chapter relate to understanding personal values and how to make ethical choices.
- **Chapter 4: Developing Customer Focus**—This chapter has been moved to Part 1 of the textbook and has been reorganized to improve flow. Added to the chapter are the topics of customer service skills, problem solving, nonverbal communication skills, effective listening, human relations, and customer service skills when dealing with email, the telephone, and social media.

Part 2: Communication—The Key to Your Success

- **Chapter 5: Improving Communication Skills**—This is a significantly redesigned chapter. The chapter covers both verbal and nonverbal communication skills as well as written communication skills. A new topic in this chapter is a discussion of Canada's anti-spam legislation.
- **Chapter 6: Communicating with Technology**—This chapter has been significantly redesigned and edited. This chapter covers global communication tools, the use of the Internet, workplace collaboration tools, the use of the telephone, and security risks and solutions in today's digital age. New topics include intelligent mobile hotspots, specialized software, cloud storage and computing, browser settings, Internet searches, and file transfer protocols, and there is an expanded discussion on security risks and solutions.
- **Chapter 7: Developing Effective Presentations**—Updates in this chapter include more examples of the different types of presentation you will be asked to create in their roles. As well, a discussion of Canadian copyright laws and accessibility when preparing presentations is included. There is an expanded discussion of software applications and add-ons to create presentations. In addition, a new topic of how to properly present materials when using webinars has been added.

Part 3: Administrative Support—Your Responsibilities

- **Chapter 8: Handling Mail and Using Reprographic Equipment**—Images in this chapter have been updated.
- **Chapter 9: Maintaining Financial Records**—Updates in this chapter include an expanded discussion on payroll processing, deductions, and Canada Revenue Agency requirements. In addition, figures and images have been updated.
- **Chapter 10: Managing Physical and Electronic Records**—This chapter has been reorganized to improve flow. New topics include the legal requirements for maintaining legal and medical records and for maintaining records in accordance with PIPEDA. In addition, figures and images have been updated.
- **Chapter 11: Planning and Organizing Meetings and Other Events**—Additions to this chapter include an expanded discussion of the different types of meetings that can take place in an organization. In addition, a new topic is included that outlines the roles and responsibilities of participants and leaders when participating or leading a web meeting.
- **Chapter 12: Coordinating Business Travel**—This chapter's updates include sections on low-cost airlines, the use of mobile apps, checked baggage requirements, and smart luggage tags.

Part 4: Planning for Your Future

- **Chapter 13: Seeking Employment**—This chapter has an expanded discussion regarding networking, including the use of social media and a 30-second introduction; how to prepare a cover letter; and the use targeted résumés. Résumé and cover letter examples have been updated. The section on evaluating a job offer has an expanded discussion on the employee benefits organizations provide.
- **Chapter 14: Becoming a Virtual Assistant**—Images in this chapter have been updated.
- **Chapter 15: Leading with Confidence**—Leadership qualities and traits have been updated in this chapter.

Key Text Features

- *Professional Profiles* open each of the four parts of the textbook. The eight profiles, all of which are new to this edition, introduce administrative professionals who, not too long ago, were students just like you. They share their stories of career advancement and success.
- *Do I Qualify?* At the beginning of each chapter, actual job postings introduce you to some of the topics in that chapter and link the chapter objectives to your future career as an administrative professional. The job postings illustrate the skills required by employers and help you

to see how the courses in your program of study prepare your for the day-to-day duties, tasks, and responsibilities you will be expected to perform on the job.

- *Learning Outcomes*, updated and revised to reflect new content, are provided at the beginning of each chapter. They are related to the skills required in the *Do I Qualify?* job postings and reveal the expected outcomes to be achieved from studying each chapter.
- *Soft Skills* (such as critical thinking, teamwork, interpersonal skills, and leadership) are consistently identified by organizations as critical skills that all employees must possess. You will be directed to include your reflections on these soft skills in your e-portfolio. You'll find the following *Soft Skills* boxed features in the text:

PART 1: **The Workplace Environment and You**

Chapter 1	Critical Thinking
Chapter 2	Conflict Resolution
Chapter 3	Business Ethics
Chapter 4	Communication Skills

PART 2: **Communication—The Key to Your Success**

Chapter 5	Ethical and Legal Considerations
Chapter 6	Continual Learning
Chapter 7	Creativity

PART 3: **Administration Support—Your Responsibilities**

Chapter 8	Teamwork
Chapter 9	Community Commitment
Chapter 10	Effective Decision Making
Chapter 11	Value Clarification
Chapter 12	Maintaining a Positive Attitude

PART 4: **Planning for Your Future**

Chapter 13	Living Your Values
Chapter 14	Self-Management
Chapter 15	Earning the Right to Lead

- *Self-Checks* appear in select chapters to test your understanding of the content. Answers to some of these are included at the end of the chapter.

Self-Check

Answer these frequently asked interview questions.

1. What can you tell me about yourself?
2. How would your previous employers and co-workers describe you?
3. How have the classes you completed as part of your major helped you prepare for your career?
4. How would you describe your personality?
5. What skills do you possess that will help you excel in this position?

- Four different *At Work* feature boxes are included in the chapters.
  - *People AT WORK* focuses on the people you will interact with on the job.
  - *Communicating AT WORK* provides tips on listening, speaking, nonverbal behaviour, and more.
  - *Technology AT WORK* addresses new technologies and issues such as security and working in the cloud.
  - *Writing AT WORK* stresses the importance of effective written communications.
- *Key Terms* are highlighted in **blue** within each chapter, listed at the end of each chapter, and then defined in the Glossary at the end of the text for ease of reference.
- *Chapter Summaries* reinforce the major points in each chapter.
- The *Critical-Thinking Activities* provide cases based on real-life situations that demand the use of critical-thinking skills.
- In *Building Workplace Skills*, career-focused projects are tied to the chapter's Learning Outcomes to help you apply the key concepts you've learned in each chapter. These projects will build your workplace skills and direct your research to maintain currency. Some projects are collaborative and provide opportunities to work with classmates in developing team-building skills. A **data file icon** is provided for activities that have a related computer file for use in the activity.
- Icons by each project indicates how the activity relates to **21st-century skills**. These skills are a set of abilities needed for success in the information age.
- Begin creating an **e-portfolio** by using some of the documents you complete in the end-of-chapter workplace skill-building projects. You will have the option of uploading the completed documents to a website where they can be easily maintained and kept up to date to use when you initiate a job search, to print out, or to save to a suitable medium so that they can be left with a prospective employer.
- Updated and expanded *Weblinks* for each chapter, which will help you in your research on new and emerging technologies, have been added to the MindTap for the textbook.

Ancillaries

Instructor Resources

The **Nelson Education Teaching Advantage (NETA)** program delivers research-based instructor resources that promote student engagement and higher-order thinking to enable the success of Canadian students and educators. Visit Nelson Education's **Inspired Instruction** website at www.nelson.com/inspired/ to find out more about NETA.

The following instructor resources have been created for *The Administrative Professional*, Fourth Canadian Edition. Access these ultimate tools for customizing lectures and presentations at www.nelson.com/instructor.

NETA Test Bank

This resource was written by Christine Doody, Algonquin College. It includes over 160 multiple-choice questions written according to NETA guidelines for effective construction and development of higher-order questions. Also included are over 130 true or false questions, over 80 matching questions, and over 50 short-answer questions.

The NETA Test Bank is available in a new, cloud-based platform. **Testing Powered by Cognero®** is a secure online testing system that allows instructors to author, edit, and manage test bank content from anywhere Internet access is available. No special installations or downloads are needed, and the desktop-inspired interface, with its drop-down menus and familiar, intuitive tools, allows instructors to create and manage tests with ease. Multiple test versions can be created in an instant, and content can be imported or exported into other systems. Tests can be delivered from a learning management system, the classroom, or wherever an instructor chooses. Testing Powered by Cognero for *The Administrative Professional* can also be accessed through www.nelson.com/instructor.

NETA PowerPoint

Microsoft® PowerPoint® lecture slides for every chapter have been created by Eva Turczyniak, Sheridan College. Each chapter has an average of 25 to 30 slides, many featuring key figures, tables, and photographs from *The Administrative Professional*. NETA principles of clear design and engaging content have been incorporated throughout, making it simple for instructors to customize the deck for their courses.

Image Library

This resource consists of digital copies of figures, short tables, and photographs used in the book. Instructors may use these jpeg files to customize the NETA PowerPoint or create their own PowerPoint presentations. An Image Library Key describes the images and lists the codes under which the jpegs are saved. Codes normally reflect the chapter number (e.g., C01 for Chapter 1), the figure or photo number (e.g., F15 for Figure 15), and the page in the textbook. C01-F15-pg26 corresponds to Figure 1-15 on page 26.

NETA Instructor Guide

This resource was written by Eva Turczyniak, Sheridan College. It is organized according to the textbook chapters and explores the main ideas of the chapter with suggested classroom activities, additional discussion items, and optional projects. Other features include answers to activities and keys to discussion items.

Offering personalized paths of dynamic assignments and applications, **MindTap** is a digital learning solution that turns cookie-cutter into cutting-edge, apathy into engagement, and memorizers into higher-level thinkers. MindTap enables students to analyze and apply chapter concepts through relevant assignments, and allows instructors to measure skills and promote better outcomes with ease. A fully online learning solution, MindTap combines all student learning tools—readings, multimedia, activities, and assessments—into a single learning path that guides the student through the curriculum. Instructors personalize the experience by customizing the presentation of these learning tools to their students, even seamlessly introducing their own content into the learning path.

Student Ancillaries

Stay organized and efficient with *MindTap*—a single destination providing access to all the course material and study aids you need to succeed. Built-in apps leverage social media and the latest learning technology. For example, you can use **MindTap** to access the following features:

- MindTap Reader, which you can use to highlight text and make notes. Your notes will flow into Evernote, the electronic notebook app that you can access anywhere when it's time to study for the exam.
- ReadSpeaker, an application that will read the text to you
- Flashcards that are pre-populated to provide you with a jump-start for review—or you can create your own
- Self-quizzing that allows you to assess your understanding
- A Reference Guide that serves as a review of grammar and punctuation rules
- Student Course Data (SCD) files that can be downloaded
- Additional projects and worksheets for each chapter
- A Business Document Formatting Guide that provides detailed instructions and fully formatted, labelled model documents that illustrate how to correctly format memos, letters, and reports you can purchase instant access at NELSONbrain.com.

What's NEW in MindTap?

MindTap for the fourth Canadian edition of The Administrative Professional features an expanded quiz bank and a variety of engaging simulations and projects that help students develop the skills that employers are looking for. Some projects are automatically graded in MindTap, and rubrics are provided for those projects that require manual grading. Examples of new simulations and projects include:

- Minute-taking video assignment
- Career goal reflection exercise
- Outlook prioritization project
- Ethics exercises featuring video, audio and email scenarios
- Dictation exercise
- Telephone instruction exercises
- Financial records assignments
- Scanning, mail sorting and mailing simulation
- Presentation development exercises
- New Cool Tools
- Reflective Essays for each chapter
- Leadership style quiz

Visit nelson.com/student to start using MindTap. Enter the Online Access Code from the card included with your textbook. If a code card is not provided, you can purchase instant access at NELSONbrain.com.

Acknowledgments for the Fourth Canadian Edition

I would like to begin by acknowledging Diane Blaney who authored the first three Canadian editions of this textbook. Thank you for your hard work and dedication to this project over the years. I am tremendously honoured to have been asked to continue with this project and update the fourth edition for the Canadian market. I would also like to thank all of the individuals who helped contribute to make this textbook and accompanying MindTap site current and up to date.

First, thank you to the talented and dedicated staff at Nelson Education: Alexis Hood, publisher, and Rianna Genore, content manager, for their support and encouragement along the way. Thank you to Dawn Hunter, a very skilled copy editor, and to Dylan Schoenmakers and Megan Watcher for their substantive edits. Also, thank you to Daniela Glass and Carrie McGregor for obtaining permissions to images to enhance the content; to Shannon Martin for her attention to detail in the content production phase; and to Jennifer Pau and her marketing team for bringing the final product to you.

Thank you also go to the following reviewers and users who provided valuable feedback through their in-depth and thoughtful comments and suggestions:

Christine Doody, Algonquin College

Dina Galanis, Durham College

Amy Gleiser, Conestoga College

Kellie Hayward, Sheridan Institute of Technology and Advanced Learning

Sheri Mankal, Fanshawe College

Janette O'Neill-Scott, Georgian College

Shannon Winterstein, Centennial College

Judy Woolridge, New Brunswick Community College

About The Authors

Dianne S. Rankin is an author, consulting editor, and developer of instructional materials for textbooks, websites, and ancillaries for education publishers. Dianne has taught at the high school and community college levels and continues to teach computer classes for businesses and organizations. She has presented at many professional conferences and has been active in the National Business Education Association and Delta Pi Epsilon. In addition, Dianne has had first-hand experience as an administrative assistant.

Kellie A. Shumack is an associate professor of instructional technology and department head of Curriculum, Instruction, and Technology in the College of Education and Auburn University at Montgomery. She has worked as an administrative assistant in the past and has taught for over 20 years at the secondary, community college, or university levels. Kellie has designed and taught numerous college courses, both in the online and face-to-face environments. She has written multiple peer-reviewed journal articles, two textbooks, and several book chapters and has presented at over 40 professional conferences. Kellie was awarded the 2012 Auburn Montgomery College of Education Excellent in Teaching Award and the 2010 Delta Pi Epsilon Outstanding Doctoral Research Award.

Eva Turczyniak joined Sheridan College in 2004 as a professor in the Pilon School of Business. Her teaching experience includes delivering a variety of courses in the office administration, legal, executive, and general programs, as well as the business diploma programs. During her time at Sheridan, Eva has developed a number of courses in different teaching formats (hybrid, face to face, and flipped). Her industry experience includes over 10 years working as a legal administrative assistant for law firms in Brantford and Toronto. Eva's educational credentials include a legal office administration diploma and a law clerk certificate from Sheridan College, as well as an Honours BA in sociology and an MA in labour studies from McMaster University.

Introducing *The Administrative Professional: Technology and Procedures*, 4ce

This edition is sharp and focused! It targets the skills and best practices needed by successful administrative professionals. The basic elements that have made *The Administrative Professional* the market leader are retained, while adding new and updated information and activities.

PART 1

The Workplace Environment and You

Chapter 1	Entering the Workforce and Becoming a Professional
Chapter 2	Managing and Organizing Yourself, Your Time, and Your Workspace
Chapter 3	Working Ethically
Chapter 4	Developing Customer Focus

In Part 1 of the text, you are introduced to the challenging world of office administration and the use of telecommunications equipment and services that are an integral component of most business transactions. You will learn about different organizational structures and the management of business and organizations, and identify what makes an organization ethical. The qualities associated with being a professional, such as maintaining a professional image through appearance, good communication and teamwork skills, and the employability skills that will be expected of you as a new employee, along with your responsibility to your employer—and theirs to you—are presented. Working ethically as an administrative professional and some steps to take in making ethical choices are outlined. You will discover methods for managing your workload, strategies for prioritizing and adjusting priorities as needed, and different approaches to managing relationships, handling stress, and maintaining a healthy work/life balance. The concept of ergonomics is introduced and guidelines are provided to help you create a safe and healthy physical workspace that reduces the risk of repetitive stress injury. Also provided are several tips on keeping a neat, well-organized, and professional-looking work area so that you can work efficiently. You will also understand the importance of customer focus, develop skills for providing effective customer service, and describe how to handle difficult customer service situations. You are entering a diverse workforce and this first part of the text will help ensure your entry into the workplace is a positive one.

2 · NEL

Part Opener

Professional Profiles provide inspiration on part opener pages. The chapters in each part are also listed.

Sheridan
Courtesy of Sheridan College

Jessica Freitas
Recruitment Coordinator

My name is Jessica Freitas, and after high school, I wasn't sure I knew what I wanted to do as a career. However, I had a knack for organization and enjoyed several aspects of the law, so it made sense to start my educational journey with the office administration—legal diploma program at Sheridan College.

I began my career as a floater, legal assistant and a few months into the new role was offered a dual role as an overflow legal assistant and backup for my manager. This role is where I developed my passion for human resources.

I decided to enroll in the human resources management certificate program at Sheridan College, which helped enhance my skills.

Currently, I am a recruitment coordinator for a professional service firm. It has offered me unlimited career growth potential. I'm in love with my job, the work I do, and the people I work with!

A challenge I have found in my career is that no matter how hard companies try to make processes and policies "black and white" there is always a large grey area. Learning to work within that grey can make or break your success.

What I find extremely rewarding is constantly learning something new and the feeling of accomplishment and pride when I find the right person for the role.

Text and photo courtesy of Jessica Freitas

A real job posting will show you examples of what in-demand skills employers will be looking for when you start your job search.

Do I Qualify?

Legal Administrative Assistant

As a national law firm, we are looking for a legal administrative assistant to support our corporate team by performing advanced, diversified, and confidential administrative duties, which include the following:

- drafting correspondence, documents, and pleadings
- interacting with clients, medical professionals, insurance adjusters, and opposing counsel
- posting time sheets and disbursements to client accounts

The successful applicant will have excellent English oral and written skills; be organized; and be able to prioritize work, take direction, and ask appropriate questions. You will be proficient in Microsoft Office applications and familiar with billing in a law office.

Career-focused Features Deliver a Dynamic and Real-World Perspective

Communicating AT WORK

Have you ever had this experience? You walk into a store and one employee stands out. That person gives you his or her full attention, walks with you to the section of the store you are looking for, and smiles at you if you happen to meet again. That employee is a professional.

Professionalism comprises numerous qualities and skills, including good judgment, initiative, discretion, organi-

Communicating AT WORK provides tips on listening, speaking, nonverbal behaviour, and more.

People AT WORK

Canada is composed of a mosaic of different cultures, races, and ethnicities. As you work in this diverse workplace, be aware of and sensitive to the various cultural differences and backgrounds of the people with whom you work, and understand that individuals, because of their different backgrounds, may view situations differently. Your openness to

People AT WORK focuses on the people you will interact with on the job.

Technology AT WORK

Using social media, such as Facebook and Instagram, is a personal activity that also impacts your professional life. The lines that once clearly defined and separated work life from personal life are now blurred by online social media. You must also be aware of your professional appearance on social networking sites such as LinkedIn.

Technology AT WORK addresses new technologies and issues such as security and working in the cloud.

Writing AT WORK

The Partnership for 21st Century Skills, a national organization of businesses and nonprofit organizations, has identified knowledge and skills it considers essential for success at work and in life. The partnership has set these standards for communicating clearly:
- Express thoughts and ideas effectively in different forms and contexts.

Writing AT WORK stresses the Importance of effective written communication.

Soft Skills relate to personal attributes, traits, and communication skills that enable individuals to be successful in their careers. At the end of each chapter, a new soft skill is introduced and explained.

Soft Skills — CRITICAL THINKING

Critical thinking can be defined as "a unique kind of purposeful thinking in which the thinker systematically chooses conscious and deliberate inquiry." *Critical* comes from the Greek word *krinein*, which means "to separate, to choose." When we think critically about a subject, we try to see it from all sides before coming to a conclusion. Critical thinking requires us to see things from perspectives other than our own and to consider the possible consequences of the positions we take.

A critical thinker does the following:

- **Describes the real issue.** Before you can solve a problem, you must be able to recognize the real problem and describe it. Break a large problem into smaller parts to help determine the main problem.
- **Distinguishes between facts and opinion.** Ask yourself whether what a person asserts as fact really *is* fact.

- **Recognizes bias.** A person who is biased can't judge something impartially because of a personal preference. Try to put aside your own preferences and look at an issue objectively. You must also look for signs of bias when you consider others' opinions.
- **Asks questions and keeps an open mind.** Stay open to new ideas and different points of view.
- **Weighs new information.** Evaluate information—and its sources—before accepting it as true.
- **Considers implications and possibilities.** Assess whether the new evidence means that you should adjust your conclusions.
- **Supports opinion with evidence.** Do not expect your opinions to be accepted without support. Explain the logical reasons for your conclusions.

End-of-Chapter Questions, Exercises, and Activities Bring it All Together...

Chapter Summary

The summary will help you remember the important points covered in this chapter.

- Time is a unique resource; it cannot be bought, sold, borrowed, rented, saved, or manufactured. It is the only resource that must be spent the minute it is received.
- Time wasters include ineffective communication, poor telephone usage, inadequate planning, interruptions, disorganization, and procrastination.
- Good time management techniques include analyzing how we use our time and establishing effective routines.
- Time management systems, such as calendars and PIM software, can help us manage ourselves in relation to our time.
- Stress is the body's response to a demand placed upon it. Chronic stress occurs when a distressful situation is prolonged, allowing no rest or recuperation for the body.
- Stress reducers include balancing work and play, knowing the difference between achievement and perfection, recognizing limits, exercising, eating right, getting enough sleep, and managing anger and time.
- Anger is a growing corporate problem; incidences of violence in the workplace have increased.

Key Terms

carpal tunnel syndrome p. 31
chronic stress p. 32
computer vision syndrome p. 31
conflict resolution p. 33
downsize p. 32
empathy p. 34
ergonomics p. 30
goal p. 23

PIM (personal information management) p. 26
priority p. 25
procrastination p. 28
rightsize p. 32
RSI (repetitive stress injury) p. 31
stress p. 32
time p. 23
time management p. 23

Discussion Items

These discussion items provide an opportunity to test your understanding of the chapter through written responses and discussion with your classmates and your instructor.

1. Identify and describe five time wasters.
2. What is PIM software, and how can it help you manage your time?
3. What is meant by ergonomics? Give five ergonomic guidelines to follow to avoid RSIs when establishing a new workstation or adapting an existing workstation.
4. What is stress, and what causes it? Identify three ways of managing stress.
5. Is all stress unhealthy? Explain your answer.
6. List and explain ways you can manage your stress.

Critical-Thinking Activity

Keri-An Mahar has worked in human resources at CanAsian for five years. She is in charge of employee benefits. Keri-An is an excellent employee—very competent, knowledgeable about human resources (she holds an MBA, with a specialty in management), loyal, dependable, and respected by her colleagues. Two years ago, a new vice-president of human resources was hired. Keri-An has tried to work with him, but the situation does not seem to improve; in fact, it worsens. He gives her inadequate information. He asks her at the last minute to prepare reports. He lies to her about company policies and directions. Then, he yells at her about violating the directions of the company. On several occa-

happen. She has talked with him repeatedly about the issues from her perspective. He seems to listen but never responds. He has never complained about her performance; she believes he is satisfied with her work. Keri-An has considered leaving the job; however, she has two more years until she is vested in the retirement system. If she leaves now, she loses all of her retirement benefits. Recently, Keri-An began to have health problems. She went to her physician, who said her illness was the result of stress. He recommended that she take at least three months off. Keri-An did so. The three months have passed, and Keri-An is ready to come back to work.

21st Century Skills

 Life and Career Skills   Learning and Innovation Skills   Information, Media, and Technology Skills   Data

Building Workplace Skills

Project 2-1 (Learning Outcomes 1 and 2)

To access the MindTap site, use the printed access card on the inside cover of your textbook. Student Course Data file Project 2-1a is a screen in your PIM software, and file Project 2-1b is an email message from Martin Albertson. After considering both of these documents, put your task list in priority order, adding the necessary items from Martin Albertson's memo. Assign each task one of four categories: "Urgent and Important," "Important but Not Urgent," "Urgent but Not Important," and "Neither Urgent nor Important." Then rank each task in the categories by assigning a 1, 2, 3, etc., to each item to place it in order within each category. This number will indicate the order in which you should proceed to work on the items. Submit your new prioritized task list to your instructor.

If available, use Outlook or another calendar software to complete this project by first entering the details from the screen image into your calendar. Next, update the calendar with the details provided in the memo. Your instructor will provide specific submission instructions.

Project 2-2 (Learning Outcome 1)

In your work with Martin Albertson, you have shared access to his planner to update his contacts and schedule. He hands you four business cards that he received at the recent national marketing conference he attended in Ottawa and asks you to enter them.

While he was out of town, you received several requests for appointments. After discussing the requests with him and receiving his approval, you enter them into his schedule.

Two data files are to be used to complete this project. The file Project 2-2a, a PDF file, contains the business cards;

the file Project 2-2b, a list of appointments. Using Outlook or another calendar software, complete all entries and make any revisions that arise because of conflicts. Prepare the contact list and a copy of the calendar in monthly format, and submit both to your instructor.

Project 2-3 (Learning Outcome 1)

On the MindTap site, file Project 2-3a is a time log form. Print out or create a page for each of the next five days. Use the hard copy forms or create a document to log the time you spend on various activities. If you are a student and employed, log the time you spend on school, part-time work, and personal activities. If you are not employed, log the time you spend on school and personal activities. Create as realistic a picture as possible.

After you finish that part of the project, analyze the way you spent your time during the five days. File Project 2-3b contains questions to help you. File Project 2-3c contains a Time Effectiveness Questionnaire, which provides general questions concerning the use of time. Respond to these items. After you have analyzed the way you use your time and considered your answers to the Time Effectiveness Questionnaire, prepare an action plan using the form in file Project 2-3d. Indicate how you will make more effective use of your time. Submit a copy of your action plan to your instructor.

Project 2-4 (Learning Outcomes 4 and 6)

A friend of yours, Indra, works in an office in your building. She is having problems. Her situation is described in file Project 2-4. Analyze her case. Follow your instructor's directions to respond to the questions following the case description. You may use the memorandum form file Project 2-4a or some other document as directed by your instructor to submit your responses.

Chapter Summary, Key Terms, Discussion Items, Critical Thinking Activity reinforce major points in each chapter.

Building Workplace Skills projects correlate to learning outcomes and 21st Century Skills

MindTap for The Administrative Professional

MindTap is a personalized teaching experience with relevant assignments that guide
students to analyze, apply, and improve thinking, allowing you to measure skills and
outcomes with ease.

- **Personalized Teaching:** Becomes yours with a Learning Path that is built with
- key student objectives. Control what students see and when they see it. Use it as-is or
- match to your syllabus exactly—hide, rearrange, add, and create your own content.

- **Guide Students:** A unique learning path of relevant readings, multimedia, and
- activities that move students up the learning taxonomy from basic knowledge and
- comprehension to analysis and application.
- **Promote Better Outcomes:** Empower instructors and motivate students with
- analytics and reports that provide a snapshot of class progress, time in course,
- engagement, and completion rates.

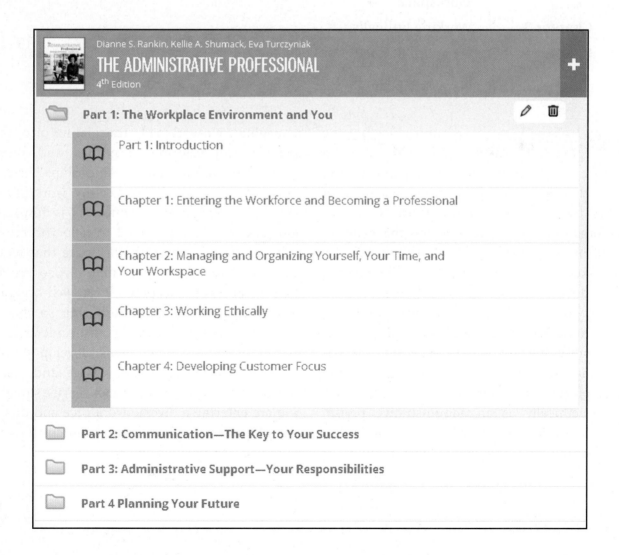

PART 1

The Workplace Environment and You

In Part 1 of the text, you are introduced to the challenging world of office administration and the use of telecommunications equipment and services that are an integral component of most business transactions. You will learn about different organizational structures and the management of business and organizations, and identify what makes an organization ethical. The qualities associated with being a professional, such as maintaining a professional image through appearance, good communication and teamwork skills, and the employability skills that will be expected of you as a new employee, along with your responsibility to your employer—and theirs to you—are presented. Working ethically as an administrative professional and some steps to take in making ethical choices are outlined. You will discover methods for managing your workload, strategies for prioritizing and adjusting priorities as needed, and different approaches to managing relationships, handling stress, and maintaining a healthy work/life balance. The concept of ergonomics is introduced and guidelines are provided to help you create a safe and healthy physical workspace that reduces the risk of repetitive stress injury. Also provided are several tips on keeping a neat, well-organized, and professional-looking work area so that you can work efficiently. You will also understand the importance of customer focus, develop skills for providing effective customer service, and describe how to handle difficult customer service situations. You are entering a diverse workforce and this first part of the text will help ensure your entry into the workplace is a positive one.

Sheridan
Courtesy of Sheridan College

Jessica Freitas
Recruitment Coordinator

My name is Jessica Freitas, and after high school, I wasn't sure I knew what I wanted to do as a career. However, I had a knack for organization and enjoyed several aspects of the law, so it made sense to start my educational journey with the office administration—legal diploma program at Sheridan College.

I began my career as a floater, legal assistant and a few months into the new role was offered a dual role as an overflow legal assistant and backup for my manager. This role is where I developed my passion for human resources.

I decided to enroll in the human resources management certificate program at Sheridan College, which helped enhance my skills.

Currently, I am a recruitment coordinator for a professional service firm. It has offered me unlimited career growth potential. I'm in love with my job, the work I do, and the people I work with!

A challenge I have found in my career is that no matter how hard companies try to make processes and policies "black and white" there is always a large grey area. Learning to work within that grey can make or break your success.

What I find extremely rewarding is constantly learning something new and the feeling of accomplishment and pride when I find the right person for the role.

Courtesy of Southern Alberta Institute of Technology (SAIT)

SAIT

Kathie Shand
Product Development Specialist, United Way of Calgary and Area

My name is Kathie Shand, and I am a product development specialist at the United Way of Calgary and Area. I attended the University of Lethbridge right after high school, with little career direction. Two years and almost 20 courses later, I felt the need for a change. I decided to enroll in the Southern Alberta Institute of Technology's administrative information management diploma program, where the inclusive culture and relevant courses enabled me to thrive.

After graduation, I began working as the administrative assistant to the president of a natural gas company. I soon moved on to another role at the same company, where I coordinated the transportation of natural gas. But I began to realize that I didn't have a real interest in the oil and gas sector, and I eventually got tired of doing something that didn't make me happy.

In May 2016, I began working as an administrative assistant at United Way of Calgary and Area. By January 2017, my role had expanded to administrative coordinator, then to program coordinator.

When a product development specialist position opened up, I saw this as a great growth opportunity.

It feels very rewarding to know that I am contributing to the work of a community impact organization and to be supported by an organization that really cares about the development and growth of its employees.

CHAPTER 1

Entering the Workforce and Becoming a Professional

LEARNING OUTCOMES

After studying this chapter, you should be able to

1. Describe the changing work environment.
2. Identify and describe the types of business organizations and workplace structures.
3. Describe the roles and responsibilities of the administrative professional.
4. Apply critical-thinking skills.
5. Describe the employability skills necessary for an administrative professional.
6. Explain why critical-thinking, decision-making, and problem-solving skills are essential to an administrative assistant.
7. Describe how factors such as appearance, communication, and teamwork affect your professional image.
8. Begin the development of an e-portfolio.

Do I Qualify?

Legal Administrative Assistant

As a national law firm, we are looking for a legal administrative assistant to support our corporate team by performing advanced, diversified, and confidential administrative duties, which include the following:

- drafting correspondence, documents, and pleadings
- interacting with clients, medical professionals, insurance adjusters, and opposing counsel
- posting time sheets and disbursements to client accounts

The successful applicant will have excellent English oral and written skills; be organized; and be able to prioritize work, take direction, and ask appropriate questions. You will be proficient in Microsoft Office applications and familiar with billing in a law office.

The World of Office Administration

In offices all around the world, the demand for administrative professionals is strong and growing. These essential office workers are respected and valued in business, industry, government, education, law, medicine, science, and the arts. Employees throughout the organization rely on administrative professionals to keep the office organized and operating efficiently.

Today, both women and men are choosing office administration as a career and as a means of advancing within a company or field. The work can be very rewarding in itself; it can also serve as an introduction to a business or an industry, from which the administrative professional can move to other positions or occupations. Either way, administrative professionals need a wide range of skills, traits, and attitudes to succeed.

To survive and thrive in this evolving workplace, you need to acquire the knowledge, skills, and qualities that allow you to become a valued part of the organization—a summary of which will eventually be incorporated into your résumé. Throughout this text, be aware of how these elements will eventually be presented in the résumé you will prepare when you begin your job search.

The Diverse Workforce

Cultural Diversity

As a nation of immigrants—one that has welcomed and accepted people from countries all over the world—Canada is becoming increasingly multicultural. **Multicultural** by definition means "relating to or including several cultures." **Culture** is defined as "the ideas, customs, values, skills, and arts of a specific group of people." Canada is a country that values diversity and respects the different cultures of all its citizens—from our own First Nations to those who have immigrated here more recently. At work you will deal with people who are diverse ethnically and culturally.

This increased diversity challenges us to find better ways to enable everyone, no matter their culture, to work to their potential. Becoming diversity competent through awareness, understanding, and acceptance of all cultures helps create an environment where we can work in a harmonious, productive business world.

People AT WORK

Canada is composed of a mosaic of different cultures, races, and ethnicities. As you work in this diverse workplace, be aware of and sensitive to the various cultural differences and backgrounds of the people with whom you work, and understand that individuals, because of their different backgrounds, may view situations differently. Your openness to different ideas and perspectives is essential. While it may not always be easy to remain open to differences, take every opportunity to practise diversity-competent behaviours that promote equity and inclusion. The results will be well worth the effort.

Gender Roles in the Workplace

More women are in the workforce today than in the past, and more than ever they are assuming positions of responsibility and authority. Positions traditionally filled exclusively by men are becoming more open to women. It is no longer valid to assume that only males will hold supervisory positions or that only women will provide administrative support. As women assume higher-level functions and as men take on administrative professional duties, we must examine our preconceptions about the way both men and women react in the workforce. People with different backgrounds and from different cultures react differently to situations. The socialization process in various cultures often encourages men and women to develop different traits. For example, if you are from North America and are female, you may have been encouraged to express your feelings openly, while males raised in North America may have been taught to keep their feelings to themselves.

Women account for almost 50 percent of today's workforce.

Notice that "may have" is used in referring to how both males and females are raised. We cannot say that all females born in North America have been socialized in this manner; neither can we say that all males have been. What is important here is that we cannot judge individuals based on a **stereotype** (a perception or an image that may be favourable or unfavourable). We cannot assume that individuals have certain characteristics because of their gender identity. You must also be mindful that not everyone identifies with a particular gender. Your role in the workplace is to be aware that stereotyping can occur and not to let your attitudes or decisions be based on these stereotypes. *Your focus must be on understanding and accepting differences.*

Shifting Demographics

Because employees are retiring at older ages, over the next two decades the workplace will comprise a variety of different generations working together. Figure 1-1 depicts the forecasted demographic shifts in the workforce. Each generation has been categorized as having unique values and characteristics. In Chapter 5 you will learn more about how these generational differences affect the workplace. We all view the world from different perspectives; to work together successfully, we need to listen closely to one another, understand one another's views, and accept individuals for who they are.

Education and Training

Changes in technology are driving the level of education required upward. In the office administration field, many employers require a diploma or an undergraduate degree as a minimum. Education is essential in landing a job, and ongoing education is a must in keeping a job.

While a formal education may be necessary for some jobs, informal education through reading, attending seminars and conferences, and being active in professional organizations is essential for maintaining currency and improving the

FIGURE 1-1

Development of Canada's Working-Age Population (15–64 Years Old)

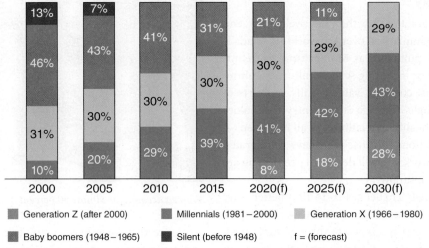

	2000	2005	2010	2015	2020(f)	2025(f)	2030(f)
Generation Z (after 2000)							
Millennials (1981–2000)							
Generation X (1966–1980)							
Baby boomers (1948–1965)							
Silent (before 1948)							

Generation Z (after 2000)   Millennials (1981–2000)   Generation X (1966–1980)

Baby boomers (1948–1965)   Silent (before 1948)   f = (forecast)

Source: Business Development Bank of Canada, "Figure 4—Millennials Are Becoming Predominant in the Workplace," *Future-Proof Your Business: Adapting to Technology and Demographic Trends*, October 2017.

knowledge and skills needed as work responsibilities change. Learning is a lifelong process. Careers of the future will be built on a commitment to lifelong learning. In addition to formal and informal learning, we learn through experience and through the mistakes we make along the way. Lifelong learning is necessary for all individuals who expect to remain productive citizens of the world. In the Professional Growth section of this chapter, we will discuss the options you have available to enhance your career opportunities through continuing education.

Your Work Environment

The work environment is constantly changing in numerous ways. Increasingly, our economy is experiencing globalization. Remote employment opportunities are growing, with the expectation that they will continue to do so. Companies are putting more emphasis on the use of teams to deliver quality products and services. The traditional workweek is changing, and part-time and temporary workers represent an increasing portion of the workforce.

Telework/Remote Employment and the Virtual Assistant

Today, many workers have traded in the traditional work environment for **telework**—work that can be performed at any place and at any time using technology. *Teleworking* is the term that broadly describes a working arrangement using telecommunications to work from a home office, a client's office, or some other location. *Teleworkers* refers to those individuals who are employed full- or part-time by an organization and work from home or some other mobile type of work environment for part or all of the workweek.

Remote employment (any working arrangement in which the worker performs a significant portion of work at some fixed location other than the traditional workplace) and the **virtual office** (the operational domain of any organization that includes remote workers) are terms used in describing the concept of work done through technology in which an individual is physically present in one location and virtually present in another. Instant messaging, virtual meetings, and email have created a niche for freelance administrative assistants, also called **virtual assistants**. These self-employed administrative assistants work from a home office to provide off-site administrative or personal assistance to clients. This arrangement is popular with individuals and small start-up companies that may not require the services of a full-time administrative assistant. You can find out more about this arrangement in Chapter 14.

Telework can be performed from virtually anywhere at any time by using technology.

The Workweek

The traditional 9-to-5 workday and five-day workweek have both undergone some changes. Hours in the workday may be flexible, and the workweek may be compressed or may involve job sharing with another individual.

With a **compressed workweek**, employees work the usual number of hours (35 to 40); however, the hours are compressed into four days (three nine-hour days and one eight-hour day).

Flextime enables an employee to work the full quota of time but at periods mutually determined by the company and the individual. Flextime helps to reduce traffic congestion at the traditional peak hours and allows employees to have some flexibility in their schedules. A **job-sharing** arrangement allows two part-time employees to perform one job that otherwise would be held by one full-time employee.

Workplace Organization

Learning about the culture, structure, and management of the organization you work for will help you perform your job better. It will help you understand the following:
- your position in the organization and your position relative to others
- acceptable behaviours and actions
- how the organization is run and why things are done the way they are
- what to expect

Office Mission, Vision, and Values

Many organizations have their own mission, vision, and values, which reflect the key beliefs and attitudes that drive an organization and define its style of doing business. A **vision statement** is an organization's roadmap and identifies what the organization wants to become. A **mission statement** defines an organization's purpose and can include its customer or market base, as well as its territory. A **values statement** outlines the behaviours and attitudes the organization will abide by when making decisions. Understanding an organization's mission, vision, and values will not only allow you to perform your job better but can also help you determine whether you want to begin your career with the organization.

Business Organizations

The businesses you work for as an administrative professional may be organized in different ways. The three basic forms are a sole proprietorship, a partnership, and a corporation.
- A **sole proprietorship** is owned and controlled by an individual. The owner receives all the profits and is responsible for all the debts.
- A **partnership** is an association of two or more people as co-owners of a business. Business decisions, profits, and losses are shared among the partners according to the terms of the partnership agreement.
- **Corporations** are legal entities formed by following a formal process of incorporation established by federal, provincial, or territorial statutes and associated regulations. Corporations may be publicly or privately owned. Public corporations are owned by investors called **shareholders** (or **stockholders**) who have purchased stock that represents a portion or share of the company.

In Canada, you may find yourself working for one of the following variations on the three basic forms of organizations:
- A **limited liability partnership (LLP)** combines the tax advantages of a partnership with the limited liability of a corporation. Professionals such as medical doctors, accountants, and lawyers often operate as LLPs.
- A **non-profit corporation** is an organization formed to engage in civic, charitable, educational, or artistic endeavours. Examples are hospitals, schools, charities, and arts organizations.
- A **government entity** carries out the functions of a provincial, territorial, municipal, or federal government. Examples are government agencies, public schools and universities, municipal departments, and numerous other departments, commissions, bureaus, and boards.

Formal Organizational Structures

Large companies usually are under the control of a board of directors that is charged with looking after the interests of shareholders. Boards of directors guide the management of the organization by establishing policies and setting goals that are implemented by the **CEO** or **chief executive officer** of the corporation. The directors typically meet monthly or every two or three months. Directors may not put themselves

FIGURE 1-2

Organizational Chart of CanAsian Airlines

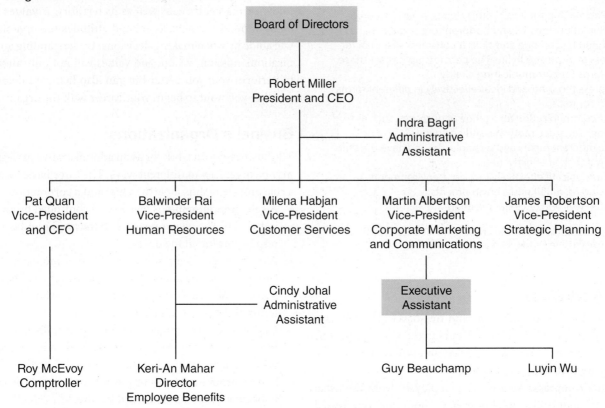

in a position in which their private interests and duties conflict with the duties they owe the company. When these interests and duties differ, a director is said to have a **conflict of interest**.

In addition to the CEO, a company may have a **CFO (chief financial officer)**, **COO (chief operating officer)**, and **CIO (chief information officer)**. These top executives may have presidents and vice-presidents reporting to them. In large organizations, managers at lower levels, such as the human resources director and the director of engineering, are responsible for day-to-day operations and for carrying out upper management's strategies and decisions and achieving the goals that have been set for the organization.

Management Responsibilities

Every organization has leaders and managers. The top executives described above are the company's key leaders, who set the direction for the organization.

Management is considered a subset of leadership, and the responsibilities associated with these two roles overlap. Although the textbook covers the characteristics of effective leaders separately from the responsibilities of effective managers, most effective managers are also effective leaders. You will learn more about effective leadership in Chapter 15. See Figure 1-2 for an example of management responsibilities depicted on an organizational chart.

The Administrative Professional's Responsibilities

With the availability of technology and the emphasis on greater efficiency and productivity through **flattened organizational structures** (fewer management levels than the traditional structures of the past) and teams, administrative professionals of today and tomorrow will find that their role is continually shifting. This shifting role generally leads to greater responsibility.

Administrative assistants support organizations in many ways. Figure 1-3 lists some of their most common responsibilities.

Job responsibilities of the administrative professional have increased in complexity and accountability and will vary depending on educational level, work experience, and even employee initiative. Many executives now answer their own voice mail and email, key in certain correspondence directly on the computer, and handle much of their own scheduling using electronic calendars. This change frees the administrative professional to take on more responsibility and become a valued member of the office team.

For years, the administrative professional's title was confined to *secretary, receptionist,* and such specialized titles as *legal secretary* and *medical secretary*. Although these titles are still used to a limited extent, today's emerging titles reflect the shifting role of the administrative professional: *administrative*

FIGURE 1-3

Typical Job Tasks and Responsibilities of an Administrative Professional

- Schedule appointments, and meet and greet visitors and clients
- Answer, screen, and transfer incoming phone calls
- Compose and key written responses to routine inquiries
- Prepare and modify documents (correspondence, reports, drafts, memos, and emails)
- Process (open, sort, and distribute) incoming mail
- Process (fold, seal, and stamp) outgoing mail
- Manage social media and update website information
- Maintain electronic and physical filing systems and retrieve documents and data as requested
- Schedule and coordinate meetings, appointments, and travel arrangements for managers or supervisors
- Prepare agendas for meetings, and record, compile, transcribe, and distribute minutes of meetings
- Resolve administrative problems and respond to inquiries
- Perform general support duties, including photocopying, faxing, and mailing
- Maintain office supply inventories
- Recommend equipment and software purchases
- Coordinate maintenance of office equipment
- Perform calculations related to expense reports, budgets, invoices, purchase orders, and petty cash
- Work with outsourcing companies
- Train office support personnel
- Conduct research as directed by the supervisor; prepare accompanying presentation visuals
- Provide computer and software training
- Solve day-to-day problems within the role of the administrative professional

The administrative professional today may have the responsibility of training colleagues or managers in new technologies.

the culture and structure of your organization and about the group or department you support and your role in the group.

What Do Administrative Professionals Do?

Most administrative assistants are required to be at the office during business hours, generally working 37.5 to 40 hours a week. Some may work part-time, but rarely do administrative assistants work from home; by its nature, their work is office-centred. The administrative professional is almost always expected to be in the office to respond to requests and keep things running. There are exceptions, of course, such as working at an off-site conference, but most administrative assistants are responsible for covering home base.

Employability Skills 2000+

To be a successful administrative professional in this world of technology and rapid change, you need certain skills and qualities. Employers expect all their employees to have the knowledge and skills they need to do their jobs and the interpersonal skills needed to work well with co-workers and customers.

Organizations seek employees who are responsible and accountable for completing the work assigned to them. They want people who manage their time well, have strong thinking and problem-solving skills, and are committed to advancing the goals of the organization.

In 2000, the Conference Board of Canada first published **Employability Skills 2000+**. This profile, which has been regularly updated, identifies the critical skills needed in the workplace, whether you work on your own or as part of a team. These skills are grouped into three broad categories:

- **Fundamental skills.** The skills needed as a base for further development. They include the ability to communicate, manage information, use numbers, and think and solve problems (critical thinking).

assistant, *executive assistant*, *marketing assistant*, *payroll assistant*, *human resources assistant*, and *office manager*.

Although job roles and responsibilities differ among the positions, certain skills and knowledge sets are essential in all administrative professional roles; these will be emphasized throughout this course. The terms **administrative professional** and **administrative assistant** will be used consistently throughout the text to denote this workplace support person.

Understanding Your Organization

The most valuable administrative professionals know a great deal about the company or organization they work for and the department or group they support; they begin to accumulate this knowledge even before they are hired. A variety of sources are available for acquiring this knowledge and some basic information about the industry in general: company publications (brochures and annual reports), the company website, the business section of local newspapers, and articles in financial publications. Chapter 13 describes information you should gather about a company or an organization before applying for a job. Once hired, observe your supervisor and co-workers; they are valuable resources for learning about

- **Personal management skills.** The personal skills, attitudes, and behaviours that drive one's potential for growth. They include the ability to demonstrate positive attitudes and behaviours, to be responsible and adaptable, to learn continuously, and to work safely.
- **Teamwork skills.** The skills and attributes needed to contribute productively. They include the ability to constructively contribute to projects and tasks and to collaborate with others.

Fundamental Skills

You will be better prepared to progress in the world of work when you can communicate, manage information, use numbers, and think and solve problems.

Communicate

The workplace runs on efficient conversations and emails in which ideas are exchanged, questions are answered, and decisions are made. You need to be able to express your thoughts and ideas effectively when speaking and writing, and to be skilled in asking questions. You also need to listen well to ensure you understand what others are saying and to be aware of their attitudes and intentions.

You will learn about effective speaking, listening, writing, and presentation skills in Chapters 5 and 7. It is very important to develop and improve these skills throughout your career. In survey after survey, year after year, employers rank strong communication skills top among the skills they look for most when hiring.

Manage Information

Success today demands that you be technologically competent. You must be able to choose and use appropriate technology to locate, gather, and organize information, and to apply knowledge and skills from various disciplines to analyze the data. Chapters 6 and 8 will help you develop these important skills.

Use Numbers

Using numbers effectively involves the ability to decide what needs to be measured or calculated; to observe and record data using appropriate methods, tools, and technology; and to make estimates and verify calculations. These skills are important not only in our working life but also in our personal life. Chapter 9 will introduce you to these skills.

Think and Solve Problems

Every workplace has problems and challenges. Most are small, but some are large and can have a substantial effect. Your employer will expect you to use your critical-thinking skills to anticipate and prevent problems. When they cannot be prevented, you will need to be able to work out ways of solving them. A person who thinks issues through and can help solve problems is a valuable employee. The ability to analyze situations critically will help you see the bigger picture—the events that are causing the change—so you can respond positively and productively. The abilities to think critically, solve problems, and make decisions are valuable skills that can be practised and improved.

Every workplace faces problems and challenges. While avoiding problems is best, there will be times when change occurs and problems may not be solved or stay solved. When that happens, understanding and applying a problem-solving approach will help find appropriate solutions. Effective problem solvers

- identify or define the problem or the purpose
- collect information by observing the problem in action
- determine the options or alternatives using brainstorming techniques
- establish criteria for the solution and choose the best option when making a decision
- evaluate the solution

Problems will arise daily, and decisions will need to be made. The ability to make decisions enhances your productivity at work. Effective decision making is covered in detail as the soft skill in Chapter 10. Briefly, to make a good decision, you must do the following:

- Determine your goal. What change do you expect as a result of the decision?
- Identify barriers to meeting the goal.
- Determine strategies to overcome the barriers.
- Evaluate the costs, benefits, and consequences of each strategy. What is the worst that could happen? What is the best that could happen? If there are risks, are they worth the result?
- Choose the best strategy.

After you implement the decision, evaluate the outcome. Use that information to help make the next decision.

Personal Management Skills

Demonstrate Positive Attitudes and Behaviours

As an administrative professional, you must deal with people, problems, and situations with honesty, integrity, and personal ethics. Chapter 3 will help you better understand the importance of working ethically. You must also recognize your own and other people's good efforts. Positive behaviours include showing interest, initiative, and effort in all the tasks that you are asked to complete.

Be Responsible and Adaptable

As an efficient administrative professional, you must

- organize your time, minimize your stress, and manage your workload
- establish priorities, determining what needs to be done first

- organize your workstation and files, whether they are visible or electronic
- organize your time so your work flows smoothly and tasks are finished as needed

Being well organized enables you to use your time well, keep track of documents and projects, prioritize tasks, and finish projects on time. Because you support others in the office, your organizational skills can make any workplace more efficient and effective. If you are disorganized, the entire office may suffer from the confusion and delays that disorder creates. Chapter 2 will help you understand more about these important skills and give you a chance to practise them.

Learn Continually

Lifelong learning is a philosophy that you should embrace. As new technologies continually enter our society and the workplace and the roles of administrative professionals change over time, you need to stay abreast of these trends and to continuously learn and grow to remain current in your field. The Professional Growth section of this chapter will outline ways that you can learn continually in your career.

Work Safely

As an employee, be aware of your own personal safety and understand the health and safety practices and procedures at your place of employment. The Canadian Centre for Occupational Health and Safety outlines the responsibilities of both employers and employees to ensure workplaces are safe and abide by government legislation. Workplace safety encompasses many aspects, such as hazard control, violence in the workplace, scent-free workplace policies, emergency planning, and WHMIS/GHS (Workplace Hazardous Materials Information System/Globally Harmonized System) training.

Teamwork Skills

Work with Others

Many tasks in today's workplace are accomplished by groups or teams. The word **team** can be traced to the Indo-European word *deuk*, meaning "to pull"; and, obviously, if teams are to be successful, then individual team members must pull together. Teamwork is the soft skill addressed in Chapter 8. Successful teams in the work environment include groups of people who need one another to accomplish a given task. By definition, an administrative professional is a team member who helps and supports others. Teamwork skills are very similar to interpersonal skills in that they require you to understand, accept, and respect the differences among your team members. Teamwork also demands that you

- behave courteously to all team members
- build strong relationships with your team members so the team's goals can be accomplished

- learn collectively with your team; start with self-knowledge and self-mastery, but then look outward to develop knowledge and alignment with your team members
- take responsibility for producing high-quality work as an individual team member and encouraging a high-quality team project

Interpersonal Skills

For years, surveys have shown that more employees lose their jobs because of poor interpersonal skills than because of poor technology skills. As an administrative professional, you come into contact with numerous people. Within the company, you work with co-workers, your immediate supervisor, and other executives. Contacts outside the company include customers and other visitors to your office, all with different backgrounds and experiences. If you are to be effective, you need to understand and accept others and be able to work with them. Interpersonal skills are like most of our other skills. We must constantly develop and improve these skills.

Take the interpersonal skills Self-Check presented here and compare your answers with the suggested responses at the end of the Self Check Box. Where do you need to improve? Commit now to improving these areas during this course. You will have an opportunity to learn more about the importance of interpersonal skills and to continue to develop your skills throughout this course.

SELF-CHECK Ⓐ

Respond to the following comments with yes or no.

1. I understand that differences exist in cultures, races, and ethnicities.
   Yes ❑   No ❑
2. I respect others' differences in culture, race, and ethnicity.
   Yes ❑   No ❑
3. I expect all individuals to react to situations just as I do.
   Yes ❑   No ❑
4. I listen carefully when others are talking.
   Yes ❑   No ❑
5. I ignore body language when others are talking.
   Yes ❑   No ❑
6. I am conscious of the words I use in my written communications.
   Yes ❑   No ❑
7. I avoid dealing with conflict.
   Yes ❑   No ❑
8. I evaluate individuals when they are talking to me.
   Yes ❑   No ❑
9. I trust people who are older than I am.
   Yes ❑   No ❑
10. Men are better supervisors than women.
    Yes ❑   No ❑

Becoming a Professional

As an administrative assistant, you are committed to helping others function well in their own positions. To do this, you need to be able to take direction and conform to established practices and policies. You must also use good judgment to recognize potential problems, assess situations, and act creatively. A professional administrative assistant can do both of these things—help others do their jobs well and know when to take the initiative and act decisively.

Throughout this course, you will learn how to fulfill your role professionally and project a professional image. Your professionalism (or lack of it) shows in everything you do at work, and becoming a true professional is a key to your success as an administrative professional.

Communicating AT WORK

Have you ever had this experience? You walk into a store and one employee stands out. That person gives you his or her full attention, walks with you to the section of the store you are looking for, and smiles at you if you happen to meet again. That employee is a professional.

Professionalism comprises numerous qualities and skills, including good judgment, initiative, discretion, organizational ability, the ability to work independently, and a professional appearance (of your workspace and yourself). Professionals are proud of doing their work well and proud to represent their organization.

Success Qualities

In addition to the skills already identified, certain qualities are essential for career success as an administrative professional. They include the following:
- openness to change
- dependability
- confidentiality
- emotional intelligence
- integrity and honesty
- initiative
- flexibility and adaptability

Openness to Change

By accepting that change is constant—in our personal lives and in our workplaces—we are more likely to be able to cope with and perhaps even embrace it when it occurs. Part of the fear of change means dealing with the unknown. Rather than worrying about changes that will need to be made, deal with the uncertainties of change by focusing on your existing skills and experience and how you can leverage them in the new structure. Keeping a positive attitude and becoming involved

FIGURE 1-4
Handling Change

The following steps will help you to handle change effectively:
- Consider the circumstances that have led to the need for change.
- Identify the objectives to be achieved by the proposed changes.
- Create steps to achieve those objectives.
- Determine the benefits or rewards that will occur as a result of the change.
- After the change has occurred, evaluate the effectiveness of the change.

can hasten that adjustment. Change requires creativity and flexibility. Administrative professionals who are open to change and able to adapt to change have a greater chance of being successful; with the right attitude and actions, that change can even lead to new opportunities. Figure 1-4 offers some tips on handling change.

Dependability

Dependability means being trustworthy. It means being at work on time if you are working at an established location. If you are engaged in telework, it means being productive in performing your job. Dependability is the willingness to put in additional time on important assignments. It also means doing what you say you will do, when you say you will do it.

Confidentiality

As an administrative professional, you may have access to information that is extremely sensitive. For example, when working in a medical or legal environment you will have access to confidential patient and client information. Protecting the **confidentiality** (secrecy or privacy) of the information received or the confidences shared may even be a legal requirement. In highlighting the importance of this aspect of the job to new employees, many firms will require employees to sign a confidentiality agreement. The following are just two ways in which the confidentiality of information may be violated:
- discussing private information with a family member or on a cellphone or over lunch with a colleague or friend
- leaving confidential information on your desk or an employee file open on your computer

Emotional Intelligence

Emotional intelligence refers to the capacity to develop self-awareness, self-discipline, and empathy in ways that affect your relationships with others. It influences the way you work, from how you make decisions to your social awareness of others in the workplace. Emotional intelligence has five key components:

1. *Self-awareness* or the ability to recognize and understand your own emotions and the effects of your own actions, moods, and emotions on others.

2. *Self-regulation* is knowing how to express your emotions appropriately.
3. *Social skills* involve interacting well with others. An important aspect of emotional intelligence is using active listening and verbal and nonverbal communication skills to build relationships and connections with supervisors and colleagues. (You will learn more about these skills in Chapter 5.)
4. *Empathy* is the ability to understand how others are feeling and to use this knowledge to respond appropriately.
5. *Motivation* is an incentive to act—a move to action. This incentive can be either an **intrinsic motivation** (internal) or an **extrinsic motivation** (external). The emotionally intelligent person is generally intrinsically motivated—seeking ways to improve, to learn, and to grow rather than extrinsically motivated by external recognition or monetary rewards.

Integrity and Honesty

Integrity is defined as "the adherence to a code of behaviour." In the workplace environment, the code of behaviour means in part that you must be honest. It means you do not take equipment or supplies that belong to the company for your personal use. It means you spend your time on the job performing your job duties—not making and receiving personal phone calls or writing personal emails. It means you uphold high standards of ethical behaviour. You do not engage in activities in which your morals or values may be questioned. The focus of Chapter 3 is on the ethical organization and the ethical employee.

Initiative

Initiative is defined as "the ability to begin and follow through on a plan or task." Initiative is taking the tasks you are given and completing them in an appropriate manner. It means having the ability to set appropriate work goals for yourself. The most highly valued administrative professional has the ability to analyze a task, establish priorities, and see the work through to completion. The professional who takes the initiative to make suggestions to the employer about needed changes or revisions is a valued member of the team.

Flexibility and Adaptability

Earlier in this chapter, you learned about the importance of being able to work with a diverse workforce. You also learned that work environments vary from workplaces of the past. All these continuing changes demand flexibility (being responsive to change) and adaptability (capable of making adjustments).

What Is a Professional?

A **professional** looks, speaks, writes, and behaves in a manner that reflects well on both the employer and the employee. A professional sets an example for others through a strong work ethic, positive attitude, and self-confidence.

Strong Work Ethic

One of the most valued traits in an administrative assistant is a strong **work ethic**. A person with a strong work ethic does not need to be externally motivated. Arriving at work on time and meeting deadlines are two of the basic values behind a strong work ethic. Your employer should be able to rely on you to take the initiative to begin and complete projects with little supervision. Employers value administrative professionals who stick with a project until it is done and done well. Always give your employer your best effort, no matter what may be going on in your personal life.

A strong work ethic does not mean that you avoid social interaction in the workplace but that you keep it under control. Your relationships with co-workers are essential to your success, so you want to be friendly and sociable without letting such interactions keep you from your work.

Positive Attitude

Human resources experts know that a worker's attitude is as important as skills for success on the job. If you come to work in the wrong frame of mind, your negative attitude can affect your performance all day. It can also influence those around you. Others want to be around you when you have a positive attitude. They are more likely to cooperate with a positive co-worker than with one who brings a negative attitude to work. Think about jobs you have had or group class projects on which you have worked. You probably preferred working with others who were enthusiastic and positive about the task.

Everyone has occasional complaints about work or co-workers, but do not let any resentments you have affect your work. Such behaviour only perpetuates problems. It can also make matters worse. No one wants to listen to the worker who seems to be always complaining about problems instead of trying to fix them. You may encounter problems you cannot solve, but they should not affect your overall attitude and performance.

Find ways to accept situations you cannot change. Your workplace may not be perfect, but you can overcome many problems by taking pride in yourself, your work, and your organization, doing everything in your power to make it better. Be part of the solution, not part of the problem.

Self-Confidence

Having **self-confidence** means you believe in yourself and your abilities. Most of us become self-confident over time through learning, growing, and refining new skills. When you are constantly striving to improve, you will have small successes that will build your self-confidence. Give yourself credit when you do something well. Everyone makes mistakes and everyone has weaknesses. Both are part of the learning process. Forgive yourself when you make mistakes.

When you do not understand something, be sure to ask questions rather than hide your confusion. When you are open to learning new information, new procedures, and new skills, you will not need to impress others with how much you already know. You can share your knowledge with others without feeling that you need to impress them by knowing everything. No matter how long you have been on the job, the people and situations around you can always teach you something that will make you a better worker.

Your Professional Image

Presenting a professional appearance to your co-workers and outsiders is essential to your success. Your appearance, speech, writing, and conduct all have an impact on how professional you appear. Familiarize yourself with the organization's dress code, if it has one.

Appearance

Arrive at work every day looking clean, tidy, and well-groomed. Being *well-groomed* generally means the following:

- Your hair is clean, trimmed, and combed. If you are a man, you are clean-shaven or your beard or moustache is neatly trimmed.
- Your teeth are brushed and breath is fresh.
- You are freshly bathed and use deodorant.
- You use scented products sparingly or not at all.

It may not seem fair, but people often judge others by how they look. We form first impressions during the first few seconds of meeting someone. Because not much can be said in this short time, this early judgment is based mostly on appearance. Whether or not they realize it, people may think that the quality of a person's work will match the quality of the person's appearance. Your appearance may be seen as reflecting your attention to detail, your level of motivation, and your sense of commitment and professionalism. The clothes you wear

may also shape your own attitude and confidence level. For example, when you dress more casually, you may also tend to behave more casually.

A professional image is more than dressing appropriately, however. A positive personal appearance without the necessary skills and qualities is meaningless. If the administrative professional expects to succeed, he or she must combine an appropriate personal appearance with the necessary skills and qualities presented in this chapter. A professional image is a combination of all these areas.

Technology AT WORK

Using social media, such as Facebook and Instagram, is a personal activity that also impacts your professional life. The lines that once clearly defined and separated work life from personal life are now blurred by online social media. You must also be aware of your professional appearance on social networking sites such as LinkedIn.

Keep in mind that the information you reveal, the words you use, and the images you post online are there for many to see. Don't trust your reputation to ever-changing privacy settings provided and sustained by a company that has its own interests. Make a point to check privacy settings frequently and maintain the mind-set that all posts are potentially public. Make sure your online images, profiles, and words are ones you would want a potential employer and your co-workers to see. Making jokes that might be offensive, expressing yourself in an unprofessional way, or showing yourself in silly or compromising situations may seem like harmless fun when you are in school. However, that sort of image can reflect badly on you in the workplace. Don't let the anonymity of social media lure you into posting something you wouldn't say or show to someone face to face.

Professional Growth

With the workplace constantly changing, you must be willing to continue to learn and to commit to continual professional growth by

- attending classes at a college or university (either onsite or online)
- attending seminars and workshops provided by your company, outside firms, or professional organizations
- finding a mentor
- reading business or professional periodicals
- participating in professional organizations
- volunteering your time and expertise to organizations in your community

Professional Organizations and Certifications

Participating in a professional organization can enhance your career by giving you opportunities to network; you can learn

The administrative professional dresses in appropriate business attire and is always well groomed.

valuable information from interacting with colleagues in your field. Local chapter meetings, national conferences, online forums, and other venues offer opportunities for professional growth. Several professional organizations have accredited programs for administrative professionals:

- The *International Association of Administrative Professionals (IAAP)* is the largest and best-known association for office and administrative professionals, which may have a local chapter in your area. This international organization offers opportunities to become accredited as a certified administrative professional (CAP) or to earn organizational management (OM) certification.
- *ARMA International* is an association for information management professionals. This association sponsors the certified records manager (CRM) designation, a certification designed for experienced professionals with management-level responsibilities.
- The *Association of Administrative Professionals* is a Canadian association that offers certification as a qualified administrative assistant (QAA) through programs offered at several postsecondary institutions across Canada.
- The *Project Management Institute* provides a variety of certifications for individuals seeking to become specialists in project management. As an administrative professional, you may be asked to work as a project assistant, and obtaining PMI certification can expand your employment opportunities. The entry-level certification is to become a certified associate in project management (CAPM), and the PMI provides further specialized certification in this field. Review the organization's website to learn more about these certifications.

Professional organizations often provide access to websites, articles, newsletters, and seminars that can help you improve your skills. Links to several administrative and other industry-related associations can be found on the MindTap site that accompanies this textbook.

Certificates are also helpful in advancing your career and professional image. For example, Microsoft offers three levels of *Microsoft Office* certification: specialist, expert, and master. There are also other certifications available from Microsoft, which endorse server, desktop, database, and developer skills. Adobe and other companies offer certifications for their software products. These certificates demonstrate that you have specialized skills, which will potentially expand your job opportunities.

Looking Forward

The procedures you learn and the skills you acquire in this course and other courses in your program of study can form the basis of a future transition to working in other specialized fields. You can build on these core competencies through on-the-job experiences and by participating in online or continuing education studies. Office and administrative professionals often pursue a field of specialization after completion of their initial certification, for example, to become a legal secretary/legal administrative assistant, medical office assistant, or executive office manager.

Legal Secretary or Legal Administrative Assistant

Working in the legal field, whether in a law office or the legal department of a large corporation, can be both fascinating and challenging. Legal secretaries/legal administrative assistants provide valuable administrative support to ensure that law firms function efficiently. Responsible for liaising with clients, they schedule appointments and respond to questions from clients, perform conflict searches, diarize or record court dates, transcribe notes from dictation, and prepare legal and court documents. Legal secretaries/legal administrative assistants are in high demand, which means they often command the highest salaries of all administrative professionals. Some will build on their knowledge and experience by continuing their studies to eventually become a paralegal.

Medical Office Assistants

Knowledgeable about medical terminology and doctors' practices, medical office assistants (MOAs) perform administrative, clerical, and in some cases clinical duties in a doctor's office, clinic, or other medical setting. Responsible for liaising with patients, they schedule appointments, gather and verify patient information, collect specimens, and may also take patients' vital signs. MOAs also file charts, keep patient records up to date, use specialized billing programs to invoice local government health services, and, depending on the environment, may also perform medical transcription. Because of our aging population, this specialized field is expected to continue to grow and expand.

Executive Assistant/Executive Secretary

Responsible for carrying out the administrative duties of executive management, executive assistants may support the work of directors, executives, or many managers all at once. They may be responsible for coordinating meeting plans from start to finish, including preparing agendas and taking minutes, organizing and coordinating the creation and publishing of correspondence; preparing departmental budgets, and liaising between executives, management, and clients. The duties of the executive secretary may include planning and organizing events, from a small department lunch up to a large holiday party or even an extensive four-day conference, which requires competency in event planning. Computer proficiency at the advanced level will provide executive assistants

FIGURE 1-5

Looking Forward: Core Competencies for Legal, Medical, and Executive Assistant Careers

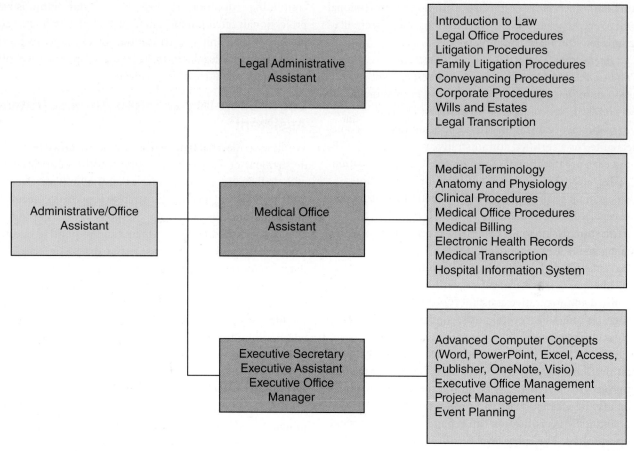

with the superior knowledge required for such positions as office manager or even executive assistant to the company president or CEO.

For administrative professionals who have already acquired competencies in keyboarding, numeracy, communications, computer applications, and customer service, the specialized courses outlined here will provide the core competencies to work professionally in these specialized fields. For the core competencies for legal, medical, and executive assistants, see Figure 1-5.

Soft Skills

Soft skills relate to personal attributes, traits, and communication skills that enable individuals to be successful in their career. Organizations consistently state that soft skills are critical skills that they are seeking in their employees when

making hiring decisions. At the end of each chapter, a new soft skill is introduced and explained. After reviewing each soft skill, spend some time reflecting on how you would be able to achieve and demonstrate the soft skill. This exercise will help you prepare when seeking employment. In Chapter 13, when you are preparing a cover letter and résumé, include the soft skills you have. In addition, understanding your soft skills will help you prepare for interviews where you will be asked to demonstrate and provide examples of your soft skills.

Critical thinking, the soft skill featured in this chapter, is reinforced in each chapter in this textbook. The Critical-Thinking Activity and Building Workplace Skills projects found at the end of each chapter require that you demonstrate your continual growth in critical thinking. A workplace situation is described in each Critical-Thinking Activity. You will be asked to critically analyze this activity and determine how it should be handled.

Soft Skills

CRITICAL THINKING

Critical thinking can be defined as "a unique kind of purposeful thinking in which the thinker systematically chooses conscious and deliberate inquiry." *Critical* comes from the Greek word *krinein*, which means "to separate, to choose." When we think critically about a subject, we try to see it from all sides before coming to a conclusion. Critical thinking requires us to see things from perspectives other than our own and to consider the possible consequences of the positions we take.

A critical thinker does the following:

- **Describes the real issue.** Before you can solve a problem, you must be able to recognize the real problem and describe it. Break a large problem into smaller parts to help determine the main problem.
- **Distinguishes between facts and opinion.** Ask yourself whether what a person asserts as fact really *is* fact.
- **Recognizes bias.** A person who is biased can't judge something impartially because of a personal preference. Try to put aside your own preferences and look at an issue objectively. You must also look for signs of bias when you consider others' opinions.
- **Asks questions and keeps an open mind.** Stay open to new ideas and different points of view.
- **Weighs new information.** Evaluate information—and its sources—before accepting it as true.
- **Considers implications and possibilities.** Assess whether the new evidence means that you should adjust your conclusions.
- **Supports opinion with evidence.** Do not expect your opinions to be accepted without support. Explain the logical reasons for your conclusions.

Chapter Summary

The summary will help you remember the important points covered in this chapter.

- Working in today's diverse workplace requires that you are aware of and sensitive to the various differences in culture, gender, age, and backgrounds of the people around you and that you respect their different perspectives.
- Professional attitudes, values, and skills include a strong work ethic, a positive attitude, self-confidence, the ability to handle change and accept criticism, the use of positive self-talk, and organizational skills.
- Largely as a result of changing technology, administrative professionals are assuming more responsibility and performing a wide and expanding range of tasks to keep offices running efficiently and smoothly.
- Successful administrative professionals work with integrity, respect confidentiality, display initiative, and are honest, dependable, flexible, adaptable, and open to change. They are self-confident and possesses a strong work ethic, a positive attitude, and emotional intelligence.
- Employers expect administrative assistants to apply critical-thinking skills when solving problems and making decisions.
- *Employability Skills 2000+* identifies the fundamental, interpersonal, and teamwork skills required to be successful as an administrative professional.
- To be seen as professional, you must be appropriately dressed and well-groomed every day.
- Professional growth can occur through attending classes or seminars and workshops, reading business periodicals, and participating in professional organizations.
- Careers of the future will be built on a commitment to lifelong learning.

Key Terms

administrative assistant p. 9
administrative professional p. 9
CEO (chief executive officer) p. 7
CFO (chief financial officer) p. 8
CIO (chief information officer) p. 8
compressed workweek p. 7
confidentiality p. 12
conflict of interest p. 8
COO (chief operating officer) p. 8
corporations p. 7
critical thinking p. 17
culture p. 5
dependability p. 12
emotional intelligence p. 12
Employability Skills 2000+ p. 9
extrinsic motivation p. 13
flattened organizational structures p. 8
flextime p. 7
government entity p. 7
initiative p. 13
integrity p. 13

intrinsic motivation p. 13
job-sharing p. 7
limited liability partnership (LLP) p. 7
mission statement p. 7
multicultural p. 5
non-profit corporation p. 7
partnership p. 7
professional p. 13
remote employment p. 6
self-confidence p. 13
shareholders or stockholders p. 7
sole proprietorship p. 7
stereotype p. 5
team p. 11
telework p. 6
values statement p. 7
virtual assistants p. 6
virtual office p. 6
vision statement p. 7
work ethic p. 13

Responses to Self Check A

1. Yes
2. Yes
3. No
4. Yes
5. No
6. Yes
7. No
8. No
9. Yes
10. No

Discussion Items

These discussion items provide an opportunity to test your understanding of the chapter through written responses or discussion with your classmates and your instructor.

1. Explain how the workforce and workplace are changing. What do these changes suggest for you as a future employee?
2. How is our current work environment changing? How is the administrative professional's role changing?
3. Identify the three basic types of business organizations. Brainstorm what you consider to be the advantages and disadvantages of working in each of these types of environments.
4. Why are interpersonal and communication skills especially important for someone in an administrative assistant role?
5. Describe the qualities that make a worker a professional.
6. Explain why critical-thinking, decision-making, and problem-solving skills are essential to an administrative assistant.
7. Describe a professional appearance, and give examples of clothing or grooming that are inappropriate in the workplace.

Critical-Thinking Activity

You are employed at CanAsian Airlines. You were asked to be part of a team that looks at the improvement of internal communication, and you took the assignment seriously. Before the first meeting, you had identified several communication problems that seem to be ongoing in the organization. At the meeting, you raised several issues: failure to respond promptly to email, failure to respond to voice mail, and airline ticket customers who have long waits when attempting to buy tickets by phone. Two of the individuals who work in your department became upset. They assumed that your statements referred to situations you had encountered with them. They exploded in the meeting, making these comments:

> I can't answer the email you send me within the hour. Get off my back.
> The next time you have a complaint about me, talk with me personally.

The manager in charge of the airline ticket sales department asked exactly what you meant by customers having "long waits" when attempting to buy tickets. He did not seem upset but was merely asking for clarification of your comment.

You responded to the two individuals in your department by stating that you were not talking about individual cases; you were attempting to identify problems that needed to be addressed so that customers can be better served. You answered the manager's question with, "I don't know the exact length of time; I have just heard complaints." Since the meeting did not get off to a good start, you feel responsible. You want to be a contributor to the process. What should you do? Think through the following items and prepare your responses.

- What is the problem?
- Do the upset employees have cause to be concerned about your behaviour?
- Should you talk to these employees before the next meeting? If so, what should you say?
- Did you have enough information about the customer ticket issue to mention it at the meeting? How should you handle this type of issue in the future?
- How should you identify problems or issues that are negatively affecting office communication?
- How can you present problems or issues at the next meeting without causing the volatility you experienced at the last meeting?

Remember, your task is to critically analyze the situation given here. Before you attempt to answer the questions, review the section Think and Solve Problems.

Building Workplace Skills

The Company

While completing projects throughout this course, you will be working for CanAsian Airlines, 2300–888 3rd Street SW, Calgary, AB T2P 4C4. CanAsian was formed as the result of a merger in March 2015 between CanAir, founded in 2000 in Calgary, Alberta, with only 30 employees, and China Airlines, founded in 2005 in Beijing, China, with 40 employees. Figure 1-2, earlier in the chapter, shows the organizational chart of CanAsian Airlines. Both airlines had grown, and after the merger, CanAsian Airlines now employs more than 39 000 people. The Canadian head office is located in Calgary at the address given above. The China head office is in Beijing.

Net earnings have experienced a slight drop from the combined net earnings of the two companies before the merger. The company is currently developing strategies to increase its overall market share by decreasing labour costs and providing certain incentives. It is looking at adding a frequent flyer program for the China operation and improved in-flight customer service for the total company.

Your Role

Your job title is executive assistant. You report directly to Martin Albertson, vice-president of corporate marketing and communications in Calgary. Since the merger, executives in both companies have been discussing how they might assume more social responsibility in the head office cities. They intend to take an active role in the educational, environmental, and social concerns of the community, in both Canada and China. Before the merger, each community saw the airline as a good corporate citizen, and the executives want to ensure things stay that way. Although their profitability picture has been good since the merger, there has been a slight downturn. As a result, the Calgary head office has laid off 50 employees in the corporate office. The result has been a lowering of staff morale; however, steps have been taken to make the employees feel more a part of the decision making.

Your duties are extremely varied. They include assisting Martin Albertson to set up meetings with government and educational leaders within the local communities to determine issues of common concern. At one point, you travelled to China with your employer and two other support staff to help set up a community conference. This trip was the only time you have travelled outside the company; however, you do communicate frequently with staff at the China office through fax, email, and computer conferencing. Your other duties include the following:

- researching and preparing all types of correspondence
- organizing your employer's schedule
- scheduling meetings
- making travel arrangements
- handling the mail
- filing correspondence
- supervising two assistants

You have two assistants who report to you—Guy Beauchamp (who has been working for CanAsian Airlines for just over a year) and Luyin Wu (who has been working for CanAsian Airlines for six months).

Project 1-1 (Learning Outcomes 1 and 3)
Online Project

TECHNOLOGY   CAREER

Browse the Web for the following information:

- Find articles on the changing office; at the IAAP website (www.iaap-hq.org), check the magazine *OfficePro*.
- Review the Statistics Canada website (www.statcan.ca) and find the job market report for legal administrative, executive assistant, and medical assistant positions. Prepare a short summary of the articles, giving the Web addresses; submit your summaries to your instructor.
- Research information on standard legal forms that might be used when an organization requires employees to sign a confidentiality agreement in a legal, medical, and general office environment.

Project 1-2 (Learning Outcomes 1 and 3)
Collaborative Project

CAREER

In teams of two or three, interview two administrative professionals. You do not need to interview these people in person; you may choose to do it by email. Ask the following questions:

- What are your roles and responsibilities?
- What skills and qualities do you need to be successful?
- What types of technology changes have occurred in your organization in the past five years? Two years?
- Describe the diversity of personnel within your organization. Have there been any issues in dealing with this diversity? If so, what were those issues and how were they handled?

Report your findings verbally to the class.

Project 1-3 (Learning Outcome 2)
Business Organization

INNOVATION   CAREER

Select a business to research. The business can be one with which you have some familiarity, such as a local company, or a large, nationally known company. If possible, talk to employees, read newspaper or magazine articles, or search the Internet to find information about the company. Create a short report that gives the following information:

- company name
- structure (partnership, corporation, etc.)

- main company location(s)
- primary products or services offered
- corporate culture (values, mission statement, causes supported, or other information from the About Us, History, or similar pages on the company website)

In your conclusion, indicate whether you would like to be employed by this organization and explain why or why not. Submit your report to your instructor.

Project 1-4 (Learning Outcomes 6 and 7)

CanAsian hired a new records clerk last fall, and you were assigned responsibility for her orientation and for mentoring her. Moira is a quick learner, and she is efficient and organized. She is neat and well-groomed, but she has an outrageous punk hairstyle and an eyebrow ring. The receptionist is leaving, and Moira has asked your advice about applying for the position. As Moira's mentor, what will you say to her? Share your thoughts with a small group (three or four) of your classmates. Compile the ideas from your group and share them with the rest of the class.

Project 1-5 (Learning Outcomes 5 and 8)

From the Student Course Data files, download and review the file Project 1-5 which provides some information on portfolio creation. With this project, you will begin the development of an e-portfolio, which you will add to throughout this course.

For this first project, review the brochure *Employability Skills 2000+* produced by the Conference Board of Canada (www.conferenceboard.ca). List the skills you already possess and those you need to acquire. Compare the list of skills needed with the skills listed in this textbook and/or in other courses in your current program of study. Prepare a table

that summarizes these important skills and identify in which chapter and/or course you will acquire them.

Create a folder in which you plan to save the materials for your e-portfolio. Some of the contents of your portfolio will be reflective, as you focus on acquiring these employability and other skills, while others will be examples of the quality of work you want to display to a prospective employer.

Create a folder within your e-portfolio folder for your ongoing reflections. Title this first reflection "Acquiring Employability Skills." You will perform a self-assessment at the end of the course to determine whether you have acquired these necessary skills.

Project 1-6 (Learning Outcome 3)

In Microsoft Word create a three-column table with seven rows. Title the table **Administrative Professionals**. Label the columns as shown:

Skills, Attitudes, and Traits	Importance	Ways to Improve

Using the information in this chapter, list in the first column what you consider to be the six most important skills, qualities, attitudes, and traits administrative professionals need. In the second column, explain why each skill, quality, attitude, or trait is important. In the third column, describe how you plan to improve your abilities in each of the six areas during this course and over the course of your studies.

Project 1-7 (Learning Outcome 1)

- Review the Canadian Centre for Occupational Health and Safety website (www.ccohs.ca). In groups, select a health and safety program to review in detail. Using Microsoft PowerPoint, create a presentation to record your findings, which you will present to your classmates.

Make the Grade with MindTap

Stay organized and efficient with **MindTap**—a single destination with all the course material and study aids you need to succeed. Built-in apps leverage social media and the latest learning technology. For example:

- ReadSpeaker will read the text to you.
- Flashcards are pre-populated to provide you with a jump start for review—or you can create your own.
- You can highlight text and make notes in your MindTap Reader. Your notes will flow into Evernote, the electronic

notebook app that you can access anywhere when it's time to study for the exam.
- Self-quizzing allows you to access your understanding.

Visit nelson.com/student to start using MindTap. Enter the Online Access Code from the card included with your text. If a code card is not provided, you can purchase instant access at NELSONbrain.com.

CHAPTER 2

Managing and Organizing Yourself, Your Time, and Your Workspace

Do I Qualify?

Marketing Administrative Assistant

Marketing firm seeks administrative assistant to join our award-winning team. The ideal candidate will be a dynamic, communications generalist who thrives in managing multiple tasks and meeting deadlines throughout the day. A valued and committed member of the team, you possess:

- strong written and oral communication skills
- proficiency in Microsoft Office and Adobe Acrobat
- the ability to manage your time and work effectively and independently preparing correspondence, presentations, reports, special projects, and related material as requested

Your job duties will include:

- tracking department schedules and projects
- scheduling and tracking contract due dates
- reviewing projects after completion to assess the efficiency of processes
- scheduling and facilitating meetings

The knowledge age in which we live is producing more stress in individuals than ever before. The price of this increased level of stress is high for both the individual and the organization. Stress may lead to psychological disorders, such as depression, anxiety, and insomnia, as well as physical issues such as ulcers, headaches, high blood pressure, colitis, diabetes, and even heart disease. Every week, millions of people take medication for stress-related symptoms. 70 percent of employees in Canada are concerned about their mental health and safety in the workplace.[1] Excessive stress and related problems are estimated to cost the Canadian economy $51 billion every year in absenteeism, lost productivity, accidents, and medical insurance.[2] According to the 2010 General Social Survey, 27 percent of Canadian workers described their lives and work as stressful.[3]

In this chapter, you will learn how to manage your workload and time, organize your workspace, control your anger, resolve conflict, and ultimately reduce your stress.

Manage Yourself

As you grow in experience throughout your career, you will continue to gain a greater understanding of how to organize and manage yourself and your workload to avoid creating unnecessary stressors. One of the first activities in understanding yourself is to consider where you want to be in the next five or ten years. Setting clear, attainable goals is a key to success in your private life and in your work life, and each helps to support the other.

According to a common expression, if you do not know where you are going, you will not know when you arrive. You need to determine what is important to you and clarify the results you are seeking. Focusing on exactly what you want to accomplish helps you decide how to achieve the desired results.

Set Goals

A **goal** is an objective, a purpose, or an end to be achieved. The meaning of the term includes any result you are trying to achieve, whether physical, intellectual, professional, or financial. It is important to write your goals down, as this provides concrete direction and clear purpose. Setting clear, attainable goals is one of the keys to success in both your private and professional lives, and each helps to support the other.

Align Your Goals with the Organization

In your career as an administrative professional, your role is to support others. You are part of a team working toward common goals that will be reached more easily if your own goals directly and indirectly support those of others. First look at the main goals for the company and determine what role your supervisor and other team members have in achieving those goals. Then align your goals with those of your supervisor and team. Your main goal may simply be to free up the time of others by offering assistance to them. If goals are not in sync, they can work at cross-purposes, reducing the chances of success for everyone involved. Knowing that you have made a significant contribution to the successes of others can be very rewarding.

Personal Goals

Personal goal setting is also important. This goal setting can take the form of deciding what your career goals are—what you want to be doing and where you want to be in five or ten years, or where you want to live.

You may have a long-term goal—such as becoming an office manager—which will be accomplished by completing many short-term goals along the way.

Goal Attributes

Effective goals should challenge you to reach a higher level of accomplishment and require you to do more than you have been doing. Using the S.M.A.R.T criteria, which was first presented in the 1981 issue of *Management Review*, a goal

- **must be specific**. If your goal is too vague, you will not know when you have achieved it.
- **must be measurable**. Pausing to assess and measure your progress along the way serves several purposes. Feeling

satisfaction in reaching smaller goals is important. It helps to keep you focused on what it is you wish to achieve, even if it is still a long way off. Accomplishing small steps can motivate you to keep going forward—making your more ambitious goals seem more reachable.

- **must be achievable**. Although goals should be challenging, they should not be unrealistically high.
- **must be relevant**. The goal should matter to you. It should be meaningful and worthwhile.
- **must be time-bound**. Deadlines allow us to determine when we have reached our goal. Depending on the goal, a deadline could be quarterly, semi-annually, annually, or ongoing. Look at your goals in those terms.

If you find that a certain step or strategy did not get you closer to your goal, it is time to reassess, rethink, and re-energize your efforts. Sometimes external conditions influence your goals to the point that you cannot accomplish them in the time frame you have set. When this occurs, revise your goal or establish a different time frame for completion.

People AT WORK

Office Manager

As an administrative professional, you may work under the supervision of an office manager. Office managers plan, coordinate, and supervise the work of administrative assistants and other support staff. They develop schedules, plan assignments, set deadlines, and oversee work to ensure it is done properly and on schedule.

Office managers frequently monitor and adjust workloads and job responsibilities to ensure that work is done efficiently. They may redesign job duties, shift them from one person to another, and create or eliminate job positions with the approval of company managers. Many companies fill office manager positions by promoting an employee from their administrative or office support staff.

Manage your Workload

Time is a unique and finite resource. Every one of us receives the same 24 hours a day to manage our lives in relation to our professional and personal goals. Although we can neither speed the clock up nor slow it down, we can learn to manage the details of the way we use our time.

Time management refers to the way we manage ourselves and our tasks in relation to the finite time we have. Many of us do not understand our time wasters, much less how we spend our time, and as a result, we may not be taking steps to manage ourselves more effectively in relation to our time.

Handle and Manage Time Wasters

Some of the biggest time wasters at work are disorganization and failure to do tasks efficiently. By organizing your work and finding efficient ways to do it, you can reduce this waste and save yourself a good deal of time. Review the list of common time wasters in the table below and consider which ones could have affected you.

Now that you have considered some of the time wasters we all face, you can understand that constant work is needed to do a better job of managing yourself in relation to the time that is available. When we pay attention to effective time management techniques, we often find that not only do we seem to have more time to get our tasks done but we also reduce the stress in our lives.

Record and Analyze How You Spend Your Time

Although you might think you know exactly how you spend your time, most people do not. By periodically documenting how your time is spent, you might be surprised at what activities are actually taking up your time. The following steps might help you to discover some of your personal time wasters.

Step One—determine how you spend your time by charting on a time log the amount of time you spend in various daily activities for a one-or two-week period. Figure 2-1 is an example of a time log you can use.

FIGURE 2-1

Time Log

DAILY TIME LOG		
Name _____ Day _____ Date _____		
Time	**Activity/ Interruptions**	**Comments**
8:30–8:45	Retrieved messages	
8:45–9:15	Aaron stopped by to discuss staff luncheon	Could have had a 10-minute chat online

Time Wasters	Example	Result
Ineffective communication	You misunderstood or did not clarify your supervisor's instructions about a letter to a client.	You required additional time to rewrite the letter; the client is unhappy and an account could have been lost.
Poor telephone techniques	You were unprepared when taking a message.	Your supervisor will not know what action to take in response to the message or, worse yet, will call the wrong person or the wrong number and will then need you to resolve the issue.
	You were unprepared when placing an outgoing call—you do not have the necessary details at hand.	You waste not only your time but that of the person called because you must locate the necessary information and replace the call.
	You take or place personal calls during work hours.	You do not demonstrate your professionalism.
	You use the telephone when email or an instant message would be a better choice.	You do not demonstrate your ability to choose an appropriate communication medium.
Inadequate planning	On Friday afternoon, your supervisor gives you what appears to be a brief report with a Monday afternoon deadline. You do not immediately review the project; by the time you get started early Monday afternoon, you quickly realize the job involves more than you had anticipated.	You are embarrassed, and your supervisor is disappointed when you must advise her that you are unable to meet the deadline. This oversight has a domino effect, first affecting your supervisor's plans, which then leads to her disappointing her supervisor or a client.

(Continued)

FIGURE 2-1

Time Log (continued)

Time Wasters	Example	Result
Interruptions	A client who is well known to you arrives at the office a few minutes early for an appointment and begins to chat about a recent function you both attended, or a co-worker stops by your workspace to discuss a work-related issue but once his concerns are addressed, he remains and begins to chat about his weekend mountain biking trip.	In both cases, the task you were working on has been interrupted, and you may need to take some additional time to refocus.
Disorganization	Your desk has a pile of folders on it with their contents spilling out; material for half-finished projects are scattered across the top of your desk; or a stack of documents to file is piled on top of the filing cabinet.	You are unable to locate required information in a timely manner. Deadlines are not met, and decision making is hampered or delayed.
Procrastination	You are assigned a large project that seems overwhelming. Because you worry about the size of it, you postpone getting started.	Leaving your work to the last minute creates stress for everyone involved.

Step Two—analyze your time log to discover ways in which you can improve the management of your time. Each day ask yourself these questions.

- What was the most productive period of the day? Why?
- What was the least productive period of the day? Why?
- Who or what accounted for interruptions?
- Were these interruptions expected? Did they occur at an expected (daily or weekly) time?
- Can the interruptions be minimized or eliminated?
- What activities needed more time?

Step Three—prepare an action plan. The purpose of the plan is to set goals for yourself as to how you will increase your time management efficiency. Using some of the following techniques will help you.

Prioritize Your Work

Many times, you will not be able to do everything you are asked to do in one day. To distinguish between the more important and less important jobs and determine the order in which they should be completed, you need to establish priorities. A **priority** is something that merits your attention ahead of other tasks. When prioritizing your work, it can help to organize tasks into four categories (as seen in Figure 2-2) that reflect both importance and urgency. An *urgent* task is one that requires immediate attention. An *important* task is one that you or your company places value on, a task that leads to growth or opportunities. Figure 2-2 shows examples of these categories. This system was developed by Stephen Covey.

It is not unusual for established priorities to change from day to day and from hour to hour, depending on the needs of your company and your department. Your top priority may have been completing the sales report; however, if your supervisor asks you to do something they consider more urgent,

FIGURE 2-2

Time Management Categories

A **URGENT AND IMPORTANT**
- Getting rid of a computer virus
- Booking plane reservations for your supervisor's last-minute trip
- Preparing for your annual performance evaluation next week *Checking voicemail*

B **IMPORTANT BUT NOT URGENT**
- Developing a relationship with the new paralegal
- Researching new virus protection software
- Planning the presentation you will give next month *checking email*

C **URGENT BUT NOT IMPORTANT**
- Filing correspondence
- Helping a co-worker move her office
- Rescheduling patient appointments that are three months away because your supervisor has just told you that he will be on vacation that week

NEITHER URGENT NOR IMPORTANT
- Going through four-year-old correspondence files
- Surfing the Internet for sales on office supplies
- Shopping for a new pair of jeans at lunch

© 2017 Cengage Learning

realign your tasks and priorities to match those of your supervisor. Move that sales report down a notch. Finish your supervisor's priority as efficiently as you can and then refocus on the sales report.

Prepare Daily To-Do Lists

Making lists of tasks you need to address can be a very effective way of organizing your work. A daily to-do or task list is a simple and invaluable tool. You can tell at a glance what you need to accomplish that day, in what order, and which tasks can wait until another day if necessary. A simple paper list works well for many people. Others like to keep a list in their word-processing or personal information management software so they can use program features to easily reorder items.

Review and adjust your task list periodically during the day and again before you leave work at the end of the day, taking a few moments to prepare your task list for the next day. To create this list, randomly record all the tasks, activities, and projects that you need to accomplish. Then review your list. Using the techniques discussed above, organize your tasks into four categories that reflect importance and urgency. Use your list, with priorities in place, to arrange papers on your desk in priority order, as well as your telephone and email messages.

Choose the method that works best for you.

Try to organize your to-do list to include variety in the tasks you are completing. Build in opportunities for regular breaks. As you complete the tasks on your to-do list, mark them off. Doing this will give you a sense of accomplishment and call your attention to what still needs to be completed. When preparing your task list for the next day, transfer any items not completed, and use them as the basis for the next day's list.

Use a Planner

You have probably used a planner in school or at previous jobs. Whether print or electronic, a planner is essential for organizing your work and for tracking appointments and other commitments for your supervisor or other workers.

Your office may require you to use a certain type of planner or planning software. Electronic planners are applications that are a component of **PIM** or **personal information management** software. Once installed on your computer network or mobile device, PIM can be used to do much more than categorize, colour-code, and track your task list—it can also be shared. In addition, it can also manage your schedule, track and keep detailed histories of your business contacts, and handle documents you have downloaded from the Internet or from other sources. Documents sent as PDF attachments or Web links can be easily attached to calendar entries or flagged for follow up. Reminders for recurring activities and tasks can be stored easily with one entry, filtered or sorted into categories, and then viewed by day, week, or month. With scheduling features and built-in reminders, electronic calendars, when used to their full potential, lend themselves very well to computer desktop organization. File folders for electronic files, Web shortcuts, and so on, can be placed on the computer desktop, which creates a paperless bring-forward file that can be easily deleted or moved when tasks are completed.

Most offices today are networked for file sharing. Calendars and tasks can be quickly and easily shared (see Figures 2-3 and 2-4) with people and can be accessed on mobile devices. When sharing a calendar, owners control and determine the levels of access to be granted to others. For example, in a large office you could choose to share your calendar details with your supervisor and perhaps two other administrative professionals on your team. For you to be able to see the details of their calendars, they would need to grant reciprocal sharing rights to you. Extending sharing rights means that specific details of appointments can be viewed and anyone with shared access can add, revise, or delete appointments; create new or delete existing contacts; and add notes or other details to these calendars. If you suddenly had a personal emergency and had to leave work, a printout of the calendar and task list would assist your co-workers in determining the tasks on which they should focus.

Two popular and widely used PIM software packages are Microsoft Outlook (calendar and contact management software that comes as part of the Microsoft Office suite) and Google Calendar. Planning templates are also available in the Microsoft Office suite. Planner templates are also available in word-processing and spreadsheet applications.

If you use an electronic planning system, invest some time in learning about their many features. Take a course at your local college or university, use the software help feature, take an online tutorial or webinar, or check out a book from the library.

Make a backup copy of your planner data. If you use a paper-based planner, photocopy the essential pages. When deciding how often to make a backup, consider the impact if you lost the data, including the time and effort it would take to replace it. What is most important is that you find or create a system that works for you and that you will use regularly.

FIGURE 2-3

Shared Calendar in Microsoft Outlook

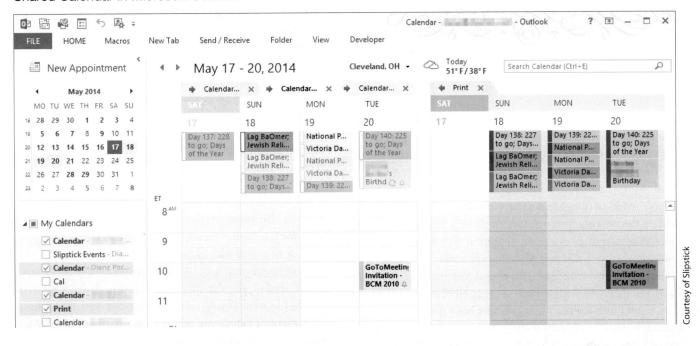

Courtesy of Slipstick

FIGURE 2-4

Shared Task List in Microsoft Outlook

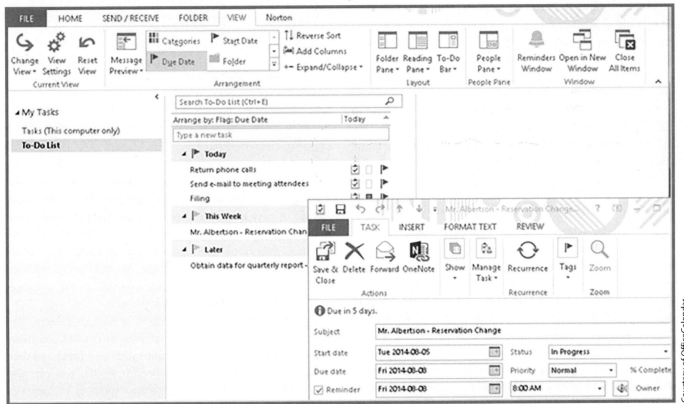

Courtesy of OfficeCalendar

Conquer Procrastination

Procrastination is the postponement or needless delay of a necessary project or task. Many of us are guilty of procrastination. We do so for a variety of reasons—worrying about the size of the project, being afraid of failing, or lacking interest. We do not want to admit to any of these reasons, so we make excuses, such as having no time to get started, having too many other projects, lacking the necessary materials to complete the job, needing additional advice from a supervisor, or believing there is more than sufficient time and therefore no rush to begin.

The first step to getting something done is starting. Pick one area where procrastination plagues you and conquer it. If you always put off filing, and too often find yourself with two or three weeks of filing stacked on your desk or have difficulty locating documents, you need to specifically include filing in your list of priorities. Make an appointment with yourself in your calendar so that this important task is not delayed.

Recognize that you have developed the habit of putting things off, then take steps to correct the habit. Even if you know you cannot finish a project that you have been postponing, give yourself a deadline and promise yourself that, until it is finished, you will dedicate yourself to it for half an hour a day or some other length of time that suits your schedule and your attention span. If possible, blocking time in your calendar daily may help—such as first thing in the morning before your supervisor arrives or before the time your daily duties begin. The main idea is to find time when you expect to have the fewest interruptions.

When planning to work on a large project, try to anticipate what could go wrong and what you might do to prevent problems along the way. Break the project into smaller tasks and focus on one at a time so that tasks seem more manageable and you get the reward of making progress. Set some deadlines, then tackle the most difficult ones first.

Do not let perfectionism paralyze you; do not be afraid to make mistakes. Any job has its difficult and boring tasks. Try to think of more efficient ways to manage them. Discipline yourself to work on them a little at a time.

Organize Files, Paper, and Email

Piles of letters, memos, and other documents can accumulate quickly. If you have ever found yourself rereading a piece of paper or shuffling it from the top to the bottom of the stack several times, you are not alone. Most of us have done the same thing. You open a piece of mail and put it in a pile, thinking, "Oh, this can wait." The pile quickly grows into an overwhelming mountain of items you thought could wait.

Many time management experts claim that handling paper repeatedly is the biggest paperwork time waster. They advise that you should handle each piece of paper just once. Read it, route it, file it, or answer it. Get it off your desk as quickly as possible. While this advice is helpful, it is not always possible, practical, or even desirable. What you should do when you receive a document is to decide how you will handle it:

- Act on it at once if it needs immediate action or if you have the time.
- Keep it on hand if you will deal with it later that day.
- If it doesn't need to be dealt with that day, and if you have more pressing priorities, determine a time when you will handle it and note it in your to-do list or planner. You may find it helpful to have an action file for items that won't be dealt with immediately but will be addressed in the next few days.
- If the document isn't your responsibility, forward it to someone who can handle it.
- If the document needs to be stored, do so at once, if possible. Non-urgent filing can wait, but set a specific time for it so it doesn't accumulate. Place it in a sorting strip or in a "pre-file" folder where documents are partially organized according to the master file list. Then if it is needed, you can quickly locate it in the sorting strip or pre-file area. Think before you create a new folder for a document or before you add it to an existing folder. Will you really need to refer to it again?
- If you don't need the document, destroy it.

Technology AT WORK

Your telephone system probably allows you to assign a code or number for a phone number you frequently call. If you take the time to program the system with shortcuts, which may be single digits, you can dial the telephone numbers you have entered without entering the entire number.

Machines can also be programmed to send a message with a single command to each person in a group, such as your company's board members, specific team members working on a project, or heads of departments. It takes some time to set up group numbers for telephones, but in the long run, programming them into the device will save you time and effort.

Email programs allow you to set up folders for organizing messages you need to save. Depending on the kind of work you do, it may help you to have folders named "From John Jones" or "From Su-kyong Kim" so that you can quickly find messages you need. You can also set up folders for emails related to a specific issue or task, such as an "Employee Benefits Committee" folder where you put all the messages from any sender that relate to that project.

Emails can be organized by date, sender, or subject. You can personalize the way your email program makes you aware of new messages (often in bold until you open them and then in normal text after they have been opened). You can also flag important messages with various symbols to help you find them. Many programs also automatically place incoming messages into predetermined folders if instructed to do that.

You will learn about organizing, managing, retaining, and disposing of paper and electronic files in Chapters 8 and 10.

Streamline Repetitive Tasks

In most jobs there are certain tasks that you do over and over again. Over time, you are likely to get faster at doing them and to find ways of performing them more efficiently. Think actively about ways to streamline this sort of work. Observe what your co-workers do, or ask their advice.

Luckily, both hardware and software can help you to work more efficiently by automating all or part of the process. As you get to know various software systems, you will also learn how to automate certain steps to speed up keyboarding and/or entering data. There are dozens of shortcuts and automations for commands in word-processing software, which you have probably mastered in keyboarding classes.

You are also probably familiar with creating templates in word-processing software to speed up the keying of documents. These tools will be covered thoroughly in Chapter 5.

In spreadsheet software, such as Microsoft Excel, you can use macros to record, save, and run an automatic series or sets of commands or steps. This will enable you to format rows, columns, cells, functions, and calculations with fewer steps. You can find excellent online training on how to use macros in all of your worksheets so that the cells, formats, and formulas are in the document without your having to enter each command in a series yourself.

In your email program, set up your address book to include groups. It will be much easier to communicate quickly with a group of people by selecting the group instead of individual email addresses.

Writing AT WORK

Email and instant messaging (IM) can make work more efficient—but they can also create work, unless you use them thoughtfully.

Sometimes people send more messages about a topic than they need to because it's so quick and easy to do.

While email is often the quickest and easiest option for contacting someone, that isn't always the case. Sometimes making a phone call takes less time than composing a message. Similarly, a face-to-face conversation might save several emails going back and forth.

Minimize Interruptions

Interruptions are a normal part of the day for an administrative professional. They come from a variety of sources—email, phone calls, and visitors—and can become frustrating time wasters. Your responsibility is to maintain positive relationships with colleagues and clients, which can involve some personal finessing

on your part. Making visitors feel comfortable and welcome does not mean you must entertain them while they are waiting to see your supervisor. The same is true for co-workers who stop by your workspace to visit. Certainly if a co-worker comes by on a work-related errand, engage briefly in friendly conversation. But try to not spend a lot of time in excessive chatting. Controlling or minimizing these types of interruptions is crucial to using your time effectively. See Figure 2-5 for some suggestions.

FIGURE 2-5

Controlling and Minimizing Interruptions

EMAIL

- If your email program is not set to notify you each time a new message is received, check it regularly but not constantly. Determine an appropriate interval to check your email (hourly, every other hour, or as frequently as you and your supervisor determine is necessary).
- Respond to emails courteously, clearly, and concisely. Be direct and specific.
- Do not let emails take the place of personal contact unless that is the preferred choice of your supervisor and colleagues.

TELEPHONE

- Give and record correct information during telephone calls.
- Identify yourself or your supervisor and state the reason for your call.
- Group multiple outgoing calls and make them when people are most likely to be available.
- If the person called is not in, ask when they will return or leave a concise voice mail message, identifying yourself and providing a brief summary of the reason for your call.
- When taking a message or screening incoming calls for your supervisor, determine who is calling (repeat the name and phone number) and the nature of the call. Confirm accuracy by spelling the caller's name and repeating the message to the caller.
- During work hours, make personal calls only when they relate to an emergency.
- Use email and fax as an alternative to leaving and receiving phone messages.

VISITORS

- Set up appointments for visitors. Discourage people from dropping by unexpectedly to see you or your supervisor.
- Make visitors welcome but continue with your work as soon as you can.
- Discourage co-workers from dropping by to socialize. For example, you can stand when they enter your workspace, or keep your hands over your keyboard or pen in your hand to silently indicate your responsibility to work during working hours.

Workstation Organization

A neat and orderly desk is especially important to administrative professionals because their workspace tends to be in a high-traffic area where more people are likely to see it. The impression your work area makes on your co-workers, clients, customers, and the general public reflects on the professionalism of your organization.

Overall Appearance

For a professional look, keep personal items at your workstation at a minimum. A family picture, a plant, or a mug might be fine, but don't overdo it, and follow any rules set by your organization.

Your desk should be clean and your work area free of dust. Your organization will probably have staff or a service that cleans employees' workstations, but you will want to keep your area looking clean throughout the day as well.

Keep your work area arranged efficiently—with everything within reach if used frequently or placed in a drawer if not. This will make your desk look orderly and keep you from being distracted by extraneous items that could get in your way.

Having an efficient and clean workspace will give a good impression to others about your quality of work. A chaotic workspace might communicate the wrong message to your supervisor, especially if you're from different generations.

Organizational Aids and Supplies

A trip to any office supply store will reveal a wide variety of organizing systems and tools from planners (discussed earlier in this chapter) to fasteners, notebooks, filing systems, and sticky notes. Every worker can benefit from a planner. You will learn over time from your own experience which other devices and supplies help you to stay organized.

Many administrative assistants find it helpful to have an inbox and outbox on their desks. With an inbox, your supervisor and co-workers will know where to put a document for your attention if you happen to be away from the desk or on the telephone. An outbox may be all you need for finished documents and projects that will be forwarded to others.

If your work is too complicated to rely on an outbox, a vertical file may help you to keep track of things. In this handy file, you can keep sturdy, wide folders of outgoing work by category. For example, you may have one file labelled "To Be Signed," another labelled "To Be Notarized," and others labelled for specific attention, such as "To Be Discussed with Supervisor," "To Be Entered in Database," or "To Be Scanned."

This sort of system will keep items from getting lost in the outbox pile and will remind you of the next step in the process. If you want to clear your desk completely at the end of the day, save a deep drawer where you can store this vertical file.

For some people, different coloured files or colour-coded labels help to distinguish certain types of projects from others. It may also help you to use colour-coded stickers on documents indicating that you have completed handling them and they are ready for the shredder or recycle bin.

A clear, orderly filing system is essential to any productive office. You will learn how to manage, organize, and maintain files in Chapter 10.

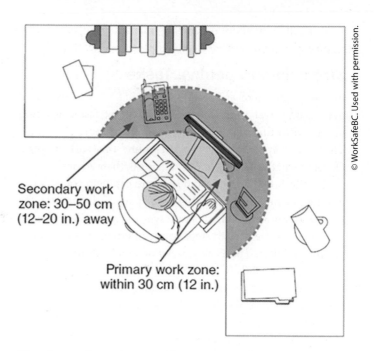

Secondary work zone: 30–50 cm (12–20 in.) away

Primary work zone: within 30 cm (12 in.)

Place frequently used items in the primary work zone and infrequently used items in the secondary work zone.

Your Ergonomic Workspace

The term **ergonomics** refers to the study of the fit between people, the tools they use, and the physical setting in which they work. The Canadian Centre for Occupational Health and Safety includes ergonomic hazards as a type of workplace hazard that can cause harm. When your workspace is set up correctly, you may be less likely to suffer from headaches, neck and back pain, and the resulting stress that can accompany these symptoms. A comfortable and ergonomically designed workspace can help you to be more productive and reduce injury, which can be caused by placing your body in awkward positions. While no solution is one size fits all, use the checklist in Figure 2-6 to help assemble an ergonomic workstation that minimizes injuries.

FIGURE 2-6

Checklist for an Ergonomic Workstation

- Your workstation is organized so that everything, including the keyboard, is within easy reach. No strain is placed on any part of your body when accessing equipment and supplies.
- A task (desk) light compensates for insufficient ambient light when reading at your desk.
- Your computer monitor is directly in front of you.
- The top of the screen is at eye level. A viewing distance of 55 to 60 cm from the eye to the computer is maintained. The monitor is parallel to overhead lights and at right angles to windows.
- The light on your computer screen is sufficiently bright.

FIGURE 2-6

Checklist for an Ergonomic Workstation (continued)

- The keyboard and mouse are positioned 60 to 63 cm from the floor (approximately 5 cm below the desk surface) to accommodate proper keyboarding techniques.
- When keyboarding, correct hand and wrist positions are achieved. A 90-degree angle is naturally formed when arms are close to your body, bent at the elbow, and wrists are in a straight line with the forearms. Shoulders are relaxed and wrists are not bent to the side or resting on anything, except a wrist rest if needed, and only finger movements are used to strike the keys.
- Your mouse fits your hand and is placed at the same level and to the side of the keyboard—close enough so you do not have to reach a long distance.
- Your chair is sturdy—five legs are better than four.
- The chair seat and backrest move independently of each other.
- Your back is adequately supported. The height and angle of the backrest on the chair is adjusted to support the hollow in your lower back.
- The correct chair height from the floor is achieved. Your knees rest slightly lower than your hips and your feet are flat on the floor to decrease the pressure on your lower back.
- A footrest is used if you cannot reach the floor once your chair is raised to accommodate a correct keying posture.
- Armrests on your chair are adjusted to the same level as your desk to alleviate the pressure in your neck and shoulder area when keying.
- Armrests are adjustable to accommodate changes to the angles of wrists and elbows.

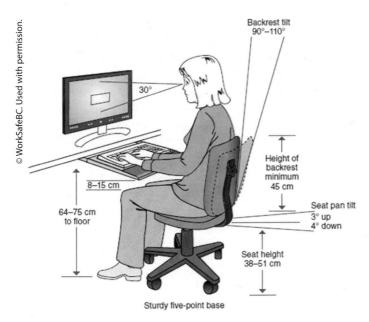

© WorkSafeBC. Used with permission.

Ergonomic workstation

Ergonomic Health Issues

RSI (repetitive stress injury) is caused by repeated performance of certain physical actions over a period of time. Also known as overuse disorders, RSIs such as carpal tunnel syndrome, computer vision syndrome, and back problems can affect your health and cost you or your organization many dollars in lost work and insurance claims.

Carpal tunnel syndrome is one type of RSI. This condition occurs through the compression of the median nerve, a large nerve that passes through a tunnel in the wrist composed of bone and ligaments. Symptoms include a gradual onset of numbness and a tingling or burning in the thumb and index and middle fingers. Other types of overuse disorders, which occur as a result of sitting at the computer for long periods, include **computer vision syndrome** (from glare) and back problems or pinched nerves in the neck and shoulder area (from chairs that are not the right height or configuration for the user).

When deciding on your computer peripherals, check out ergonomic and/or wireless keyboards and mice. Some features of ergonomic keyboards include

- a split keyboard
- a built-in wrist rest
- a detachable wrist rest

Take frequent breaks. You can help to prevent RSIs by taking a one-minute break every 20 minutes, a short rest period (10–15 minutes) every two or three hours, and standing up every 30 minutes. If you are stiff when you get up from your chair, take breaks more frequently to increase your circulation. To relieve strain on eye muscles, try looking away from the screen for a short period of time every 30 minutes and try focusing on distant objects occasionally. A break reminder application, known as WorkSafe Sam, is available from the WorkSafeBC site. It provides stretching tips to help reduce eye and muscle strain for office workers and can be downloaded, installed, and configured to pop up on your screen and remind you to take regular breaks. (A link to this application is provided on the MindTap site for this textbook.)

Ergonomic assessments are often conducted in larger firms when employees begin a new job or when they transfer to another position in a different office location. After an assessment is completed, workstations with standard desk heights and chairs set at standard positions can be adjusted to suit individual needs, thus ensuring that the workstation and the individual are in balance and potential RSIs are minimized.

A more detailed computer workstation checklist in PDF form is included in the WorkSafeBC booklet *How to Make Your Computer Workstation Fit You*.

More information on setting up an ergonomically sound workspace is available on the websites of the Canadian Centre for Occupational Health and Safety or your provincial or territorial equivalent, such as WorkSafeBC.

For a fee, you can also participate in an online course in office ergonomics where you will learn to recognize the early signs of discomfort that can arise while working with office equipment, learn the factors responsible for such discomfort, and participate in activities that will help you in assessing, controlling, and preventing ergonomic problems and injuries. Links to these sites are provided on the MindTap site.

Stress and Anger—A Major Malady

Time, stress, and anger are closely related. When we are angry, we become stressed. Personal conflict and anger in the workplace come from many sources.

As knowledge continues to expand rapidly and ever-changing technology becomes the rule rather than the exception, we must constantly learn new ways of performing our jobs. As businesses **downsize** (reduce the number of employees) and **rightsize** (determine the most efficient and effective number of employees and organizational structure), we may lose our jobs and even change our careers. As telework becomes a reality for more and more employees, we must adjust to working in very different conditions than in the past—often by ourselves. Such situations force us to deal with change and to embrace change if we are to be successful workers in this millennium. All these occurrences can and often do contribute to stress.

Stress is the body's response to a demand placed on it. Our wants, needs, and desires are derived from stress of some kind. Stress cannot be avoided; in fact, we would not want to avoid all stress. If you never felt a need to achieve, you would not go to school. If you never felt a need to contribute, you would not accept a challenging job. This type of stress is known as healthy stress. Healthy stress can and does have a positive impact on our lives. However, when stress becomes chronic, it is a negative health factor. **Chronic stress** occurs when a distressful situation is prolonged, allowing no rest or recuperation for the body; negative stress can cause physical and emotional problems. Chronic stress can also lead to emotional problems such as depression, withdrawal, deep-seated anger, loss of self-esteem, and self-rejection.

Causes of Negative Stress

In addition to the change factors in our society that can cause stress, there are numerous other causes of negative stress. Some of the more common causes are discussed here.

Work Overload

Productivity is a key word in all organizations today. In order to compete in an international market, organizations are experiencing the need to be more productive; at the same time, they are expected to reduce costs. Employees are often asked to produce more in less time with a greater degree of accuracy than ever before; thus, employees often find themselves working long hours.

Family Demands

In the majority of families today, both parents work. Parents must balance the pressures of their jobs with spending time with children and juggling household demands with other responsibilities.

The divorce rate in Canada continues to be high, and single-parent homes are not uncommon. The responsibility for raising children may fall on one parent. The responsibilities at home, along with the pressure of having to make enough money to meet the needs of the family, can cause stress.

© PeopleImages/iStock

Families include seniors who may require special care.

Despite increased stress in our lives, we are living longer than ever before. Many times, this long life means that families include older family members who may require special care. Adult children may need to devote time and energy to assisting their own parents in adapting to new living arrangements. Dealing with the challenges of senior family members can be difficult for everyone involved.

Communicating AT WORK

Do not encourage family and friends to call you at work, and also avoid making personal calls while on the job. There are, of course, exceptions. Your child's school may call to advise you that your child has a fever. Your employer will understand that you need to take this call. In most cases, however, the needs of family and friends can be handled before and after business hours.

Economic Pressures

Even dual-career families may find it difficult to make ends meet. Individuals may work longer hours or take second jobs to bring in additional money for household needs. Single parents, too, may find themselves struggling to meet the financial needs of the family.

Workplace Conflicts

Personality conflicts sometimes occur within the office. Many people try to avoid or ignore conflict, but it usually does not go away; it merely gets worse. Conflict resolution skills are always important in workplace situations, and as an administrative professional you should develop these important skills. When you are faced with conflict, address it; engage in **conflict resolution** (addressing and dealing with issues in a positive manner). Conflict resolution is the soft skill featured in this chapter. Suggestions for resolving conflict are given in Figure 2-7. Consider these suggestions and try to implement them as you work with others.

FIGURE 2-7
Suggestions for Resolving Conflict

- Identify what is causing the conflict. Is it power, resources, recognition, or acceptance? Many times, our needs for these items are at the heart of the conflict.
- Determine what each person needs or wants. Ask questions and be willing to listen to the other person. Everyone feels a deep need to be understood. In satisfying that need in the other person, you may be able to lessen the conflict. If you do not understand what the other person is saying, paraphrase what you think you hear and ask for clarification. Be open to what the other person tells you.
- Identify points of agreement. Work from these points first. Then identify the points of disagreement.
- Create a safe environment by establishing a neutral location and adopting a tone that is accepting of the other person's views and feelings. Acknowledge the other person's feelings. Behind their anger may be fear. Let the other person tell you how they are feeling.
- Watch how you position yourself physically in the room. Remember, you have a more difficult time competing with someone sitting next to you than with someone who is across the table or room. A circular seating arrangement may be appropriate if you have several individuals involved in a conflict.
- Do not react. Many times individuals act too quickly when a conflict occurs. Step back, collect your thoughts, and try to see the situation as objectively as possible.
- Do not seek to win during a confrontation. Negotiate the issues, and translate the negotiation into a lasting agreement.
- Listen actively. Watch the person's eyes; notice his or her body language.
- Separate people from the issue. When the people and the problem are tangled together, the problem becomes difficult to solve. Talk in specific terms rather than general terms.

Stress Reducers

Although we cannot avoid all negative stress and anger, we must guard against it becoming a prevalent part of our lives. Healthy individuals find ways to get rid of negative stress so their bodies will not be damaged. Here are some stress and anger reducers for you to practise.

Take Care of Yourself

To be effective on the job, you need to feel well. Make sure that you maintain a healthy diet, control your weight, exercise, and get enough sleep.

A healthy diet has a number of benefits. It can help you feel well and reach or maintain your ideal weight. In addition, a healthy diet may reduce your risk of cardiovascular disease, type 2 diabetes, osteoporosis, stroke, certain kinds of cancer, and other medical problems. It is also essential in the management of many other diseases.

Make time for exercise, even if it's only walking. It's no secret that exercise helps you manage your weight. It also improves your mood, boosts your energy level, and helps you sleep better.

Taking care of yourself also means making time for activities that you enjoy. The demands of work, family, and other obligations can consume large amounts of time. Setting aside time for yourself is not selfish. It will help you maintain a good work-life balance and perform better on the job.

Exercise has many benefits.

Life Management

Your employer understands that you have a personal life and that it can often be difficult to juggle private and professional responsibilities. The more organized you are in your private life, the more energy you will have to focus on work. The more order you put into your professional life, the less it will interfere with life at home.

You should also spend some time thinking about your negative emotions and what triggers them. When you understand what sorts of things make you impatient or angry, you can better control those emotions when they begin. Controlling your emotions is very important in both personal and work relationships. When you control your emotions, you can step back and consider the best way to respond, instead of impulsively reacting.

Workplace Wellness Programs

The Canadian Centre for Occupational Health and Safety has created a Comprehensive Workplace Health and Safety Program that provides organizations with guidelines and suggestions on how to create a healthy environment for their employees. These ideas may include flexible work schedules, fitness programs, stress management, individual goal setting, personal empowerment, and personal growth. Be aware of the services available to you through your employer to maintain your overall well-being.

Many organizations also have an employee assistance plan (EAP), which is a confidential counselling service. Employees can seek professional assistance from psychologists or psychiatrists. These trained individuals can help you discover the causes of your stress and provide guidance and suggestions on how you can alleviate it. If, however, an EAP is not available at your place of work, check with your family physician; they can provide sources of assistance.

Success in a World of Change

Time and stress management go hand in hand, each contributing to the other. If we do not set realistic goals, or if we fail to manage our workload well, we can become stressed; if we are stressed, we cannot achieve our goals or manage our time well.

To thrive in the business world today, we must master the multitude of changes that come our way in the form of technology, and we must be productive and happy in our work. If we are stressed to the point of being burned out on the job, angry a large part of the time, and finding too few hours in the day to accomplish what must be done, it is difficult to realize our full potential. By putting to use the techniques presented in this chapter, you have a chance to succeed on the job and to thrive in a world of change.

We can actually gain new energy by taking time to play. As adults, we may have forgotten how to relax and, with complete abandon, enjoy the world around us. Some experts writing in the field of creative energy urge us to take "joy breaks"—to stop for two to five minutes to play when we feel overtired or non-productive. We might even have toys at our desk—putty, a Slinky, a kaleidoscope. These toys are small enough to keep in your desk. Just a few minutes of working the putty, moving the Slinky back and forth, or looking at the various shapes in the kaleidoscope can release stress through relaxation, pleasant thoughts, and smiles.

Forward-thinking, progressive companies across the country are recognizing the importance of laughter for their employees; if their employees are going to be productive and happy, they must help their employees use humour in the workplace. Studies have shown that humour can increase productivity and decrease absenteeism, but, more importantly, it can lead to better job satisfaction. Stanford University researcher William Fry has found that laughing 100 times a day is equivalent to 10 minutes of exercise on a rowing machine. A good, hearty laugh pumps air into the lungs, increases oxygen intake, and causes muscles to relax. Laughter can even cause blood pressure to drop. After a hearty laugh, a person enters a deep state of relaxation that can last as long as 45 minutes.[4] A chuckle also helps. So take a few minutes each day to read your favourite cartoon in the newspaper or to notice the funny antics of your co-workers. Laughter really is good medicine.

Another way to quickly reduce tension and loosen up muscles that tighten during long hours working at your computer is to take a short exercise break. You might keep athletic shoes at your desk, and during a five- to ten-minute break, climb stairs or take a brisk walk outdoors. Or you might simply do some stretching or meditation exercises while seated or standing at your desk. Search the Internet for *desk exercises* to view videos demonstrating activities that can help to relieve stress and muscle strain. Such physical activity allows you to release built-up tension, open blocked thinking, and trigger creative ideas.

Soft Skills

CONFLICT RESOLUTION

When the attitudes of openness, empathy, and equality are employed to help resolve conflict, they can provide growth opportunities for all involved.

OPENNESS

Be open to what others think and feel. Also, state your feelings and thoughts openly without being negative. In other words, use "I" statements about how you feel and what you think should happen.

EMPATHY

When others are speaking, listen with **empathy** (identifying with and understanding another's situation, feelings, and motives). Express your concern and support for the other person's opinions. Be willing to change your position if others present appropriate reasons for doing so. In other words, do not be closed to the opinions of others.

EQUALITY

Give other people time to express their feelings. Evaluate all ideas equally. Do not base your opinion of an idea on whether the person is a friend of yours or whether you like or dislike the individual. We learn from hearing what others think and feel. We close ourselves from learning when we ignore the ideas of others.

Chapter Summary

The summary will help you remember the important points covered in this chapter.

- Time is a unique resource; it cannot be bought, sold, borrowed, rented, saved, or manufactured. It is the only resource that must be spent the minute it is received.
- Time wasters include ineffective communication, poor telephone usage, inadequate planning, interruptions, disorganization, and procrastination.
- Good time management techniques include analyzing how we use our time and establishing effective routines.

- Time management systems, such as calendars and PIM software, can help us manage ourselves in relation to our time.
- Stress is the body's response to a demand placed upon it. Chronic stress occurs when a distressful situation is prolonged, allowing no rest or recuperation for the body.
- Stress reducers include balancing work and play, knowing the difference between achievement and perfection, recognizing limits, exercising, eating right, getting enough sleep, and managing anger and time.
- Anger is a growing corporate problem; incidences of violence in the workplace have increased.

Key Terms

carpal tunnel syndrome p. 31
chronic stress p. 32
computer vision syndrome p. 31
conflict resolution p. 33
downsize p. 32
empathy p. 34
ergonomics p. 30
goal p. 23

PIM (personal information management) p. 26
priority p. 25
procrastination p. 28
rightsize p. 32
RSI (repetitive stress injury) p. 31
stress p. 32
time p. 23
time management p. 23

Discussion Items

These discussion items provide an opportunity to test your understanding of the chapter through written responses and discussion with your classmates and your instructor.

1. Identify and describe five time wasters.
2. What is PIM software, and how can it help you manage your time?

3. What is meant by ergonomics? Give five ergonomic guidelines to follow to avoid RSIs when establishing a new workstation or adapting an existing workstation.
4. What is stress, and what causes it? Identify three ways of managing stress.
5. Is all stress unhealthy? Explain your answer.
6. List and explain ways you can manage your stress.

Critical-Thinking Activity

Keri-An Mahar has worked in human resources at CanAsian for five years. She is in charge of employee benefits. Keri-An is an excellent employee—very competent, knowledgeable about human resources (she holds an MBA, with a specialty in management), loyal, dependable, and respected by her colleagues. Two years ago, a new vice-president of human resources was hired. Keri-An has tried to work with him, but the situation does not seem to improve; in fact, it worsens. He gives her inadequate information. He asks her at the last minute to prepare reports. He lies to her about company policies and directions. Then, he yells at her about violating the directions of the company. On several occasions, Keri-An has yelled back at him; she never felt good about the situation when she allowed these outbursts to

happen. She has talked with him repeatedly about the issues from her perspective. He seems to listen but never responds. He has never complained about her performance; she believes he is satisfied with her work. Keri-An has considered leaving the job; however, she has two more years until she is vested in the retirement system. If she leaves now, she loses all of her retirement benefits. Recently, Keri-An began to have health problems. She went to her physician, who said her illness was the result of stress. He recommended that she take at least three months off. Keri-An did so. The three months have passed, and Keri-An is ready to come back to work.

What suggestions would you make to Keri-An to decrease the stress on her job?

21st Century Skills

  Life and Career Skills
CAREER

 Learning and Innovation Skills
INNOVATION

 Information, Media, and Technology Skills
TECHNOLOGY

 Data
DATA FILE

Building Workplace Skills

Project 2-1 (Learning Outcomes 1 and 2)

TECHNOLOGY   DATA FILE

To access the MindTap site, use the printed access card on the inside cover of your textbook. Student Course Data file Project 2-1a is a screen in your PIM software, and file Project 2-1b is an email message from Martin Albertson. After considering both of these documents, put your task list in priority order, adding the necessary items from Martin Albertson's memo. Assign each task one of four categories: "Urgent and Important," "Important but Not Urgent," "Urgent but Not Important," and "Neither Urgent nor Important." Then rank each task in the categories by assigning a 1, 2, 3, etc., to each item to place it in order within each category. This number will indicate the order in which you should proceed to work on the items. Submit your new prioritized task list to your instructor.

If available, use Outlook or another calendar software to complete this project by first entering the details from the screen image into your calendar. Next, update the calendar with the details provided in the memo. Your instructor will provide specific submission instructions.

Project 2-2 (Learning Outcome 1)

TECHNOLOGY   DATA FILE

In your work with Martin Albertson, you have shared access to his planner to update his contacts and schedule. He hands you four business cards that he received at the recent national marketing conference he attended in Ottawa and asks you to enter them.

While he was out of town, you received several requests for appointments. After discussing the requests with him and receiving his approval, you enter them into his schedule.

Two data files are to be used to complete this project. The file Project 2-2a, a PDF file, contains the business cards; the file Project 2-2b, a list of appointments. Using Outlook or another calendar software, complete all entries and make any revisions that arise because of conflicts. Prepare the contact list and a copy of the calendar in monthly format, and submit both to your instructor.

Project 2-3 (Learning Outcome 1)

TECHNOLOGY   DATA FILE

On the MindTap site, file Project 2-3a is a time log form. Print out or create a page for each of the next five days. Use the hard copy forms or create a document to log the time you spend on various activities. If you are a student and employed, log the time you spend on school, part-time work, and personal activities. If you are not employed, log the time you spend on school and personal activities. Create as realistic a picture as possible.

After you finish that part of the project, analyze the way you spent your time during the five days. File Project 2-3b contains questions to help you. File Project 2-3c contains a Time Effectiveness Questionnaire, which provides general questions concerning the use of time. Respond to these items. After you have analyzed the way you use your time and considered your answers to the Time Effectiveness Questionnaire, prepare an action plan using the form in file Project 2-3d. Indicate how you will make more effective use of your time. Submit a copy of your action plan to your instructor.

Project 2-4 (Learning Outcomes 4 and 6)

CAREER   DATA FILE

A friend of yours, Indra, works in an office in your building. She is having problems. Her situation is described in file Project 2-4. Analyze her case. Follow your instructor's directions to respond to the questions following the case description. You may use the memorandum form file Project 2-4a or some other document as directed by your instructor to submit your responses.

Project 2-5 (Learning Outcomes 4 and 6)

Ahmad, a friend of yours who has worked for CanAsian for two years, is extremely unhappy in his job. He has confided in you about the office situation and has asked for your analysis of what is happening. His situation is described in file Project 2-5. Follow your instructor's directions to respond to the questions following the case description. You may use the memorandum form file Project 2-5a or some other document as directed by your instructor to submit your responses.

Project 2-6 (Learning Outcomes 4 and 6)

Collaborative Project
Online Project

Work with three of your classmates on this project. Using the Web, search for a recent article on each of the following topics:

- controlling stress
- managing anger
- using wellness programs

Summarize the articles and present your findings to the class. Turn in a written report of your findings to your instructor; cite all your references.

Project 2-7 (Learning Outcome 3)

As an administrative professional, you are likely to spend a lot of time working at a computer. If you follow ergonomic guidelines in arranging your workstation and using your computer equipment, you will work more comfortably and will be less likely to develop medical problems such as back pain and carpal tunnel syndrome.

Visit the Canadian Centre for Occupational Health and Safety (CCOHS) or the equivalent website for your province or territory to learn about ergonomics for computer workstations. Links to the CCOHS and CanOSH (a Web portal of links to Canadian occupational health and safety information) sites are provided on the MindTap site. Follow the guidelines at these sites to arrange your workstation at school, work, or home to follow ergonomic guidelines. Create a report summarizing your findings and describing the results. Submit your report to your instructor.

Project 2-8 (Learning Outcomes 1 and 2)

Your company recently hired a new administrative assistant, Maryam Arjmand. On her first day, you stopped by her desk to meet her. During your conversation, you told her to let you know if you could do anything to help her settle in. Since then, Maryam has called you whenever she has a question. Sometimes the questions are about items that are urgent; but on other occasions, they are not. Assisting her usually takes just a few minutes, but sometimes it takes longer.

Maryam probably calls you about eight times a day. Helping her so much is affecting your ability to get your work done. Two administrative assistants work in Maryam's department, and you know they would be happy to help her. Maryam, however, doesn't know them very well and is more comfortable asking you. How can you continue to assist Maryam and to encourage her to ask questions about things she doesn't understand while limiting the inroads that her interruptions make on your time?

Discuss this situation with two of your classmates and brainstorm some solutions. Share your ideas with the class.

Project 2-9 (Learning Outcomes 4 and 6)

Share with your classmates some methods of relieving stress and how you have handled conflict in your own life. Then add to your e-portfolio that you began in Chapter 1 by describing how you plan to control your stress and resolve conflict in the future. In preparing this plan, do the following:

- Identify the stressors that you currently have in your life. These stressors may be at home, at school, or at the office.
- Provide examples of conflict in your life.
- Identify ways you can relieve these stressors and manage the conflict.
- Identify situations that currently make you angry.
- Identify ways you can manage that anger.
- Identify ways you will seek to control stress, manage anger, and resolve conflict in the future.
- Identify some of the ideas that you have heard from your classmates that you will consider implementing.

Save this document in your Reflections folder under an appropriate file name.

Make the Grade with MindTap

Stay organized and efficient with **MindTap**—a single destination with all the course material and study aids you need to succeed. Built-in apps leverage social media and the latest learning technology. For example:

- ReadSpeaker will read the text to you.
- Flashcards are pre-populated to provide you with a jump-start for review—or you can create your own.
- You can highlight text and make notes in your MindTap Reader. Your notes will flow into Evernote, the electronic notebook app that you can access anywhere when it's time to study for the exam.
- Self-quizzing allows you to access your understanding.

Visit nelson.com/student to start using **MindTap**. Enter the Online Access Code from the card included with your text. If a code card is not provided, you can purchase instant access at NELSONbrain.com.

Endnotes

1. "Workplace," Mental Health Commission of Canada, https://www.mentalhealthcommission.ca/English/focus-areas/workplace, accessed August 3, 2018.
2. "The Sanofi Canada Healthcare Survey 2014," Sanofi Canada, http://www.sanofi.ca, accessed January 2014.
3. Susan Crompton, "What's Stressing the Stressed? Main Sources of Stress among Workers," Statistics Canada, https://www.statcan.gc.ca/pub/11-008-x/2011002/article/11562-eng.htm, accessed August 3, 2018.
4. Andrea Atkins, "Laughing Matters," *World Traveler*, November 1997, pp. 53–56.

CHAPTER 3

Working Ethically

Do I Qualify?

Administrative Assistant

National nonprofit organization seeks legal assistant to support the work of its legal affairs department. The ideal job candidate must have:
- excellent written and oral communication skills
- understanding of and commitment to the mission and philosophy of the company
- excellent interpersonal skills
- flexibility and adaptability
- ability to maintain confidentiality of sensitive information
- effective time management skills, organizational abilities, and attention to detail
- experience with federal, provincial, and municipal lobbying and gift/gratuities rules

LEARNING OUTCOMES

After studying this chapter, you should be able to:

1. Explain the importance of ethical behaviour in the workplace.
2. Identify characteristics of ethical businesses and organizations.
3. List and describe basic workplace standards as found in the Canada Labour Code.
4. Identify traits of an ethical administrative professional.
5. Define the steps necessary for ethical change.

The ethics of business enterprises affects our society greatly. Highly successful business leaders are quoted in the news, and their behaviour is observed and often emulated by others, not only in the business world but also in the nation and the world at large.

The influence of business on society and the influence of corporate leaders on individuals are not always positive. For example, poorly run businesses and leaders who misuse their power and authority can lead to inferior products and services, environmental pollution, unsafe working conditions, unfair treatment of employees, and various other unethical behaviours. When business leaders behave irresponsibly, our society and individuals within it are often the losers. For example, in 2015 Volkswagen deceived regulators and customers by admitting they modified their vehicles in order to be able to cheat emissions testing. This scandal cost the company millions of dollars and tarnished its reputation. In 2017, Loblaw Companies Ltd. was found to have engaged in an industry-wide bread price-fixing scheme that resulted in a class action lawsuit being filed against the company.

In this chapter, ethics is considered a **pragmatic** topic—one not only to be understood conceptually but also to be practised on a daily basis. This chapter will help you to understand the significance of ethics in the workplace and the responsibility you have as an administrative professional.

Characteristics of Ethical Organizations

Employees are more likely to enjoy going to work each day when they know they will be treated fairly, they will not be harassed, and the other workers will play by the rules. Employees expect their employer to pay them well and treat them fairly. Companies that do neither can expect to have a high turnover rate, which adversely affects the business. Owners, including shareholders, have an interest in the company showing a profit. Investors expect the company to be open and honest about its financial condition. Customers who buy the company's products and services provide the financial resources for making a profit. Pleasing its customers with an excellent product or service and standing behind that product or service are top priorities for successful businesses. Maintaining an ethical climate is in the best interests of a business or an organization.

Several characteristics distinguish ethical organizations. They include being honest, visionary, and environmentally and socially responsible; being committed to diversity and intolerance of discrimination within the organization; providing a safe and healthy environment for workers; offering fair and equitable pay; and respecting the law. Many organizations today have written vision or mission statements that clarify the directions and values of the organization. Such statements let the employees know the directions of the organization, what it values, how it intends to live those values, and what is and is not considered to be ethical behaviour within the organization.

Royal Bank of Canada, a Canadian organization consistently on the *Fortune* 500 list, has an extensive code of conduct that applies to all employees and directors (see Figure 3-1); the Code "protects employees, clients and RBC by providing a common understanding of what's acceptable and what's not. It is a resource that helps us understand what's expected and why."[1]

In the spirit of the code, RBC provides this advice to employees if they encounter a potential conflict of interest:

- Think about how your actions will look to others.
- Disclose activities up front, especially if you are unsure about potential conflict.
- Talk to your manager or local compliance group if you have any questions.

FIGURE 3-1
Royal Bank of Canada Code of Conduct

OUR VISION AND VALUES

RBC's Values define what we stand for everywhere we do business. They are reflected in our behaviour and the way we build relationships and deliver value to all our stakeholders—clients, employees, shareholders, communities and others we deal with. Guided by our shared Values and united in a common purpose, we can achieve our strategic goals and accomplish great results.

We demonstrate our Vision—**To be Among the World's Most Trusted and Successful Financial Institutions**—by living our Values in the decisions and actions we take every day. These five Values set the tone for our culture and unify us across geographies and businesses:

CLIENT FIRST

We will always earn the right to be our clients' first choice.

- Put client needs above our own whatever our role, to build lasting relationships
- Listen with empathy, understand client needs to offer the right advice and solutions
- Bring the best of RBC to deliver excellent value and differentiated client experiences

COLLABORATION

We win as One RBC.

- Believe in each other and trust in teamwork and colleagues' intentions
- Share knowledge, listen, and teach to learn and achieve more together

- Look beyond ourselves to see the bigger picture for opportunities and solutions

ACCOUNTABILITY

We take ownership for personal and collective high performance.

- Be bolder, reach higher, act with courage to realize potential and make a difference
- Own it; seek out accountability and empowerment to grow and excel
- Be curious and learn continuously to build skills and careers

DIVERSITY & INCLUSION

We embrace diversity for innovation and growth.

- Speak up for inclusion and empower people to grow and achieve more
- Seek out and respect different perspectives to challenge conventional approaches
- Identify and act on the opportunities and needs that client diversity brings

INTEGRITY

We hold ourselves to the highest standards to build trust.

- Be respectful, transparent and fair in all relationships
- Stand up for what we believe; speak with candour; constructively challenge
- Build trust of clients, colleagues and community partners by listening to and understanding their interests and needs

Source: Royal Bank of Canada, Code of Conduct (2018). Royal Bank of Canada website. Reproduced with permission of Royal Bank of Canada.

Being Socially and Environmentally Responsible

Social responsibility refers to the obligation of a business to contribute to the greater good of the community. Communities rely on the support of local companies for financial stability and growth. Businesses have a legal and ethical obligation not to harm the citizens of the community. This obligation includes properly disposing of harmful wastes and using pollution controls for factories. An ethical company is a good neighbour.

Businesses make choices about pollution, employee health and safety, the sponsorship of charitable endeavours and employee volunteer programs, and other issues and needs. Organizations may choose to give employees time off for volunteering or a convenient way to financially support worthy causes. After the September 11 attacks, the 2016 Fort McMurray wildfires in Alberta, and the flooding in Houston following Hurricane Harvey in 2017, corporations were among the first to send millions of dollars in aid for people in need.

Business executives who are socially and environmentally responsible are constantly aware of the possible dangers in their businesses and take all necessary precautions to see that the environment is not polluted. They pay attention to government regulations that address the careful disposal of hazardous materials and implement programs to recycle paper, plastics, electronics, and other items. Ethical organizations work to preserve the environment for future generations by reducing the impact of their operations on the environment. When involved in new construction, they give top priority to cutting down as few trees as possible and protecting wetlands and other areas that are environmentally important. They adopt alternative energy sources, such as solar, wind, or methane, and may use hybrid or electric vehicles in their fleets.

Being Committed to Diversity

A diverse workforce benefits companies in several ways. It helps them meet the needs of their global customers and an increasingly diverse Canadian population. Studies have shown that groups and teams with diverse members are more creative and make better decisions. Diversity also helps a company attract and retain talented employees.

Ethical organizations go farther than the law requires. They make hiring decisions based on merit and are committed to providing equal employment opportunities. They create environments that are attractive to all employees. They provide diversity training for their employees and hold managers accountable for consistently supporting and ensuring diversity.

Being Intolerant of Discrimination

Businesses are made up of people; people who bring their own particular prejudices to the workplace. **Prejudice** is defined as "a system of negative beliefs, feelings, and actions." These beliefs, feelings, and actions are based on *learned* categories of distinctions, *learned* evaluation of these categories, and *learned* tendencies to act according to certain beliefs and feelings. Prejudice can lead to acts of **discrimination** (treatment or consideration based on class or category rather than individual merit). Discrimination may occur in many forms; some of the most commonly seen forms of discrimination are based on race or ethnicity, gender, sexual orientation, and age. Discrimination may also involve sexual harassment.

Racial/Ethnic Discrimination

Racial/ethnic tensions will always exist in a multicultural country like Canada. All organizations must comply with laws that promote equal treatment and prohibit discrimination. The Canada Labour Code (CLC) and subsequent regulations form the primary source of federal employment and labour law. Additionally, at the provincial and territorial level, numerous statutory provisions govern the employer/employee relationship. Human rights codes established at the provincial level state that every person has a right to equal treatment with respect to employment without discrimination based on race, ancestry, place of origin, colour, ethnic origin, citizenship, creed, sex, age, record of offences, marital status, family status, sexual orientation, or disability. Figure 3-2 lists areas of prohibited discriminatory practices identified in federal law.

FIGURE 3-2

Prohibited Discriminatory Practices

- Discriminatory hiring, firing, or treatment in the course of employment
- Discriminatory employment applications, advertisements, or inquiries
- Discriminatory membership practices by employee organizations
- Discriminatory policies or agreements by employee or employer organizations
- Maintenance of gender-based wage differentials
- Freedom from sexual and other kinds of harassment in the workplace

Gender Discrimination

The federal Employment Equity Act provides for employment equity for women, Indigenous peoples, people with disabilities, and members of visible minority groups. We recognize in our society today that very few occupations are gender-specific. Employers may not advertise a job specifically for a man or a woman unless bona fide occupational requirements require a person of a specific gender—for example, if the position involves modelling men's clothing. Hiring decisions must be based on whether the individual has the knowledge and skills needed for the job, not on whether the person is male or female.

Also, employee pay cannot be based on whether a person is male or female. Provincial and territorial employment standards legislation and the federal CLC prohibit pay discrimination on the basis of gender. Men and women performing work in the same establishment under similar conditions must receive the same pay when their jobs require equal skill, effort, and responsibility.

Provincial and territorial human rights codes also prohibit discrimination based on sexual orientation and gender identity/expression. Gay, lesbian, bisexual, and transgender organizations have become active in helping to ensure that the rights of individuals are not violated on the basis of their sexual preference or gender identity and expression.

Age Discrimination

No distinction can be made in age, either in the advertising or hiring process or after an employee is on the job. For example, an organization cannot print a job vacancy notice that specifies a particular age or age range for applicants. At one time, many companies in Canada had a mandatory retirement age. Forcing an employee to retire by reason of age is considered to be a human rights issue. In 2012, an amendment was made to the Canadian Human Rights Act that abolished mandatory retirement. Figure 3-3 lists steps for handling harassment or discrimination.

FIGURE 3-3

Steps for Handling Harassment or Discrimination Issues

- Know your rights and know the laws. Know your organization's position on discrimination and harassment, the activities considered to be legal under your provincial or territorial human rights code, and your employer's responsibility toward you.
- Keep a record of all harassment and discrimination infractions, noting the dates, incidents, and witnesses (if any).
- File a formal grievance with your company. Check your company policy and procedure manual or talk with the director of human resources concerning the grievance procedure.
- If no formal grievance procedures exist, file a formal complaint with your employer in the form of a memorandum describing the incidents, identifying the individuals involved in the harassment or discrimination, and requesting disciplinary action.
- If your employer is not responsive to your complaint, your province or territory may have human rights offices that can assist you. Search online for the address and telephone number of the Human Rights Commission office nearest you where you can file charges of discrimination.
- Talk to friends, co-workers, and relatives. Avoid isolation and self-blame. You are not alone; harassment and discrimination of all types occur in the workplace.
- Consult a lawyer to investigate legal alternatives to discriminatory or harassing behaviour.

Maintaining a Policy against Harassment

Harassment in the workplace may be present in several forms. It is generally defined as conduct that demeans, humiliates, or embarrasses a person, leading to a hostile work environment. Bullying is one form of harassment that has moved from the school playground into the office. Both the Canadian Human Rights Act and the CLC protect employees from harassment in the workplace.

Sexual harassment, a specific type of harassment, has been defined in the CLC as "any conduct, comment, gesture or contact of a *sexual nature* that is likely to cause offence or humiliation or that might, on reasonable grounds, be perceived as placing a condition of a sexual nature on employment or on any opportunity for training or promotion." Three criteria can be used to determine whether sexual harassment exists:

1. Submission to sexual conduct is either implicitly or explicitly a condition of employment.
2. Employment decisions affecting the recipient are made on the basis of the recipient's acceptance or rejection of sexual conduct.
3. The conduct has the intent or effect of substantially interfering with an individual's work performance or creates an intimidating, hostile, or offensive work environment.

Division XV.1 of Part III of the CLC makes the organization responsible to "make every reasonable effort to ensure that no employee is subjected to sexual harassment" by issuing and publishing to all employees a policy statement concerning sexual harassment.

The organization is liable for the behaviour of its employees whether or not management is aware that harassment has taken place. The organization is also responsible for the actions of non-employees on the company's premises. Because of these liabilities, many organizations have published policy statements that make it clear to all employees that harassment of any kind is a violation of the law and of company policy. These statements generally include a clearly defined grievance procedure so an employee has a course of action to take if harassment does occur.

Supervisors can help to create a workplace free from sexual and other forms of harassment by

- applying and promoting high standards of integrity, conduct, and concern for all employees.
- leading by example. Social behaviour should not become confused with behaviour that is considered appropriate in the workplace.
- ensuring employment decisions are based on merit.
- educating employees as to the activity that constitutes sexual harassment; let everyone know that sexual harassment will not be tolerated. Sexual jokes, teasing, or innuendo should not become a routine part of the work environment.

- ensuring that employees who feel they are victims of sexual harassment are aware of the options available to them in addressing these issues. They should not fear punitive action or retaliation against them as a result of lodging their complaint.
- identifying a person that employees can contact confidentially with any concerns and complaints about sexual or other harassment issues.
- investigating every complaint promptly and thoroughly.
- observing the language and behaviour of fellow supervisors and advising them if their actions may be perceived by others as sexual harassment.

People AT WORK

Sexual Harassment Compliance Officer

If you work for an organization that provides training for employees on the activities that constitute sexual harassment, you may receive your training from a sexual harassment compliance officer. Sexual harassment compliance officers provide policy information and guidance when an organization responds to incidents of sexual harassment. An officer takes complaints of sexual harassment and sex discrimination and investigates each complaint thoroughly. They provide remedies and works with external representatives regarding complaints. The sexual harassment compliance officer also works with management to provide a working environment free of sexual harassment and sexual discrimination.

Providing for Persons with Disabilities

Persons with disabilities can face biases based on their physical challenges and may be treated differently because of their disabilities. The ethical organization abides by federal, provincial, or territorial human rights statutes, acts, or policies in fulfilling their duty to accommodate. In 2018, the Canadian federal government tabled the first national accessibility law which, when enacted, will be referred to as the *Accessible Canada Act*. In addition, Ontario, Manitoba, and Nova Scotia each has its own specific accessibility legislation that outlines the requirements organizations have to ensure their workplaces are accessible. The objective of the statutes, acts, or policies is to eliminate barriers that prevent full participation of existing and potentially new employees in the workforce. In addition to physical barriers, other barriers to employment include unnecessary job requirements and unequal access to training and development. The ethical organization

- provides access to all facilities for people who have physical challenges
- provides the proper equipment, workspace, and training and development
- ensures that initial employment practices do not discriminate against people who have physical challenges

"Duty to accommodate" requires the employer to make every effort to accommodate employees with disabilities, unless to do so would create undue hardship on the employer. In determining undue hardship, an employer may take into consideration the health of the employee, safety, and costs.

Involvement in the Community

The ethical organization recognizes the needs of its community and assists with meeting these needs when possible. For example, the organization might

- provide tutors for elementary and high-school students
- engage in mentoring programs for troubled youth
- work with colleges and universities in providing intern experiences for students
- provide computers (or other technology the business manufactures) to schools
- serve on community boards and commissions
- participate in the local chamber of commerce
- contribute to community charities
- provide leadership to solicit funds for worthy causes, such as for children who have disabilities, health care for people who are indigent, and shelters for people who are homeless
- assist with arts and other programs by providing leadership and/or monies

Respect for the Needs and Rights of Employees

Promoting employee productivity is important to the ethical organization. An ethical organization understands that employees have needs, such as the need to know the values and directions of the company, what is expected of them, and so on. Figure 3-4 illustrates some ways the organization can meet the needs of employees.

FIGURE 3-4

Meeting the Needs of Employees

- Provide employees with a copy of the values and goals of the organization; ask that managers review these documents with their employees.
- Encourage managers to consistently distribute important information about the organization.
- Help employees set achievable goals that are consistent with the goals of the organization.
- Administer employee performance evaluations fairly.
- Support employees in learning new skills.
- Reward employee creativity.
- Challenge employees to generate new ideas.
- Encourage collaboration and cooperation among employees.
- Establish teams to work on significant organizational issues.

An ethical organization also understands that employees have rights. Three such rights are the right to due process, the right to organize, and the right to privacy.

Right to Due Process

Generally, employees make a conscious effort to contribute to an organization. In return, they expect to be treated fairly by an organization. People would not choose to work for an organization if they did not think they were going to be treated fairly. **Employment at will** (the doctrine that allows employees to be fired for good cause or for no cause) has been and still is an employment doctrine upheld by some organizations. In an unethical organization, adherence to such a doctrine can cause irreparable harm to employees. For example, companies have been known to call long-time employees into a supervisor's office, tell them they no longer have a job, and send them home immediately with no severance package and loss of all benefits. The doctrine of employment at will has come under considerable attack and, in most organizations, is being replaced by the right to due process. **Due process** means that managers impose sanctions on employees only after offering them a chance to correct the organizational grievance. An ideal system of due process is one in which employees are given

- a clearly written job description
- organizational policies and procedures
- the assurance that all policies and procedures will be administered consistently and fairly without discrimination
- a commitment by top management that managers will be responsible for adhering to the values and morals of the organization
- a fair and impartial hearing if the rules are broken

Right to Organize

Approximately one-third of the Canadian labour force is represented by a trade union. Under federal, provincial, or territorial labour relations legislation, every person is free to join a union of their own choice and to participate in its lawful activities. With more than a half-million members, the Canadian Union of Public Employees (CUPE) is Canada's largest union.

Labour unions are instrumental in ensuring that the rights and benefits of employees are upheld. Employees join unions to have a stronger, collective voice in resolving the issues that arise in the workplace. They resolve such issues through negotiations and collective agreements, without which many employees could be at an economic disadvantage. These collective agreements enhance existing federal, provincial, and territorial employment standards.

Right to Privacy

Canada's Personal Information Protection and Electronic Documents Act (PIPEDA), or similar legislation implemented provincially or territorially, provides the ethical organization with guidelines regarding the individual employee's right to privacy. Certainly, an organization has the right to information about an employee that affects that individual's performance. For example, if a physical illness no longer allows an employee to perform his or her job, the employer has a right to know about it. However, the employer does not have the right to know about illnesses that do not affect job performance. Similarly, an employer does not have the right to know about a person's political or religious beliefs. In fact, in a job interview, the employer cannot ask questions about marital status, age, organizations to which the person belongs, where the person was born, the spouse's employment status, and so on. These questions are illegal. If an organization acquires information about an employee's personal life while doing a legitimate investigation, the organization has an obligation to destroy the information, especially if the data would embarrass or in some way injure the employee. Also, an organization must give employees the right to give or withhold consent before any private aspects of their lives are investigated.

Adherence to Workplace Standards

Occupational health and safety legislation in Canada outlines the general rights and responsibilities of the employer, the supervisor, and the worker. In addition to federal legislation that applies to employees across the country employed by the federal government, each province and territory has its own legislation. You can read more about the specific legislation in your province or territory by accessing the CanOSH (Canadian Occupational Safety and Health) website from the link provided on the MindTap site.

An ethical organization abides by the CLC and other statutory provisions at the provincial or territorial level that confer upon employees certain minimum standards of employment. Figure 3-5 provides an overview of the topics covered by employment standards legislation. Specific requirements may vary by province or territory.

Establishing and Living Organizational Values

Many organizations today establish vision and value statements and make these statements available to their employees and to the public by posting them on websites and distributing them in organizational publications. Here are excerpts of mission/vision/value statements from two organizations: Horizon Health Network in New Brunswick and Royal Bank of Canada.

FIGURE 3-5

Topics Covered by Employment Standards Legislation

MINIMUM WAGES

The minimum wage rates payable to most workers varies across provinces and territories. In 2018, the minimum wage rate in Alberta was $15; in Saskatchewan, $11.06; in Nova Scotia, $11; in Ontario, $14; and in Nunavut, $13.

HOURS OF WORK

While some provinces or territories may authorize hours in excess, generally the legislation provides that no employee shall work more than eight hours per day or 48 hours per week. In Quebec, the Act defined 40 hours per week to be a regular workweek for any employee.

OVERTIME

Overtime generally at a rate of one-and-a-half times the regular rate of pay is paid to employees who work in excess of approximately 40 hours per week. At the request of an employee, some employers may provide time off in lieu of overtime pay.

PUBLIC HOLIDAYS

Under federal, provincial, and territorial law, employees are entitled to five paid public holidays each year: New Year's Day, Good Friday, Canada Day, Labour Day, and Christmas Day. Federal employees also receive paid days off for Easter Monday, Victoria Day, Thanksgiving Day, and Boxing Day; many non-federal employees also get these holidays. Some provinces recognize Remembrance Day in November, a civic holiday in August that is known by specific names in each province, and a Family Day in February.

VACATION PAY

After one year of service with an organization, an employee is entitled to two weeks' vacation with pay (except in Saskatchewan where it is three weeks and Quebec where it is one day per month worked). At the employer's discretion, this vacation may be taken at a time mutually convenient to the employee and employer, and may occur within ten months of commencement of employment.

MATERNITY LEAVE

Provincial and territorial laws vary, but upon four weeks' written notice, female employees are entitled to 17 weeks of unpaid maternity leave, provided the employee has been employed for a minimum number of weeks immediately preceding the estimated delivery date. Unemployment insurance benefits are available to employees on maternity leave. On her return, the employee is entitled to reinstatement in her former position or to be given a comparable position in the same location and with the same wages and benefits.

PARENTAL LEAVE

Upon four weeks' notice, an employee who has been employed a minimum number of weeks is entitled to 37 weeks of parental leave. This leave is available to male and female employees, and, in the case of a female employee, may immediately follow a maternity leave. At the end of the parental leave, an employee is entitled to be reinstated to the same or comparable job at the same rate of pay, with the same benefits and seniority accrued as of the date of the commencement of the leave.

COMPASSIONATE CARE LEAVE

Compassionate care benefits are a component of Employment Insurance. Benefits may be paid up to a maximum of eight weeks to a person who needs to be absent from work in order to care for a family member who is gravely ill and at risk of dying. No provision is made for paid leave as the Code provides job security only. However, some financial support may be available through the Employment Insurance Act to qualified employees.

EQUAL PAY FOR EQUAL WORK

Employees who perform substantially the same kind of work in the same establishment where the performance of duties requires the same skill, effort, and responsibility must have the same rate of pay. Difference in pay rates may exist where the differential is based on any factor other than sex, such as seniority or meritocracy.

BENEFIT PLANS

When in place, they must be furnished to all employees with no differences based on age, sex, or marital status.

Sources: Compiled from various sites, including "Statutory Holidays in Canada," www.statutoryholidays.com/index.php; "Minimum Wages in Canada," Canada Online, http://canadaonline.about.com/od/labourstandards/a/minimum-wage-in-canada.htm; "The Canada Labour Code," http://laws-lois.justice.gc.ca; "The Canadian Human Rights Commission," www.chrc-ccdp.ca, accessed August 2011.

Horizon Health Network

Our Vision: Exceptional care. Every person. Every day.

Horizon, through our staff, physicians and volunteers must seek to be more than simply adequate . . . to exceed the expectations for every person who looks to us for service and to do this for each and every interaction with our patients and visitors. . . . Nothing short of aspiring to give exceptional care will allow us to do our very best.

Our Mission: Helping People Be Healthy

. . . We achieve best results through placing our patients and clients at the centre of our health delivery system.

Our Values: At Horizon, the following values guide how we work together and serve our patients, their families and each other
- We show empathy, compassion and respect.
- We strive for excellence.
- We are all leaders, yet work as a team.
- We act with integrity and are accountable.[2]

Royal Bank of Canada
- Our Vision: To be among the world's most trusted and successful financial institutions
- Our Values: Client first: We will always earn the right to be our clients' first choice

- Collaboration: We win as ONE RBC
- Accountability: We take ownership for personal and collective high performance
- Diversity & Inclusion: We embrace diversity for innovation and growth
- Integrity: We hold ourselves to the highest standards to build trust
- Our Mission: Helping clients thrive and communities prosper[3]

Once you know the company mission/value statement, it is your responsibility to behave in ways that support the mission. If you find yourself in a company where you cannot support the mission or values, it is time for you to find another position.

Maintaining a Safe and Healthy Environment

The public expects an organization to behave in ways that protect and maintain a safe and healthy environment for its customers and the community it serves. Additionally, the ethical organization is committed to providing and maintaining a safe and healthy environment for its employees.

Over the past few years, incidences of violence in the workplace have increased. In fact, workplace violence has become such a large problem in North America that the Occupational Safety and Health Administration in the United States and the Canadian Centre for Occupational Health and Safety have both published specific guidelines on this issue, and legislation exists in both countries. This legislation in Canada, known as "due diligence" legislation, when applied to occupational health and safety means that an employer will take all reasonable precautions to prevent injuries or accidents in the workplace. Due diligence is defined as that level of judgment, care, prudence, determination, and activity which a person would reasonably be expected to exercise under particular circumstances. This duty applies to all situations that are not covered by other, specific workplace legislation.[4]

Many organizations have workplace violence prevention programs, which include helping individuals learn how to deal with and de-escalate conflict. Why is this happening? Experts suggest that the following issues may contribute to increased anger and violence: ignorance of other cultures and the belief that we are being treated unfairly.

An ethical organization upholds the provincial or territorial regulations and acts that require employers to furnish a place of employment free from recognized hazards that can cause death, injury, or illness to employees. Such is the case with smoking and substance abuse.

Smoking

Studies have shown that smoking can be extremely dangerous to an individual's long-term health and that exposure to second-hand smoke can cause emphysema and lung disease.

All provinces and territories in Canada have legislation that prohibits smoking in indoor public spaces and workplaces. Provinces such as Ontario have updated their legislation to expand second-hand smoke to include cannabis and vapour. Because this legislation is not federally enacted, differences do exist at provincial, territorial, and municipal levels in terms of the definition of second-hand smoke, the provision of ventilated smoking rooms and the distance from a building's entrances and exits at which smoking is banned.

Substance Abuse

Substance abuse refers to the use of alcohol or drugs to an extent that is debilitating for the individual using the substance. Drug and alcohol users are absent an average of two to three times more than other employees and perform at about two-thirds of their actual work potential. Their absence and reduced performance affects all employees, by reducing overall productivity in the workplace. Shoddy work and material waste are evident, and mental and physical agility and concentration deteriorate with substance abuse. Even small quantities of drugs in a person's system can cause deterioration of alertness, lack of clear-headedness, and slower reaction speed, which often result in serious workplace accidents.

The Ethical Administrative Professional

At work, you will face many ethical choices. Some of these choices will be easy to make. The right or wrong answer will be clear. For others, the answer will not be so easy. Many of the characteristics of an ethical organization are also considered ethical characteristics of employees within the organization. While each person has their own core values, values that are widely shared by ethical employees include respect (for the organizational structure, diversity, clients and customers, and the privacy of others), honesty, fairness, responsibility, and compassion.

Personal Values

People rely on their personal values when making ethical decisions. While each person has their own core values, some values are widely shared. Five of these common values are honesty, fairness, respect, responsibility, and compassion.

- **Honesty.** Be honest. Don't deceive, cheat, or steal. Consider how you feel when someone lies to you. Being honest means not only telling the truth but also giving the relevant information.
- **Fairness.** Being fair means acting without prejudice or favouritism. Be fair in your dealings with co-workers, customers, and supervisors. Listen to others. Don't blame others, and do not take advantage of others.

- **Respect.** To have respect for others means that you regard everyone with consideration and care. Respect cultural differences and diversity in the workplace. Try to understand differences in opinions and find common ground and consensus in decision making. Respect also means listening with an open mind to the opinion of others. Learning to be tactful is very important in showing respect. The more respectful you are toward others, the more respect they will show toward you. It is possible to have disagreements without disrespecting each other. There will be some people at work whom you like more than others, but you must be respectful to everyone.
- **Responsibility.** Take responsibility and be accountable for your duties and actions. Always try to do your best. When you make a mistake, own up to it and correct it.
- **Compassion.** Be kind and considerate toward others. Show understanding and caring for your co-workers. Send thank-you notes, sympathy notes, and congratulations notes when appropriate. Try to put yourself in another person's situation to understand how that person might act and feel. Avoid hurting others' feelings.

Respect for the Organizational Structure

While organizations today have fewer layers than in the past, an organizational structure and a reporting line are usually identified in an organizational chart. Being respectful of the organization means that when you have issues or concerns, you do not go over your supervisor's head—that is, you do not consult their superior. If you have an idea that you believe will help the productivity of the office; if you cannot meet a deadline on a project; or if you have problems with someone who reports to you, talk with your supervisor. Keep them informed on all significant items.

Respect for Diversity

Just as the ethical organization is committed to diversity, so too is the ethical employee. The ethical employee accepts and respects the diversity of all people—whether that diversity is in ethnicity, race, gender, or age. The ethical employee understands that there is no place in the office for telling jokes that have racial, ethnic, or gender overtones.

Respect for Clients and Customers

As an administrative professional, you must be respectful of your clients and customers. In business, follow the adage "the customer is always right." While you should not take this statement literally—a customer may be wrong; after all, everyone makes mistakes—in the context of service to the customer, they are always considered to be right. Advocate within the company on behalf of your client, to gain the needed information or, if at all possible, provide the service your client needs. Value the client's time; do not waste it by keeping them on the phone for too long or by being late for an appointment. Treat every client and customer as a VIP (very important person). Remember, without clients and customers, the company would not be in business and you would not have a job.

If you have occasion to help entertain customers and clients—you may be asked to take an out-of-town customer to dinner—keep the situation on a purely professional basis. If gifts from clients and customers are offered to you, check the policy of your organization before accepting. Certainly a small gift may be appropriate, and you can accept it graciously; however, as a matter of ethics, you should not accept an extremely expensive gift.

Respect for the Privacy of Others

Respect the privacy of others within the office by maintaining the confidentiality of information that is formally protected in federal and provincial or territorial legislation and information that is not formally protected but that people assume is private. For example, if someone confides a personal matter to you, do not spread the "juicy gossip." If you have access to personnel files that contain confidential information about others, keep the information confidential. You may at times be given information that is not specifically labelled "confidential," yet should not be passed on to others. Be sensitive to the handling of this information. Do not hide behind the rationale "But I was not told it was confidential." Use your common sense. Ethical conduct dictates that you are always discreet. Remember the Golden Rule: Treat others as you would want to be treated.

Do not go over your supervisor's head; talk with them about issues.

Gossip divides people and forces employees to take sides. Do not be a part of the gossip circle.
- Do not pass on half truths
- Verify information before repeating it
- Do not divulge company business under any conditions
- Make your gossip good news gossip
- Consider the image that others have of you. What do you think of co-workers who spread malicious gossip or talk about confidential information?

Dealing with Workplace Politics

In a truly ethical world, office politics would not exist. Unfortunately, we do not live in such a world and probably never will. Workplace politics are fed by networks of individuals where whom you know can be more important than what you know. Favours may be handed out on the basis of the existing networks.

So what do you do about workplace politics? When you begin a new job, notice what is happening around you. Be aware of the power bases. Be aware of who knows whom and their relationships. Then hold on to your own value system. Do your job to the best of your ability. Do not gossip about office politics. Use your awareness of the power bases to get your job done. In other words, do not fight a power base when you know you cannot win. Spend your energies in doing what is right. Generally, when you hold on to your values and perform your job extremely well, you will be recognized and respected for who you are.

Making Ethical Choices

For some ethical problems, the right choice isn't immediately clear. Suppose, for instance, that your supervisor, whom you like and respect, has a problem with alcohol that is affecting her work. You have to choose between telling the company and protecting your supervisor. When you are in situations like this, you can follow a set of steps to help you reach a good decision:

- Evaluate the problem and understand the options.
- Know the stakeholders. The consequences will affect them.
- Strive to do the right thing. Don't be driven by the desire for immediate gratification.
- Be in harmony with your employer's values.

Ethical training teaches that limiting yourself to *either-or* choices is a mistake. There may be other choices available that will allow a more ethical way to proceed. In this example, you might investigate the company's policies regarding substance abuse. It may turn out that your company works with the employee to address the problem rather than dismissing that person. You might choose to disclose the information to someone in authority at the company whose judgment you trust. You may think about your relationship with your supervisor and decide that you can talk with her about the problem and suggest that she seek help.

Working Ethically

Most people want to work ethically. They want to do the jobs they've been hired to do and to live up to the expectations of their supervisors, co-workers, and customers. When things are going well, working ethically can be easy. It's when circumstances aren't ideal that the temptation to lie, cut corners, or cover up can arise. As an administrative professional, you will sometimes be overworked. You will be under pressure to meet deadlines and produce results. You will experience stress from your job or your personal life. These situations occur for everyone, and they will also occur for you. You need to prepare yourself so you can handle them without losing your sense of perspective or taking actions that you will regret.

Honesty

Dishonesty at work is a common ethical problem. Dishonesty means not only lying but also withholding information or misrepresenting the truth. These actions are always unethical; they are also sometimes illegal. Be honest with your supervisor, co-workers, and clients. When you make a mistake that your supervisor needs to know about, tell your supervisor, even if you think it makes you look bad. Be honest with customers. For example, if clients or patients are waiting for appointments and you know there will be an hour's delay, say so.

Confidentiality

As an administrative professional, you will work with private and sensitive information. Working ethically means protecting the confidentiality of that information. Protecting confidentiality is also sometimes a legal requirement. In Canada, PIPEDA outlines how private sector organizations handle, use, and disclose personal information. If you work in a health care facility, for example, you will be prohibited from sharing a patient's medical information without the patient's written consent, except in certain circumstances. Similar protections exist for client information in legal offices. Company information, as well as personal and financial data of employees and clients are often subject to confidentiality in many other types of businesses.

While breaches of confidentiality are sometimes intentional, they can also occur through ignorance and carelessness. Take the time to make yourself thoroughly aware of the ways in which confidentiality needs to be protected in your office. Learn the requirements of the law, and always follow standard company procedures for storing, maintaining, and releasing confidential data.

Working ethically also means maintaining confidentiality of information that isn't formally protected but that people assume is private. Forwarding someone's e-mail to another reader without first getting permission from the writer is an example of unethical behaviour.

Taking Credit for Other's Work

Working ethically also means not taking credit for work that isn't your own. When this is done, it is plagiarism. Like breaches of confidentiality, plagiarism is sometimes intentional, but it can also occur through carelessness or lack of understanding. The most common cause of plagiarism is lack of time. It is easy, when you have much work to do or are under a deadline, to hastily write down material from a source and to forget to note that it is a quotation. And people are often not aware, for instance, that copying and pasting material from the Internet is plagiarism and is often also a violation of copyright laws. Always provide the source for the following kinds of information, regardless of the medium in which it is provided:

- direct quotations
- paraphrases or restatement of material in your own words
- factual information that isn't widely available or generally known
- photographs, images, tables, and figures

Writing AT WORK

How can you apply ethics in your workplace writing? Here are several suggestions:
- Make sure your content is accurate. Check and recheck your facts.
- Honesty is important. Avoid questionable language.
- Under no condition should your writing contain obscenities or off-colour language.
- Use the editing process as a means of ensuring your messages are courteous and professional. Setting aside a document and reviewing it later will help you from sending messages that you will later regret.
- Take pains not to offend any group in your writing, and avoid language that could be perceived as sexist.
- Don't use humour, unless you know your correspondent well. Keep in mind that many jokes can be offensive to different people or groups.

Petty Theft

Employee theft costs companies billions of dollars each year. For retailers, losses from employee theft exceed those from shoplifting. Taking home notebooks, copy paper, staplers, and other office supplies is stealing. So is using an office copier for personal copying. Duplicating company software to use at home is illegal and unethical. Using the company mail system to mail personal packages is stealing from the company and is also unethical.

Misuse of Time

The importance of attending to company business while at work was discussed in earlier chapters. Surfing the Internet, reading or writing personal email, browsing through catalogues, and reading the news should be done away from work. It is appropriate to have a little communication on matters that are not related to work with other employees. Occasional personal phone calls are usually permissible. Abuse of that privilege is unethical.

Calling in sick when you are not is a common unethical practice. Attendance is extremely important. When employees aren't at work, their work doesn't get done; other people may need to do it for them. Employee absences affect co-workers and supervisors. Coming in late and leaving early can become a bad habit, as can taking extended breaks or lunch hours.

Substance Abuse

Drug and alcohol abuse in the workplace is not tolerated. Employees who abuse drugs or alcohol use more sick days, are late more often than other employees, are less productive and efficient, are more likely to be injured on the job or injure someone else, and cause low employee morale. Some companies have mandatory drug testing before employment. If there is an accident on the job, a drug test may be required.

Personal Behaviour Outside Work

Unethical behaviour outside work can wreak havoc on your professional life. Posting inappropriate personal information on social networking sites should be taken seriously. Some job recruiters search for applicants' names on these sites and on the Internet at large. In some cases, applicants aren't hired and employees are fired for posting provocative photos, making inflammatory statements, or making disparaging comments about their job or workplace on social media.

Employees can also be fired for doing something illegal in their personal lives. Examples are being caught with illegal drugs or receiving a citation from the police for driving while intoxicated.

For the most part, companies do not try to dictate what their employees do in their personal lives. A few companies, citing rising health care costs, forbid their employees from smoking, drinking, and using drugs not only in the workplace but also outside it. These companies sometimes do blood tests to detect any violations of their policies regarding drugs. Such companies usually have a policy about drinking, smoking, or drug use that prospective hires know before they accept a position with the company.

Technology AT WORK

It is unethical to use company time for personal business. Are you spending time on these sites instead of performing work?
- social networking sites
- news sites
- banking sites
- entertainment sites
- shopping sites
- sports sites
- auction sites
- stock trading sites
- employment sites

Ethical Change

Not all individuals and organizations are ethical. Such a statement is not meant to be negative. It merely suggests the inevitable—we do not live in a perfect world. We do live in a world in which employees make ethical mistakes but, in the majority of instances, consistently strive to improve themselves and the organizations in which they work. Ethical organizations require that people within the organization behave ethically, including top management and all individuals throughout the organization. The process of achieving ethical change requires understanding, a systematic approach, commitment, cooperation, and hard work.

Factors Supporting Ethical Change

The organization and individuals committed to ethical change can take certain practical steps to produce the change. These steps include the following:
- Determine the ethical change needed.
- Determine the steps required to achieve the objective.
- Practise the new behaviours.
- Seek feedback on the change.
- Reward the individual or group involved.
- Evaluate the effects of ethical change.

Ethics—The Choice Is Yours

Although you cannot influence the ethics of an entire organization unless you are in upper management, you can carefully check out an organization's ethics before you accept a position. How do you check out an organization's ethics? Here are a few suggestions:
- Read the organization's Web page information. Does it mention the ethics of the organization? Does it mention a commitment to diversity? Does it mention a commitment to the external community? What types of programs does it offer for employees?
- Check the history of the organization. Has the organization ever made headlines for behaving unethically?
- Talk with acquaintances who work for the organization. Ask them to describe the ethical environment of the company.

As an individual employee, you can commit to behaving in an ethical manner. You can decide to follow the ethical stances mentioned in this chapter. You will
- respect the organizational structure
- respect diversity
- respect clients and customers
- respect others' privacy
- be honest
- accept constructive criticism
- consider office politics
- make ethical decisions
- be dependable

You can also promise yourself that if for some reason (beyond your control) your organization begins engaging in grossly unethical behaviours, you will seek employment in another organization. Peter M. Senge, in his book *The Fifth Discipline*, tells the story of the frog: If you put a frog in a cup of tepid water, it will not jump out; the temperature is comfortable. If you heat the water gradually over time until it is boiling hot, the frog will stay in the water and die. The frog adjusts to the temperature as it increases and does not notice the difference in the environment or the threat to its safety. The moral of the story is this: Unless you are committed to observing the ethical behaviour of an organization and behaving in an ethical manner yourself, you may stay in an organization that becomes unethical and find yourself supporting those unethical behaviours to the detriment of your own value system and career growth. Commit now to "jumping out" of unethical waters before you "die" in them.

A Case Study

Consider this example of a setting in which ethical change is needed and is addressed within the organization.

Determine the Ethical Change Needed	As an administrative professional, you have two people reporting to you—Guy Beauchamp and Luyin Wu. You have been asked to lead a ten-person team that will be looking at the hiring practices of administrative professionals. Presently CanAsian's number of minorities employed in this category is not consistent with the number of available minorities in the area. Of the administrative professionals presently working for CanAsian, 7 percent are Indo-Canadian, 3 percent are Latin-American, and 2 percent are Asian. The statistics for Calgary show that the availability of administrative professionals is Indo-Canadian, 25 percent; Latin-American, 10 percent; and Asian, 5 percent. The task of the team is to examine how CanAsian might change these statistics to be more representative of the area. You ask both Guy and Luyin to work with you on the team.
	At the first meeting, Guy makes several statements that are interpreted by the team as being negative concerning the need for change. Luyin says nothing but exhibits body language that suggests she is upset with Guy. You believe you must try to help them modify their behaviours or the team will not be successful. You determine that the following ethical changes are needed:
	• Guy needs to demonstrate greater acceptance of all diversity.
	• Luyin needs to state her opinions in meetings in an open but non-confrontational manner.
Determine the Steps Required to Achieve the Objective	After thinking through the situation, you decide to approach each person individually and discuss the following:
	Guy—Discuss with Guy the importance of CanAsian improving its diversity statistics and ask his opinion of how this might be done. Ask him to prepare his ideas before the next team meeting and to review his ideas with you. In this example, the team leader recognized that the approach to Guy must be positive, not negative. The team leader did not berate him for his behaviour but asked for his help on the completion of the team report.
	Luyin—Discuss with Luyin the importance of stating her opinions in an open manner at the team meetings. Let her know you value her opinions and want to hear from her. Remember that Luyin is Chinese, and it may not be easy for her to state her opinions openly.
	You also decide to clarify the objectives with the entire group at the next meeting, presenting the objectives positively.
Practise the New Behaviours	Give Guy and Luyin a chance to behave differently from the way they did in the last meeting by asking Guy to share his suggestions for improvement (that you have reviewed together before the meeting). If Luyin does not voice her opinions, ask for her response. Reward Guy and Luyin for doing a good job by publicly praising both of them.
	After clarifying the objectives for the group, ask whether anyone has questions and discuss whatever issues are raised.
Seek Feedback	Ask a trusted member of the committee to evaluate both your behaviour and the behaviour of the team, and to then make suggestions for changes. If necessary, you might have a consultant observe the group and offer suggestions to team members for successfully completing their tasks. The team leader may also engage in team-building exercises with the group.
Reward the Individuals and the Group	Assuming Guy and Luyin show positive changes in their behaviour, reward them for their growth. Let them know you appreciate their work on the committee, that they did a good job, and that the results of their work will make CanAsian a better place to work. In addition, reward yourself for your work with the team. You deserve to be proud of your insights and willingness to work with the individuals. Mentally add this success to your list of strengths.
Evaluate the Effects of the Ethical Change	Observe whether the team's recommendations result in greater diversity in the numbers of administrative professionals who are employed. If not, you might want to discuss the problem with the human resources director.

Ethics is a systematic study of moral conduct, duty, and judgment. Ethics can be thought of as guidelines or accepted beliefs about what is right or wrong, good or bad. These beliefs are reflected in business ethics, which applies these principles to day-to-day decisions and activities in the workplace.

People's decisions and actions each day affect how others perceive them. Can others depend on you to act fairly? Do they consider your decisions to be based on a thoughtful process? Do they count on you to do the right thing? In a similar way, the reputation of a business is affected by the decisions and actions of its employees, managers, and owners.

Certainly, ethical behaviour has always been important for organizations and individuals, and understanding business ethics is especially important for administrative professionals because of the nature of this trusted position. Administrative assistants are knowledgeable about confidential information and sensitive issues.

The use of technology and the level of connectedness existing today through social and other forms of media means that we are now more immediately aware of unethical practices. For example, if an airline crash kills hundreds of people and the cause is faulty equipment because of improper maintenance by the airline, we learn those facts almost immediately; similarly, news travels quickly when a company puts a food product on the market with an additive that may cause illness or even death. And when Enron filed for bankruptcy in 2001, secretive insider partnerships were disclosed that had been used to hide millions of dollars in corporate debt. This disclosure was due in part to ethical employees who blew the whistle on the illegal activities. The term *whistleblower* now applies to ethically minded employees who bring to light the indiscretions of their organization.

Technological advances in medical science have expanded to the point that ethics now represents a major consideration. Some of the ethical questions being debated include the following.

1. Does an individual have the right to determine when they die and to seek assistance with death?
2. How long should a seriously ill patient be kept alive through artificial means?
3. Is it ethical to use stem cells derived from embryos and fetuses in medical research?

These questions have implications for various health professions, pharmaceutical businesses, and individuals.

Obviously, these ethical questions represent only a few of the many issues we face. As technology opens new vistas, ethical questions will continue to occur. The point here is that we require, now and in the future, wisdom on the part of business leaders and individuals who are employed by businesses to face and solve the ethical issues that will confront us. An important aspect of this wisdom is **morality** (a set of ideas of right and wrong). All of us must strengthen our own ethical understandings and moral **integrity** (consistently adhering to a set of ideas of right and wrong), both within and outside the workplace.

Chapter Summary

The summary will help you remember the important points covered in this chapter.

- Ethics are guidelines or accepted beliefs about what is right or wrong, good or bad. Business ethics apply these principles to day-to-day decisions and activities in the workplace.
- The lack of ethical behaviour by a business can affect our society and the individuals within it.
- Advances in technology and the immediate coverage of business practices through social media have resulted in higher awareness of ethical standards.
- The ethical organization respects the needs and rights of employees, is honest, visionary, committed to diversity, and socially and environmentally responsible.
- The ethical employee is honest, dependable, and cooperative; respects the organizational structure, diversity, others' privacy, clients, and customers; and makes ethical decisions.
- As an individual, commit to behaving ethically; and, when necessary prepare to leave an organization that is unethical.

Key Terms

discrimination p. 41
due process p. 44
employment at will p. 44
ethics p. 52
integrity p. 52

morality p. 52
pragmatic p. 39
prejudice p. 41
sexual harassment p. 42
substance abuse p. 46

Discussion Items

These discussion items provide an opportunity to test your understanding of the chapter through written responses or discussion with your classmates and your instructor.

1. Why is ethical behaviour important for businesses?
2. List and explain six characteristics of the ethical business.
3. List and explain characteristics of an ethical employee.
4. Can ethical change occur? If so, how?
5. What factors often impede ethical change?

Critical-Thinking Activity

Martin Albertson, your supervisor at CanAsian, gives his expense accounts to you each month. Your responsibility is to put the information on a form and return the form to him. Once he reviews and signs the form, you send it to the president for signature. Last month, you noticed Mr. Albertson included alcoholic beverages on the expense report (under the category of food and beverage). This month you noticed he did it again, and you remember the same thing occurring several months ago. Company policy specifically states that an employee cannot be reimbursed for purchases of alcohol. You believe it is merely carelessness on the part of your supervisor; you believe in his honesty. However, you are beginning to wonder whether you are engaging in unethical behaviour by not calling his attention to these items. Mr. Albertson has always been clear about your responsibility for knowing and adhering to the policies and procedures of the company.

1. What is the problem?
2. What is your role in the issue?
3. How should you handle the situation?
4. Have you been behaving ethically by not calling it to his attention? If your answer is yes, explain your position.

Building Workplace Skills

Project 3-1 (Learning Outcomes 1, 2, and 4)

INNOVATION   CAREER

Collaborative Project

Along with three of your classmates, interview two executives concerning the following:

- The importance of ethical behaviour
- The characteristics of an ethical organization
- The traits of ethical employees

As you are interviewing the executives, determine whether their organizations have a vision or mission statement or code of ethics. If so, ask if you may have a copy of the statement or code. Present your findings to the **class**. Take notes during the interviews so you can report your findings accurately.

Project 3-2 (Learning Outcome 5)

INNOVATION   CAREER   DATA FILE

Read the case study for this chapter, which can be found in the document Project 3-2a, and respond to the questions given. Submit your answers to your instructor in a short memorandum using the memorandum form provided in file Project 3-2b.

Project 3-3 (Learning Outcome 4)

INNOVATION   CAREER   DATA FILE

Locate the sound file Project 3-3, Exchange from the Student Course Data files, on the MindTap site. Play the file to hear a short conversation between Mark and his supervisor, Ms. Ramirez, and a second conversation between Mark and his co-worker, Courtney. What unethical workplace behaviours are taking place? Did Mark make the right decision?

Project 3-4 (Learning Outcome 2)

INNOVATION   TECHNOLOGY

Use the Internet to find and report on three companies that have codes of ethics on their websites. What is the code of ethics of each company? Does the company provide a list of values? Does it outline an ethics policy with respect to hiring, the environment, social responsibility, or other ethics topics? Write a summary of each company's code of ethics and any values and ethics policies. Be sure to cite your sources appropriately.

Project 3-5 (Learning Outcome 2)

INNOVATION   CAREER

Collaborative Project

You are the administrative assistant to the director of human resources. The company is going to institute an ethics training program, and she has asked you to research programs and identify three good prospects. The programs should cover common ethical problems encountered in an office environment, particularly related to confidentiality. Work in a small group to research and choose the programs. Assemble materials from the programs you have selected for the director's review, and write an evaluation that compares them.

Project 3-6 (Learning Outcome 4)

TECHNOLOGY   DATA FILE

You are responsible for maintaining the supply cabinet. You have noticed that some supplies are diminishing at a rate more quickly than seems reasonable. You suspect that they are being taken for personal use. Additionally, you have noticed that a few of the staff are consistently arriving to work a few minutes late. They appear to feel that it doesn't matter. Locate the file Project 3-6. Create a spreadsheet in Microsoft Excel. Enter the data provided and complete the calculations to see how much these types of employee theft could cost a fictitious company of 30 employees over one week. Over a year? Does this change your opinion?

Prepare a report for Mr. Albertson that can be circulated to all staff. Attach your spreadsheet.

Project 3-7 (Learning Outcome 2)

TECHNOLOGY   CAREER

Use library resources or the Internet to find *Maclean's* magazine's most recent annual listing of the ten best companies to work for in Canada. Pick three of the companies, and write a paragraph on each one explaining why it was picked as one of the best companies to work for.

Make the Grade with MindTap

MINDTAP

Stay organized and efficient with **MindTap**—a single destination with all the course material and study aids you need to succeed. Built-in apps leverage social media and the latest learning technology. For example:

- ReadSpeaker will read the text to you.
- Flashcards are pre-populated to provide you with a jumpstart for review—or you can create your own.
- You can highlight text and make notes in your MindTap Reader. Your notes will flow into Evernote, the electronic

notebook app that you can access anywhere when it's time to study for the exam.

- Self-quizzing allows you to access your understanding.

Visit nelson.com/student to start using **MindTap**. Enter the Online Access Code from the card included with your text. If a code card is not provided, you can purchase instant access at NELSONbrain.com.

Endnotes

1. "Code of Conduct," Royal Bank of Canada, December 2017, http://www.rbc.com/governance/_assets-custom/pdf/RBCCodeOfConduct.pdf, accessed August 3, 2018.

2. "Strategic Plan 2015–2020," Horizon Health Network website, http://en.horizonnb.ca/media/616051/horizon_strat_plan_english_jan28.pdf, accessed February 2015.

3. "Purpose, Vision, Values, and Goals," 2018, Royal Bank of Canada, http://www.rbc.com/aboutus/visionandvalues.html, accessed July 21, 2018. Reproduced with permission of Royal Bank of Canada.

4. "OSH Answers: OH&S Legislation in Canada—Due Diligence," Canadian Centre for Occupational Health and Safety website, www.ccohs.ca/oshanswers/legisl/diligence.html, accessed August 2015.

CHAPTER 4

Developing Customer Focus

LEARNING OUTCOMES

After reading this chapter, you should be able to

1. Explain the differences between external and internal customers.
2. Define customer focus and describe strategies for developing customer focus.
3. Develop skills for providing effective customer service.
4. Describe how to handle difficult customer service situations.

Do I Qualify?

Executive Assistant

Insurance agency seeks an administrative assistant to provide customer service support for established and prospective clients. Candidate must:

- provide excellent customer service to all internal and external clients
- possess strong organizational skills and excellent communication skills
- be capable of working effectively with people in difficult situations
- maintain a database, process forms, and prepare correspondence
- handle incoming phone calls and emails
- be proficient in Microsoft Office

Importance of Customer Focus

While organizational goals may vary from business to business, the major goal of all organizations is to make a profit. To achieve this goal, customer service is vitally important in every organization. A **customer**, also known as a *client* or *buyer*, is someone who buys or uses the products or services of a company or an organization. **Customer service** is often defined as the ability of an organization to consistently give customers what they need *and* what they want. As an office worker, you may feel that the idea of customer service does not apply to you, that it applies only to those working in retail or sales. However, successful businesses and organizations are those that are committed to providing high-quality service to all their customers. This attitude and commitment is called **customer focus**.

Organizations with a customer focus know the importance of providing excellent customer service to attract and maintain customers. Customer service is not simply a job or a department; it is a way of thinking within an organization.

One such organization is the Disney Corporation; the basis of its philosophy is providing quality customer service that not only meets but exceeds expectations. Applying this philosophy to other businesses is easy—whatever you do, it must be of the highest quality and always with the needs of your clients foremost in your mind. Make every contact with clients or customers one that makes them feel valued and important. Over the years, many companies from around the world have sent their managers to the Disney Institute to learn how to adapt the Disney approach to their own organizations. You may want to consult a book published by the Disney

Institute, *Be Our Guest: Perfecting the Art of Customer Service* by Theodore Kinni; many other books are available on the topic of customer focus.

As an administrative professional, a significant part of your day-to-day activities will involve interacting with external customers or clients, as well as with members of your own organization (internal customers). Good communication skills in your personal interactions are an important aspect of projecting a positive image of your company.

Disney is well known for its customer-first philosophy.

Internal and External Customers

Although many people are aware of the importance of providing service to external customers, individuals sometimes forget the importance of internal customer service. All of the techniques and strategies that make for effective external customer focus apply equally to internal customers.

Internal Customers

Internal customers are departments or employees within an organization who use the products or services provided by others within the organization.

For a business to provide good external customer service, effective internal customer service is essential. The relationships among managers, employees, associates, and peers are all important when developing an internal customer focus. Developing strong relationships with those who depend on you to provide answers or services is essential to creating an environment that puts customers first. By developing positive relationships with internal customers, you show that you value their importance to the organization. Excellent internal customer service can lead to employee satisfaction, employee loyalty, employee retention, and a higher level of external customer service. Employees in the printing services department of a company, for example, serve the needs of other employees. These employees are the internal customers of the workers in the printing services department. Without the services this department provides, others in the company would not be able to do their work. Even employees who have no direct contact with external customers, like those in printing services, must have a customer service focus for the entire organization to be effective.

External Customers

Everyone within an organization has a role to play in developing an environment that is focused on the customer or client. The most recognized **external customers** of a business or organization are the people or other organizations that buy or use the products and services provided by the organization. Other visitors to the workplace may be representatives of businesses who want to provide a service or sell a product to your firm. In all cases, these visitors to your workplace should be treated courteously.

You should know your supervisor's preferences and expectations regarding how to handle visitors. For example, your supervisor will usually want immediate access to be granted to certain people, such as the president of the organization, the chairperson of the board, a valuable client or customer, or a distinguished civic official. Learn about your supervisor's preferences by determining

- who will be seen immediately regardless of how busy your supervisor is at the time
- whether friends or relatives should be included in this group
- whether there are certain people your supervisor *will not* see under any circumstances
- how to handle job applicants or sales representatives (e.g., referring them to the human resources or purchasing department)
- when introductions should be made for visitors new to the office
- whether a particular time of day is set aside for seeing visitors

Nonprofit Organizations

Nonprofit organizations and government entities provide products or services to groups of people without seeking financial gain; any revenue earned helps to further the organizations' public goals. Even though these organizations may not be trying to make a profit, effective customer service is important for achieving their goals.

Consider public schools as an example. The goal of an elementary school may be to provide quality instructions in a safe, friendly environment that is conducive to learning. School staff members must consider the students' needs and wants (provide effective customer service) if they are to accomplish their goal. In this example, the students, their parents, and the community as a whole are the customers. All are stakeholders in the benefits or burdens of a successful or failed education system. A customer focus in this case does not mean profits for the school but can mean profits (economically and as a society) for the community.

People AT WORK

Customer Service Representative

Customer service representatives are responsible for providing outstanding customer service and technical support to both internal and external customers.

Many companies employ customer service representatives who work in person with customers in a traditional office setting. Other organizations provide access to customer service representatives by telephone, email, or Internet.

Customer Focus Strategies

External customers who are not satisfied with the service they receive are likely to take their business elsewhere in the future; customers who are pleased with the service they have received are more likely to buy from the company again. Increased sales and profits can be a major benefit of providing effective customer service and can lead to customer satisfaction, customer loyalty, and customer retention. Excellent customer service can also minimize external customers' filing formal complaints against the organization which can tarnish the reputation of the organization and decrease profits and sales. In Canada, external customers have the following avenues to file formal complaints against organizations and professionals:

- the Better Business Bureau for complaints related to a variety of business practice areas
- the Law Society of Ontario for complaints related to legal professionals
- the College of Physicians and Surgeons in each province or territory for complaints related to medical professionals

A successful administrative professional understands the importance of customer focus in all business relationships. Some strategies (plans of action for achieving goals) for developing a customer focus include showing respect for customers and going out of your way to seek their input in resolving

problems and issues. Taking responsibility for errors or mistakes, providing a complete explanation, and following up on issues will ensure that you maintain effective relationships with your customers or clients.

Showing Respect for Customers

You may have heard the statement "the customer is always right." Although the intent of the statement is to show the importance of customers, the statement should not be taken literally. Customers are people, and people are not always right. If a customer does come to you with a concern, give it serious attention.

The customer deserves to be treated fairly and with respect, to have complaints or questions heard, and to be provided with an explanation if there is a question about a product or service. Show the customer that you are sincere and serious about providing assistance.

Seeking Customer Input

Problems can provide learning opportunities for you and your organization. An effective customer focus strategy is seeking input from customers. A customer concern or complaint is really a request for action. If you listen to customers, they will often have ideas about how to solve the problem. Doing something special or extra that is not required as part of your job can help the company maintain a valued external customer and may also help you to build a good relationship.

Have you ever been disappointed in a product or service that you purchased? When you brought your concerns to the attention of a customer service representative, did they listen intently to your concern? Were you offered a solution to your problem and perhaps given something extra for your trouble? Perhaps you purchased a sweater from an online store, and the company sent the sweater in the wrong colour. When you called the customer service line, the representative explained how to return the incorrect merchandise and gave you a voucher for 20 percent off your next order. This positive interaction likely made you feel valued and that your continuing business was important to the company.

Use problem situations to obtain information from customers. Asking for customers' feedback gives them an opportunity to participate in the process of improving a situation. Sometimes a customer will recognize issues that you may not see and suggest ideas about how a problem can be avoided in the future. Allowing the customer to participate in solving a problem is a positive step toward re-establishing goodwill.

Customers today often access social media and company websites to provide unsolicited feedback. As an administrative professional, one of your roles may be to monitor your social media sites and feeds, and to acknowledge and respond to customer concerns.

Go the Extra Mile

Giving a customer more than is expected is a way of setting your company or product above the others. Although keeping customers happy is important, never do anything that violates company ethics or standards to keep a customer happy. Know the actions you can take to maintain customers, such as giving discounts on orders or reduced fees, by talking with your supervisor ahead of time. Look for ways to say yes to what the customer wants so that doing business with your organization will be easy.

Maintain Effective Relationships

Getting to know people within your organization will help you know whom to contact or whom to refer a customer to when you have a question about how to assist a customer. Always be appreciative of the help of others, and let them know they are important.

When you are helpful and provide assistance to your internal customers, the natural result is often that they will provide you with excellent internal customer service as well. These two-way relationships can continue to grow and develop into solid working relationships built on customer-focused practices.

Taking Responsibility

When you make a mistake, do you admit it or try to hide it? If you answered honestly, you probably had to say that there have been times when you did not admit you had made a mistake. Everyone occasionally makes an error, and admitting it can be difficult for anyone. However, refusing to admit to being wrong can damage your reputation and label you as being dishonest.

When you or your company makes a mistake, the key is to apologize quickly for the error and then solve the problem. Take the time to determine what went wrong and how you can prevent the same mistake in the future. If you skip this step, it's possible you will repeat the mistake.

Learn from the positive situations as well; take time at the end of the day to think through what went right. Document the procedures or strategies that worked well, and use them in similar situations later.

Explaining the Situation

Have you ever been in a situation in which you spoke clearly, articulated well, and gave details, and yet the individual to whom you were talking still did not understand you? For most people, the answer is yes. Why did the person not understand your meaning? Perhaps the person is not using the same frame of reference as you are. Explain issues or points clearly and fully to your customers. Do not assume the customer already has all the information related to the issue or problem. Apply effective listening techniques and give the person an opportunity to let you know whether they understand by asking, "Does this make sense to you?" This question gives the individual an opportunity to tell you whether or not you have been clear in your communication.

Following Up on the Issue

Once a problem has been solved, it is imperative to follow up by checking with the customer to determine whether the solutions have been implemented. The most effective problem solving has little or no value if the solution was never implemented.

A customer remembers the end result. Despite receiving excellent service throughout the resolution process, if the problem is not resolved, that is all the customer will remember. If you need more time to implement a solution, phone to let the customer know you have not forgotten the issue; doing so will go a long way toward maintaining customer satisfaction.

Be Positive and Helpful

A positive customer service encounter starts and ends with a positive attitude. The attitude you display is often as important as the answers you give and the actions you take. Show your positive attitude by attempting to help customers even when you do not have all the answers. People will come to you for help and be more eager to help you if you have a positive attitude. Treat all people individually with the same eager attitude of helpfulness, and encourage suggestions for how you can improve.

Customer Service Skills

Whether you are dealing with customers in a face-to-face situation or by telephone, email, or websites, you can develop skills that will help you have successful interactions. Several skills you will need when working with customers are discussed in this section.

Problem-Solving Skills

Problem solving is at the centre of all great customer service. Regardless of your effectiveness as an administrative professional, problems will arise with internal or external customers. Although there are some customers who are difficult to please, most of them are not interested in making your job more stressful. Most customers simply want you to provide information or help them solve a problem.

Satisfied customers may or may not tell anyone about you or your organization, but unhappy customers will likely share their frustrations and experiences with others. Keep your customer focus, and take care of any issues that arise promptly and with a smile.

After determining that a problem exists, follow a systematic method to solve it. Steps for solving problems are discussed in more detail in this section.

When solving a problem, talk with people who can provide information about the issues.

Identify the Problem

Attempt to understand the problem. This is often the most difficult step in the process. When defining the problem, ask yourself: What problem am I trying to solve? What will be the outcome of this problem? Sometimes the true problem will be difficult to identify. You may need to complete part of the next step, collecting information, before you can correctly identify the problem.

Collect and Analyze Information

Collect and analyze information related to the problem. To do this, you must ask a series of questions related to the problem you have identified. The more information you can collect, the more likely you are to solve the problem quickly.

Look for patterns, trends, or relationships in the data you have collected. Your goal is to develop a clear understanding of the problem and related issues before trying to determine a solution.

Determine Options

The next step in solving a problem is to generate options or possible solutions. Sometimes the problem will be unique, and it will be challenging to develop a solution. Other times, it will be a problem you have seen before, and you may rely on past solutions when determining your course of action.

If a problem has occurred frequently in the past, your company may have collected information or developed specific policies related to the problem. This information can be helpful in finding a solution.

Evaluate and Implement

Effective problem solving requires that you evaluate each of the options you have defined as possible solutions. Sometimes the best alternative will be obvious, and other times it will be difficult to make that determination.

The positive and negative results of a particular solution should be considered from both the company's perspective and the customer's perspective. You should consider both when making your decision. Once your evaluation is complete, implement the best option.

Evaluate the Solution

After a solution has been implemented, it should be evaluated. Evaluation helps you decide whether you have made the right decision for the immediate situation. It also helps you improve your problem-solving skills for the future.

Communicating AT WORK

Internal space boundaries (the area of space separating you from others) can affect your communication with others. These boundaries can be based on both cultural and individual preferences.

In some cultures, people tend to have small interpersonal space zones. People get close together to talk, and little personal space is preferred. People in other cultures, however, place a different emphasis on personal space. These people may prefer to have more distance from others.

When you are working with customers, respect their personal space preferences. If you get too close, you will notice that the customer feels uncomfortable. They may back away from you. Honour the customer's personal space zone by standing a comfortable distance away.

Nonverbal Communication Skills

Nonverbal communication consists of messages you convey without words. These messages can be as important as the words you speak. Nonverbal communication can occur through eye contact, facial expressions, and other means. You can develop effective nonverbal communication skills to aid you in communicating with customers.

Eye contact is a powerful form of nonverbal communication. It lets customers know that you are interested and attentive to what they are saying. It may also convey compassion and caring. Avoiding eye contact may suggest a lack of concern or lack of honesty. When dealing with customers, you should make eye contact frequently. Customers may perceive that you are not interested in what they are saying if you do not periodically make eye contact with them.

Facial expressions, such as a warm smile, can be valuable in communicating with customers. A smile signals that you care about the customer and are eager to help. Typically, a smile indicates happiness. However, if the customer is extremely upset, a smile can signal that you are laughing at the individual, suggesting to the customer that you are not taking the issue seriously.

If a customer is angry or upset, maintain a facial expression that shows interest but will not be perceived as mocking. Facial expressions that show interest and attention will increase your credibility with customers and make them feel important.

Effective Listening Skills

The importance of listening effectively when dealing with customers cannot be overemphasized. Listening shows that you care about your customers and respect their questions and concerns. Listening says to customers that you believe they are important.

Listening is more than hearing what the speaker is saying. Effective listening requires that you be focused on understanding what the other person is saying and not on what is happening around you.

When listening to someone, allow the person to complete a thought before you begin to respond. Do not interrupt the speaker. Listen for pauses that may indicate the speaker is finished talking before you respond. Chapter 5 provides more information about listening skills.

Human Relations Skills

Human relations skills are abilities that allow us to interact with others effectively. These abilities are sometimes called *people skills*. Showing respect for others, having empathy for others, and showing support for the skills and ideas of others are demonstrations of human relations skills.

Customer service is more than saying the words the customer wants to hear. It involves both the words you say and the way you say them. When talking with internal or external customers, your tone of voice is very important. Your voice can convey concern, respect, and compassion. Most importantly, your words must sound sincere.

Empathy is understanding or showing concern for someone's feelings or position. It is the ability to imagine yourself in the other person's situation. Empathy does not involve agreeing or disagreeing; it involves attempting to understand the other person's point of view.

Being able to show genuine empathy for a customer who is describing a problem will help you gain or keep the customer's trust. An **empathy statement**, such as "I can imagine it is frustrating when equipment does not operate as expected," is a declaration that acknowledges how the customer is feeling without admitting or denying fault. Using empathy statements can help defuse a customer's feelings of anger or frustration.

Face-to-Face Customer Service Skills

In many large organizations, a receptionist initially greets all external visitors to the workplace. Other than through telephone communication, this initial contact may be the first experience that the customer or client will have with the company, so it is important that it is a positive one. The receptionist may record the name of the visitor, her or his company affiliation, the nature of the visit, the person the visitor wants to see, and the date of the visit. The receptionist may then bring the visitor inside or notify the administrative professional that the visitor has arrived. If it is a first-time visit, your job may involve going to the reception area and then escorting the visitor to your supervisor's office.

Even though the receptionist may already have greeted the visitor, your role as an administrative professional is to welcome them to the organization. Greet the person graciously and use the visitor's name if you know it. Everyone appreciates being called by name, and doing so informs visitors that you care enough to make an effort to remember their name.

If you have never met the visitor, introduce yourself and identify your position in relation to your supervisor, for example, as "Ms. Albertson's administrative assistant." Extend your hand to the visitor as you do so. If the person seems inclined to avoid physical contact, simply drop your hand to your side, smile, and ask the client to be seated.

Business greetings in North America have become relatively informal and may even begin with a hug if the person is a close friend or long-time acquaintance. You may find that your supervisor greets some individuals in this informal manner. As an administrative professional, you do not initiate such an intimate greeting with someone entering your office, though if a visitor chooses to greet you in a familiar manner you may respond accordingly. If a visitor initiates a physical greeting that makes you uncomfortable, greet them warmly while politely declining physical contact. Avoid making guests feel awkward.

In small companies, you may be on the front line, greeting all visitors to your workplace and directing them to the correct individual within the organization. Always give a visitor your immediate attention. If you are on the phone when a visitor arrives, make eye contact and, when appropriate, ask the caller to hold while you greet the visitor. Tell the visitor you will assist them in just a moment. Return to your telephone call and finish as quickly as possible. It is discourteous to leave someone standing at your desk while you finish filing papers, preparing a report, or talking on the phone. If you must answer the telephone when a visitor is at your desk, excuse yourself.

Email Customer Service Skills

As an administrative professional, you will probably communicate with internal and external customers through email.

Greet people with a smile and a handshake.

Handling email effectively is an important part of developing a customer focus. Steps for writing effective email messages are presented in Chapter 5.

Designate specific times during the day to check and answer your email messages. Determine the scheduled times based on the volume of messages you receive. For example, if much of your job requires handing email from customers, you may need to check your inbox every hour or every half hour. However, if a small part of your job requires handling email questions, you may want to check your email only three or four times a day. Keep in mind that the customer should be served in a timely, caring, and efficient manner, but you shouldn't let the constant flow of email messages control your time or affect your ability to respond to other customers.

At times, responding to difficult customer email requests or complaints can be frustrating and challenging. At these times, just imagine that your supervisor will be copied on the email. This will help clarify your tone as patient, helpful, and respectful.

Telephone Customer Service Skills

The telephone is an important workplace tool. As an administrative professional, you must be effective in your telephone communication skills, or you may make customers angry or lose customers for your organization.

A telephone conversation is sometimes challenging because you cannot see the person with whom you are speaking. You must put a smile in your voice by using a friendly tone. Speak at an appropriate volume, pitch, and speed. Ask questions tactfully, and respond calmly even when the caller is loud or angry.

Follow these guidelines for effective telephone communication:

- Listen for facts.
- Search for subtle meanings.
- Be patient.
- Repeat back to the customer what you believe the customer said.
- Act to handle the problem or issue.

Always assist the customer to the best of your ability. Ask questions about anything that is not clear to you. Let the customer know what will happen next, especially if you cannot solve the problem or answer the questions right away.

Conclude every telephone call in a positive manner. At the end of every conversation, thank the caller and ask if there is anything else you can do to help. Effective telephone communication skills are discussed in Chapter 6.

Writing AT WORK

Using positive words will create a positive environment when dealing with customers. Evaluate the words you use in your written interactions with customers. Examples of words to use and words to avoid are shown below:

Words to Use	Words to Avoid
Can	Can't
Please	Never
Yes	You have to
Do	Not my job
Will	Won't
Thank you	Sorry
Appreciate	I don't know

Internet and Social Media Customer Service Skills

Customer service on the Internet is a way of life. Businesses use their websites as well as a variety of social media platforms (Facebook, Instagram, Twitter, and LinkedIn) as vital avenues for sales and customer service. Many companies at the very least offer customers the option of searching for answers to their questions on the company website. This option, called Web self-service, may be in addition to or as an alternative to contacting customer service representatives by telephone. Typically, this service allows customers to use the same tools and knowledge databases that customer service agents within the organization use to help customers find answers.

Depending on the social media platform used, customers can also learn about the products and services of a customer and obtain answers to questions they have about your organization. In addition, social media platforms provide customers with opportunities to communicate directly with the organization. These interactions can be positive but there also may be customers that are dissatisfied with the service they have received. When responding to these inquiries, ensure you follow the customer service strategies and customer service skills outlined earlier in this chapter.

Handling Difficult Situations

When you work with organizations that value customer service, treat each customer with respect, and follow the suggestions that have been given in this chapter about working with customers. However, there are times when you will encounter individuals who behave inappropriately. You need to understand how to respond when difficult situations arise.

Technology AT WORK

Some companies offer a live chat feature as part of their web-based customer service. Customers can exchange text messages with staff members in real time. This option is effective for low to moderate product support and offers a personalized service that may be less expensive for the company than telephone support. Customers appreciate getting answers to questions quickly.

Some companies make live chat available while customers are searching the website, during the order process, or after a sale. Allowing customers to ask questions while ordering may result in fewer returned products because customers are better informed when placing orders.

Handling Conflict

One of the best customer service techniques is avoiding problems. This can be accomplished by being proactive with customers. Learn to anticipate customers' needs and provide solutions to their concerns before they ask. Be polite; show empathy (as mentioned earlier) and understanding of an issue to help prevent a customer from becoming angry. Sometimes it is not possible to anticipate concerns or avoid problems. When that happens, conflict may occur.

Effective customer service involves learning how to handle conflict. When dealing with customer conflict, listen carefully to customers' problems or concerns. Work hard to make your customers happy, even if it means fixing something that you do not think is a major concern.

Accept the blame on behalf of your company or department, even if the problem or mistake is not your fault (and certainly if it is your fault). When possible, offer more than one solution to allow the customer to feel in control.

Handling Difficult Customers

Some people will be difficult no matter how helpful and professional you are. Sometimes a customer is upset or angry for reasons that have nothing to do with you or the company.

When a customer is angry, take a deep breath and tell yourself to stay calm.

- Although you can control your own behaviour, you cannot control the actions of others. Sometimes a customer will get angry even when you do your best to prevent it. People react angrily for a multitude of reasons, many of which may not relate to the particular customer service issue you are speaking with them about. Do not take it personally; usually the customer is not angry at you. Try to defuse the anger as quickly as possible by listening to the customer's concerns. Use empathy statements to show you understand the gravity of their issue. Think of a time when you needed sympathy and understanding and then treat the angry customer with the same care you experienced or needed during that time.

- Acknowledge the situation to the customer and ask what you can do to solve the problem or make the situation better. Sometimes just asking the question will get the situation back under control. At other times, making an apology is the best approach. If you (or your company) has made a mistake, apologize for the error and then correct it, if possible. If correcting the error is not possible, perhaps you can offer some form of compensation to keep the customer's goodwill. Remember to stay within company guidelines in such a situation.

Dealing with Abusive Customers

Some customers go beyond simply being angry or frustrated and become abusive. Usually, you cannot help an abusive customer until she or he calms down. As you would with someone who is difficult, do not let yourself become angry, as this behaviour will merely escalate the situation.

Look for points of agreement with the customer and voice your agreement. This technique generally works well, and you can then begin to help solve the problem with the customer. If the customer continues to be abusive, you may have to ask the customer to call back later when they can discuss the issue calmly.

Many organizations have a policy concerning difficult or abusive telephone situations. Find out what the policy is and observe it. Some companies have a recorded announcement telling callers that the call may be recorded for customer service quality or training purposes. Customers may be less likely to make threats or inappropriate comments when they know the call might be recorded.

Soft Skills

COMMUNICATION SKILLS

Effective communication skills are an integral skill that every administrative professional should strive to achieve and continuously improve. In your role, you will be required to communicate with customers, clients and co-workers on a daily basis. Communication skills can be placed into three categories:

- verbal communication—the ability to effectively speak and listen
- written communication—the ability to effectively write and read written communications

- nonverbal communication—the ability to communicate and understand individuals without the use of words or verbal communication, including body language, unspoken understandings, and cultural and environmental conditions that may affect communication between individuals

In Chapters 1 and 5, communication skills are outlined, and tips and strategies to enhance your communication skills are provided.

Chapter Summary

The summary will help you remember the important points covered in this chapter.

- An organization that has a customer focus demonstrates effective customer service in its interactions with internal and external customers. Providing excellent customer service is important for success in businesses and other organizations.
- When receiving workplace callers, know your employer's preferences and expectations. Your employer will usually see certain people without an appointment. Your employer may also decide *not* to see certain people.
- Appropriate techniques for receiving office visitors include the following:
  - Greet the visitor with a handshake.
  - Determine the purpose of the visit.
  - Make the wait pleasant by offering the visitor a beverage and reading material.
  - When speaking with the visitor, use his or her name.
  - Introduce the visitor to your supervisor, if appropriate.
  - Do not be discourteous to callers—even the difficult ones.
- Understanding how to respond to difficult or abusive customers will help you provide effective customer service even in difficult situations.
- Strategies that you can use to develop a customer focus include showing respect for customers, seeking customer input, taking responsibility, explaining the situation, and following up on issues.

Key Terms

customer p. 56
customer focus p. 56
customer service p. 56
empathy p. 61

empathy statement p. 61
external customers p. 57
human relations skills p. 61
internal customers p. 57

Discussion Items

These discussion items provide an opportunity to test your understanding of the chapter through written responses or discussion with your classmates and your instructor.

1. What is customer focus? Why is it important for the success of businesses and other organizations?
2. List eight techniques for effectively handling the workplace visitor.
3. What is the difference between internal customers and external customers? Give an example of an internal customer and an external customer.
4. Describe three strategies you can use to develop a customer focus.
5. What steps should you take to solve a customer service problem?

Critical-Thinking Activity

Your friend Leslie Page works as an administrative assistant at the Palms Dinner Theatre. She handles records for sales of season tickets. Today, Mr. Bronson and his wife came in with two guests for the matinee performance. When the Bronsons and their guests found two of their seats occupied, they turned to Leslie for assistance.

Mr. Bronson indicated that he had purchased four season tickets. After checking on the computer, Leslie noticed that two of the tickets were returned in January and a credit was issued. When she relays this information to Mr. Bronson, he indicates that the tickets that were returned were for a show two months ago, not for today's performance. Although Leslie wants to be helpful, there is not a lot she can do. Once the original tickets were released (and the credit issued), the tickets were resold. In addition, the table seating for today's matinee performance is sold out. All Leslie can do is offer the Bronsons and their guests four seats in the gallery at the back of the theatre.

Mrs. Bronson is angry and insists on sitting in their original seats. She demands that Leslie remove the individuals from her seats. How should Leslie handle the situation?

21st Century Skills

 Life and Career Skills
CAREER

 Learning and Innovation Skills
INNOVATION

 Information, Media, and Technology Skills
TECHNOLOGY

 Data
DATA FILE

Building Workplace Skills

Project 4-1 (Learning Outcomes 1, 2, and 3)

INNOVATION   DATA FILE

You receive the following visitors in your office today. How would you deal with each situation? Write a memorandum to your instructor, using the memorandum form on the MindTap site (access to which is provided with the printed access card on the inside cover of your textbook) file Project 4-1, and state what you would do.

1. A sales representative comes in and asks for an appointment to see your supervisor; your supervisor has told you he does not like to see sales representatives.

2. Your supervisor has been called out of town unexpectedly. He scheduled an appointment with Mr. Chlebovec for 11 a.m. but failed to tell you about this appointment. You forgot to check his calendar. Mr. Chlebovec comes in at 10:50 for his appointment.

3. A woman comes in to see your supervisor. She refuses to give her name or the purpose of her visit. However, she says the matter is urgent. She seems upset.

4. Ms. Nicole Botha comes in to see your supervisor. Ms. Botha has an appointment at 11 a.m., and it is now 10:55 a.m. Your supervisor has had an extremely busy morning, and he is now in a conference that will last until 11:20 a.m.

5. R. T. Yip is in your supervisor's office. He had an appointment at 2 p.m. It is now 3 p.m., and your supervisor has an appointment with Ms. Carol Haile. Ms. Haile has arrived.

6. George O'Casey arrives at 3 p.m. for his appointment with your supervisor. Upon checking your appointment book, you find that Mr. O'Casey's appointment is for 3 p.m. tomorrow.

Project 4-2 (Learning Outcomes 1, 2, and 3)

TECHNOLOGY

Create a newsletter that includes tips and strategies for providing effective customer service. The newsletter should be one to two pages. Use the contents of this chapter and any other sources of information on this topic you can find on the Internet or other publications. Note the source information for these articles. Review newsletters you have received or examples you find online to help you format the document. Design and create an appropriate masthead (the block of identifying information usually positioned at the top of the page). Include at least two graphics and one bulleted list in the body of your newsletter. Follow instructions provided by your instructor for submission of this project. Add this document to your e-portfolio.

Project 4-3 (Learning Outcomes 3 and 4)

CAREER   DATA FILE

Locate the sound file Project 4-3 Customer Call from the data files. The file is a recording of a conversation in which a customer, Nina, calls Atkins Computers to talk with a customer service representative about a problem with a printer. Listen to the entire conversation. What did Roberto, the customer service representative, do correctly? What could he have done better? What could the customer have done differently to make the experience more positive? Work with a partner to write a new script implementing your suggestions and then record the new conversation.

Project 4-4 (Learning Outcomes 2 and 3)

INNOVATION   TECHNOLOGY

You are an administrative assistant at E&C Kitchen Sales. Seven salespersons work at the organization. After discussing effective customer service skills with the staff, your supervisor, Mr. Mendoza, wants to determine whether the salespeople are putting these skills into practice. He has asked you to create a survey so customers can provide feedback on their experiences. The survey should include questions on the customer service skills and strategies discussed in the chapter, including nonverbal communication, friendliness, a positive attitude, effective listening, and empathy. Using Google Forms, create a survey and provide the link to your instructor. Use the link provided on the website with this textbook or search the Internet if you need assistance with using Google Forms.

Project 4-5 (Learning Outcome 3)

INNOVATION   TECHNOLOGY

Your company plans to begin working with similar companies in Spain, Germany, and France. Over the next few months, all employees will work with employees from the partnering businesses. Since nonverbal communication is an important part of internal customer service, your supervisor has asked you to research the differences and similarities in nonverbal communication in those countries. Include information on handshakes, personal space, facial expressions, and two other types of nonverbal communication that you identify. Prepare a Microsoft PowerPoint or Prezi presentation that your supervisor can share in your monthly staff meeting.

Make the Grade with MindTap

Stay organized and efficient with **MindTap**—a single destination with all the course material and study aids you need to succeed. Built-in apps leverage social media and the latest learning technology. For example:

- ReadSpeaker will read the text to you.
- Flashcards are pre-populated to provide you with a jump-start for review—or you can create your own.
- You can highlight text and make notes in your MindTap Reader. Your notes will flow into Evernote, the electronic notebook app that you can access anywhere when it's time to study for the exam.
- Self-quizzing allows you to access your understanding. Visit nelson.com/student to start using **MindTap**.

Enter the Online Access Code from the card included with your text. If a code card is not provided, you can purchase instant access at NELSONbrain.com.

PART 2

Communication—The Key to Your Success

In Part 1, you reviewed the Conference Board of Canada's *Employability Skills 2000+*. This profile identifies the skills you need to enter, progress, and remain in the workplace whether you are an entrepreneur working on your own or an employee working for a business or an organization. The ability to communicate effectively is one of the fundamental and basic skills that will ensure you are prepared to progress in the world of work.

The communication process—listening, speaking, writing, and nonverbal—can all be improved through constant practice. While you may not have the total responsibility for researching and writing formal reports, or for planning or delivering presentations, you may play a role by supporting your supervisor in these activities. For example, you may be asked to gather information for a report or presentation. You may also be responsible for keying, reproducing, and distributing the completed report, or developing effective visual aids to accompany a presentation.

Once you are in the workforce, you will find that your communication skills are critical to success as an administrative professional. By studying the chapters in this part and completing the activities, you will be able to identify the characteristics of effective communication techniques and understand the role you as an administrative professional play in information processing in the workplace.

CONESTOGA
Connect Life and Learning

Krista Allen

Administrative Assistant, School of Business Administration, Conestoga College

My name is Krista Allen, and I work in the School of Business Administration office at Conestoga College as an administrative assistant. As it is for many people, the journey to my current role was not without obstacles.

I began a career in restaurant management but quickly realized that it was not for me. I decided to apply to the office administration—executive program at Conestoga College; it seemed like a good fit for my skill set, as well as something that would work well with the lifestyle I envisioned for myself and my growing family. I entered the program in January 2011. Over four semesters, I maintained a 4.0 GPA, while working 40-plus hours a week as the assistant manager at a local restaurant. I graduated in 2012 with honours and distinction. I was offered my current position at Conestoga College in November 2013.

The School of Business Administration office is vibrant and fast-paced, and I am constantly presented with unique challenges. On a given day, I may have to provide software training to a colleague, schedule a meeting with people from different departments, fix the photocopier, order catering, make travel arrangements, prepare meeting minutes, and help a student rearrange their timetable. I am constantly learning and always adapting. It is challenging and hectic, but it is also rewarding and certainly never boring!

Josephine Williams

Food Service/Facility Support Clerk, Oakville-Trafalgar Memorial Hospital

My name is Josephine Williams, and I am a 34-year-old mother of two children. In 2010, the company where I had worked for five years eliminated the night shift, and I was laid off.

I applied for numerous jobs, but nothing panned out. I decided to go back to school. I attended triOS College for the medical office assistant program.

I graduated with honours following nine months of hard work and intense studying. But I was back to square one—job hunting again! Eventually, I received a call for an interview at the Oakville Hospital. Two weeks later, I landed a job as a temporary part-time facility support clerk. I worked all the hours assigned to me, even short notice calls, and I earned a permanent part-time role within two months. I am now a full-time clerk II for the food service/facility support team. I couldn't be happier; I loved working at the hospital.

I have no regrets about my career. Not only did I prove to myself that I can achieve anything I set my mind to, but I also was able to show my children that they should never give up; no matter what happens in life to never give up, we can do what we want to do if we work hard and strive for greatness!

CHAPTER 5

Improving Communication Skills

Do I Qualify?

Administrative Assistant

Small manufacturing company seeks candidate with good organization and communication skills to assist management team. Candidate must:
- demonstrate effective communication skills
- work independently with minimal supervision
- be able to conduct effective Internet searches

Responsibilities include
- customer service-related phone calls
- preparing, reviewing, reconciling, and distributing invoices
- processing adjustments to customer accounts and resolving issues

Communication—A Complex Issue

You cannot be effective in the workplace without being an effective communicator. Since the majority of the administrative professional's day involves contact with people, you will require effective communication skills. Effective communication is the ability to process and exchange ideas and feelings so both the person originating the communication and the person receiving the communication clearly understand the message. Building and maintaining effective communications are never easy. This statement is particularly true today in our complex, diverse world. People find it difficult enough to relate successfully to others who are like them. The task becomes even more complex when people are from different cultures and backgrounds, of different ages, and even from different countries.

Commit to improving your communication skills throughout this course. Commit to carefully studying the concepts presented in this chapter and to using the effective communication techniques presented.

Our global business environment, increasing technology, and the greater diversity of the people who compose the workforce are some of the forces that contribute to the complexity of communication in the workplace.

This global business environment demands that we be globally literate—that we see, think, and act in ways that are culturally mindful of the vast differences in our world. Our contacts with others may be through telecommunications—the

Internet, fax, telephone, and virtual conferencing—in addition to our face-to-face communication. Regardless of the form the interaction takes, practising effective communication techniques is imperative. Effectiveness assumes that you are

- clear concerning your own values and attitudes
- sensitive to cultural differences
- aware of gender and age issues

Values and Attitudes

Generally, we do not give much thought to how our values may differ from other people's values. We sometimes assume that everyone has the same values and then operate from this assumption. Obviously, that assumption is not true, and it can cause communication difficulties if it is not understood.

Just as you need to understand what you value, you also need to be clear about the attitudes you reflect to others. Your **attitude** is the position, disposition, or manner you have about a person or a thing. In the workplace, a great deal of attention is paid to the attitude of employees. In fact, during the formal evaluation process, an individual is often evaluated on their attitude. A positive attitude is always an asset, whereas a negative attitude is always a detractor.

Cultural Differences

Our diverse population and multinational organizations require that we be alert to and tolerant of the differences between the people with whom we work. We cannot expect that all people will react to situations in the same way. Diversity can mean that significant differences exist among our values, our assumptions, and our attitudes. Consider some of these cultural differences between people.

Trust is earned differently in various countries. If an employee in Canada or in the United States performs well on the job, the employee earns trust quickly. Superior performance equates to trusting the individual to do the job well. In Japan and Germany, trust is earned over a long period; trust may in fact be a result of an individual's family relationships or long-term knowledge.

Respect also is viewed differently in various cultures. In Asian countries, great respect is given to the older generation and to people in authority, such as political officials. In Canada, we tend to believe that respect must be earned; it is not automatically given to specific people or groups of people.

Canadian students learn from the time they enter school that class participation is important; we are taught to give our opinions. If students do not participate in class, they are considered to be uninterested or even unprepared for the class. Asian students regard teachers so highly they find it difficult to voice their own views in class. Doing so is almost a sign of disrespect to the teacher.

North Americans are considered to be demonstrative. Generally, we show our feelings easily. If we are happy, we smile a lot. If we are sad, we seldom smile. We are taught from an early age to make eye contact with people. We have certain concepts of time and **space**—it is important to be on time for business appointments; a certain amount of space or distance is maintained between people in a conversation.

Businesses that lack an understanding of our global cultural differences can easily make mistakes. Here are some examples that were costly to businesses[1]:

- McDonald's took 13 months to realize that Hindus in India do not eat beef. When it started making hamburgers out of lamb, sales flourished.
- In Africa, companies show pictures of what is inside bottles so that illiterate customers know what they are getting. When a baby food company showed a picture of a child on its label, the product did not sell very well.
- A U.S. television ad for deodorant depicted an octopus putting antiperspirant under each arm. When the ad flopped in Japan, the producers realized that, in Japan, octopuses do not have arms; they have legs.
- A U.S. firm sent an elaborate business proposal to Saudi Arabia bound in pigskin. Since Muslims consider pigs to be unclean, the proposal was never opened.
- Kentucky Fried Chicken's slogan "finger-lickin' good" translated to "eat your fingers off" in Chinese.

Remind yourself not to expect people from different cultures to behave as you do. Become diversity-competent—educate yourself about other cultures by reading books that are available in bookstores or your local library, by joining a global chat group on the Internet, and by talking with your colleagues from different cultures about their life and the differences they see in various cultures.

Gender Issues

Though the gender of an individual once held importance in terms of job roles, social and familial responsibilities, and even education and socialization, it is now generally advocated that no values, attitudes, behaviours and roles are intrinsically appropriate for males and females. Gender roles and identities have expanded over the years from those that were traditionally taught. Be respectful to individuals who identify themselves outside of the traditional male and female roles (e.g., non-binary, transgender). To ensure effective communication, address an individual using their preferred pronouns (e.g., he/him, she/her, they/them).

Age Issues

Since the requirement of mandatory retirement at age 65 was eliminated for all but a few specific occupations in certain provinces in Canada, the workforce has become more diverse and now consists of people ranging in age from 19 to those in their 70s. In coming decades, labour analysts predict that as many as six generations could be working alongside one another. Just as people who grow up in different cultures and environments have different values and expectations, so do people who are of different ages. These diverse generations and some of their characteristics have been variously labelled by writers in the field as shown in this table:

Birth Dates	Generation Name
before 1946	Silent Generation or Traditionalists
1946–1964	Baby Boomers
1965–1980	Generation X
1981–1999	Millennials or Generation Y
after 2000	Generation Z

As writers have categorized these generations by age group, they have also studied how these generations behave and have assigned certain values and characteristics to each. Tom Brokaw, in his best-selling book *The Greatest Generation*, discussed the common values held by the men and women of the Silent Generation as duty, honour, courage, service, and responsibility for oneself.

- **Baby Boomers**, skeptical about politics and the status quo, have grown up in an era of reform. They are confident, independent, and self-reliant. Possessing a strong work ethic and commitment to their workplace, they often remain with a single employer throughout their working lives. They are optimistic and team-oriented but are neither afraid of confrontation nor hesitant to challenge established practices.
- **Generation X** are more tolerant and more open to diversity and alternative lifestyles than previous generations. They readily embrace differences in religion, race, and ethnicity. They are spiritual and relational, and value good friends. They are more willing to change jobs to get ahead and less committed to one employer. They appreciate a work-life balance—they work to live; they do not live to work.
- **Millennials** grew with technology, and their values and characteristics have been shaped by the technological revolution. They are entrepreneurial, goal-oriented, and adept at multitasking, and they expect immediate feedback and rewards. They seek meaningful work and, like Generation Xers, appreciate a work–life balance.
- **Generation Z** is the newest generation to be classified. They are likely to be more independent, needing less direction because of their immediate access to information and the answers they need. At young ages, they were already highly connected through mobile devices in a seamless cloud-based world of friends, data, and entertainment; they will likely expect to be able to work, learn, and study whenever and wherever they want.

Individuals who grow up in different times may have different values. Recognizing these different values does not give anyone the right to characterize or make judgments about individuals based on their ages. What is important is that, in the workforce, we must recognize possible differences that are due to age and then address these differences in positive ways.

As you work in this diverse world comprising multiple values, cultural differences, and gender and age issues, your challenge is to develop diversity competence by doing the following:

- Recognize that these differences occur.
- Constantly seek to understand these differences.
- Understand their implications for communication.
- Grow your ability to communicate with all people.

To grow in your ability to communicate, you must understand the communication process and the barriers to effective communication. Additionally, you must continually practise effective communication techniques.

The Communication Process

Communication occurs when a message is sent by one person and received and understood by another person. Communicating effectively is essential to successful business operations and is the first skill listed in the Conference Board of Canada's *Employability Skills 2000+*. As an administrative professional, you must communicate with co-workers, clients, and vendors to achieve the company's goals. Advertisements and product information on websites must be current, correct, and sensitive to the needs and attitudes of customers of different cultures, interests, and abilities. Customer requests and questions must be answered clearly and promptly to maintain goodwill.

Improving your communication skills will help you create messages that are clear and effective. Good communication skills may also help you get and keep a job. Employers understand the importance of these skills. When discussing job candidates, "by far, the one skill mentioned most often by employers is the ability to listen, write, and speak effectively. Successful communication is critical in business."[2]

The communication process involves a message, a sender, a channel, a receiver, and feedback.

- A **message** is the idea being presented by the sender of a communication. It is a symbol or group of symbols that conveys meaning, such as a thought or an idea. For example, a letter contains words that are written symbols. These words convey a message to the reader.
- The **sender** is the person who creates the message and transmits it via a channel. In the previous example, the sender is the person who writes the letter.
- A **channel** is a means by which a message is sent, such as a letter or an email, or speaking in person or by telephone.

- The **receiver** is the person for whom a message is intended; the person who receives the message, such as the recipient of a letter or an email message.

Gestures and other nonverbal behaviours can also send messages. When a person (the sender) says hello, smiles, and extends a hand toward you (the receiver), that person is sending a message that he or she is glad to meet you. **Feedback** is a return message sent by the receiver. When you smile and say, "Pleased to meet you," you are giving feedback. Feedback helps the sender know whether the message was understood correctly, as illustrated in Figure 5-1.

FIGURE 5-1
The Communication Process

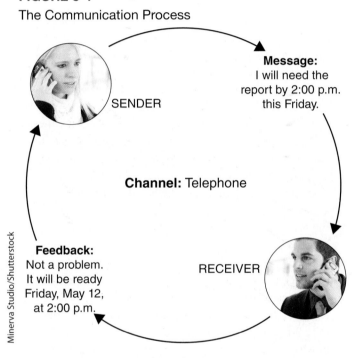

SENDER

Message:
I will need the report by 2:00 p.m. this Friday.

Channel: Telephone

RECEIVER

Feedback:
Not a problem. It will be ready Friday, May 12, at 2:00 p.m.

Minerva Studio/Shutterstock

Communication Barriers

For effective communication to take place, the message must be understood as the speaker or writer intends. If the listener or reader interprets the message differently, problems may occur. For example, suppose you receive an email message from your manager on Thursday morning telling you that you need to finish a project by next Friday. To your manager, the term "next Friday" means the following day. However, you interpret the message as meaning that the project is due on Friday of the following week. Your manager will be disappointed when the project is not completed the next day, and you will be disappointed to learn that you did not understand the message as intended. You are both the victims of a communication barrier. A **communication barrier** is anything that interferes with successful communication. Communication barriers can be internal or external.

Internal Communication Barriers

In the exchange with your manager described above, an internal barrier prevented the message from being understood. In your previous experience, the term "next Friday" has meant Friday of the following week—not the next Friday to occur. Because of your previous experience, you interpreted the message to have a different meaning from what the originator intended.

Other examples of internal communication barriers include mental or emotional distractions, biases, and lack of motivation.

- When you are worried about something or emotionally distressed, you may have trouble focusing on a message. As your mind wanders, you may miss part of the message.
- If you have a negative bias toward the topic, it may be difficult to accept positive comments. For example, if you had a bad experience with two printers of the same brand, you probably have a negative bias toward that brand. Claims of glowing performance for that printer will be difficult for you to believe.
- Lack of motivation means that you have no reason either to be interested in or to try to understand a message. If you think, for example, that a new company policy being discussed will not apply to your department, you may not pay close attention to the discussion. You may miss part of the message or misunderstand a point of the message because you are not listening carefully.

External Communication Barriers

External communication barriers include noise, poor lighting, extreme room temperature, or uncomfortable seating. Noise may make it difficult to hear or to read and focus on a message. Poor lighting, a room that is too cold or warm, and an uncomfortable chair are examples of physical barriers that can distract an originator or a receiver, hindering communication. Language can also be an external communication barrier. When the originator and receiver do not speak the same language, communication can be difficult.

Overcoming Communication Barriers

Originators and receivers should make an effort to recognize and overcome communication barriers. External barriers are often easier to overcome than internal barriers. For example, if noise is a problem, you may be able to move to a quiet location to read a message. You may also be able to adjust lighting, seating, or room temperature to prevent these physical conditions from being a distraction.

Some internal barriers can be difficult to overcome. If you are ill, you may need to postpone your participation until a later time. If you have trouble focusing on a message because you are sleepy, take a break, and walk about the room or open a window to get some fresh air. This activity may help you to feel refreshed and ready to receive the message.

People AT WORK

Training Specialist

Training specialists direct training activities in response to company and employee requests. They may conduct orientation sessions and arrange on-the-job training. They may also develop training for the use of new equipment or software.

Many companies have ongoing training programs to help employees improve their job skills. Seminars may be offered periodically on topics such as effective customer service and working in teams.

The training specialist may seek help from other employees, including you, or outside experts when needed. For example, the training specialist might ask you, as an expert in using Microsoft Access, to help train other employees to use this program.

When communicating with someone, be aware of how well the person knows the language you are using. For example, if English is your first language and you are speaking with someone whose first language is Japanese, you should use standard English in your message. Avoid using acronyms, informal terms, or expressions that the receiver might not understand.

Listening Skills

Most of us are not excellent listeners. Essential to effective communication, listening is an acquired, learned skill. In the words of author Robert Louis Stevenson, "All speech, written or spoken, is a dead language, until it finds a willing and prepared listener."[3] **Listening** is hearing and trying to understand the message. Listening is THE most valuable verbal communication skill. Being an effective listener can help you be more productive and improve your relationships with others. A first step toward becoming an effective listener is to understand the type of listening that is appropriate for particular situations. Listening can be categorized as casual listening or active listening.

Casual Listening

Casual listening is hearing and trying to understand what is being said with the objective of relating to others. When chatting during lunch with a colleague, you use casual listening to understand what is being said and to help respond appropriately. You typically do not focus on analyzing what is said or trying to remember every detail of the conversation.

Active Listening

Active listening is more goal-oriented than casual listening; it is listening for the meaning as well as the words of the speaker. When listening actively, you have a definite purpose in mind. The four types of active listening are described below.

- **Informative listening** is used when you want to hear, understand, and remember the information being presented. For example, when you listen to a manager or co-worker give instructions for completing a task, you are using informative listening.
- **Evaluative listening** is used to hear, understand, and judge what is being said. You may evaluate whether the information is useful, accurate, or interesting. For example, suppose you listen to a salesperson describe a product. As you listen, you will evaluate the message to decide whether you accept or reject it.
- **Emphatic listening** is used to hear, understand, and offer feedback that shows you have understood the message. Understanding the message does not necessarily mean that you agree with the speaker. The feedback you offer indicates only that you understand the message. Customer service associates often use emphatic listening to let callers know their complaint is understood. When a customer calls to complain about a printer, they know the message has been understood when the customer service associate says: "I'm sorry you are having trouble getting the printer to work properly." The associate can then ask questions and offer advice to try to solve the problem.
- **Reflective listening** is used to hear, understand, and offer feedback that helps the speaker think about feelings or objectives. The feedback should not be judgmental; rather, it should prompt the speaker to think or question further. Prompts, open-ended questions, and restatements of what the speaker has said are useful in giving feedback with reflective listening. Suppose a co-worker says to you, "I am at a loss about how to tackle this project." A response that shows reflective listening might be, "So you're not sure where to begin. Tell me more. What's your understanding of the goals of the project?" This feedback reflects what the speaker has said and prompts the speaker to think further about the project and his or her objectives.

Listening Effectively

An effective listener prepares to listen by removing internal and external listening barriers. When someone approaches you at your desk or in a meeting, stop talking or working on tasks. Clear your mind of distracting thoughts and give the speaker your full attention. As the speaker begins talking, quickly determine the type of active listening that will be appropriate. Is the speaker giving you instructions? If so, informative listening is appropriate. Does the speaker seem worried or upset? Emphatic listening may help you communicate effectively in this situation.

Do not let biases or previous experiences keep you from listening with an open mind. Perhaps you have heard a speaker present ideas at several meetings and have found none of the ideas helpful. This meeting might be different. Do not miss important information because you prejudge a speaker or a topic. When receiving instructions from someone or listening to someone speak in a meeting, quickly note questions that you will ask later to help clarify points you do not understand.

When you begin thinking about your response while another person is still speaking, you could easily miss part of the message. A nod or an encouraging smile can show the speaker that you are interested. By restating important points of the message at an appropriate time, you verify that you have understood the message.

Communicating AT WORK

Follow these tips for effective listening:
- Focus on the speaker and the message.
- Use the appropriate type of casual or active listening for the situation.
- Keep an open mind and do not prejudge the speaker or the message.
- Keep your emotions in check. Do not let an emotional response to a message distract you from listening.
- Wait until the speaker pauses to begin framing your response.
- At an appropriate time, ask questions to clarify the message you heard.
- Offer feedback to the speaker.

Verbal and Nonverbal Communication

The way you speak—not just what you say—makes an impression on listeners. The nonverbal cues you use can add to or detract from the message you send to receivers. Using the proper degree of formality when talking with co-workers and clients is also important.

Using the proper degree of formality for different communication situations will make listeners more open to receiving your message. The degree of formality that is considered appropriate when speaking with co-workers, managers, and clients varies across companies. In some companies, co-workers (and managers, in particular) are addressed more informally by their first names. Observe the custom followed at your company. However, do not be overly friendly or informal with co-workers or clients you do not know well even if you address them by their first names.

Be especially sensitive to the degree of formality you use when talking with co-workers or clients from other cultures. In many parts of Canada, direct and concise communications are considered appropriate. For example, you might say to a co-worker, "Great. Call me when you have the final results." To a client or co-worker from another culture, this message may seem abrupt or rude. A more appropriate message might be, "That's great news, Mr. Haddad. Will you please call me when you have the final results."

© Dragon Images/Shutterstock.com

Use an appropriate degree of formality when talking with co-workers or customers.

Verbal Communication Skills

Verbal communication is the process of exchanging ideas and feelings through the use of words. Always use proper grammar when speaking with co-workers, clients, and others in the workplace. Using improper grammar and slang expressions detracts from your professional image and could be confusing to those whose first language is not English. Factors such as pitch, tone, volume, and rate of speech can affect your verbal communications. Also important is using the proper degree of formality when talking with co-workers and clients. Verbal skills used in giving a presentation are discussed in Chapter 7.

Pitch

Pitch is an attribute of sound that can be described as high or low. Someone who is nervous or frightened may speak in a high-pitched voice as their throat tightens. Listeners may be less likely to believe your message when you speak in a high-pitched voice.

On the other hand, people who speak in a comfortably low-pitched voice tend to project calmness and control. Listeners are more likely to have confidence in a speaker using a low-pitched voice. If you are nervous or tense as you prepare to speak at a meeting or with a client, make a conscious effort to relax your body. Drinking something warm will help relax your vocal cords so you can speak in a low-pitched voice.

Tone

Tone is an attribute of voice that conveys the attitude or emotional state of the speaker. The same words spoken in different tones can convey different meanings. For example, the words "that's great" spoken in a friendly and enthusiastic tone convey a positive message. The same words spoken in a sarcastic or frustrated tone convey quite a different meaning. Be aware of your tone of voice to be sure you are sending the message you want to send.

Pace and Volume

When you speak too quickly or too slowly, the listener may either miss part of your message or become frustrated and lose interest. Listening to someone who is speaking too loudly can also be frustrating for a listener. On the other hand, speaking in a voice that is so low that people consistently ask you to repeat yourself can cause a different sort of problem. If listeners feel they are embarrassing you by asking you to repeat yourself too often, they may just give up and your message will be lost. Be aware of this type of feedback and make a conscious effort to increase the volume of your voice so that you are speaking at a medium pace and at a volume that ensures your message can be received and understood.

Nonverbal Communication Skills

Nonverbal communication is sending a message without spoken or written words. An example of nonverbal communication is **body language**—body motions, gestures, and facial expressions. Nonverbal symbols can affect or even alter a message. A job candidate in an interview who sits up straight, makes eye contact with the interviewer, and looks interested in the conversation reinforces the message that they are interested in the job and the company. A candidate who slumps in the chair, does not make eye contact, and is not focused on the discussion sends the nonverbal message that they are not interested in the company or the job. Even though the candidate may express interest, nonverbal cues contradict the spoken words. When nonverbal cues do not support a verbal message, the listener is more likely to accept the nonverbal message. Be aware of your body language so that your nonverbal messages reinforce your verbal messages.

Nonverbal communication symbols have different meanings from culture to culture. For example, the "okay" sign made by placing the forefinger and thumb into a circle and raising the remaining fingers has a positive meaning in North American cultures. However, in some other cultures, this gesture is considered offensive. People in different cultures feel differently about the use of personal space. Standing less than a metre away when talking with someone is a comfortable distance for people in some cultures. In other cultures, this distance is too close and will make the listener feel uncomfortable, as if their space is being invaded. A listener in this situation may keep backing away from the speaker and have difficulty focusing on the message. Learn about the nonverbal cues of people from other cultures with whom you communicate so that you can send the appropriate nonverbal messages.

Written Communication Skills

Is written communication as important in the workplace today as it was in the past? The answer is a resounding yes. In fact, because email is so widely used in today's offices, administrative professionals probably compose more original written communications now than ever. Written communication in all its forms remains extremely important.

Emails, letters, memos, and reports are among the major communication documents in the workplace. Depending on the effectiveness of the writer, these documents may create goodwill or ill will for the organization—and the writer. To be a truly effective administrative professional, you need to add another communication skill to your list of qualifications—the ability to compose effective business documents.

As you begin your career, you may be asked to prepare emails, interoffice memoranda, and routine correspondence, such as a letter requesting information. As you learn more about the organization and demonstrate your writing skills to your employer, the complexity and number of your writing assignments will probably increase, and your employer may ask you to compose letters in draft or final form for their signature. No matter what type of position you hold, written communication skills are invaluable to both you and the organization. You should establish a goal now to become an excellent communicator through the written word.

The basic types of written messages that the administrative professional prepares are emails, memoranda, letters, and reports.

- **Emails.** An email is generally a very short communication—it should be no longer than what is visible on one computer screen without scrolling.
- **Memoranda.** Although email has become the communication vehicle of choice for most interoffice correspondence, memoranda are still written, particularly when the message is longer than a paragraph or two.
- **Letters.** Letters are more formal than memos and emails. They represent the company to customers, clients, and prospective customers and clients.
- **Reports.** The reports that are prepared in the workplace may be informal reports of two or three pages, or they may be formal reports containing a table of contents, the body of the report (with footnotes or endnotes), appendices, and a bibliography.

Organizational Skills

Writing effectively is a process that involves planning, composing, editing, proofreading, and publishing messages. Each stage of the process is important in creating an effective message.

Planning

Before beginning to write any message, take time for some planning, which will save time and reduce frustrations. Ask yourself the W questions: Who? What? When? Where? Why?

- Who needs to receive the communication?
- What is the objective of the communication?
- What information is needed before writing the communication?
- When will the information be provided or required?
- Where should the information be sent?
- Why is the communication being written?

If you are working on a formal report, make an outline before beginning. If you are new to writing letters, you can help organize your thoughts by making random notes on a notepad or on your preferred computer note-taking program, such as Microsoft OneNote. Just as you would work with your to-do list, jot down ideas randomly; place them in order when you begin to compose the message. As you become more experienced in writing letters and informal reports, you may need to create only a mental outline of what you want to write; a formal report, however, will likely require an outline.

Adjust the Message for the Receiver

Your message will be more effective if you adjust the message for the reader. Consider the reader's needs, wants, and interests as they relate to the message. Then state your message in a way that addresses these needs or interests. To help you identify the reader's needs or wants, ask questions such as these: What are the ages, genders, backgrounds, and biases of the readers? What knowledge or experience related to the message topic do the readers have? Will the readers consider the message to be positive, neutral, or negative news?

Writing with the reader's needs and interests in mind is called the *you* approach. The first example shown in Figure 5-2 is not written with the you approach. The second example uses the you approach and will be more appealing to the reader. When using the you approach for email messages, memos, and letters, the first paragraph of the message typically begins with *you, your,* or the person's name.

Composing

Composing is writing a message based on the objectives and plan developed for the message. A complete business message typically has an opening, one or more developmental paragraphs, and a closing.

- The opening paragraph identifies the subject of the message.
- The developmental paragraphs supply supporting details.
- The closing paragraph ends a message. This paragraph may summarize earlier points of the message, ask the reader to take some action, or try to build goodwill.

Organize the Message Content

Message content can be organized using the direct, indirect, or persuasive approach, depending on the anticipated reader reaction. Use the direct approach when the message, such as a job offer or congratulations on a promotion, is one the reader will be pleased to receive or when the message is expected to have a neutral effect on the receiver, such as a message requesting or relaying information. Use the indirect approach when reader is expected to react negatively, and use the persuasive approach when attempting to prompt the reader to take some action.

Direct Approach

When using the **direct approach** the message content will:

- Begin with the reason for the correspondence.
  Do you sell an all-in-one printer, scanner, telephone, and copier?

- Continue with whatever explanation is necessary so the reader will understand the message.
  If so, please provide me with the capabilities of your product and the price.

- Close with a thank you for action that has been taken or with a request that action be taken by a specific date.
  I need the information by January 15; please respond using the address given in the letterhead. Thank you for your assistance.

The direct approach would be appropriate for an email message to a co-worker confirming that you can complete a task. Figure 5-3 shows an email message written using the direct approach.

Indirect Approach

At times, you must write messages refusing either a request or an appointment or in some way saying no to a person. Using

FIGURE 5-2

EXAMPLE 1	EXAMPLE 2
We have decided to approve the loan application for a mortgage on the home at 234 Maple Avenue.	Your loan application has been approved for a mortgage on your new home at 234 Maple Avenue.

© Cengage Learning

Writing with the reader's interest in mind, as in Example 2, is called the you approach.

FIGURE 5-3

Email Message That Uses the Direct Approach

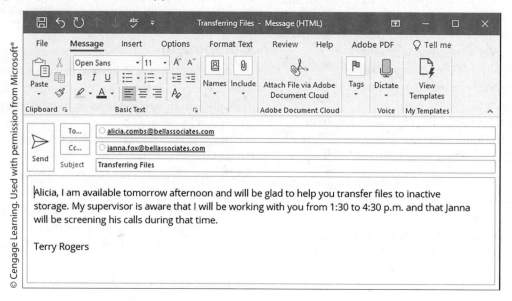

© Cengage Learning. Used with permission from Microsoft®

an **indirect approach** will help the recipient accept the decision and understand your concern. You can leave the recipient with a positive impression when writing indirect messages if you:

- Begin with an opening statement that is pleasant but neutral.
  Your plan to build a fund for a new arts centre in the community is commendable. I hope you are able to meet your goal.

- Review the circumstances and give the negative information.
  Every year CanAsian contributes several thousand dollars to important causes. However, even though your proposal is a worthy one, we have already expended this year's budget. If you are still in need of our help next year, please let us know. We will be happy to consider a proposal from you.

- Close the message on a pleasant and positive note.
  Good luck in your efforts. Our town needs more civic-minded groups such as yours.

Figure 5-4 is an example of a letter using the indirect approach.

Persuasive Approach

When you want to convince someone to take a specific action, such as persuading a busy executive to speak at a conference or, when you want to change an indifferent or negative reader reaction, the **persuasive approach** is appropriate. By using this indirect approach with its special characteristics you

can, ideally, change the reader's initial negative or indifferent attitude to a positive one.

Using the *you* approach to do so, you would:

- Begin with "you" or "your."
  Your role as an administrative professional is often challenging. You deal with conflict, unhappy customers, changing technology, and numerous other challenges daily. Would you like to know how to handle these challenges effectively and keep your frustration level down?

- Continue by creating interest and desire.
  If you answered yes to these questions, our monthly publication, The Effective Administrative Professional, will help you. It is packed with techniques and suggestions for handling office situations.

- Close by asking for the desired action.
  You can have this publication in your office every month for only $48 per year. That is a very small amount to pay for lowering your frustration level and making your job more rewarding. Fill in the information on the enclosed card, and return it by January. Your early return will guarantee you one free month of the subscription. We look forward to counting you as one of our many satisfied subscribers.

Note that when you are in this initial phase of writing a document, do not be concerned about proofreading or formatting; these tasks can interrupt your creative thought processes. Get your ideas down; make corrections and do your formatting in the next phase, when you are editing the document.

FIGURE 5-4

Block Letter with Open Punctuation That Uses the Indirect Approach

Bell and Associates

304 Fernwood Ave. | Truro, NS B2N 0E3 | 606.555.0147 | www.bellassociates.com

October 24, 20--

Dr. Alan Mossavi
63 Normandy Avenue
Truro, NS B2N 3J6

Dear Alan

Your invitation to speak at the seminar on December 15 is an honour. I know that your students will benefit from hearing professional in the marketing field discuss the latest trends in marketing products.

Unfortunately, the demands on my time are currently very heavy. Our company is introducing a new product line next year, and I am developing a marketing campaign to be launched on January 1. Handling this campaign along with my other duties leaves me no time for speaking engagements this fall, so I must refuse your request.

Have you met Harmony Ming, one of our marketing assistants? Ms. Ming is very knowledgeable about our company's marketing efforts and the latest trends in product marketing. I have not spoken to her about your request, but I think she may be available. Her telephone number is 902.555.0157. You might wish to invite her to take part in the seminar.

Sincerely

Alexander Ramon

Alexander Ramon
Vice President of Marketing

xx

Editing

Editing is reviewing and revising a message to improve its form and content. To be effective and to accomplish its goal, written communication in any form—instant message, email, memorandum, letter, or report—must be clear, concise, complete, courteous, and correct. Figure 5-5 describes messages with each of these characteristics. Review your messages with these characteristics in mind.

When you are editing a document, especially for a co-worker, or working collaboratively with others, using Microsoft Word's Track Changes feature can be helpful. The Track Changes feature shows additions, deletions, and changes you make to a document. You can also add comments to a document to explain why you made a change or offer suggestions related to the document. The changes can later be accepted or rejected by you or a co-worker to create a final version of the document. Figure 5-6 shows part of a document that has been marked using Track Changes.

FIGURE 5-5

Characteristics of Effective Written Communications

Courteous	A courteous message has a positive tone and is considerate of the reader. Saying *please* and *thank you* and using the proper degree of formality help create a courteous message.
Correct	A correct message does not contain errors or imply information that is not accurate. The mechanics of the message (spelling and grammar), as well as the information itself, should be correct.
Concise	A concise message expresses ideas in as few words as possible without being abrupt or incomplete. It does not contain unnecessary elements, redundancies, or empty phrases.
Clear	A clear message gives precise information that cannot be easily misunderstood. It does not contain contradictory information.
Complete	A complete message contains all the information needed to achieve the objectives of the sender. It does not omit dates, times, locations, amounts, or other details that the reader needs to know.

© Cengage Learning

FIGURE 5-6

Microsoft Word's Track Changes Feature Can be Helpful when Editing a Document.

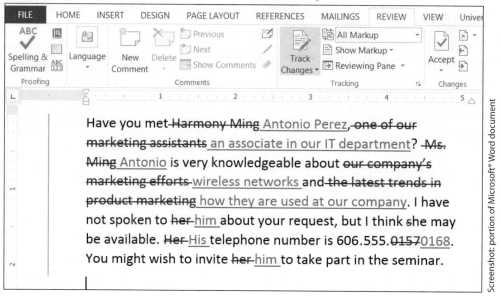

Screenshot: portion of Microsoft® Word document

Proofreading

When proofreading your message, do more than check spelling, grammar, punctuation, capitalization, and sentence structure. Consider the tone of your message; ensure it is appropriate. Check that your paragraphs are effective and the reading level will match that of your reader.

You can use the grammar and spell check features in your software program to assist in catching errors. Grammar programs can help you find grammatical errors. They flag punctuation and capitalization errors. They also let you know when you have used the passive voice. A thesaurus helps you develop your vocabulary by suggesting alternatives for words you have used frequently. Do not rely completely on this software feature. Grammar and spell check features do not catch *all* errors. For example, if you use *form* rather than *from*, the error will not be detected. When proofreading, apply your spelling skills and the knowledge of good grammar you have acquired in your communications courses. Operating systems and application software usually designate "English (U.S.)" as the default for grammar and spell check features. Be sure to change your default settings to "English (Canada)" to ensure correct Canadian spelling is identified.

Use the Track Changes feature of your software when proofreading from the screen to make corrections or insert comments that identify changes to be made. When you are proofreading hardcopy documents, add proofreaders' marks directly to the document to indicate necessary changes or corrections. Commonly used proofreaders' marks are provided in the Reference Guide that can be accessed on the MindTap site.

Technology AT WORK

Many businesses use social media to publish messages to customers and others. Social media are online tools that allow users to share information, collaborate, and interact with one another. Examples of social media include Facebook, Twitter, LinkedIn, blogs, wikis, photo and video sharing sites, and Web conferencing sites. Your company may have a social media policy that provides rules or guidelines regarding how employees may use social media for marketing, promoting events, gathering customer feedback, or other business uses.

Publishing

Publishing is sending a message to the receiver (as with a letter or an email message) or making the message available to the receiver (as with posting information on a company intranet, website, or social media site). Selecting an appropriate method for publishing a message is important. For example, a message to a co-worker that contains sensitive or confidential information should not be sent in an email message. A personal conversation or a printed memo should be used instead. When choosing an appropriate communication channel, consider factors such as

- the purpose/objective of the message
- the target audience
- the length of the message
- how quickly the information needs to be delivered
- the cost of distribution and the budget available

Types of Written Messages

Emails

Have you ever not opened an email because the subject did not seem important or you didn't recognize the sender's name? With the number of emails we receive continually growing, it is important that they be well written. Although email is considered an informal means of communication, when composing business emails, you should apply the same effective writing techniques that you use when composing other types of messages. Since people receive dozens of emails every day, take care to write your emails effectively if you expect them to be read. Pay attention to all details—including the subject line—and consider the following guidelines:

- Be appropriately formal when writing emails. The rule of thumb is to be almost as formal in a business email as you are in other forms of written communications with your employer and co-workers.
- Always include a subject line; use it to state the purpose of the message. For example, if you are sending an email about a budget meeting, the *Subject* should read "Budget Meeting, 2:30 P.M., November 1," rather than "Meeting." If you are replying to a message but are changing the subject of the conversation, change the *Subject* line. Better yet, start a new message altogether.
- Keep the message short—no longer than the length of your screen (without scrolling) is best. Be clear, concise, complete, and correct. Use complete sentences, capitalize and punctuate properly, and do not run sentences together; it is difficult to read email constructed in this manner. Insert a blank line after each paragraph. If your memo is longer than one screen, attach a separate document.
- Edit and proofread carefully. Do not send an email that contains inaccuracies or incorrect grammar. Use the program's spelling and grammar check feature and delete unnecessary phrases, words, or sentences.
- Do not send or forward spam (electronic junk mail).
- Some mail programs do not keep an attachment together when a message is forwarded. Check to ensure both the message and attachment are being forwarded together.
- **Emoticons** can be perceived as casual interactions. In business communications, they have limited use (to soften a negative message or to clarify your tone and intent). They should be used only with people you know well.
- Always capitalize the appropriate words, be specific about your needs, and use a proper closing that includes your name and title in your signature (if appropriate). See the examples below; one is too informal and inappropriate for business. The other is appropriate.

Inappropriate

jim, we need to have a meeting soon—can you arrange? i'm free next mon. thks.

Appropriate

Jim,
We need to meet to discuss our division's projected budget for the next six months. Are you available on Monday, November 14, from 9 a.m. until 10 a.m.? If so, let me know by this afternoon. We can meet in my office.
—Ed

- Include a standard text in your closing such as
This email and any files transmitted with it are confidential and intended solely for the use of the recipient. If you have received this email in error, please notify me by return mail and delete this message from your system. Any unauthorized use or disclosure of this message is prohibited.

Or
Think green. Please consider the environment and do not print this email unless you really need to.

- Assign a high priority to the message only when truly needed.
- Assume that any message you send is permanent. Even if you and the receiver delete the message, it may not be deleted from everywhere the message was stored. The message could be sitting in someone's private file or in an archive. The receiver can also forward your email to others.
- Unless they serve a specific purpose, avoid using different fonts, colours, clip art, and other graphics in an email, which can clutter it and detract from your main message. Your message can take longer to send and receive as a result, particularly if you include numerous graphics. However, when replying to a message, using coloured text to insert your responses to specific questions or comments is an effective method to use that can help to make your response more understandable.
- If you make a typo or regret sending a message, you can undo the action if the option is available in your email program. By enabling the "undo send" option in Gmail you have the option to take back a message you have just sent.
- Use cc and bcc fields appropriately. The cc field is used when you want to keep an individual informed of the contents of the email but they do not need to take any action. When an individual is added as a bcc the recipients of the "to" and cc fields are unaware who has been added as a bcc. This feature can be used if you are sending an email to a large number of individuals but you do not want everyone's email addresses exposed. A bcc is also effective

in sensitive matters. For example, if you are dealing with a customer complaint, you can add your manager as a bcc so that they are informed of how the complaint was resolved without the recipient knowing other individuals were included in the email.

In Canada, organizations must comply with Canada's Anti-Spam Legislation (CASL), which was introduced in July 2014. This legislation requires that organizations receive consent from their customers and clients if they intend to use email to promote or market their organization. Ensure you become familiar with the procedures an organization has established to comply with this legislation.

Ethical behaviour is also important in email. For example, you should not misuse the organization's email system by sending an inappropriate amount of personal email. Ethics is the soft skill topic in this chapter.

Instant Messaging

Instant messaging (IM), similar to email, is a cost-effective tool for written communications among employees of any organization. Text conversations between yourself and anyone using the same program on your contact list can happen in real time through a server connection. When you launch the program, you can see icons that indicate who on your contact list is online, who is online but not available for IM, and whether contacts are using a mobile device.

As the text version of a phone call, IM usage is growing in organizations as a supplement to both email and telephone communications. Many of the guidelines and etiquette for email also apply to IM.

Memoranda

Although email is widely used in most organizations, memoranda continue to have a place in the work environment. The hardcopy memorandum (memo, for short) generally is written when the message is fairly long (more than one screen) or the information is confidential or sensitive.

A word processing template that includes standard elements ensures that the same format is used throughout the organization. A variety of templates from Microsoft Word can be customized to include an organizational logo in addition to the heading *Memorandum* and the following required elements: To line, From line, Date line, and Subject line.

When completing the To portion of the memo, know your company preferences and follow them. Follow these general rules:

- Use the first name (or initial) and last name of the individual.
- Use the job title of the individual if it is company procedure to do so; many organizations do not use titles in memos.

- Do not use courtesy titles such as Ms. or Mr.
- If you are sending a memorandum to more than one individual, list the names in alphabetical order or by hierarchical order within the company.
- If you are addressing a memo to a group (generally six or more people), use a generic classification, such as "United Way Fundraising Team." Include a distribution list at the end of the memo giving the names of the recipients. An example of a distribution list for a memo is shown in the Document Formatting Guide available on the MindTap site for this textbook.

When distributing memos, you may use specially designed interoffice envelopes. These envelopes are reusable and are generally large enough that standard-size stationery can be inserted without folding. An example of an interoffice envelope is illustrated in Chapter 8.

The notation pc (photocopy), cc (courtesy copy), or c (copy) can be added at the end of the memo when copies are being sent to other individuals. Again, list the names of the recipients alphabetically or hierarchically, whichever is company procedure.

As with all messages, before writing a memo, take time for some planning, then gather information and apply the characteristics of effective communication. In style, memos are slightly more formal than emails but less formal than letters. Consider your audience when setting the memo's tone (informal or formal). Memos to co-workers may be informal, while memos to managers or clients may be more formal.

If a memo is more than one page long, a heading should be placed on the second and subsequent pages. The heading should include the recipient's name, the appropriate page number, and the date. An example of a second-page heading is shown in the Document Formatting Guide, which can be accessed on the MindTap site.

Figure 5-7 illustrates a memorandum. Notice the memorandum uses side headings. This approach helps the reader scan the memo quickly and easily. Such an approach also helps the writer to focus on and clarify the message.

Letters

Although organizations communicate extensively with their customers, clients, and employees via telephone, memo, email, and perhaps IM, letters remain an important method of publishing a message. Letters are more formal than memos and emails. A letter represents the company to the outside public—customers, clients, and prospective customers and clients. A well-written letter can win friends and customers. Conversely, a poorly written letter can lose customers and make enemies of prospective customers. One of your tasks as an administrative professional is assisting your employer with writing effective letters or writing letters yourself for their

FIGURE 5-7
Memorandum

Bell and Associates

304 Fernwood Ave. | Truro, NS B2N 0E3 | 606.555.0147 | www.bellassociates.com

TO: Andrea Wilson, Administrative Assistant

FROM: Karl Leinsdorf, Human Resources Manager

DATE: June 2, 20--

SUBJECT: Leave of Absence

Andrea, your family medical leave of absence request has been approved. Your leave will begin on July 1, 20--, and continue for six weeks as indicated on your leave of absence request form. The approved form is attached. The reasons for your leave of absence will be shared with your supervisor but not with other employees as you requested.

You seemed to have a good understanding of the conditions of a family medical leave when we talked last week. However, if you have any questions regarding your leave, please let me know.

Attachment: Leave of Absence Form

---

signature. Use a letter format approved by your company. Block and modified block formats are commonly used for business letters. Figure 5-4 shows a letter formatted in block style with open punctuation. Figure 5-8 shows a letter formatted in modified block style with mixed punctuation. Both punctuation styles can be used with either letter format.

Ensuring Mailability

Since letters represent your company to outside individuals, in addition to writing them well and using correct grammar, spelling, and punctuation, you must also format them correctly. If you need a quick review on letter styles and folding letters, refer to the Reference and Business Document Formatting Guides on the MindTap site.

Increase your productivity when creating letters by using formatting and other features of your word processing software, such as mail merge and envelope and label options. Mail merge is a feature that allows you to create personalized letters, labels, or envelopes for large mailings. The mail merge operation creates new documents that contain the text of a main file with data from a data file inserted at specified locations in the main document. Using mail merge is an efficient way to create letters for several recipients when only a small amount of data specific to each recipient changes with each letter.

By using your cursor to select the recipient's address in a letter, you can automatically generate envelopes or labels. Using this method to create an envelope saves time and ensures that exactly the same name and address appear on both the letter and the envelope. You can print the envelope or add it to the document for printing later. Similar procedures can be followed to create a mailing label. You will be given

options to select the label size and to print a full page of the same label or a single label.

Your supervisor may, on occasion, return a piece of correspondence to you, informing you of an error that must be corrected before it can be mailed. Ensure your effectiveness as an administrative professional by paying attention to all details in correspondence before submitting it to your supervisor for signature.

Reports

Many types of reports are prepared in the workplace. Some reports are informal and contain only two or three pages. Other reports may be formal reports with a table of contents, bibliography, and appendices in addition to the body of the report.

A summary of a report may be presented orally, in addition to distributing the report electronically or in print. Creating oral presentations and visual aids is discussed in Chapter 7.

The writing process for reports is the same as for other written messages—plan, compose, edit, proofread, and publish—with one exception. The writer may need to do research to find the information needed to compose the report.

The administrative assistant's role in preparing reports varies:

- You may have the responsibility of keying and formatting the report, producing the final copies, and distributing the report.
- You may help with the research.
- You may draft some or all portions of the report.

Since formal or long reports often require much time and effort to prepare, it is especially important that the writer

FIGURE 5-8
Modified Block Letter with Mixed Punctuation in Direct Order

Office Solutions

4540 Eastgate Boulevard, Victoria, BC, V8P4A7   250.555.0125

May 12, 20--

Ms. Janet Waldon
Johnson Company
3574 Kennedy Avenue
Victoria, BC V8P 4A7

Dear Ms. Waldon:

Thank you for inviting me to make a presentation on document printers. We have seve ral models of ink jet and laser printers for sale, and I will be happy to present information about them to your company. A brochure describing our most popular printer is enclosed.

Your suggested time for the presentation, 3 p.m. on May 20, is convenient for me. I will provide information on several printers. I will also bring three printers that I think would be good choices for your company based on the information you have given to me. You will be able to see these printers in action and judge the quality of the printouts. I will also provide the information on the cost of refill cartridges that you requested.

Please call me if your company has any special printing needs that we have not discussed so I can address those needs in my presentation. Iwill call you on May 19 to reconfirm our meeting at your company location.

Sincerely,

Anita Diaz

Anita Diaz
Sales Representative

tr

Enclosure

c   Scott Marlin, Account Manager
        Alicia Stokes, Buyer

---

identify the objective of the report clearly and consider the audience for the report. For a long or complicated report, a timeline should be developed to set deadlines for completing stages of the research and report composition.

Research for Reports

Most reports involve some type of research. The research may be **primary research**—the collecting of original data through surveys, observations, or reviewing and analyzing data. For example, suppose your manager asks you to create a report on the use of company sick days. You might need to review the attendance records for all employees for the past five years to determine whether use of sick days has been increasing or

decreasing. Your report might include a graph that shows total sick days used for each of the last five years. The report might include other information that you calculate, such as the percentage increase or decrease in the use of sick days and the time of year when the most sick days are used.

The report may also require **secondary research**—finding data or material that other people have discovered and reported via the Internet, books, periodicals, and various other publications.

Suppose you are asked to conduct research for a marketing plan for a new product your company plans to sell. You could research the demographics of the target market area to find the number of people living in the area. You could also find information about the ages, races, genders, education, and income levels of the area residents. Using this information, the report writer can make recommendations for marketing strategies that will appeal to the target buyers. When using information discovered from secondary research, be sure to give proper credit to the source of the information by using footnotes or endnotes. Do not reprint copyrighted material without the consent of the copyright holder.

Writing AT WORK

When proofreading, look for these common errors in written messages:
- missing or repeated words
- transposed words
- incorrect amounts or dates
- incorrect use of words
- incorrect or missing punctuation
- incorrect capitalization
- incorrect grammar
- incorrect spacing or placement of document parts

During your research, it is important to determine the credibility of the company or individual providing the information that you find and to note the date of the article or study. Information found in print or on the Internet is not necessarily reliable or current. Ask yourself these questions to help you evaluate the credibility of sources: Who wrote the information? What education or expertise does the person have? Is the person representing a respected organization? Is the information current? Is the information biased toward a particular viewpoint?

When using secondary research in reports, you must properly document your research sources. The Document Formatting Guide on the MindTap site includes a section on documentation. Information is also provided on **MLA style** (Modern Language Association), **APA style** (American Psychological Association), Web style, and traditional documentation styles.

Formats for Reports

An informal report may have only one or two parts: either just the body or the body and an **executive summary** (a one- or two-page summary of the report). An informal report may also be formatted as a memo. In the memo format, the name of the person requesting the report appears in the To line, the report writer in the From line, and the title in the Subject line. When the report contains more than one page, side headings, similar to those used in a formal report, may be used to identify the sections of the report. An informal report is written in a conversational style using personal pronouns such as *I, you, me, we*, and *us*.

The executive summary is useful for a reader who does not need a detailed understanding of all aspects of the report, but who does need to know the major findings and recommendations. Readers can use the executive summary to preview the report to determine whether they want to read a certain portion or the entire report.

The executive summary
- describes the background—why the report was necessary and identifies the problem or issue
- summarizes the report's major findings—what was discovered through the research
- itemizes the recommendations being made as a result of the discoveries

The formal report normally deals with a more complex subject, is longer than the informal report, and requires more time and preparation. Formal reports are generally written in manuscript format and contain several parts, which may include an executive summary, title page, table of contents, body, bibliography or reference section, and appendix. Not all reports will contain all these parts.

Your company may have a particular format that you will be expected to use for formal reports. Refer to the company's style guide for documents if one is available. If a style guide is not available, review reports in the company files to see the formats that have been used for other reports.

Formal business reports usually follow these guidelines:
- **Title page.** The title page contains the title of the report; the writer's name and title; the organization, department, or division name; and the date the report is being submitted.
- **Table of contents.** A table of contents is optional, but is generally included when a report is long. The table of contents lists major sections and the first page number of each section. The table of contents helps the reader quickly locate specific sections of the report.
- **Manuscript style.** The body of the report includes a main title and side headings to identify parts of the report. Software features such as the Title and Heading styles in Microsoft Word are typically used to ensure consistency in the format of titles and headings.
- **Paragraph formatting.** Use 1 or 1.5 line spacing with 10 or 12 points of blank space between paragraphs. The paragraphs are not indented.
- **Visual aids.** Tables, charts, or other visual aids may be included in the report body or in an appendix.
- **Footnotes, endnotes, or internal citations.** Ensure the report properly cites sources of material and the authors of material used in the report. Footnotes appear at the bottom of the page where the reference is made. Endnotes are grouped at the end of the document. Internal citations appear within the context of the document.

- **Bibliography.** At the end of the report, a references page lists all sources used in writing the report. Each entry includes the complete name(s) of the author(s), the title of the book or periodical, the date of publication, the publishing company, and the page numbers.

- **Appendix.** Use an appendix to provide additional details or related information mentioned in the report.

A sample business report appears in the Business Document Formatting Guide found on the MindTap site for this textbook.

Soft Skills

ETHICAL AND LEGAL CONSIDERATIONS

You were introduced to the importance of ethical behaviour in Chapter 3. Almost every day, we hear on television or read in a newspaper about business ethics. Ethical problems are difficult to resolve precisely because no rules exist to determine when something is ethical or unethical. Every organization and individual must make that decision independently.

In written correspondence, you, as an employee of an organization, must be honest, must maintain confidentiality (not divulge organizational business outside the organization), and must be loyal (act in the employer's interest). The organization must also act ethically regarding its public responsibilities. Organizations must tell the truth about their products and services and not mislead the public. For example, airlines have an ethical obligation to the public to meet the scheduled flight times unless circumstances such as weather or mechanical problems arise. They also have an ethical obligation to be honest with the public as to why a flight is late. Automotive companies have an ethical obligation to the public to present correct written specifications of all vehicles. Not-for-profit organizations have an ethical obligation to present in writing to the public how their dollars are spent to achieve their public goals.

In written correspondence (newspaper ads, TV ads, marketing letters, brochures, and so on), organizations have legal obligations that are covered by various laws, including copyright, trademark, contract, and liability laws. These laws are also applicable to email messages. For example, email users must abide by the fair dealing rule of copyright law when forwarding copyrighted materials obtained from the Web. The fair dealing rule is very specific about when something can and cannot be used, and provides guidelines about materials used in a commercial or not-for-profit nature, the length of the copied work in comparison to the entire document, and so on. Unless the legal obligations of organizations are carefully observed in all written materials, the organization faces the consequences of costly lawsuits, loss of the public's goodwill, and loss of business.

Chapter Summary

The summary will help you remember the important points covered in this chapter.

- To be effective in the workplace, you must be an effective communicator. Effective communication is the ability to process and exchange ideas and feelings so the person originating the communication and the person receiving the communication clearly understand the message being communicated.
- A communication barrier is anything that interferes with successful communication. To improve communications, senders and receivers can try to overcome internal barriers and external barriers.

- To be an effective verbal communicator, you should know the appropriate use of the four active listening skills—informative listening, evaluative listening, emphatic listening, and reflective listening.
- Writing is a process that involves planning, composing, editing, proofreading, and publishing messages. Each stage of the process is important in creating an effective message.
- Administrative assistants may be expected to write memos and letters for a manager's signature. They may format and distribute reports, write informal reports, or help with research for reports.

Key Terms

active listening p. 74
APA style p. 85
attitude p. 71
body language p. 76
casual listening p. 74
channel p. 72
communication p. 72
communication barrier p. 73
direct approach p. 77
editing p. 79
emoticons p. 81
emphatic listening p. 74
evaluative listening p. 74
executive summary p. 85
feedback p. 73
indirect approach p. 78

informative listening p. 74
listening p. 74
message p. 72
MLA style p. 85
nonverbal communication p. 76
persuasive approach p. 78
pitch p. 75
primary research p. 84
receiver p. 73
reflective listening p. 74
secondary research p. 84
sender p. 72
space p. 71
tone p. 76
verbal communication p. 75

Discussion Items

These discussion items provide an opportunity to test your understanding of the chapter through written responses or discussion with your classmates and your instructor.

1. What elements are involved in the communication process, and what is the role of each element?

2. What is a communication barrier? Give examples of internal and external communication barriers.
3. List four types of active listening, and explain the purpose of each type.
4. List and explain three elements of nonverbal communication.

Critical-Thinking Activity

Yuan Liang is a manager for CanAsian Airlines. He was transferred from China shortly after the merger of the two companies. He speaks English; however, he has never lived outside China, although he had visited Canada several times before his transfer. He is having difficulty understanding the culture. Although you do not report to Mr. Liang, your employer, Mr. Albertson, has assigned you to work on a quality team chaired by Mr. Liang. In the first team meeting,

you made several suggestions to Mr. Liang and the committee. Mr. Liang smiled and nodded in agreement with your suggestions; the team also voiced agreement. However, when the minutes from the meeting were sent out, you found no indication that your suggestions would be implemented. During the second meeting, Mr. Liang started the discussion with the same problem as was discussed at the last meeting—the one you thought had been resolved. After some discussion within the group (without your participation), you stated that you did not understand why the topic was being discussed again since you thought the group had agreed on a resolution at the last meeting. Mr. Liang only smiled and continued the discussion. However, after the meeting, he contacted your manager and told him you had embarrassed him before the group. Mr. Albertson called you in and asked you to explain the situation; he stated that you should have told him your concerns about the meeting. You are angry and also defensive—angry with Mr. Liang because he did not talk with you and angry with your supervisor because he seems to be questioning your integrity.

Using several of the critical-thinking techniques presented in the first chapter, ask yourself these questions:
- Am I recognizing the cultural differences that are involved?
- Is my position on this issue reasonable and rational?
- Have I tried to understand the situation from Mr. Liang's point of view?
- With those critical-thinking concepts in mind, answer these questions:
- How should I have handled the situation?
- What can I learn from this situation?
- Should I talk with Mr. Liang about my feelings?
- What should I say to Mr. Albertson?

21st Century Skills

 Life and Career Skills
CAREER

 Learning and Innovation Skills
INNOVATION

 Information, Media, and Technology Skills
TECHNOLOGY

 Data
DATA FILE

Building Workplace Skills

Project 5-1 (Learning Outcomes 1 and 3)

INNOVATION

Recently you attended a seminar on improving writing skills. The speaker arrived late and seemed flustered and disorganized. You wondered whether his presentation would also be disorganized. At first the room was quite comfortable, but as the room filled with people, it became too warm. When the speaker turned down the lights to show his presentation, you had to fight to stay awake. Maybe you should not have had such a large lunch. The speaker faced the screen at the front of the room as he discussed points on the slides. The portable microphone he was wearing occasionally omitted a shrill squeak as he moved around at the front of the room. You learned a couple of new ideas for improving your writing, but on the whole, the seminar was not a very enjoyable experience.

What are the internal communication barriers in this scenario? What could you do to help overcome these barriers? What are the external communication barriers in this scenario? What could the speaker do to help overcome these barriers?

Project 5-2 (Learning Outcome 3)

Collaborative Project

INNOVATION   DATA FILE

Open and read file Project 5-2a on the MindTap site, access to which is provided with the printed access card on the inside cover of your textbook. With a team of three or four of your classmates, discuss the case provided; then answer the questions given at the end of the case by writing a memorandum to your instructor, using the memo form in file Project 5-2b. List the members of your team in the From section.

Project 5-3 (Learning Outcome 2)

INNOVATION   DATA FILE

Test your informative listening skills. Locate the sound file Project 5-3 from the data files. Play the file to hear some assignments from your supervisor. Play the file only once. Take notes as you listen, but do not pause the recording or replay the file. Working from memory and your notes, list everything you can remember from listening to the instructions. List any questions you would ask your supervisor about the assignments if you were given the opportunity. Now play the sound file again. Were you able to list all parts of the assignments? Were any of your questions answered as you heard the instructions again?

Project 5-4 (Learning Outcomes 1 and 3)

You work as an administrative assistant in the human resources department of your company. In the course of keying documents and taking messages for your supervisor, you have learned that the company is planning to downsize 15 employees. As you are having lunch with two co-workers, the conversation turns to rumours that the company is considering laying off employees.

"Surely you must know what's going on," says your friend Marsha. "Won't you give us a hint?"

"Come on," says Tim, when you hesitate to answer. "You know you can trust us not to say anything."

What is your responsibility to the company in this situation? To your co-workers? What would you say in this situation? You want to do the right thing and stay on good terms with your co-workers.

Project 5-5 (Learning Outcomes 1 and 3)

You are relatively new at your position as an administrative assistant at TKO Manufacturing. You work with the controller, Mr. Sakimoto, and the staff of the accounting department. Mr. Sakimoto speaks and writes English as an additional language. He seems sensitive regarding his command of the language, and everyone on his staff is careful not to correct his minor speech errors.

You have noticed that Mr. Sakimoto sometimes makes errors in grammar or in stating common expressions in the letters he writes. You would be happy to review his letters and correct these errors for him. How can you approach this subject with Mr. Sakimoto in a way that will not cause him embarrassment?

Project 5-6 (Learning Outcome 4)

Mr. Albertson has been asked by Dr. Greg Lee, president of Mount Royal University, to do a presentation on business ethics at a national conference for business executives scheduled on November 10 from 3 to 4 p.m. CanAsian is having a meeting of its executive management team (from Canada and its international locations) on November 8, 9, and 10. The meeting will conclude at noon on the 10th. Mr. Albertson has decided to ask Yang Su from the China office to join him in the presentation. The presentation will be made by a panel with each participant allotted approximately 20 minutes to discuss international business ethics. A question-and-answer session will follow the presentations.

Write a memorandum to Mr. Su asking him to participate; the memorandum may go out with your name on it. Use the memorandum form in file Project 5-6 on the MindTap site, access to which is provided with the printed access card on the inside cover of your textbook.

Project 5-7 (Learning Outcome 4)

Mr. Joey Premdas of Floater Staffing Inc., 401–5920-1A Street SW, Calgary, AB T2H 0G3, asked you to participate in a panel discussion on the topic of effective communications in the workplace. You would like to do so, but your current workload is extremely heavy. Write a letter to Mr. Premdas declining his request. Print your letter on the letterhead stationery available on the MindTap site, file Project 5-7.

Project 5-8 (Learning Outcome 4)

Three emails are on the MindTap site, Project 5-8a, 5-8b, and 5-8c. Review these emails, determining what is wrong with each one. Then rewrite each email as it should be written, using the email forms on Project 5-8d, 5-8e, and 5-8f. Make a copy of your three emails, and submit them to your instructor.

Project 5-9 (Learning Outcome 4)

You work for the Hospital for Sick Children in Toronto, which specializes in research and treatment for illness and disabilities in children. Write a letter to be sent to someone who has donated money to the hospital in the past. Use the indirect approach for this persuasive letter. Thank the person for giving in the past and helping to make treatment of ill children possible. Point out that a large part of the hospital's operating funds comes from donations. Ask the person to send a donation as part of a matching funds campaign. A generous patron will match all the funds donated by individuals up to $50 000. Suggest donation amounts of $100, $500, $1000, or more. However, indicate that any donation amount will be appreciated. Indicate that the funds from this campaign will be combined with other donations to help pay for treatment of children who are ill or injured. The donation must be received within one month from today. Indicate that a reply envelope is enclosed with the letter. Research the address for the hospital and create a letterhead. You are writing to Mrs. Alma Chaney. Make up an address for her from your local area.

Project 5-10 (Learning Outcome 4)

TECHNOLOGY   CAREER

At a recent department meeting, someone mentioned the attention that Earth Week and going green are getting in the media. Another person noted that green initiatives can save money as well as enhance the reputation of a company. Your manager, Ms. Adderely, asked you to do some research and write a short report (two to three pages) about ways an office can implement green practices. The report should also recommend at least three ways that your office can go green. The changes you recommend should be both practical and cost-effective for the company. Use footnotes and endnotes to document the sources of information you use in the report. Include a title page and a references page. Use the format shown for a business report in the Reference Guide of this textbook. Partner with a classmate for the editing and proofreading phase of this writing project. Read your classmate's report and use Track Changes to mark any errors that you find. Use a comment to indicate any section that is unclear or to offer other suggestions for improvement. Ask your classmate to do the same for your report.

Make the Grade with MindTap

Stay organized and efficient with **MindTap**—a single destination with all the course material and study aids you need to succeed. Built-in apps leverage social media and the latest learning technology. For example:

- ReadSpeaker will read the text to you.
- Flashcards are pre-populated to provide you with a jump-start for review—or you can create your own.
- You can highlight text and make notes in your MindTap Reader. Your notes will flow into Evernote, the electronic notebook app that you can access anywhere when it's time to study for the exam.
- Self-quizzing allows you to access your understanding.

Visit nelson.com/student to start using **MindTap**. Enter the Online Access Code from the card included with your text. If a code card is not provided, you can purchase instant access at NELSONbrain.com.

Endnotes

1. Robert Rosen, Patricia Digh, Marshall Singer, and Carl Phillips, *Global Literacies: Lessons on Business Leadership and National Cultures* (New York: Simon & Schuster, 2000), p. 174.
2. Randall S. Hansen and Katharine Hansen, "What Do Employers Really Want? Top Skills and Values Employers Seek from Job-Seekers." Quintessential Careers, http://www.quintcareers.com/job_skills_values.html, accessed May 22, 2011.
3. Robert Louis Stevenson, "On Listening & Writing," Quotations, The International Listening Association, http://www.listen.org, accessed May 22, 2011.

CHAPTER 6

Communicating with Technology

LEARNING OUTCOMES

After studying this chapter, you should be able to:

1. Explain the value of global communication tools.
2. Describe the tools and methods used for collaborating in the workplace.
3. Describe effective techniques for telephone communication.
4. Identify security issues and solutions for protecting computer data.
5. Demonstrate a commitment to continual learning in our technological age.

Global Communication

Technologies for communicating on a global level are expanding and constantly changing. As an administrative professional, many of your daily tasks will involve gathering data, processing data into usable information, and then sharing the information with your supervisor, co-workers, suppliers, and customers. You will also use global communication tools, such as a telephone, a computer, a mobile device, a local area network, a collaborative website, and the Internet, to help you complete these tasks.

Telecommunications is the transmission of electronic information (text, data, voice, video, and images) from one location to another. Having accurate and timely information is essential for businesses wanting to remain competitive in today's global economy. As an administrative professional, you will use telecommunication tools for many of your daily tasks—gathering data, processing data into usable information, and then sharing the information with your supervisor, co-workers, suppliers, and customers.

Computers

Desktop and laptop computers change constantly and allow businesses and individuals to stay connected personally and professionally. You will use a computer in your job as an administrative professional undoubtedly more than any other tool. The Windows operating system is the most used in business; however, Apple's iOS is standard in some industries, such as graphic design, and it continues to gain in popularity.

Mobile Technologies

Tablet computers, smartphones, and intelligent mobile hotspots allow the administrative professional to be more mobile and productive in many environments.

Tablet Computers

A **tablet computer**, commonly shortened to tablet, is a wireless mobile device with a touch screen panel that operates by touch or stylus and keyboard. The Apple iPad, Microsoft Surface, and Samsung Galaxy are examples of tablet computers. These devices differ from a laptop computer primarily by their touch-screen interface and smaller slate-type style and size.

Tablets are constantly evolving, with options including convertible tablets (a laptop with a 180-degree rotating screen that lays flat for the slate style), hybrid tablets (a laptop whose display can be removed to form a tablet), or rugged tablets (tablets with extreme hard drive protections and a rugged case for punishing conditions).

As an administrative professional, you may use a tablet computer for duties such as managing or sharing files, recording notes or video of meetings, or responding to email.

Smartphones

A **smartphone** is a cellular phone with the power and many of the features of a tablet computer. Smartphones have a touch-screen interface and the capability to run software to do things such as record video, take pictures, manage a calendar, or send and receive email. An administrative professional with a smartphone and cellular access can easily connect with their supervisor, co-workers, suppliers, and customers, regardless of location. For example, an administrative professional who is waiting in line at the post office can still answer email and eliminate a backlog of communication while out of the office.

Mobile Applications

A **mobile application** (app) is software that is designed to run on a portable device, such as a tablet or a smartphone. Mobile apps often mirror the functionality of software on a desktop or laptop but with some limitations.

Apps give the administrative professional the ability to remain productive while away from the desk. Common mobile apps used by administrative professionals include calendars, email, shared files, notes, lists, schedules, and up-to-date maps and yellow pages.

Intelligent Mobile Hotspots

An **intelligent mobile hotspot** is a portable Internet connection and is another way to keep your devices connected all

A *variety of mobile technologies are used in the office environment.*

the time. The hotspot can come in the form of a small portable device or can be a feature available on a smartphone. The mobile hotspot makes Internet access possible through a cellular network.

Administrative professionals may use mobile hotspots to keep laptops, tablets, or smartphones connected to the Internet or may maintain a mobile hotspot for others. Mobile hotspots need power through a charged battery or optional power cord.

Data Storage

Computers use two types of data storage—primary storage (or main memory) and secondary storage. The three types of primary storage are **random access memory (RAM), read-only memory (ROM)**, and **flash memory**. RAM storage, which works very fast, is used to temporarily store and run software program instructions and to store data currently in use. Purchasing the highest RAM capacity you can afford ensures that, as new applications come on the market, your computer will be able to handle them. When the computer is turned off, RAM contents are lost.

ROM storage holds basic operating instructions needed when a computer is turned on. The computer battery ensures that these necessary instructions are not lost when the computer is turned off. Some computers and devices, such as cellphones and smartphones, use flash memory to store these basic start-up instructions.

Your computer uses secondary storage memory the same way you use a file cabinet—to organize, store, save, and retrieve software and data files. A hard disk drive is an internal storage device physically mounted into your computer console that is intended to remain in place indefinitely. The amount of storage you need depends on the programs and type of data with which you intend to work. The amount of memory available has steadily increased in direct relation to its declining cost.

If you require additional storage capacity, you can plug one or more external hard drives into a USB port on your computer. Two secondary storage devices that allow you to remove data from the hard disk but still retain data files are optical disk and flash memory devices. An optical disk is a thin, round, plastic disk that can be read from or written to using laser technology; two examples of optical disks are CDs and DVDs, both of which are available in two options: read-only (CD- or DVD-ROM) and read/write (CD- or DVD-RW).

A flash drive, also known as a jump drive, keychain drive, pen drive, or thumb drive, can be used on any computer by plugging it into a **USB** port. This small, portable secondary storage device is about the size of a package of gum with storage capacities that range from 4 to 128 gigabytes (GB). With a flash drive's read/write capability, data can be stored, retrieved, and deleted from this storage device as easily as from a hard drive.

Software

The hardware components that make up a computer system could not function without the instructions it receives from operating system software and application software.

A computer's **operating system** provides the connection between you, the computer's hardware, and the application program. In understanding how an operating system works, consider this analogy. When you turn the key in your car, the motor starts. You merely perform the one function, without being aware of the various electronic parts and the interrelationships among them that are needed for the motor to start.

Operating system software works in a similar manner. It translates your instructions—entered by keyboard, mouse, or touch—into a form that can be understood by the computer. When you turn on your computer, the operating system gets the computer ready to receive your additional commands, which generally come from application software programs. Without an operating system, you are unable to use any application software program. Existing operating systems—such as Microsoft Windows, Android, Linux, and iOS for Macs—are continually being modified and revised, and new ones are being developed.

Application software works with operating software to perform specific tasks. For example, you can use a word processing program to produce a report with graphics, add tables to it using a spreadsheet program, and create a presentation that includes graphics with presentation software. These applications are available separately or bundled together in packages known as application or productivity suites. In a suite, components of the individual applications have a consistent user interface, making it easier to learn new features and to share content between files that have been created by separate applications.

Some of the software programs that can be purchased for installation on your computer and are available from Microsoft and IBM include the following:

- **Microsoft Office.** Available by annual subscription or one-time purchase. The subscription version includes the full suite of Word, Excel, PowerPoint, Access, Outlook, OneNote, and Publisher as individual applications. The one-time purchase version for PC or Mac each include some but not all of these applications.
- **Quicken.** A financial management program for personal and small business use.
- **Sage 50 Accounting.** An accounting software program used by small businesses for managing cash flow and monitoring expenses, creating invoices, making bill payments, and generating a payroll.

Software application programs such as these are continually revised and updated. In addition to the application programs that can be purchased and installed on single workstations or local networks, thousands of free software packages are available on the Web. As an administrative professional, you may be asked to review and test new or free versions to determine their suitability for your organization.

Administrative professionals who specialize in health services or legal industries will also be exposed to **specialized software**. In health services, Accuro, Nightingale, and Epic are software applications used in medical offices and hospitals to maintain medical health records. In the legal field, Conveyancer, DivorceMate, PCLaw, ACL, and ProLaw are software applications used to manage and produce legal documentation to support various practice areas.

Cloud Storage and Cloud Computing

In cloud computing, the **cloud** (a remote network of servers that provide a service or run applications) is another term for the Internet. **Cloud computing** means using files and applications over the Internet. An office may use a cloud computing system to run software applications and store files remotely. In this case, each local computer is not accessing the software or storing files on the local hard drive. It only has to run the interface software that communicates with the remote computers (the cloud). Microsoft Office 365 is one example where all the features of Office are available through an annual renewable subscription.

Accessing information in this manner allows the user to obtain files or programs from any computer, tablet, or smart device with Internet access. For the administrative professional, this feature is especially helpful if working from multiple devices during the day or if access to files is needed while on the go. **Cloud storage** allows for efficient dissemination of information as well, such as sending files from a smartphone while away from your desk. Team members can work together to create and revise documents as they would on a local shared workspace.

The application software in some productivity suites can be used as an interface to a shared workspace. The software works in combination with Web server technologies.

Networks and the Internet

A network comprises two or more devices connected for the purposes of communicating and sharing both information and resources. Sometimes these communications occur within an organization's private network; other times they occur globally over the Internet. When using a private network, all authorized users have access to current data stored in one central location on their network. For example, product information stored on a private network permits authorized employees access to common information, which, when retrieved, is current and timely. A network administrator manages the installation of all software and a regular backup of files is stored on the network.

A private network that covers a small geographical area and links computers, printers, and other devices within an office, a building, or several nearby buildings is known as a local area network, or LAN. When expanded across a city or region, such as linking several city or regional campuses of a college or university, then it is known as a metropolitan area network, or MAN. International businesses link their offices around the world with a private network known as a wide area network, or WAN.

Intranets and Extranets

An **intranet** is a private network that uses Web pages and other Web technologies. It looks and operates much like pages on the World Wide Web. An intranet is accessible only by an organization's employees through their LAN. Intranets are used to share information that needs to be quickly and easily disseminated, such as company policies and in-house newsletters. Individual departments and groups may use the intranet to share and revise documents.

An **extranet** also uses Web technologies but is available to certain individuals, companies, and others outside an organization. Access to an extranet is controlled by usernames and passwords. These same usernames and passwords also control what users can see and do on the extranet. You are making use of an extranet when you connect to your financial institution to review your account activity. Extranets are also used by health institutions to access medical records, or by businesses to allow shareholders to view financial information.

The Internet

A worldwide public collection of networks linking business, government, and educational agencies and individuals, the Internet has revolutionized the way people communicate and the way business is conducted. Organizations around the world use the Internet to communicate with vendors and customers, to sell their products and services, and to provide customer support after the sale. According to the Internet World Stats website, more than three billion people worldwide use the Internet.[1]

The World Wide Web, known simply as the Web, is a part of the Internet that consists of computers called Web servers. Web servers store multimedia documents called Web pages that can contain text, graphics, video, audio, and links to other Web pages. The application software used to access and view Web pages is called a **Web browser**. Firefox, Safari, Microsoft Edge, and Google Chrome are examples of Web browsers.

Because of the millions of pieces of information available on the Web, one of the biggest challenges is finding data that is both reliable and meets your needs. *Search engines* have been developed to help with this process, and they are updated frequently to keep up with the new pages being submitted. Figure 6-1 lists several search engines you might find helpful as you surf the Web.

FIGURE 6-1
Web Search Engines

These search engines can help you find information quickly on the Web. Search engines are continually searching the Web for new pages.

- Google Canada (www.google.ca)
- Bing (www.bing.com)
- Yahoo! (www.yahoo.com)
- Yahoo! Canada (www.ca.yahoo.com)
- Ask (www.ask.com) lets you ask a question in natural language and get a list of links to sites that may have the answer
- HotBot (www.hotbot.com)
- Dogpile (www.dogpile.com) compiles search results from other search engines such as Google, Yahoo!, Bing, and Ask
- SearchEurope (www.searcheurope.com) searches for sites in Europe

Browser Settings

Each Web browser has features which make navigating Web pages easy, efficient, and secure. Regardless of which Web browser you prefer to use, many will have the following common features:

- **Navigation bar.** Back, Forward, Refresh, and Home buttons to navigate through Web pages
- **Cache.** A copy of each Web page viewed is stored in cache
- **Breadcrumbs.** Keep track of the path you took to reach a Web page
- **Favourites/Bookmarks.** The ability to save Web pages you view frequently or want to store for future reference
- **History.** Keeps track of the Web pages you visited in a day, week, or month
- **Pop-up blocking.** Prevents distractions from appearing on your screen such as pop-up advertisements or advertisements that appear in a separate window
- **Private browsing.** Browsing mode that permits you to browse the Internet without tracking history
- **Sync feature.** The ability to connect your desktop and mobile device so that you can access your bookmarks/favourites and browsing history on all your devices

It is recommended to review your preferred Web browser's help section to explore these features further, as well as to learn about additional unique features available in that particular browser.

Internet Searches

In your role as an administrative professional, you will search the Internet to find information. For example, you may need to find a hotel for your supervisor to stay in for a meeting in another country or to research new software your organization may be interested in implementing. Regardless of what you are searching for, there are various techniques that can ensure successful search results.

Keywords or Search Phrase

Web searches are commonly done using **keywords** (one or more words) or a **search phrase** (multiple keywords). Many search engines use a **predictive search feature** where an algorithm based on the most popular searches is used to predict what you are searching. The search engine will return a list of **hits** or links to Web pages that match your keywords or search phrase. Figure 6-2 outlines some search phrases and keywords used to search for information on buying a new laptop and how the search can be modified to provide the best search results.

Wildcard Character

If your search still returns too many hits, you can use wildcard characters, such as an asterisk or question mark, to narrow your search.

- **Asterisk (*).** Asterisks are usually added at the end of a word which will result in a search for derivations of a word. For example, keying motivat* will return searches for motivate, motivational, motivated, and motivation.
- **Question mark (?).** Inserting a question mark represents a single character in a word. This is frequently used when there are words spelled with different variations. For example, keying favo?rite will return searches for favourite and favorite.

Boolean Operators

To produce better search results, include **Boolean operators** in your search phrases or keywords. Boolean operators are words or symbols that identify a relationship between the keywords. Figure 6-3 outlines examples of how Boolean operators can be used.

FIGURE 6-2

Example of Search Engine Criteria for a New Laptop

Keywords or Search Phrase	Search Engine Results	Possible Changes
looking for a new laptop	list of hits is too extensive	add the word "Lenovo"
looking for a new Lenovo laptop	list of hits is still too extensive	remove the verb and common words "for" and "a"
new Lenovo laptop	list of hits is still too extensive	use quotation marks
new "Lenovo laptop"	Lenovo listed	

FIGURE 6-3

Boolean Operators

Boolean Operator	Example	Search Results
AND	iPhones AND laptops	hit list displays devices that are iPhones and laptops
OR	laptops new OR used	new or used laptops will appear
NOT or minus symbol	iPhone smartphones NOT accessories iPhone smartphones -accessories	only iPhone smartphones will appear; not accessories
quotation marks	"iPhone smartphones"	hit list displays results with the exact phrase iPhone smartphones

© 2017 Cengage Learning

Advanced Search Forms

Some Web browsers also have search forms to assist in narrowing and simplifying searches. Figure 6-4 shows an example of Google's Advanced Search form. You will see that this search form allows you to include or exclude words and other search criteria, you can specify a specific language or country to include in your search, you can limit your searches to specific domains (e.g., .gov or .org), and you narrow results based on when the last update occurred.

Evaluating Online Sources

In recent years, there has been increasing discussion about the rise of misinformation appearing on social media platforms and the Internet. When conducting Web page searches, evaluate the online sources. To evaluate online sources, you can apply the **CARS checklist**. CARS stands for:

Credibility. Locate the author of the article or Web page, and conduct a Web search to confirm their credentials and background are authentic and reliable.

Accurate. Accurate information is up to date, detailed, and comprehensive and is supported by cited research or sources. If the information is vague or missing, determine what, if any, sources have been provided and confirm their validity.

Reasonable. Is the information you gathered reasonable rather than being characterized as extreme or excessive? The information you gather should be objective. Determine if the author provides various points of view and does not use biased language to express their point. In addition, determine if the author has a potential conflict of interest. For example, the author is promoting a specific software application and you determine that they also sell this software as their occupation. This would be deemed a conflict of interest.

Support. Are there credible sources provided for the facts and pictures found in the article or Web page? A lack of credible sources to support claims made by the author are simply the opinions of the author and should not be considered fact.[2]

FIGURE 6-4
Google Advanced Search Form

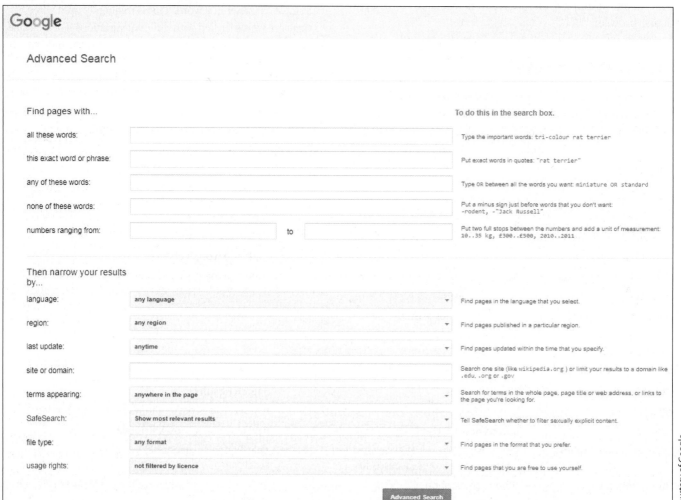

Troubleshooting

As you work with both computer hardware and software, problems are going to occur. One of your tasks as an administrative professional is to solve as many of your problems as possible. You need to become adept at troubleshooting (tracing and correcting problems). To be an effective computer troubleshooter, you should know the following:

- the operating system your computer uses
- the functions of software packages you are using
- the assistance available to you within the organization in which you work (Is there a technician who can help you? If not, is there an administrative professional competent on the package you are using?)

When you are working on a particular software program and encounter problems, you can take some basic steps. As an example, the following troubleshooting assistance is available for most software programs:

- A context-sensitive Help feature allows you to ask questions and provides information on many topics.
- Online help from the software manufacturer is often available using instant messaging or by permitting them remote access to your computer.
- Third-party manuals are available to help you learn new programs and answer many questions you might have. These manuals are available in most bookstores and online.

Workplace Collaboration Tools

As an administrative professional, you will spend many hours collaborating with others to accomplish a variety of tasks, such as creating and revising documents. Productivity software such as Microsoft Office contains basic collaboration tools that allow you to schedule, host, and participate in meetings in person, over the phone, or via video chat and send and receive email. Productivity suites also include features for routing documents across a network to co-workers who can then review, revise, and return them.

Networks enable several other useful electronic tools essential for collaboration—email, shared workspaces, weblogs, blogs, and Web conferencing. The network, Web-based software, and cloud software used for workplace collaboration are commonly referred to as **groupware**. Groupware examples include Microsoft SharePoint Services, Novell GroupWise, IBM Notes Google Apps, Jive Software, and EMC Documentum eRoom.

Email

The most popular and indispensable workplace communication and collaboration tool is email. Email messages

- can be composed, sent, and delivered in minutes
- are sent when convenient to the sender and read when convenient to the recipient
- can be used to transfer files across the network as email attachments
- can be accessed from numerous locations and devices
- provide a low-cost method of communication
- can be saved as a permanent record of a business activity

Email Software

Email software is used to store an electronic address book, and to create, send, receive, retrieve, reply to, and save email messages. Incoming messages are downloaded from the mail server to an Inbox folder on your computer. In addition to enabling you to create custom folders, by default it will also contain folders for temporarily storing outgoing messages, copies of sent messages, drafts of messages not yet sent, and messages you have deleted. Some examples of email software are Novell GroupWise, Microsoft Outlook, and Mozilla Thunderbird.

Web Mail

Another way to access email is through a Web browser. Popular Web-based email services include Gmail by Google, Yahoo! Mail, and EarthLink Web Mail. Web-based email has the advantage of portability. You can access a Web-based email account from any computer or mobile device that has a Web browser and access to the Internet.

You learned in Chapter 5 that when email messages are sent in the workplace, email guidelines and etiquette must be considered. Another important consideration is email ethics.

Technology AT WORK

Screencasting means recording the activity on your computer screen, capturing both video and audio. Screencasts are used in business to show clients, prospective customers, and co-workers how to use a product or service. These short movies can be provided via email or a website and serve as a valuable productivity tool for the administrative professional. Various types of software or Web tools perform screencasting. Some tools are free, and others require purchase. Tools also vary in the features that are available, including the length of the video and whether editing or captioning is possible. The MindTap website for this textbook has links to several current options in screencasting software and Web tools.

Instant Messaging

An **instant message** is an electronic message that opens in a small window on a recipient's computer screen. Although instant messages are quick and easy to use, some workers find it a distraction to have instant messages popping up on their screen. However, as a workplace collaboration tool, it has some real advantages. Instant messaging usually leads to a faster response than email and can be quicker than making a phone call. It also supports text, video, and audio messaging, and greatly enhances collaboration in the workplace through its ability to transfer electronic files as attachments or to remotely access the computer screen of a colleague to troubleshoot a problem or share data.

In terms of disadvantages, instant messaging has a limited ability to keep a record of messages, and organizations may be concerned by the possibilities of unauthorized interception of messages or of sending viruses within attachments. Also, exchanging personal messages during work hours can lead to lost productivity. As a result, businesses are increasingly establishing company-wide procedures for using instant messaging in the workplace. Some have installed network software to monitor and secure employees' instant messages, while others have turned the attachment feature off and permit only short text messages to avoid these potential problems.

Shared Workspaces

Using Microsoft OneDrive, Dropbox, or Google Drive can create a shared workspace—that is, a virtual work area hosted by a Web server and accessed via a Web browser. Team members who have been granted access are able to work together in the shared workspace to create and revise documents, view the status of projects, and share project calendars. Features of a shared workspace include the following:

- names and contact information for each team member
- links to other Web-based information needed by the team members
- document libraries containing stored documents related to the specific project
- tasks assigned to each team member and each task's status

The application software in some productivity suites can be used as an interface to a shared workspace. The software works in combination with Web server technologies.

File Transfer Protocol

File transfer protocol (FTP) is a method of transferring data from one computer to another. The word *protocol* in this term means the rules that the computers use to communicate with one another. The rules used allow files to be uploaded and downloaded to computers directly and safely. As an administrative professional, you may be responsible for managing files using this method.

Online Discussion Groups, Wikis, and Blogs

A discussion group is an online forum in which participants discuss or monitor information on a specific topic. Discussion groups include newsgroups (virtual bulletin boards), mailing lists (email newsletters), and Web-based forums (messages posted via a Web browser). Businesses use mailing lists and Web-based forums to provide customer service and to make customers aware of products and services. Professionals can use discussion groups to connect with peers and stay updated with the latest information in their field.

A **wiki** is a website or group of Web pages on which anyone can add, edit, or delete content. An example of a wiki is Wikipedia, a popular Web-based free encyclopedia to which anyone can contribute. Contents of wikis may not necessarily be supported by facts, so you should never use a wiki as your only source of information or data. Wikis can, however, provide a good subject overview and, when sources are provided, a starting point for further research. In the workplace, businesses host wikis on their secure intranets to enable work groups to build knowledge bases on specific work-related topics.

A **blog** is a Web-based journal in which participants express their opinions, thoughts, and feelings. Posting to a blog is called *blogging*. Although a wiki and a blog are both Web-based, they are used differently. Unlike postings to a wiki, postings to a blog are added chronologically and generally follow conversational threads or ideas. Postings to a blog may be monitored by a moderator and edited to remove inappropriate content. Examples of public blogs include those hosted by reporters and columnists at online news sites.

Businesses use public blogs and social media such as Facebook, YouTube, Instagram, and Twitter to create forums for exchanging information. Some examples include the following:

- Private blogs hosted on a company intranet can help work groups manage their projects.
- A blog site hosted by an application software manufacturer enables users who are testing a manufacturer's latest software version to share their testing results with other testers; they also can share ways to use and troubleshoot the software and can suggest software updates and new features.
- A business can set up a Facebook account to present a human face to customers and to provide an opportunity for people who like the brand or product to share their opinions.
- Small business owners such as those who own restaurants can use Twitter to connect with new customers through tweets and to update existing clients and customers on promotions and events.

Virtual Meetings

Virtual meetings use telecommunication technology tools to provide opportunities for workplace collaboration. By choosing to collaborate using teleconferencing, video conferencing, or Web conferencing, users save time and money. See Chapter 11 for more details on these technologies.

Reprographic Equipment

Reprographic equipment refers not only to the process of making copies but also to any piece of equipment that makes copies of an original. Most offices have digital multi-functional equipment that includes the features of a printer, scanner, fax machine, and copier. Chapter 8 outlines the functionality of this equipment in greater detail.

Social Networking

Social networking sites, such as Facebook, Twitter, Instagram, and LinkedIn, are popular ways to stay connected in today's society. **Social networking** is the use of a particular website to find others with similar interests. Businesses use social networks to gain access to people who might purchase their products or services. As an administrative professional, one of your duties might be to monitor or update the company's social networking page or profile.

As a collaborative tool, some organizations use public, private, or secret social networking pages to stay in contact with customers, provide product information, advertise services, gather data from focus groups, or collaborate among employees to complete a common project.

Maintaining Calendars

Working as an administrative professional, you will be responsible for maintaining a calendar for your direct supervisor or for several people. Two commonly used calendaring systems are Microsoft Outlook and Google Calendar. Be aware of the personal preferences of each member. Just as your supervisor may have a preference for handling visitors to the office, they may also have a preference for dealing with the daily routine. They may want to maintain their own calendar and just let you know what is scheduled each day, or may want you to maintain the schedule on their behalf. As an administrative professional, you may be responsible for scheduling appointments, maintaining a record of the appointments your supervisor has personally scheduled, and coordinating these appointments with other scheduled activities.

Commonly, two types of information are recorded when maintaining calendars—appointment data and reminder information. As an administrative professional managing your supervisor's calendar, you will enter not only business appointments and events but also other, more personal events, such as birthdays, anniversaries, and so on. If you are using an electronic calendar, it is easy to edit details of an appointment.

The calendar is also useful for identifying blocks of time dedicated to work on major projects or reports. If your supervisor uses a mobile device to record appointments while out of the office, they can sync their calendar to ensure appointments are up to date. As discussed in Chapter 2, the calendar can also be used for noting reminders to yourself or your supervisor. Check the reminders daily and again at a specific time each week to see that everything has been done.

Scheduling Appointments

An **appointment** is a time set aside for people to discuss an issue. When it comes to scheduling appointments, understand your supervisor's preferences and know which appointments should be given preference and how much time should be allocated for each appointment. If you have entered regularly occurring appointments or meetings into the calendar, when a request for an appointment is received, you can be sure to avoid conflicts in the schedule.

Requests for appointments are usually received in one of three ways—by telephone, by email or mail, or in person.

- **When appointments are requested by telephone**, determine the purpose of the appointment to ascertain whether your supervisor is the most appropriate person. To reduce any margin of error, confirm that you and the caller have identical information by repeating the time, date, and place of the appointment to the caller as you enter it into the calendar. Obtain and record the caller's telephone number or email address in the event you might need to change any of the details of the appointment. If required, provide the caller with directions to your office.
- **Appointments requested by email or mail** will normally contain the requisite information of who, what, when, and where, and as a result you may be able to enter the specifics into the calendar and provide a confirmation to the sender that the appointment has been scheduled. Incoming mail or email may contain announcements about meetings or conferences of interest to your supervisor. Make a note of these on the calendar and draw them to your supervisor's attention.
- **When an individual is in the office personally making the request**, you can provide a reminder of the date and time established.

Confirming appointments is a regular activity for administrative professionals working in medical or law offices. Check the policy in your office or the preference of your supervisor to learn whether you are expected to confirm appointments.

Cancelling Appointments

If your employer cannot keep an appointment, it is your responsibility to cancel it. Appointments may be cancelled by a telephone call or by an email. Be sure to give a reason and offer to reschedule. A detailed explanation is not necessary. For example, you might say, "Mr. Albertson has been called out of town unexpectedly and will be unable to keep the appointment. May I schedule another appointment for next week?"

List of Appointments

Depending on your supervisor's preference, you may be expected each day to prepare a list of appointments and gather the necessary materials. This task can be done either at the end of the previous day or first thing every morning. Reviewing this list serves as a quick reminder for you and your supervisor when you arrive at the office and should include the time, purpose of the appointment, name and affiliation of the caller, and any necessary reminders or materials. If you are using an electronic system, the list of appointments can be quickly and easily printed out along with any recorded daily reminders.

Electronic Calendars and Online Appointment Systems

In a networked environment, it is possible to link all calendars (or just those relating to a specific group) within the organization, giving each person access to multiple calendars. You will find the task of maintaining current schedules for your supervisor and yourself is much more efficiently accomplished using the networked calendar since you can enter appointments, tasks, and reminders; maintain histories, agreements, and connections with clients; cancel appointments; and easily rearrange schedules as events change (see Figure 6-5).

One of the advantages of networked or shared calendars quickly becomes evident when attempting to arrange a meeting with a larger group. For example, arranging a meeting of four or five people means you must first choose a time when all the required people will be available and when a meeting room is available. This step may require a phone call or email to each person. Next you need to read the replies and compare them to determine which time is mutually convenient before confirming with everyone.

Using scheduling software in a networked environment makes finding a meeting time and place simple. You enter the names of the participants, the tentative date, the tentative time, the length and location of the meeting, and any resources that may be needed. The software reviews the calendar of each potential participant—whether there are 2 or 22—as well as the required resource (the meeting room). If there are conflicts, you are notified. You can then decide whether to schedule the meeting as tentatively planned or leave the program to determine a time suitable to all.

Online appointment software that puts the convenience of making appointments in the hands of the client or customer is very useful for a sole proprietorship or a partnership. This Web-based software provides clients and customers with 24/7 access to schedule their own appointments online. You establish the parameters so that clients see only your availability when choosing a time convenient to them. The appointment calendar can be embedded into a company website, can apply to various locations or multiple users, and can also be set up to email automatic reminders to clients. It can also be synced

FIGURE 6-5

Outlook Calendar in One-Week View with Current/Next Month and New Appointment Screen Displayed

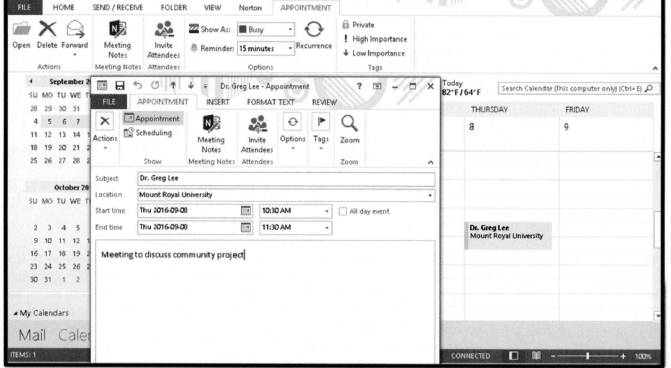

with a mobile device so that you are able to view an appointment schedule that is always current. Search the Web for *online appointments* to see what is current in this software and to view demos or download trial copies.

Transcription

While transcription was once a widely used method of creating business documents, and is still used regularly in medical or legal environments, fewer executives today use dictation as an input method for document production. Because of the user-friendly nature of word processing software, email, and IM, executives are able to draft messages and send the documents through the network to the administrative professional who is then responsible for proofreading and formatting the text of the documents.

For executives who do not possess keyboarding skills, however, dictating reports and other documents is often a preference, simply because they can speak more quickly than they can type. It is possible, therefore, that as an administrative professional you may find yourself responsible for either transcribing notes made by your supervisor or dictating on behalf of your employer.

Transcription Equipment

A wide range of dictation and transcription equipment and software are available, from digital dictation systems and apps for smartphones. Executives who travel or whose job responsibilities are in the field may use handheld portable dictation devices or their smartphones to record reminders, documents, and instructions when not in the office.

Mobile and desktop digital dictation units are illustrated in Figure 6-6 along with the foot pedal and headset, which are used for transcription. These units contain adjustable volume,

FIGURE 6-6

Mobile and Desktop Digital Dictation Units with Transcription Headset and Foot Pedal

- Express Scribe
- Phillips Dictation Systems

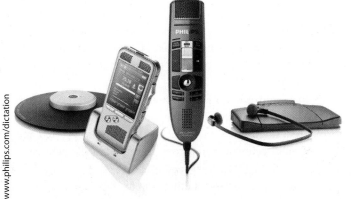

Photos/Videos: Speech Processing Solutions GMBH. www.philips.com/dictation

tone, and speed controls so that the playback can be modified for the individual transcriptionist. A digital display indicates the total dictation time, and audio tones sound to indicate the location of dictated instructions.

Computer-based systems are another option for dictation and transcription. Once the appropriate dictation software is loaded onto the computer or smartphone, the originator dictates using a computer, a portable handheld recorder, or other telecommunication device and then transmits the recordings via email, the Internet, or the company intranet. Transcription software, which includes features such as variable-speed playback, foot-pedal or hand-control operation, file management, and more, must be installed on the computer being used by a transcriptionist. This transcription software can be controlled using the keyboard (with **hot keys**—user-defined combinations of keystrokes that provide quick access to a command or menu) or a foot pedal or hand control.

Speech Recognition

Many medical offices and hospitals are utilizing speech recognition software to transcribe medical records. Dragon Naturally Speaking is the most common software application used by health practitioners. The health practitioner dictates into a microphone and the software automatically transcribes the information. As an administrative professional, you would be responsible for editing the documents to ensure accuracy.

Telecommunications

Telecommunications means the transmission of electronic information (text, data, voice, video, and images) from one location to another. Telephones are a common telecommunication tool. You will find a variety of telephone equipment in the workplace, including standard phone sets, cordless sets, conference call speakers, and headsets to use with computers and software. Common features on business phone sets include buttons for answering multiple phone lines, built-in speaker phones, displays to view caller identification information, and programmable buttons for setting up call management features. Popular call management features include call forwarding, call waiting, holding, conferencing, redialling, transferring, and speed dialling.

IP Telephony

Voice over Internet protocol (VoIP), or **IP telephony** (te-lef-uh-nee), continues to change voice communication. IP telephony transmits voice over a private network or a public IP network, such as the Internet. The primary advantage of IP telephony for business is reduced cost. Sending and receiving voice messages over the Internet or a private network eliminates long-distance phone charges, as PC-to-PC calls can be completed from almost any place in the world at no charge. Businesses can also reduce service and maintenance costs by supporting just one network—the IP network—instead of operating separate networks for data and voice. Other IP telephony advantages include the following:

- Users are not tied to one area code and may even be given a choice of area codes by their service provider.
- When moving to new office space or a new city, phone service no longer needs to be transferred.
- Voice mail can be routed to a computer's electronic mailbox.
- Phone numbers kept in a user's contact management software can be dialled from a computer.

IP telephony is available for the home office in two ways: a standard telephone can be plugged into an adapter that is plugged into your network router; or, freeware such as Skype can be used with a headset connected to your computer. Once the freeware has been downloaded and installed on your computer or smartphone, you can call other Skype users around the world. A small fee is charged for calling cellphones and landlines. To learn more about Skype, visit the website. A link to the website is provided on the MindTap site for this textbook.

IP telephony also has some disadvantages. Although IP telephony voice quality is continuing to improve, in some circumstances, it may not be equal to voice quality on a standard phone line. A high-speed Internet connection is required, and connection reliability depends on an Internet service provider's reliability.

Call Management Skills

As an administrative professional, you will communicate by phone daily with many people without ever seeing or meeting them. Regardless of the calling technology you use, remember that good human relations skills are crucial to making a positive impression of you and your company.

Be Attentive and Discreet

Listen carefully to what the other person says. During the conversation, avoid typing or flipping through pages—these sounds can easily be heard. Give the caller your undivided attention and do not interrupt. If the caller is unhappy about some situation, allow them to explain. Most of a person's anger may be dissipated in telling the story. It is easier to handle an unhappy person after you have listened to the problem. Use good listening skills to:

- Listen for facts and feelings.
- Try to understand what the speaker is saying, both from the words and from the tone of voice.
- Search for hidden or subtle meanings.
- Be patient.

Communicating AT WORK

Be discreet when you must tell a caller that your supervisor is unavailable. Explain that your supervisor cannot answer their phone—but do not say too much. You may say, "Ms. Portosky is away from the office now. I expect her back in approximately an hour. May I have her call you when she returns?"

Never say, "Ms. Portosky is not here yet" (at 10 a.m.), "She's gone for the day" (at 2 p.m.), or "She's out sick" (at any time of day). A good rule to remember is to be helpful about when your supervisor is returning without specifying where the supervisor is or what they may be doing.

Use Correct English and Avoid Slang

Pay attention to your English and pronunciation. Slang is neither businesslike nor in good taste. Figure 6-7 gives you some suggestions to avoid using slang.

FIGURE 6-7

Slang and Replacement Words

Avoid Saying	Instead, Say
yeah	certainly
ok	yes
uh-huh	of course
bye-bye	goodbye
Huh?	I beg your pardon.
	I did not understand.
	Would you please repeat that?

Take Messages Completely and Accurately

Although paper phone messages can be lost or misplaced, many offices still rely on them to manually record incoming messages or voice mail recordings. Two options that may be purchased from your local stationery supplier are single-sheet message pads and books with self-duplicating sheets. Whether the phone message is created manually or electronically, ensure that all the necessary information is captured (see Figure 6-8). Incomplete messages can be very frustrating for the recipient. If you are not given all the information, ask the caller. Repeat the message to the caller so you can be certain it is accurate.

Your organization may have a computer-based system for recording and delivering telephone messages. Similar in format to a single-sheet message pad, it can be completed and emailed to a recipient, and a copy is automatically generated and archived. PHONEslips (see Figure 6-9) is an example of a computer-based message taking system. A program-specific

FIGURE 6-8

A Completed Telephone Message

When taking a telephone message, record the following information:

- the caller's name spelled correctly (If you are uncertain of the spelling, ask the caller to spell it. If the spoken letters are difficult to distinguish over the telephone, use words to help identify letters.)
- the caller's company's name
- the complete (10-digit) telephone number
- the date and time of the call
- the exact message
- your initials or name so the recipient can contact you if there are questions

FIGURE 6-9

Computer-Based Messaging System

PHONEslips, an add-in application for Outlook, eliminates the need to use message pads.

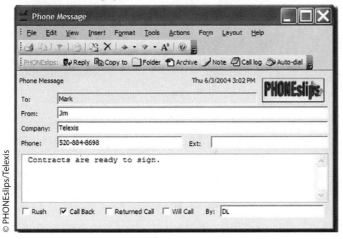

© PHONEslips/Telexis

toolbar gives instant access to all its features, and messages can later be instantly retrieved from the archive for follow-up and for scheduling reminders. Messages can also be automatically forwarded to a cellphone so an important message is never missed.

Use the Caller's Name

It is flattering to the caller to be recognized and called by name. Frequent responses such as, "Yes, Mr. Valentine, I will be happy to get the information" and "It was nice to talk with you, Ms. Keiba" indicate to callers that you know who they are and that you care about them as individuals.

Ask Questions Tactfully

Care should be used in asking questions. Ask only necessary questions, such as, "May I tell Mr. Albertson who is calling?" or "When Mr. Albertson returns, may I tell him who called?" Never ask, "Who's calling?" People can be offended by such

a blunt question. If your employer is not in or cannot take the call, ask about the nature of the call, as you may be able to handle the call yourself or refer it to someone else. For example, you may say, "If you tell me the nature of your call, perhaps I can help you or refer you to someone who can."

Speak Distinctly and Clearly

Make sure the caller can understand what you say. Speak in a normal voice at a moderate rate—one that can be heard comfortably. If your duties include considerable time on the telephone, a headset provides an ergonomic alternative to a regular telephone handset. Hands-free wireless headsets using Bluetooth technology are also available. They allow more freedom of motion and can be worn—and calls answered— when you are away from your desk.

Handle Problem Calls

Most individuals are pleasant over the telephone, especially when you are courteous to them. Occasionally, you may have a caller who has had a difficult day or for some other reason is unhappy. Sometimes you can defuse an angry caller by taking the time to listen to the situation. Do not become emotionally involved in the situation. Remember that the caller is not angry at you but at a situation or an event.

After you have listened to the caller's story, try to help solve the problem. For example, you can suggest a solution or tell the caller you will have someone who can solve the problem return their call. Do not put the person on hold or mishandle the call by transferring it to an individual who cannot help. Such actions may make the person angrier.

At times, a caller may refuse to give you their name. You should discuss this situation with your supervisor and understand exactly what you are expected to do. However, if you are unsure about what to do, put the person on hold and explain the situation to your supervisor. They can then decide whether to speak to the caller.

Do Not Discriminate

Have you ever found yourself being nicer over the telephone to the president of your company than to a caller you do not know? If the answer is yes, make a point of being friendly before you know who is on the other end of the line. Try saying to yourself, "A friend is calling," before answering the phone. When addressing anyone, use terms that show respect. Use inclusive language, and avoid making assumptions about gender identity, sexual orientation, ethnicity, age, or ability.

Incoming Calls

The call management skills covered in the previous section apply to all calls. Here are some special techniques for handling incoming calls.

Answer Promptly

Never consider the telephone call an interruption in your workday. When your telephone rings, answer promptly—on the first ring if possible and certainly by the third. Consider the telephone call as your job calling. You may lose a potential customer if you are slow in answering the telephone.

Identify Yourself and Your Organization

Most businesses and supervisors have specific procedures for answering the telephone. If you work in a large organization, chances are you will not be the first person to answer any given call. In large businesses, calls are often routed first to a person whose job it is to greet visitors, whether by telephone or in person. This person identifies the company and then routes the incoming call to the appropriate party, which may be a supervisor's administrative professional. For example, as the administrative professional for Mr. Albertson, you would answer his line with "Mr. Albertson's office, Rebecca Martin." If you are answering calls that have not been routed through a receptionist, you would identify the organization or department. You might say, "Good morning. CanAsian Airlines, Rebecca Martin." or "Good afternoon, Advertising Department, Rebecca Martin."

Transfer Calls Carefully

Each telephone system is different; be certain you know how to transfer calls on your system. Callers dislike being told their call will be transferred and then being disconnected because of incorrect transferring procedures. Before you transfer a call, explain to the caller why you must do so. Make sure the caller is willing to be transferred. For example, you might say, "Mr. Albertson is out, but Travis Figimara can give you the information. May I transfer you to Mr. Figimara?" If company policy permits, you may also want to give the caller the extension or complete number of the person to whom the caller is being transferred in case the transfer fails. The caller can then call that person directly without having to call you again.

Place Calls on Hold

A caller may sometimes request information that you do not have at your fingertips. You may need to check with someone else or access your files to get the information. You may be answering your supervisor's line because they are not available to take a call. If you must place the caller on hold until your supervisor is available or until you retrieve the necessary information, do so only with the caller's permission.

Do not assume that a caller is willing to be placed on hold. You may say, "I need to pull the information from my files. Would you like to hold for a moment while I get it, or shall I call you back?" or "Mr. Albertson is on another call, would you like to hold?"

If the caller agrees to hold, try to get back to the person as soon as possible. Nothing is more irritating to a caller than to be left on hold for a long time without an update on your progress. When you return to the line, let the caller know you are back by saying, "Thank you for waiting." Some guidelines suggest you should check in and update the caller on your progress every minute. If you are delayed in getting the information, go back to the person on hold and ask if they want to continue to hold or leave a message; apologize for the length of time it is taking.

Answer incoming calls promptly, using a friendly tone of voice.

Handle Multiple Calls

You may be responsible for answering more than one telephone line. If so, at times you will be answering a call on one line when another line rings. When this happens, you must remember that the caller on the second line does not know you are already on the phone. The caller is expecting to get an answer immediately. Excuse yourself politely by saying to the first caller, "May I put you on hold for a moment? I must answer another line." Be brief—ask the second caller to hold while you complete your first call or ask for a number so you can call back as soon as you finish the first call. Then return to the first caller with, "Thank you for waiting." Your responsibility is to handle all calls as quickly and efficiently as possible.

Screen Calls

Many executives have one telephone number that is published for callers and another, inside number that is not published. The executive typically uses the inside number to make outgoing calls; the number may also be given to close friends or family members. In an activity commonly referred to as *gatekeeping*, the administrative professional may be expected to screen calls that come from the published number, by determining who is calling and why, and then diverting those calls the executive will not take, such as unsolicited sales calls. If your supervisor is not in or cannot take the call, ask about the nature of the call so you can handle it or refer it to someone else. For example, you may say, "If you tell me the nature of your call, perhaps I can help you or refer you to someone who can."

If someone else in the organization can handle the call, transfer it to that person, but only after first requesting permission from the caller to do so. If no one is available to take the call, either take a message, or courteously let the person know that your employer is not interested. One response might be, "I appreciate the information; however, Mr. Albertson is not interested in pursuing the matter at the present time."

Writing AT WORK

When answering the telephone for another person, write complete and accurate messages.

Messages may be created in word processing software and printed or attached to an email for the recipient. Messages may also be recorded manually using paper message pads.

When writing a message, be careful to include all the needed information as listed below.

Repeat the message to the caller so you can be certain it is accurate.
- the caller's name spelled correctly (ask the caller to spell their name if you are not certain how it is spelled)
- company name
- telephone number (with area code)
- time of call
- exact message text

Set Up a Message When You Leave Your Desk

Technology offers several options for handling calls when you are away from your desk. For example, you can record a message on your system and set it to automatically forward your calls to your voice mail. Your voice mail greeting should be customized and updated regularly to include the current date and a message that informs callers when they can expect to receive a return call. You can also set your system to forward your calls to a cellphone, a pager, or a co-worker. If a co-worker will be taking your calls, let them know where you can be reached and what time you will be back. If your supervisor is also away, tell the co-worker in general terms where your employer is and when they will be back. For example, you might say, "Mr. Albertson is in a meeting and will be available around 3 p.m."

Follow Up

If you say to a caller that you will call back with information, do so. You can also help your supervisor to remember to follow up on phone calls. Following through enhances your reputation for reliability and trustworthiness; when you fail to follow up, the result may be a cancelled order or a lost customer. Use your chosen reminder system to keep track of these items and, when necessary, provide a tactful reminder to your supervisor to follow through. Your assistance will be appreciated.

Mobile Phone Etiquette

If you are working offsite with a client or customer and you receive a call on your cellphone, interrupting your work to answer may seem discourteous to the client or customer. Taking these calls conveys the impression that you have something more important to do than helping the client. When working with others, be courteous by setting your cellphone to silent mode. If you must keep your cellphone on due to an urgent call you are expecting, be sure your co-worker or client knows about it. You might say, "We may be interrupted by a call I must take, but I promise to be as brief as possible." If the call comes through, excuse yourself and do keep the conversation short.

When you are in a meeting, do not use your cellphone to read messages, send email or text messages, or play games. The people in the room with you deserve your full attention. If your eyes stray to your phone, others will likely notice and may be offended.

Show your respect for others when using your phone in a public place or an open work area by keeping your voice low so as not to disturb others around you; by using discretion when discussing private matters or sensitive topics that may be overheard by others; and by turning your cellphone off or setting it to silent mode in one-on-one interactions and during meetings, classes, and other public events.

Outgoing Calls

As an administrative professional, you will often be responsible for placing calls for your supervisor; you will also be making business calls yourself. Handling outgoing calls professionally is just as important as handling incoming calls professionally.

Place Calls Properly

Supervisors usually place their own calls to save time and to create a favourable impression. However, some people may prefer that you place calls on their behalf. If so, identify your supervisor before you transfer the call. For example, you might say, "Mr. Albertson of CanAsian Airlines is calling." Then transfer the call to Mr. Albertson's line.

Ensure that your supervisor is available to take the call before you place it and that they have not placed another call in the interim. For example, before you place the call, you might say, "Mr. Albertson, are you going to be available for a few minutes? I want to place the call you requested to Mr. Chen."

Plan Your Call

Before picking up the phone, take a few minutes to plan your call. Keep in mind its purpose and what you intend to say. You can avoid an unnecessary follow-up call by assembling beforehand any necessary files or reference documents that you might need during the call.

Your call may be answered first by a receptionist or the administrative professional to the person you are calling. Identify yourself and your organization and state your purpose clearly and concisely. For example, you might say, "This is John Chin of CanAsian. I'm calling to verify Dr. Lee's attendance at the committee meeting tomorrow at 3 p.m. in Conference Room A." If you are transferred to the person you are calling, be prepared to identify yourself again and to restate the purpose of your call. You may exchange pleasantries with the individual you are calling; however, the main purpose is to get your message across without wasting the other person's time.

Frequently Called Numbers

A file of frequently called numbers is an excellent time saver. For quick reference, program these numbers into your phone system or store them in the contacts section of your personal information management software.

Note the Time Zone

The multinational nature of business means that calls are made frequently to various locations across the country and around the world. Time zone differences must be taken into consideration when placing these calls. Canada has six time zones—Newfoundland, Atlantic, Eastern, Central, Mountain, and Pacific, which are shown in Figure 6-10. The World Clock website gives times for locations around the world. The MindTap site has a link to this site.

FIGURE 6-10
Canadian Time Zone Map

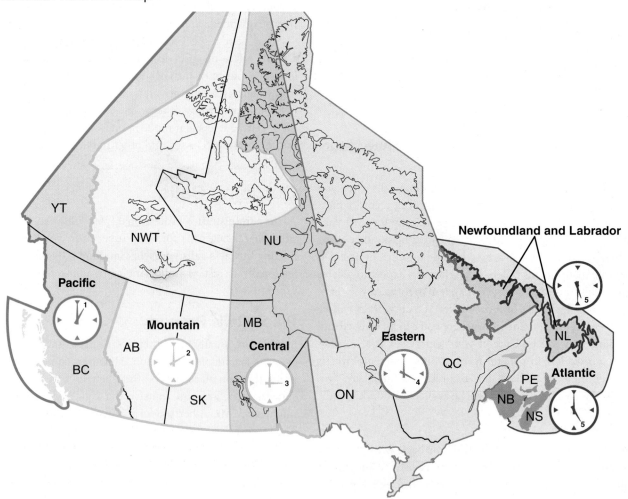

Voice Mail

Voice mail or **voice messaging** is an efficient method of managing incoming calls when the call recipients are unavailable. The voice mail feature plays a recorded announcement and records voice messages. Most workplace telephone systems use voice mail for inside calls between employees and for calls from outside the company.

Some voice mail systems provide automatic notification that messages are waiting for the mailbox owner via his or her email or smartphone. Many voice mail systems also support message broadcasting, or sending the same message to multiple voice mailboxes.

The proper use of voice mail in the workplace increases productivity and saves time and money. Workers can leave a voice message instead of placing repeated calls to someone who is not available. Voice messages are to the point, eliminating extraneous conversation.

Caller Instructions

As an administrative professional, you may be assigned the task of setting up your telephone system's voice mail announcement—the first message a caller may hear when calling your company.

- Begin by identifying the company.
- Provide the most important information or answer the most frequently asked questions, such as hours of operation, fax number, website, street address, and postal code.
- If your voice mail system has multiple levels of call routing, give callers no more than four options. Callers strongly dislike trying to follow a maze of instructions to record their messages.
- Keep caller instructions short—aim for less than 15 seconds.
- When recording step-by-step instructions, refer to the end result first—then explain what action to take. For example, you may say, "To transfer your call to our receptionist, press zero."
- Be certain your instructions tell the caller how to reach a person. Callers dislike becoming lost in a voice message system that never allows them to speak to a person.

Your voice mail's outgoing message is very important, as it can create either a favourable or an unfavourable impression. A well-crafted announcement succinctly provides key information, such as your name, in-office or out-of-office information, and whom to contact if the call is urgent. The sound and tone of your voice message greeting should make a favourable impression. When recording your outgoing message, vary your vocal tone; do not talk in a monotone and try to eliminate background noise that could interfere with your message.

Keep It Current

The message your callers hear represents you in your absence. Your voice mail message should be timely and professional. During extended absences, if appropriate, provide sufficient details to ensure effective customer service. Hearing an outdated message is very frustrating for a caller. Change the message frequently; if your schedule changes from day to day, change your message daily; if your schedule changes during the day, periodically update it so that callers have some idea when they might expect to receive a return call.

Leaving a Message

When leaving a voice message, keep it short and to the point. Include your name and company, a number where you can be reached, and a brief statement of the purpose of the call. Ask for a return call if that is what you want. Speak slowly and distinctly. Do not include sensitive or confidential information in a voice message. Repeat your name and number at the end of the message so that the recipient will not need to replay the message to double-check the information.

Security Issues, Risks, and Solutions

An unaware employee can be an organization's greatest weakness when it comes to data security. Criminals may gain access to company information (or an individual's) in a variety of ways, including email, browsers, social networking sites, weak passwords, mobile devices, poor data security, Wi-Fi usage, and the cloud.

Your computer has a great value to criminals for crimes such as data theft (like client social insurance numbers or medical information), identity theft, or to harm others (like sending spam).

Securing your files, equipment, online presence, and company information is very important for the company where you work and for you personally. Cyber criminals target individuals and organizations with state-of-the-art tools and techniques designed to capitalize on simple tasks, such as clicking on a link or opening an attachment. Protect your organization, yourself, and others by always assuming you are a target. Pay attention to your instinct—if something doesn't seem right, it probably isn't.

Email

Email is a powerful tool the cybercriminal can use—mainly because we use email so much in our professional and personal lives. **Phishing** is emails used by cyber criminals pretending to be someone known and trusted, such as a friend or a bank. For example, you might receive an email that pretends to be from a well-known bank requiring you to click on a link and log in or else have your account frozen. The link to the website looks real, and the logos appear authentic; however, the criminal who sent the email just wants your bank account login information. Another example is of an email with an attachment from a seemingly legitimate organization. The source proves to be a cybercriminal sending infected attachments. In many of these attempts, the hackers not only want your information, but they also want to infect your computer with a virus that hacks your browser and takes over your computer.

A more targeted attack by cyber criminals is called spear phishing. **Spear phishing** is a specific scam that involves email sent to only a few people within an organization. These emails are very personalized and require more research by criminals.

Email from trusted sources, such as a friend or a co-worker, could be problematic as well if the trusted source has been hacked. Always be cautious when anything appears suspicious.

Here are some tips for protecting computer equipment and yourself:

- Before you click on a link, use the mouse-over feature (don't click just roll your cursor over the link) to see what the link says so that you can verify it is real. If you believe it's from a reputable source, go to the site in your Web browser, not via the email.
- If there's any doubt about an email, call the person to verify.
- Anything with a generic salutation, such as "Dear Customer," is suspect.
- Only open attachments you are expecting.
- Be wary of email that has spelling or grammatical errors, especially if it's from a seemingly reputable organization.

Browsers

Since we primarily interact with the Internet using a browser, criminals try to use this as a way to gain access to information. As you visit websites, you may unknowingly encounter a stealthy tool that can lead to attacks that may take control of a browser or a computer. Most browser software has safe guards in place to prevent such tools from taking over your computer. Known malicious websites are denied access to your computer, and warnings are posted for you. Don't connect to a website if your browser warns you not to, and always make sure you are using the most current version of your browser (including plug-ins). Use the highest security setting you can on the browser if possible.

There may be times when you need to download and install new software; these downloads could have viruses. To prevent infection, make sure antivirus software is actively scanning any new files that you download from the Internet; don't install plug-ins or add-ons unless you really need them. Contact your organization's IT support if you are unsure whether your antivirus software is working properly.

Social Networking

Social networking (Facebook, LinkedIn, etc.) is a popular way to stay connected but can pose problems for your organization or your own personal security. Privacy controls on these sites can be confusing and complicated and may change without your knowledge. The primary way to protect your employer and yourself on social networking sites is it limit the amount of personal and professional information you post. Never post on any website confidential information about the organization you work for.

Mobile Devices

Smartphones and tablets are popular, useful, and powerful and can also put you at risk. Only install apps that you need, and ensure that they are from trusted sources. Back up and update your devices regularly. Attacks you find via email can also be texted and infect the apps on your devices. Be careful when using Wi-Fi and Bluetooth. Disable both when not using them. It is important to turn off Bluetooth discoverable features when not in use. If you lose your device, someone else will have access to your information. Use passwords and remote wiping options if available. Notify your organization's IT support if you lose a mobile device owned by the company.

Passwords

Good passwords are hard to guess (not your pet's name or your birthdate). Use passwords that are easy to remember, and make them as long as possible. In a passphrase, you use multiple words in a password, such as "caffeineiscoming." Use numbers, uppercase letters, and symbols in your passwords, and be creative. For example, replace the letter "a" with the "@" symbol, replace the letter "o" with the number zero, or use an exclamation mark. Being creative means the previous "caffeineiscoming" example becomes "C@ffeineisc0ming!"

Also consider how you use your passwords. Don't use your bank password to access YouTube, Gmail, or Twitter accounts. If you have too many passwords to remember, consider a password manager; this is a program that securely stores your passwords, and you only have to remember the passwords for your computer and the program. Check with the IT department of your organization to be sure this option is permissible at your organization. Never give your password to anyone— not even a co-worker.

If you are travelling, do not log onto your work network or bank account using a public computer. Some computers have programs that capture keystrokes, so your information could be compromised.

Change your password immediately if you believe it may have been discovered. When possible, use online accounts that offer two-factor authentication (also known as two-step verification). In **two-factor authentication**, you must use more than a password to login. For example, some also require a code texted to a smartphone.

Wi-Fi Security

Wi-Fi Internet access is popular and convenient but does come with some inherent security issues. Potentially, everything you do while using Wi-Fi can be monitored. Unsecured public Wi-Fi networks are to be avoided. Never access your work network or bank account using an unsecured Wi-Fi network. If possible, install a **virtual private network (VPN)** on any computer that connects to a Wi-Fi network. VPNs allow you to work online more securely by using encryption. Never install a Wi-Fi network at work without permission to do so.

Data Security

What hackers most want is the sensitive information that is stored on your computer or other devices. Sensitive information could be social insurance numbers, credit card numbers, medical records, or other personally identifiable information. As an administrative professional, you may handle this type of information on a daily basis. Remain sensitive to its value to criminals as you consider the security of your computers or mobile devices. Only use systems or methods your organization approves when storing, using, or moving sensitive information. Do not use cloud storage (such as Dropbox or Microsoft OneDrive) for sensitive information unless you are permitted by your organization to do so. Before you move or transfer sensitive information using a flash drive or external hard drive, for example, gain permission first.

Never put sensitive information in an email unless you have first verified the identity of the person. Never leave your computer without first password protecting it. Destroy unwanted sensitive data in the manner prescribed by your organization.

Cloud Storage

Cloud storage comes with risks because your organization is storing information at an unknown location that you don't control. Before using cloud storage at work, get permission and understand the organization's policies regarding cloud storage. Remember that because files may be shared using cloud accounts and accessed by other people on other computers, your devices are more susceptible to viruses.

Protecting your Hardware and Software

You must remain constantly vigilant to protect yourself and your company from security risks. Spam-blocking or filtering software can be installed on servers and individual computers in an attempt to block spam. Email software generally contains some features you can customize to manage these unwanted messages. Antivirus software helps protect both your computer from becoming infected and your files from being corrupted or lost. It can also detect existing viruses and clean your computer so that any found viruses will not spread. Always use up-to-date antivirus software from a reputable vendor that is capable of scanning your files and email messages for malevolent software. Norton Security, shown in Figure 6-11, is an example of software designed to control security risks. It includes an auto-update feature that downloads profiles of new viruses so that it can check for them as soon as they are discovered.

FIGURE 6-11

Norton Security Software

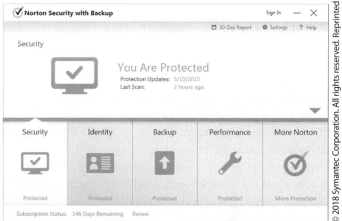

Anti-spyware software scans your computer; spyware can be removed from your machine so it no longer poses a threat.

A **firewall** filters the information coming to your computer from the Internet, permitting communication only with sources you know and trust. Without it, any personal information stored on your computer or distributed using the Web may be accessed for as long as your computer is connected to the Internet. You can restrict the traffic coming through your firewall by identifying trusted sites in your Internet browser. By disabling the file sharing feature in your operating system, you can prevent others from being able to download or view your files or documents. Some ISPs include firewall protection as part of your contract.

Taking the following steps can help you to keep your computer data secure:

- Back up and carefully store important information so that a copy exists if the data are lost or corrupted.
- Protect hardware and data by assigning effective passwords.
- Log off the computer or network before you leave your desk to prevent unauthorized users from accessing information.
- Do not open email attachments from people you do not know.
- Update and run your antivirus and anti-spyware software regularly.
- Log in to your online accounts regularly.
- Regularly check your online bank statements and credit card statements to ensure all transactions are legitimate.

Computer Ethics

Computers have spawned some behaviours that are unethical or questionable. Just as we need to be vigilant about behaving ethically at work, we need to be certain we are living the organization's values and our personal values as we perform computer work. One problem that has become pervasive with computers is the illegal copying of software. People often rationalize that computer software companies are getting rich anyway, so it is okay to copy software for their personal use. In Canada, computer software is defined as a literary work and is therefore covered by the Copyright Act that protects original literary, artistic, musical, and dramatic works.

In addition to the copying of software being unethical and illegal, it can bring viruses into the computer system. Companies and individuals who copy software deprive themselves of both the benefits of technical support provided by many software companies and the ability to buy upgrades at reduced rates. There is, however, one legal exception to copying—one backup copy of software may be made. In Canada and the United States, organizations and individuals who are caught illegally copying software can be tried and fined. Penalties can include imprisonment or fines for the unauthorized reproduction or distribution of software.

It is unethical to use a computer to gain entry into a company's databank; in fact, it is theft. You might ask, "If I produced the data for the company, isn't it my property to do with as I please?" The answer is no; it is not your property unless you have specifically negotiated an arrangement with your company that allows you to retain the rights to the property. The property rights belong to the company whose resources have been used to develop the product—in other words, they have paid you or others within the company a salary or a commission to develop the product. To usurp any property rights, including the right to use the property, is a form of property theft and is unethical.

The Future of Telecommunications

The evolution of telecommunications promises to continue, with access to all types of data, video, audio, text, and graphics at faster speeds than we are currently experiencing. In addition, telecommunication companies will continue to both merge and expand their services, delivering telecommunication services that connect people to people and people to machines in a multitude of ways.

Soft Skills — CONTINUAL LEARNING

This chapter reinforces the importance of continual learning in our technological age. Changes in technology occur at a rapid pace. Even though great care has been taken to include the latest information here, it may soon become outdated. As a result, we must all be continual learners if we are to be productive workers and citizens in our society. Years ago, Alvin Toffler said in his book *Future Shock* that the educated person of tomorrow is the person who has *learned how to learn*. That statement is particularly relevant today and will continue to be relevant for many years. Here are some suggestions for you as you commit yourself to continual learning:

Since none of us can keep all the newly emerging information in our heads, learn how to find and where to look for what you need—take time to explore the Internet, computer periodicals, and books.

Develop an inquiring mind. When you do not understand something, ask questions. Do not be afraid to admit that you do not have all the answers. Part of ongoing learning is accepting what you do not know and being willing to do something about it.

Commit to continuing your formal education. Take classes offered by your organization or classes offered at a college or university. Take a course online—many colleges and universities now offer a wide variety of these courses that you can complete at a convenient location and time.

Devote time to learning. Learning does take time, but the results are well worth it.

Chapter Summary

The summary will help you remember the important points covered in this chapter.

- When telecommunication tools such as laptops, tablets, and smartphones are connected to a network, they make sharing information fast and affordable.
- Computers, mobile technologies, networks, and cloud computing are global communication tools.
- Email, instant messaging, shared workspaces, FTP, discussion groups, wikis, blogs, video and Web conferencing, and social networking are workplace collaboration tools.
- Using good human relations skills leaves a positive impression of you and your company with a caller.
- Voice mail is an efficient method of managing incoming calls when the call recipients are unavailable.
- IP telephony has the advantage of reduced cost compared with other methods for long-distance calls.
- Users should be aware of security risks and take steps to reduce exposing themselves to viruses and other risks.
- Be aware of ethical computer behaviour and appropriate etiquette when using telecommunication devices.
- Make a commitment to continual learning.

Key Terms

application software p. 93
appointment p. 99
blog p. 98
Boolean operators p. 95
CARS checklist p. 96
cloud p. 93
cloud computing p. 93
cloud storage p. 93
extranet p. 94
file transfer protocol (FTP) p. 98
firewall p. 109
flash memory p. 92
groupware p. 97
hits p. 95
hot keys p. 101
instant message p. 97
intelligent mobile hotspot p. 92
intranet p. 94
keywords p. 95
mobile application (app) p. 92
online appointment software p. 100

operating system p. 93
operating system software p. 93
phishing p. 107
predictive search feature p. 95
random access memory (RAM) p. 92
read-only memory (ROM) p. 92
search phrase p. 95
smartphone p. 92
social networking p. 99
spear phishing p. 108
specialized software p. 93
tablet computer p. 92
telecommunications p. 91
two-factor authentication p. 108
USB p. 93
virtual private network (VPN) p. 109
voice mail or voice messaging p. 107
VoIP (voice over Internet protocol) or
IP telephony p. 101
Web browser p. 94
wiki p. 98

Discussion Items

These discussion items provide an opportunity to test your understanding of the chapter through written responses and discussion with your classmates and your instructor.

1. Explain the differences among the Internet, an intranet, and an extranet.
2. Describe two mobile technologies and how they might be utilized in the workplace.
3. Explain the difference between operating system software and application software.
4. Describe three tools an administrative professional could use to collaborate.
5. What are some steps you can take to combat security risks and keep computer data secure?
6. Describe two ethical problems involving computers that may occur in organizations.

Critical-Thinking Activity

Guy has been working at CanAsian Airlines as your assistant for slightly over a year. When he started with the company, you gave him the Policy and Procedures Manual for CanAsian, which includes a section on computer ethics. This section makes clear that all computers are the property of CanAsian and are not to be used for the personal use of employees. Yesterday, your supervisor, Martin Albertson, asked you why Guy had worked overtime the evening before. Mr. Albertson said that as he was leaving, at about 7 p.m., he noticed that Guy was still at his desk. He walked over to say goodnight and noticed that Guy was working on some type of project that did not appear to be related to CanAsian work. You had to answer that you knew nothing about it but that you would look into it. This afternoon, you asked Guy why he had worked late the evening before. He stated he had volunteered to prepare a mailing list for a community organization of which he was a member but he did not have a computer at home. You thanked him for giving you the information and left to mull over what you should do. Guy has been an exceptional employee—he never misses work; he is always on time; his work is done promptly and accurately; he

is polite and understands confidentiality. In fact, in his yearly review last month, you gave him an outstanding rating.

When you gave him the policy and procedures manual, you did not go over it with him, but you did ask him to read it. After thinking about it overnight, you went back to Guy the next morning and asked him if he had read the policy and procedures manual. When he answered yes, you asked him why he had violated the company policy on using computers for personal business. Guy told you the manual did not discuss personal use of computers. He pulled it from his desk and showed you that there was no section on computer ethics. Now you are in a real quandary. Address the following items:

- Do you believe you made a mistake in giving Guy an incomplete policy and procedures manual? Do you believe Guy is lying to you? Explain your answers.
- How should you handle the situation?
- How can you be certain in the future that employees understand and adhere to the policy and procedures manual?
- After talking with Guy, what will you report to Mr. Albertson?

21st Century Skills

 Life and Career Skills
CAREER

 Learning and Innovation Skills
INNOVATION

 Information, Media, and Technology Skills
TECHNOLOGY

 Data
DATA FILE

Building Workplace Skills

Project 6-1 (Learning Outcomes 1 and 2)

Online Project

CAREER TECHNOLOGY

Using one of the search engines listed in this chapter research one or more of the following:

- Suggestions or freeware available for IP telephony. Compare the features they offer for free with those they offer for a small cost.
- Characteristics of two or more shareware software programs. Compare their features and cost.
- Implementation of social media by businesses to connect with clients, customers, and employees.
- Several sites on the Internet offer free blog services. Locate such a site by keying *free blog* in an Internet search

engine. Review several sites from the list. Compare the individual features offered and the cost.

Present your findings orally to the class, or write a report of your findings, documenting your resources. Submit your report to your instructor.

Project 6-2 (Learning Outcome 2)

INNOVATION TECHNOLOGY

You've been asked to prepare a departmental newsletter. With a partner, brainstorm ways to collaborate digitally using some of the tools mentioned in this chapter. Research collaborative sites, and prepare a list of links and descriptions for your instructor.

Project 6-3 (Learning Outcome 2)

With your partner from Project 6-2, choose two tools to explore further. Individually, each of you should explore one of the tools (such as a blog, a wiki, or a video conferencing site) and then create a short screencast explaining the tool. The companion website for this textbook has helpful links to assist you. Provide your screencasts to your partner as well as your instructor.

Project 6-4 (Learning Outcome 1)

Refer to the instructions in file Project 6-4 on the MindTap site, access to which is provided with the printed access card on the inside cover of your textbook. Numerous changes must be made to Project 6-4a. If you do not know how to make the changes, use the Help icon on your software package to troubleshoot. Print out a copy of the document with the changes you made. Using the memorandum form Project 6-4b on the MindTap site, write a memorandum to your instructor and provide the readability level. This project could be added to your e-portfolio as evidence of your ability to revise a document and use the help feature of your software package.

Project 6-5 (Learning Outcome 3)

Write scripts for the following scenarios, and then make audio recordings for the telephone calls. Make up details as needed. Be sure to be professional and follow the information given in this chapter.

a) You receive a call for your boss. They aren't in and you don't know when they'll be back.

b) Your boss is not coming in because their child is sick. You have to apologize and reschedule their 10:30 a.m. appointment for any time tomorrow afternoon.

Project 6-6 (Learning Outcome 2)

Make an infographic of workplace collaboration tools. Provide the link to the graphic or a file to your instructor. Possible websites are provided on the MindTap website for this textbook.

Project 6-7 (Learning Outcome 5)

Prepare another section of your e-portfolio; describe how you will commit to continual learning throughout this course. Refer to the suggestions in your text on continual learning before you prepare your plan. Save your self-improvement plan in your e-portfolio under an appropriate file name.

Make the Grade with MindTap

Stay organized and efficient with **MindTap**—a single destination with all the course material and study aids you need to succeed. Built-in apps leverage social media and the latest learning technology. For example:

- ReadSpeaker will read the text to you.
- Flashcards are pre-populated to provide you with a jump-start for review—or you can create your own.
- You can highlight text and make notes in your MindTap Reader. Your notes will flow into Evernote, the electronic notebook app that you can access anywhere when it's time to study for the exam.
- Self-quizzing allows you to access your understanding.

Visit nelson.com/student to start using **MindTap**. Enter the Online Access Code from the card included with your text. If a code card is not provided, you can purchase instant access at NELSONbrain.com.

Endnotes

1. "Usage and Population Statistics, June 30, 2014," Internet World Stats, http://www.internetworldstats.com, accessed March 30, 2015.

2. Robert Harris, "Evaluating Internet Research Sources," Virtual Salt, https://www.virtualsalt.com/evalu8it.htm, accessed December 12, 2016.

CHAPTER 7

Developing Effective Presentations

LEARNING OUTCOMES

After studying this chapter, you should be able to:

1. Plan, research, and write presentations.
2. Develop visual aids for presentations and meetings.
3. Release your creativity.
4. Practise and deliver effective verbal and visual presentations.
5. Conquer presentation fears.

Do I Qualify?

Administrative Assistant

Advertising agency needs an administrative assistant to provide support for three account executives. Good human relations and organizational skills are essential in this position. The job involves:

- handling verbal and written communications
- managing customer records and other files
- managing calendars and schedules
- tracking, documenting, and communicating issues, resolutions, and action items to management
- developing electronic slide presentations
- performing other duties as assigned

As an administrative professional, you will have many opportunities to speak in front of small groups. Your job may include working with small teams and presenting the teams' reports to groups in your organization. You may be asked to develop electronic slides to use as discussion aids for meetings or for someone else to use in a presentation. A **presentation** is a speech, lecture, or seminar that may be delivered in person or via the Internet or another network. A presentation delivered remotely may be recorded and made available for later viewing online. You may also develop slides to use in webinars. A **webinar** is a seminar presented over the Internet or other networks, such as a company intranet. (An **intranet** is a private computer network that looks and performs much like sites on the Internet.)

A presentation may be delivered by one person or by a team.

As you become active in professional organizations, such as the International Association of Administrative Professionals (IAAP), or progress in your career and assume greater responsibilities, you may have the opportunity to assume leadership roles. In these positions you may present to smaller or larger groups. Therefore, developing your presentation skills is essential for your professional growth.

Many people experience presentation anxiety, commonly called stage fright. Presenters often lack the confidence and skill to make effective presentations. With proper planning and practice, you can develop effective presentation skills and overcome presentation anxiety. You can also learn techniques for developing effective slides to use as visuals for meetings, webinars, and other presentations. The planning steps in this section are important when you give a presentation, prepare visual aids, or help develop a speech that someone else will present.

Creativity

Creativity is having the ability or the power to cause to exist. Creativity is a process. It is a way of thinking and doing. It is a way of making new connections or new links. It is solving a problem in a new and different way. Creativity is important not only for producing effective presentations but also for dealing with the constant change that is occurring in offices today. In fact, creativity and change are closely linked. Creativity is needed to respond successfully to change, and creativity results in change. For example, when giving presentations, you probably have a goal of educating your audience about a certain concept or idea. Assume you are giving a presentation to your workgroup on developing empowered teams. You have two basic goals:

- to help the audience understand the importance of teamwork in today's workplace
- to help the audience understand how to develop empowered teams

In other words, through your presentation, you hope to effect change within the organization.

People AT WORK

Marketing Manager

A marketing manager develops plans and strategies for how a company will promote and sell its products or services. Specific job duties may include directing or doing research, planning or conducting surveys on customer satisfaction, and estimating the expected demand for a product.

Marketing managers typically develop and give presentations to company managers, business partners, and customers. If you are an administrative professional who works with a marketing team, you may be asked to help do research and develop these presentations. If you work in another area of the company, you may be asked to provide information on products or services to the marketing team.

Keep in mind that to "be creative and innovative in exploring possible solutions" is one of the skills listed in *Employability Skills 2000+*. Also, survey results show that employees' creative thinking is one of the soft skills most highly desired by organizations. Employers clearly understand that successful employees are ones who can creatively solve the problems they face.

Bring Your Personal Creativity to the Office

Begin to ask questions in your work environment. Through asking and finding answers, you may discover a more creative, more productive way to do the work of the organization. As you practise thinking creatively, you will find that you will have both successes and frustrations. Do not lose your creativity when problems arise. You probably need it then more than ever. Now, let's look at how you can put creativity into action in developing and delivering presentations.

Planning a Presentation

Preparing an effective presentation takes time and involves the same steps you studied for planning a written message. Planning means gathering materials and organizing your thoughts, developing your ideas, and finding unique ways in which to express them. Using your creativity in the process will help you put together a memorable presentation that holds the audience's attention and communicates your message.

The planning steps outlined in this section are just as important, whether you are helping develop a presentation that someone else will deliver or creating one you will deliver yourself. Presentation skills combine written and verbal communications and, much like the written communication skills covered in Chapter 5, developing them is an ongoing process. You also must learn techniques for researching and developing effective slides to use as visuals for meetings and presentations.

Begin Early

Ensure you give yourself plenty of time to prepare an effective presentation. By beginning early, you can spend a few minutes every day thinking about what you want to say and writing down your thoughts. Record them and place them in a folder; then, you can review your ideas later and revise them or discard material that no longer seems relevant. In other words, you have a chance to reflect on your thoughts. Collaborative workplace tools such as Microsoft OneNote are effective in recording and storing these thoughts as they come to you.

Identify the Objective

Is the objective to inform the audience? To persuade? To inform *and* persuade? Spend some time determining the objective or goal. If you do not understand the objective of the presentation, certainly no one else will. Once the goal has been determined, write it down in one clear, concise statement. As you prepare the presentation, review the statement frequently to stay on track.

As an administrative professional, your goal in giving a presentation is usually to inform your audience. For example, if you have chaired a committee in your organization, you might give a presentation to managers on the activities of the committee. Other goals of a presentation might be to persuade or entertain. For example, you might prepare a webinar for the company intranet about the benefits of the company's new flex-time schedule and encourage employees to sign up for the program. You might speak at a luncheon for a retiring co-worker. Your purpose would be to entertain the audience by recounting anecdotes or describing the accomplishments of the retiring colleague.

Consider the Audience

Consider the characteristics of the people who will hear the presentation. Ask and answer questions such as these:
- Why are they attending the presentation?
- What do they want to learn or how can they benefit from the presentation?
- What are the **demographics** (characteristics such as age, gender, race, education, and income level) of the audience?
- What are their interests?
- What knowledge do they have about the topic being presented?

Consider the Time and Length

Ask the meeting organizer about the desired length of the presentation and when it is to be delivered. Plan a presentation that can be given effectively within the allotted time. You may have a choice of when to speak:
- Mid-morning, when listeners are alert, is often a good time to speak.
- If you will use slides that require the lights to be low, right after lunch may not be a good time. Listeners may become drowsy in the low light.
- If you are speaking at a breakfast meeting, keep the talk brief. The audience probably has a full day ahead and will appreciate a short presentation.

When planning a live webinar, consider the audience members and their locations. Will all the attendees likely be located in the same time zone? If not, when will be a time that is convenient for most people? Be sure to include the time zone designation when inviting people to the webinar or posting information about it.

Unless the audience will be actively involved in the presentation, most presentations should be no longer than 20 minutes, with 30 to 40 minutes being the maximum. For example, if the presentation is for a workshop that includes several activities for small groups, the presentation could be organized with a break for group tasks after 20 minutes.

Build in an opportunity to gather their feedback, and then continue the presentation for another 15 or 20 minutes. The presentation can end with another small group activity, or the entire group might share what they learned from the earlier activities. Part of your task in creating a presentation is to manage the topic; speaking longer than 30 minutes tends to create an environment where participants become bored and restless.

Consider time for attendee participation in live webinars as well as in presentations. For some live webinars, audience members may use a chat feature to ask questions of the presenter. The presenter may choose to answer questions as they are received or at certain intervals in the presentation. Having a colleague review questions as they arrive and forward appropriate questions to the presenter can be effective. The presenter may use polls or surveys to ask the audience members one or more questions to which they can respond during the webinar. For live informational webinars, plan to limit the time to 60 minutes, including time for questions and surveys or polls. Webinars posted on company intranets to present information to employees may be shorter, depending on the content. For longer topics, the webinars may be divided into a series of presentations.

Consider the Location

The location of the presentation and related activities are important to know. Ask these questions about the setting:
- Where will the presentation be given? In the workplace? A hotel? A conference centre? A school? How much time do you need to allow for travel to the location?
- Are other activities scheduled before or after the presentation? You need this information so you will know when the room can be set up and when you must remove any material or equipment after the presentation
- What is the size of the room? What is the configuration of the seating? If the audience is small, should the audience sit around a table? As the presenter, you may be able to determine the seating arrangements

If possible, check the room well before the presentation. Be certain the size of the room is appropriate. You do not want to give a presentation to 12 people in a room designed for 100 people. The too-large room will make it seem that you expected many more people. Nor do you want to give a presentation to 50 people crowded into a room designed for 25.

Talk with the person responsible for the room arrangements. Ask them to check the room on the morning of the presentation to ensure that the equipment is present, the room is clean, the temperature is pleasant, and the lighting is appropriate.

Syda Productions/Shutterstock

Select a room that is appropriate for the expected size of the audience.

Research the Topic

One key to overcoming stage fright is knowing the topic of your presentation well. When you know the topic well, you will feel more confident and less nervous during the presentation. You can also do a better job of preparing slides or handouts when you have a good understanding of the topic.

Research the topic to find the information you need. You may be able to find the information in company records or by talking with employees or customers. For example, if the presentation addresses sales trends for three company products, the information you need is probably in the company's sales records. If the presentation focuses on employee satisfaction with the company's benefits plan, you could interview employees about their thoughts on the plan or survey a targeted group for their responses.

When the topic is more general or not specific to your company, conduct research on the Internet or in a library. Be sure to record complete source information for each source you use. You may want to give the audience these details in a handout.

Writing Presentations

After you have planned and researched the topic adequately, you are ready to begin the writing process. In addition to preparing appropriate visual aids, your writing tasks include developing an opening, a strong body, and an appropriate conclusion. As you write, continue to think of ways to make your presentation interesting to your audience. If working as part of a team, determine which team members will write various sections of the presentation. Discuss how other team members will review the material written by others.

Put the main points in logical order to create an outline. This can be a formal outline or a simple list in Microsoft PowerPoint, you can also create the outline there, as shown in Figure 7-1. Record the details you want to discuss under the main points.

FIGURE 7-1

Outline for a Presentation in Microsoft PowerPoint

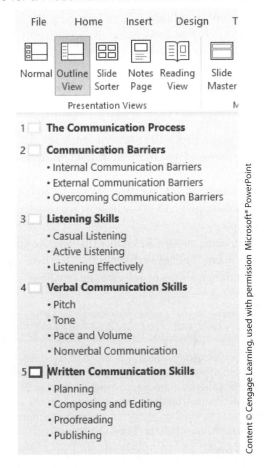

Content © Cengage Learning, used with permission Microsoft® PowerPoint

Develop an Opening

The opening should immediately engage the audience's attention and preview the message. Be creative in developing the opening. Use a relevant story or a quotation, ask a question, or refer to a current event. Begin with the unexpected and the unpredictable. If you use a joke, be sure it is in good taste and will not be offensive to any member of the audience. The opening should hold the audience's attention and, at the same time, help the presenter relax with the audience. When you are determining how to open the presentation, ask yourself these questions:

- Is there a link between the story and the presentation? Is it relevant?
- Is it a new story or joke? Will the audience members be bored because they have already heard it? Is it as succinct as possible? You do not want one-third of the time to be spent on the opening story.

However you decide to begin, remember that the purpose is to set the stage for the message. Write a strong opening that relates to the message. Then, as a transition from the opening to the presentation itself, outline the main points of the presentation—the audience needs to know what will be presented.

Develop a Strong Body

Start with the strongest points. Get to those major points quickly; do not spend time on irrelevant facts. As you develop the message, keep your focus on the audience. Keep asking these questions as you write:

- What is the message?
- Are you developing the right message for your audience?
- Are you using current examples to illustrate concepts? Do you have current data?
- Do the quotations relate to points you make? Do not use too many quotes; they can distract from the main message.
- Are you using direct language? Do not try to impress your audience with multi-syllable words or little-used terminology.
- Are you using active voice rather than passive voice? For example, say, "I believe …" instead of "It is believed …"
- Is your message sincere, relevant, and credible?

Develop a Strong Closing

The conclusion should summarize the points made in the presentation and leave the audience feeling motivated to respond in the way intended. Remember, the conclusion is the final impression on the audience. Make it forceful and positive. Leave the audience energized to work toward the goal that was established at the beginning of the presentation. A strong closing will capture the audience's attention. It helps them see the relationship between each part of the presentation—the opening, the body, and the closing. The conclusion can be a moving statement, a story, a call to action, or a challenge. Let the audience know the presentation is about to conclude by stating simply, "In conclusion …" or "The final point is…." Make the conclusion powerful but short (about 5 to 10 percent of the talk). For example, you can urge listeners to action, press them to think about new possibilities, or even make them laugh. The audience should leave thinking they have learned or have been motivated to take some action.

Developing and Using Visual Aids

A **visual aid** is an object or image that the audience can see and that will help them understand the message. When used properly, visual aids can greatly enhance the presentation and help people understand the message. Visual aids can increase the amount of information your audience remembers. People generally remember 40 percent more when they hear and see something simultaneously. Various types of objects or images can be used. Select visual aids that reinforce the message and that are appropriate for the presentation or meeting.

Objects

Objects that can be used as visual aids include natural items (plants), a piece of equipment (a sorting strip), and products (books). For example, at a meeting of company sales representatives, an effective visual aid is a new product that the sales reps will sell. If the audience is small, the object can be displayed or passed around so everyone can see it.

If the audience is large, you can place small objects on a document camera for remote viewing. A large image of the object is projected onto a screen.

Flipcharts and Posters

Posters and flipcharts are traditional types of visual aids. Although some people may consider these aids to be outdated or low tech, they can be effective in many situations.

Posters can be an effective visual aid in meetings and presentations to small groups. The poster might show an image related to the discussion or list the key points you want the audience to remember. Posters that give the session title and presenter's name are often used at the doors to meeting rooms at seminars and conferences.

If you have a printer that can handle large sheets of paper, you can achieve professional-looking results with software such as Microsoft Publisher. When you need a poster with a more professional look, you can hire an outside printer. Several Internet sites offer full-colour poster printing on high-quality paper or vinyl with a quick turnaround. You upload a file with the images and text for the poster, review a proof of the poster, and receive the printed poster within a few days.

Flipcharts are pads of large paper with pages that can be removed from the pad and displayed on meeting room walls as reminders of the discussion as the meeting progresses. This low-tech method for creating visual aids can be effective in small group meetings where listeners are asked to participate by generating questions or ideas.

Interactive Electronic Whiteboards

Mounted to a wall or floor stand, an **interactive whiteboard (IWB)** as pictured in Figure 7-2 is a large interactive display that can be connected wirelessly to a computer using Bluetooth technology or physically through a USB cable. A projected image of the computer desktop is displayed on the surface of the whiteboard.

FIGURE 7-2

Interactive Electronic Whiteboard

Monkey Business Images/Shutterstock

When using interactivity software installed on the computer, a hand (or some other pointing device) can be moved on the whiteboard surface, taking the place of a mouse or keyboard, to control the computer remotely. This software makes it unnecessary to go to the computer to activate or run a program or to annotate a presentation. The whiteboard becomes an input device creating virtual versions of paper flipcharts, including pen and highlighter options. The images drawn or the notes written on the whiteboard during a presentation or meeting can be viewed by the audience as they are created and then captured and saved to the connected computer for printing or emailing after the presentation or meeting has concluded. Optical character recognition (OCR) software can translate cursive writing on connected graphics tablet to text. Audience response system software can assist a presenter poll an audience and capture feedback onto the whiteboard.

Presentation Visuals

The most commonly used visual aid for presentations and business meetings is created with presentation software, such as Microsoft PowerPoint. Microsoft PowerPoint has a variety of add-ins such as Poll Everywhere and Office Mix that can enhance your presentations. Explore the available Office add-ins. In addition to Microsoft PowerPoint, you can use presentation software programs such as Microsoft Sway, Keynote, Prezi, and Google Slides. To increase your employability, become familiar with these various platforms.

Creating presentation slides with any of these software programs is not complicated. To be effective, however, slides should be easy to read from all locations in the meeting room. If your audience is large, you may need two screens—one screen on one side of the room and the other screen on the other side of the room. If possible, before the presentation, display the slides in the room that will be used, or a room of similar size, to ensure that viewers in the back of the room can read the slides.

The text should highlight the main points about the topic. For a live presentation, the text should not include everything you intend to say in the presentation. Follow these guidelines for creating slides:

- **Develop one slide** for every two or three minutes of your presentation. This number keeps the audience interested and does not overwhelm the listeners with visuals.
- **Include a title on each slide** and two to four short words or phrases as bullet points.
- **Do not crowd** the text or images on the slides.
- **Use graphics** (charts, photos, clip art) on some slides to help illustrate points and add interest.

FIGURE 7-3

PowerPoint Templates and Themes Help Create Effective Slides

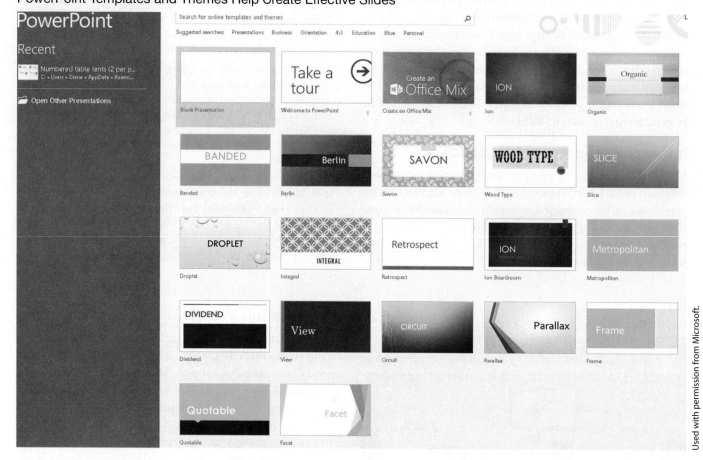

- **Use contrasting colours** for the slide background and the text. For example, use a light background with dark text or a dark background with white text.
- **Limit the number of fonts used**—perhaps one font for the title and a different font or size for the bullet points. Do not use all capital letters, which are hard to read, for bullet points.
- **Strive for a professional look.** Use design themes or templates in the software (as shown in Figure 7-3) to ensure a consistent look. You may want to include the company or organization logo on the title slide. Ensure you follow any style guide an organization may have established regarding consistency, content placement, and text treatment.
- **Be creative.** Use animated bullet points and slide transitions to add interest to the slides. Use special effects, sound, and video sparingly and only if appropriate for the presentation. Special effects should not divert the listeners' focus from the content of the presentation.

Slides created for use in a webinar may be accompanied by voice comments from a presenter or used alone. If the slides are to be used alone, they should contain all the needed information in brief, concise language. Otherwise, they should follow the guidelines given above for slides to be used in a live presentation.

Legal Requirements

When creating presentation visuals, you must abide by Canadian laws and legislation. Ensure that presentations comply with accessibility legislation at the federal level and if you work in Ontario, Manitoba, or Nova Scotia, the respective provincial legislation. In addition, if your presentation visuals use copyright-protected information such as pictures, ensure you abide by Canada's Copyright Act and properly cite and acknowledge these items in your presentation visuals and seek permission to use them, if necessary.

Handouts

Handouts can be an important part of a presentation. The simplest handouts are copies of the slides. Handouts that list the main points you will discuss and provide space for notes can be passed out at the beginning of a speech or meeting. Handouts with additional information about a topic are often distributed when the topic is introduced or near the close of the session. For example, if the presentation introduces a new health insurance plan, a handout with details about the plan would be helpful.

Handouts should be attractive, easy to read, and free of errors. If you have a complex handout that may distract the audience, pass it out just before you discuss the topic or at the end of the presentation. Let the audience know it is available and when to expect it. Knowing the notes will be available at the end of a presentation allows participants to relax and absorb the message without needing to take notes.

Once the presentation is written, put it aside for a day or two; then review it. Does the speech fit the anticipated audience? Does it meet the purpose? Is the opening creative? Will it get the audience's attention? Have you used stories and quotes appropriately, and have you spaced them throughout the presentation? Remember, if you involve the audience, they will learn. A well-selected story or quote can involve the audience. Is the presentation the proper length? Remember, it is better to be too brief than too long. (The American president Abraham Lincoln delivered one of that nation's most celebrated addresses—the Gettysburg Address—in less than five minutes.) Are your visual aids effective? Are you using an appropriate number of visuals? Do you need to rewrite any parts?

Preparing to Deliver the Presentation

As an administrative professional you may make presentations to three basic types of audiences:
- co-workers in your organization
- workplace teams containing a cross-section of people within your organization
- colleagues within professional organizations to which you belong

If you will be delivering presentations, you may, like many others, experience presentation anxiety, commonly called stage fright. Nervousness or anxiety is a normal reaction for many people when they think about presenting before an audience. Presenters often lack the confidence and skill to make effective presentations. With proper planning and practice, you can develop effective presentation skills and overcome presentation anxiety. Knowing that you are well prepared and well rehearsed can help you to decrease your nervousness, conquer those presentation fears, and ensure you give an effective presentation.

Rehearse

Make arrangements, if at all possible, to rehearse in the room where you will give the presentation. If this is not possible, try to rehearse the presentation in a room of similar size to the one in which you will speak. Learn whom to contact for help if the equipment malfunctions during your presentation.

Rehearse the presentation just as you are going to give it. For example, if you will be standing at a lectern during the presentation, then stand at a lectern during your rehearsal. If you will be using a microphone, use a microphone during your rehearsal. Find out what type of microphone you will

use. With a stationary microphone, you do not need to be concerned about holding it or whether it is correctly positioned on your clothing. Unfortunately, a stationary mic has a major disadvantage—it ties you to the lectern. In most presentations, you will want to be free to walk across the front of the room and even into the audience.

If you are using an unfamiliar laptop, bring your presentation on a flash drive, even if the presentation was emailed or uploaded to the cloud ahead of time. Having a backup copy of the presentation and handouts on a flash drive is always a good idea.

Go over your presentation completely three or four times. Speak slowly—you will speed up instinctively during the presentation itself. Then ask a colleague to listen to your practice session and provide constructive criticism. If none of these options is practical, practise in front of a mirror. With repeated rehearsals, the text becomes part of your memory; you will be more at ease since you will not likely forget an important point during the presentation.

Memorize your opening line, question, quotation, or story. Doing so will help you feel confident as you begin to speak. However, do not try to memorize the entire presentation. Use your slides or an outline to help you move smoothly from point to point as you speak in a conversational tone. Include details that you want to be sure to mention in the notes section of the slides. You can view these notes on your monitor or a printout, but they will not be visible to the audience.

iStock/Thinkstock

Dressing appropriately is important when delivering a presentation.

Use Visual Aids Effectively

As you rehearse, display the visual aids you plan to use in the presentation. Just as you will during the presentation, stand where you will not block the view of listeners. Look at the audience, not at the visual aids, as you speak. If the lights will be dimmed, try to keep the light at a level that lets the audience see both you and the slides and other visual aids. The room should have enough light for the audience to take notes.

Know how to operate the equipment, such as the laptop, remote mouse, and IWB. If you are uncomfortable showing the slides while you talk, ask someone to assist you. If you choose this approach, your assistant should rehearse with you so they know when each slide is displayed. Give the person an outline that indicates when to advance the slides, when to show a visual aid, and when to pass out the handouts.

Plan Your Attire

Several days before the presentation, determine what you will wear. The usual attire for a woman is a suit or dress; for a man, it is a suit and tie. Wear something comfortable that makes you feel good. Bright colours are perfectly okay. Avoid necklaces and earrings that are too large and distracting. Rings and bracelets are appropriate, but do not wear noisy bracelets, which can distract the audience. Coloured shirts and bright ties are fine. The colour of the suit should look good on the person. Your hair should be well groomed.

Delivering Presentations

Conquer Your Fears

First, realize that nervousness is normal. In fact, as shown by surveys, one of everyone's greatest fears is speaking before an audience. You have already learned two things to help control your nervousness—preparation and rehearsal. A well-prepared and well-rehearsed presentation can eliminate many of your fears. You know who your audience is, you know what you intend to say, and you know how you will say it.

The Day before the Presentation

Remind yourself that you have prepared well. You have followed all the steps mentioned previously: beginning early, identifying the objective of the presentation, rehearsing, and so on. Burn off some of your nervousness by exercising. Try not to push yourself to the limit with work responsibilities the few days before your presentation; when you are overly tired, you increase your chances of not doing a good job.

The Day of the Presentation

Arrive early enough to check out the microphone, the equipment, and the layout of the room. Have the name and telephone number of the contact person at the presentation venue, in case you have last-minute changes.

In the 10 or 15 minutes before your presentation is to begin, find a private place where you can relax.

Beginning Your Presentation

Your introduction should help establish that you are a credible speaker. **Credible** means believable or trustworthy. Use nonverbal cues to establish credibility from the start. Pay attention to your body language as you are being introduced. Stand or

Rehearse your presentation before a group of respected colleagues; ask for their constructive criticism.

sit up straight in a relaxed posture. Look at the speaker and then look at members of the audience.

After the introduction is completed, walk to the lectern confidently and respond to the introduction. If you are not introduced, you may need to introduce yourself. Arrange your notecards if you have them, look at the audience for a few seconds, and then begin.

You may feel calmer if you realize that the audience is much less aware than you are of any nervousness you are feeling. Also, realize that the audience is your friend; the audience wants you to succeed. If you feel your hands shaking as you begin, leave the microphone on a stand and your notes and/or glass of water on the lectern so that you do not draw attention to them.

During the Presentation

During your presentation, keep the following in mind:
- **Maintain eye contact with the audience**. If you are in a small group, look at each individual briefly. When you are in a large group, move your eyes from one side of the room to the other, concentrating for a time on each portion of the room. If you are using visuals, stand to the side of the slide when you are showing it and face the audience—talk to them, not to the projected slide.
- **Use natural gestures**. In conversations with others, your facial expressions reinforce what you are saying; the same is true when delivering a presentation. It is fine to use your arms and hands to emphasize points, but too many arm and hand gestures can be distracting to the audience.
- **Be natural; do not perform**. Speak in a normal tone of voice—not too loudly or too softly, vary your tone, and do not speak too fast or too slowly, as speaking too slowly can result in a bored listener. Articulate carefully and be animated in both your speech and your expression. For example, do not drop your *g's*; say *learning*, not *learnin'*.
- **Observe the nonverbal feedback from the audience**. Puzzled looks or blank stares are cues that the audience

does not understand what you are saying. You may need to modify the rate of your voice or give another example or two to clarify what you mean. Smiles and nodding heads are positive reactions.

- **Watch your time.** If you have been asked to deliver a 20-minute presentation, do so. Do not go over the time limit. Because you rehearsed your presentation several times before giving it, you know how long it will take. It is essential that you watch the time during your presentation; however, do not be obvious about it. Such behaviour would be distracting for the audience. Some speakers use the clock on their laptop if they are using it to support the presentation or they place their watch on the lectern where they can refer to it discreetly. Determine a plan that works for you, with no audience distraction.

Communicating AT WORK

When you speak during a meeting or a presentation, avoid using clichés. A cliché is a trite expression or phrase that has been overused to the point of no longer being effective. Using clichés can make your message seem boring or insincere. Notice the following clichés and the improved wording.

Cliché	Improved
at the present time	now
24/7	at all times
your kind letter	your letter (omit *kind*. People, not letters, are kind.)
among those present	here or present
perfect in every detail	perfect
cool as a cucumber	calm
powers that be	managers, senators, or whomever you are referring to
Words are inadequate to express how I feel about this honour.	Thank you for the invitation to speak here today.

The closing should either summarize what you want the audience to remember or ask them to take some action appropriate for the goal of the presentation. Your conclusion, summary, or call to action should clearly tie in with your opening statements and the points you made in the body of the message.

If the presentation includes a question-and-answer session, be sure to repeat the questions that have been asked so that everyone in the audience can hear the question as well as your answer. Answer questions briefly, since time for this part of the presentation is usually limited.

Do not become frustrated if someone asks a question about a point you covered earlier; the questioner may have been distracted or may not have fully understood what you said.

Answer the question patiently, and use different statements or examples from those used earlier. If you do not know the answer, say so. Take the person's name and get back to them with the answer if doing so is appropriate for the situation.

Watch the time and do not let the session run longer than the time allotted. Use the last few minutes of the session to repeat the main points or the action you want the audience to remember.

Seek Feedback

Within a day after you have finished delivering your presentation, critique what happened. Either evaluate yourself or have someone else evaluate you. You might want to videotape your presentation to help you in the critiquing process. You may also want to provide evaluation forms for the people in the audience. In critiquing yourself, keep the following in mind:

- Be kind. List the good along with the not-so-good.
- Do not try to solve too many problems at once. Pick one or two things to improve each time.
- Realize evaluation is an ongoing process.
- Give yourself credit for the improvements you make.
- Get feedback from other people; really listen to the feedback. If someone compliments you, believe it.

You or the individuals who asked you to speak may provide evaluation forms for the people in the audience. Ask to see copies of the completed forms; review them carefully. Do not let yourself become upset over a few negative comments. Know that there will always be some negatives. However, take seriously the points that are made in the critique. Before you speak again, concentrate on how you might improve your presentation techniques.

Giving Team Presentations

Teams are used extensively in businesses and other organizations. Team presentations require specific skills and offer some benefits that a single presenter does not have. Some of these benefits include the following:

- Having two or more people deliver parts of the presentation can increase and hold the audience's attention.
- Having more than one speaker brings greater experience and expertise to the presentation.
- If the audience works in small groups on a particular assignment, team members are available to mingle with the groups and provide expertise and leadership.
- One presenter can record comments or questions from the audience while another speaks.

Select the Team

Having the right combination of people on a team can make the team more effective. In some cases, you may be assigned to the team and have no input on who the other members will be. In other cases, you may be able to choose the people on the team. What should you consider when assembling a team? Here are a few suggestions to consider:

- What are the strengths and weaknesses of each person?
- What does the strength of each person add to the strength of the team?
- Do the team members collectively have a breadth of knowledge about the topic?
- What particular knowledge does each individual have? Do individual team members have the technical knowledge needed for the presentation?
- What people skills does each presenter possess? For example, is the person a team player? An effective communicator? A good listener?

A presentation team needs a strong leader who can make decisions and motivate the team. In some cases, the team may select its leader after a team discussion about the strengths and weaknesses of the group. Team members need to be willing to engage in this discussion non-defensively. If the team is going to work together for a longer period of time, management may appoint the leader. If the presentation will be delivered to an external group, the person who was initially contacted by the external group may be the leader. That person can assemble a team with members they choose.

Work Together for Success

Each team member and the team collectively should know the purpose of the presentation(s). The team leader should facilitate this session. Certain questions need to be asked and answered: What do you want the audience to know or do as a result of the presentation? What is the best way to convey the message?

Identify duties for each team member related to planning, research, writing, developing visual aids, and presenting. Set deadlines for when each task should be completed and times for when the team will meet to work on or rehearse the presentation. When deciding who will be responsible for various duties, consider each team member's area of expertise, presentation style and skill, and understanding of the audience.

Not all team members need to speak during the presentation, but everyone should be present and available to answer questions and help during small group activities. All members should review the feedback and discuss ways to improve.

Soft Skills — CREATIVITY

Clearly, there are no rigid steps to becoming creative. Remember, it is a process—a process that can be different for each individual. However, here are some steps that can help release your existing creativity.

HAVE FAITH IN YOUR CREATIVITY

First, have faith in the fact that you are creative. If you have an idea that differs from other people's ideas, do not immediately assume you are wrong. Try it out. Your idea may be the creative spark to solving a complex problem. Always maintain a spirit of inquiry. Ask questions. Do not assume that a question you have is too dumb to ask. Allow yourself the freedom to ask. Do not be uncomfortable when you do not know how something is going to turn out. By experimenting with the unknown, a wonderfully new and creative product can occur.

DESTROY JUDGMENT

As you think through a problem or an issue, do not be judgmental. Let your thoughts flow freely. Do not discard any of them. Do not let your mind tell you that an idea is no good or ridiculous. To help you destroy judgment (which, by the way, is not easy to do), pay attention to every thought you have. Notice it; hear yourself think it. If you begin to be critical of your thought, attack the judgment.

LOOK AND LISTEN

The story is told of a businessman who heard that a Zen master (who lived at the top of a mountain) knew the three basic secrets to life. Anyone who knew these secrets would live a happy, fulfilling life. The businessman climbed for two years to get to the top of the mountain. Once there, he approached the old master and asked that he tell him the secrets. The master said, "Yes, I will tell you. The first secret is pay attention, the second secret is pay attention, and the third secret is pay attention."

You may be asking, "Pay attention to what?" Pay attention to what you sense, what you think, what you hear, what you see. Pay attention to nature; pay attention to others.

ASK QUESTIONS

Michael Ray and Rochelle Myers, in their book *Creativity in Business*, report writing down the following questions that a four-and-a-half-year-old asked in less than an hour:

- What's behind a rainbow?
- What colour is the inside of my brain?
- What's inside of a rock? A tree? A sausage? Bones? My throat? A spider?
- Does the sky have an end to it?
- Why are my toes in front of my feet?

We smile when we read these questions. If you have children or younger siblings, they may have asked similar questions. As we grow up, we stop allowing ourselves to continue to ask questions. We think we should know all the answers; but, obviously, we do not. Our continuing to ask questions (whatever they may be) helps us get in touch with our creativity. Do not frighten yourself at first by asking big questions, such as "What is the nature of humans?" Give yourself permission to ask small and even playful questions. Let yourself question things you have never questioned in your adult life.

Chapter Summary

The summary will help you remember the important points covered in this chapter.

- Develop and use your creativity when preparing presentations.
- As an administrative professional, your job may include helping to develop or deliver presentations. Developing your presentation skills is important for your professional growth.
- When planning a presentation, identify the goal of the presentation; consider the audience, the time and length of the presentation, and the location; and research the topic if needed.
- Using visual aids, such as posters, whiteboards, and electronic slides, can increase the amount of information the listeners remember from the presentation.
- When delivering a presentation, focus on sharing your message with the listeners. Use the last couple of minutes of the session to repeat the main points or action you want the audience to remember as they leave the presentation.
- Teams are used extensively in businesses and other organizations. Team members should agree on the purpose of the presentation and work together to plan, research, write, and deliver the presentation.

Key Terms

creativity p. 115
credible p. 122
demographics p. 116
flipcharts p. 119
interactive whiteboard (IWB) p. 119

intranet p. 114
posters p. 118
presentation p. 114
visual aid p. 118
webinar p. 114

Discussion Items

These discussion items provide an opportunity to test your understanding of the chapter through written responses and discussion with your classmates and your instructor:

1. Why does an administrative professional need to develop presentation skills?
2. List the planning steps involved in developing a presentation.
3. What are some options you might use as an opening for a presentation? What points should you consider when selecting one of these options?
4. List some steps you might take to conquer your presentation fears.
5. Identify five techniques for preparing effective electronic presentations or slides that you consider most important. Explain why.
6. What are two benefits of giving a team presentation rather than an individual presentation?

Critical-Thinking Activity

You are a member of a local chapter of the International Association of Administrative Professionals (IAAP). You have been asked to speak at the IAAP national meeting, which will be held in Charlottetown this year. Your speech is not a keynote; you will be presenting at a session on the first afternoon of the conference from 2:00 p.m. to 2:40 p.m. You have been given the prerogative of choosing your own topic and whether or not you will present as an individual or make it a team effort. The theme of the conference is promoting professional growth. You decide you will do a team presentation; two members of your chapter have agreed to present with you. (Work with two of your classmates on this project.)

As a team, list the steps that you will need to take to select a topic and prepare the presentation. Select a topic and write an objective statement for the presentation. Develop a personal introduction for each person on the team.

Building Workplace Skills

Project 7-1 (Learning Outcome 1)
Collaborative Projects

Team Presentation

Do further planning, including needed research, to develop the team presentation on the topic you selected in the Critical-Thinking Activity. As a team, develop a strong opening for the presentation. Create an outline for the presentation body and write the body and closing for the presentation. Develop a list of five questions that might be asked during a question-and-answer session and write answers for each question.

Project 7-2 (Learning Outcome 2)

Visual Aids

Continue to develop your team presentation. Identify visual aids that will be helpful in giving the presentation. As a team, create the visual aids. Create a handout to accompany the presentation. The handout can be a printout of slides with space for taking notes or a sheet with additional details or related information.

Project 7-3 (Learning Outcomes 4 and 5)

Deliver a Presentation

Identify which part of the presentation will be delivered by each team member. Rehearse the team presentation, using the visual aids you created earlier. Deliver the presentation to your class or a group of classmates. As a team, write an evaluation of the presentation and the team's delivery, noting strong points and weak points to improve for future presentations. Use the Presentation Evaluation Form Project 7-3a. Your instructor will collect the evaluation forms at the end of your presentation and give them to you for review. What can you learn from the evaluation forms? Write a memorandum to your instructor, using the memorandum form file Project 7-3b. Detail the strengths and weaknesses of your presentation as revealed by the evaluation forms and as seen by your group. Use these headings in your memorandum: (1) Group Opinion of Strengths and Weaknesses of Presentation and (2) Class Members' Opinion of Strengths and Weaknesses of Presentation.

Project 7-4 (Learning Outcomes 1, 2, and 3)

You recently gave a presentation on ergonomics in the office at a local IAAP meeting. The goals of the presentation were to inform listeners about this important topic and to persuade them to apply ergonomic practices. The president of the IAAP chapter has asked you to provide the main points of your talk in an electronic slide show that can be posted online for IAAP members who were not able to attend your presentation.

- Do research on the topic using the Internet and other resources.
- Write an outline of the main points and the details you will include in the slides.
- Create an electronic slide show that includes a title slide and at least nine additional slides. Use appropriate photos, pictures, or graphics and animation for the slides. For each slide except the title slide, record a voice file and attach it to the slide so users can hear your comments. The voice file for each slide should be one to two minutes in length.

Project 7-5 (Learning Outcome 3)

INNOVATION

Feedback Form

As you waited for your dental appointment recently, you wrote a few notes about developing a form to request feedback from the listeners at your next presentation. Open file Project 7-5. Review the notes in this file. Think of additional questions or information you might want to include on the form. Create and print an attractive form that you can use to get feedback from the audience when you give a presentation.

Project 7-6 (Learning Outcomes 2, 3, 4, and 5)

CAREER

Add one or both of the presentations you created in Projects 7-3 and 7-4 to your e-portfolio as an example of the work you can do in preparing presentation visuals.

Make the Grade with MindTap

Stay organized and efficient with **MindTap**—a single destination with all the course material and study aids you need to succeed. Built-in apps leverage social media and the latest learning technology. For example:

- ReadSpeaker will read the text to you.
- Flashcards are pre-populated to provide you with a jump-start for review—or you can create your own.
- You can highlight text and make notes in your MindTap Reader. Your notes will flow into Evernote, the electronic notebook app that you can access anywhere when it's time to study for the exam.
- Self-quizzing allows you to access your understanding.

Visit nelson.com/student to start using **MindTap**. Enter the Online Access Code from the card included with your text. If a code card is not provided, you can purchase instant access at NELSONbrain.com.

PART 3

Administrative Support— Your Responsibilities

As an administrative professional, you will be a valued member of a team in a business or an organization where co-workers will depend on you to keep the office organized and operating efficiently. Your many administrative duties and responsibilities may include the following:

- You should understand the role an administrative professional commonly plays in creating and maintaining financial documents. This section stresses the confidential nature and importance of accuracy when preparing financial documents, and includes information about common employee benefits and required payroll deductions.
- The management of records is an important responsibility for every administrative professional. A working knowledge of common records systems—alphabetic, subject, geographic, and numeric—and the ability to determine which is appropriate will be invaluable to your organization. Choosing appropriate supplies,

equipment, and media for physical and electronic records may also be your responsibility.
- You will be introduced to various types of business meetings and formats for meetings, and will learn the importance of your responsibilities as an administrative professional in assisting with meetings. Understanding the responsibilities of all meeting participants is important if meetings are to accomplish their business goals.
- The role of an administrative professional often includes arranging for domestic or international travel—booking flights and hotel accommodations, researching travel and security alerts, handling issues while the executive is away, and completing follow-up activities after the trip.

Providing administrative support means anticipating your supervisor's needs—knowing what they want or need before they have requested it. In doing so, you can exceed expectations and help to create a professional atmosphere where everyone enjoys coming to work.

Jacqueline Stillman

Support Officer—Special Events, Office of the President, Mohawk College

My name is Jacqueline Stillman and I graduated with honours from the office administration executive business program at Mohawk College in 2015.

During my time as a stay-at-home mom, technology had advanced rapidly. When I found myself ready to re-enter the workforce, I lacked the confidence and skill set to do so. Returning to college began my journey toward a new career.

I'm currently employed as an administrative assistant and support officer in the Special Events Department of the office of the president at Mohawk College.

Each day, I take on a wide range of responsibilities such as managing and finalizing budgets, invoicing, and planning and executing events. No two days are alike, which I find very rewarding.

The biggest challenge in my role is constantly being on top of things as I am responsible for keeping my team organized and able to fulfill their responsibilities. My strong time-management and organizational skills help me succeed every day.

I am privileged to be part of a team where each of us possesses a variety of strengths and skills. I have learned first-hand that it is important for the administrative professional to possess skills such as problem solving, adaptability, time management, organization, and oral communication.

In my role, it is important to be a lifelong learner and continue to learn new technology and processes to stay current.

Marina Polonski

Clerical Associate, Humber River Hospital, Nephrology Unit

My name is Marina Polonski, and I work for Humber River Hospital's inpatient nephrology unit as a clerical associate.

In 2011, I was laid off from a job I had held for 15 years. I had no idea what I wanted to do next, but I knew I wanted to move away from a desk job. My job was task-specific and did not allow for much career growth. I decided to return to school and move into the growing medical field. In 2012, I entered the medical office administration accelerated diploma program at Seneca College, Newnham Campus.

Walking into school as a student for the first time in 15 years was certainly daunting, but my experience was rewarding and transformative. Graduating from the program with high honours taught me that it's never too late to go back to school and chase your dream career.

Working in a hospital is incredibly engaging, with new challenges every day. As the first point of contact, I need to be professional, courteous, and unfailingly patient. I work with patients living with challenging illnesses and also with their family members, who are often confused, scared, and overwhelmed.

Looking back, I couldn't be more grateful to have grown with the nephrology team over the last five years or for the journey that brought me to my new career.

CHAPTER 8

Handling Mail and Using Reprographic Equipment

LEARNING OUTCOMES

After studying this chapter, you should be able to:

1. Explain how to process incoming mail effectively.
2. Describe how to prepare outgoing mail effectively.
3. Identify classes of mail and special services available through Canada Post Corporation.
4. Describe reprographic equipment and their features.
5. Develop teamwork skills.

Do I Qualify?

Office Administration Assistant

An international company is offering an opportunity for a responsible worker in its North Shore office. In addition to screening telephone calls and office emails, duties include:

- opening, date-stamping, sorting, and delivering incoming mail to departments
- collecting, preparing, and processing domestic and international outgoing mail for all departments
- conducting transactions with Canada Post and private carriers
- printing postage and labels
- operating copier, paper shredder, and sorter
- filing and a variety of other administrative duties as assigned

Attention to detail, a strong work ethic, and the ability to multi-task and shift focus quickly are required.

For many years, mail could be defined with a fairly simple statement. Nearly all mail could be described as written information sent via **Canada Post Corporation (CPC)** to locations within Canada and abroad. Today the meaning of mail is much broader: electronic mail (email and fax) and mail delivery systems include, in addition to Canada Post, numerous private express companies, such as Purolator Inc., FedEx (Federal Express), UPS (United Parcel Service), and DHL Worldwide Express. The Internet and software packages allow users to determine the correct postage without ever leaving their desk or entering a post office. Just like express and private services, Canada Post, too, has expanded, due in part to both the exponential growth of online shopping and the expectations of business organizations that their hardcopy mail will be delivered almost as quickly as electronic mail.

The increase in electronic communication has resulted in a significant drop in both the volume of first-class mail being delivered by Canada Post and the revenue Canada Post collects. In recent years, Canada Post has responded by introducing several electronic options for customers. For example **epost**, a free, secure, online personal digital mailbox, allows individuals and businesses to access, view, and pay bills online. It can also be used as a digital safety-deposit box to store copies of important documents such as passports, insurance documents, and more.

Canada Post's **epost Connect** is a secure service that is linked to an epost account to provide the same private and confidential online secure communications services for business customers through Bulk and Collaboration options.

Does this mean we are sending less mail than in the past? Absolutely not. In fact, with the growth of online shopping and parcel shipment, we are sending more mail. But it does mean that we have drastically changed the way we communicate with each other and our expectations about effective communication. Electronic communication is a routine part of our everyday existence, and while paper mail may continue to drop in volume, for many organizations, it is still an extremely important method of communication.

An administrative professional has numerous responsibilities related to mail handling—from preparing incoming mail for presentation to your supervisor to reviewing and preparing outgoing correspondence to be mailed. After studying this chapter, you will understand your role and responsibilities regarding effectively processing all types of mail, both traditional and electronic. You will also become more knowledgeable about reprographics equipment and their functions. The soft skill you will focus on in this chapter is *teamwork*.

Handling Incoming Mail

Unanswered or misplaced mail can represent a significant cost to an organization in lost business. Your job as an administrative professional is to ensure that incoming mail is well organized and presented to your supervisor in a timely manner. If you work in a large organization, the mail is likely delivered to a central mailroom where it is sorted according to the company's departments. In addition to sorting, the mailroom may offer additional services, such as opening the mail. If the mail is opened, correspondence is not taken from the envelope, since the envelope itself may have information that the receiver needs. Mail opened in mailrooms is often processed through automatic mail openers that also count the items. This step helps a company to analyze and justify its mail costs. Mail is usually either picked up at the mailroom by the administrative professional or delivered by a mailroom attendant at set times during the day (usually in the morning and the afternoon) so employees know when to expect it.

In some cases, mailrooms may also process incoming mail using imaging technology that scans and electronically stores the contents of documents, integrating them into an electronic communication system. Colleges and universities, for example, receive thousands of applications for admission from potential students; this mail can be electronically distributed to the inbox of the appropriate department or departments. Using this technology reduces the needless copying of documents for circulation.

In small offices, a Canada Post carrier may deliver the mail directly to the office, or the company may maintain a mailbox at the post office. If the organization maintains a post office box, you may have the responsibility for picking up the mail. Once you receive the mail in your office or department, you will sort, open, read, and possibly annotate, organize by priority, and present it to your supervisor. You will also determine which items, if any, should be copied and circulated to others; such items are then prepared for distribution by attaching a routing slip.

Sorting Mail

First, do a preliminary mail sort. If several individuals work in the department, sort the mail according to the addressee. An alphabetical sorter is handy if you are sorting mail for several individuals. Once the mail is sorted, place the mail for each individual into separate stacks.

When this preliminary sort is completed, sort each person's mail in this order:

- **Personal and confidential**. The administrative professional should not open mail marked "Personal" or "Confidential." Place this mail to one side to avoid inadvertently opening it.
- **Xpresspost, Registered, or Priority**. This mail has high priority and should be placed so it is the first mail the recipient sees.
- **Regular business mail (lettermail)**. Mail from customers, clients, and suppliers is also considered important and should be sorted so it receives top priority.
- **Interoffice communications**. This mail generally is received in the distinctive interoffice envelope shown in Figure 8-1.

People AT WORK

Mail Clerk

A mail clerk typically works in the mailroom for a large organization. This person performs duties related to preparing outgoing mail and delivering mail to departments of the organization. The mail clerk may operate equipment such as a postage meter, copier, paper shredder, sealer, and sorter. They may seal envelopes or packages and apply correct postage from a postage meter or labels printed from a computer printer.

The mail clerk may conduct transactions with Canada Post, private mail carriers, or online mail vendors. In some companies, the mail clerk keeps a log of all outgoing and incoming packages. Sorting and applying bar codes and postage for bulk mailing items is another duty typically performed by a mail clerk. If you work in a large company with a mailroom, you may need to request services from a mail clerk.

FIGURE 8-1

An Interoffice Envelope

INTER-DEPARTMENT DELIVERY

Note—Cross Out Entire Line When Received and Re-use Until All Lines Are Full.

Date	Deliver To:	Department	Sent By:	Department
		◯		◯
	◯		◯	
	◯		◯	

© Costas/Shutterstock

- **Advertisements, newspapers, magazines, and catalogues**. These materials are considered relatively unimportant and can be handled after the other correspondence is answered. They should be placed at the bottom of the correspondence stack so they may be read at your supervisor's convenience.

Opening Mail

Mail may be opened in the mailroom or in the individual's office. Mail opened in an individual's office is usually opened by hand, using an envelope opener. When opening mail, follow these procedures:

- Have these necessary supplies readily available: an envelope opener, a date and time stamp, routing and action slips, a stapler, paper clips, tape, sticky notes, and a pen or pencil.
- Before opening an envelope, tap the lower edge of the envelope on the desk so the contents fall to the bottom and cannot be inadvertently cut when the envelope is opened.
- Check the envelope carefully to be certain all items have been removed.
- Fasten any enclosures to the correspondence. Attach small enclosures to the front of the correspondence. Attach enclosures larger than the correspondence to the back.

- Mend any torn paper with tape.
- If you open a personal or confidential letter by mistake, do not remove it from the envelope. Write "opened by mistake" on the front of the envelope, add your initials, and reseal the envelope with tape.

Stack the envelopes on the desk in the same order as the opened mail in case it becomes necessary to refer to the envelopes. A good practice is to save all envelopes for at least one day in case they are needed for reference; they can then be recycled or can be shredded if they contain confidential information.

Certain envelopes should be retained. Keep the envelope when you notice one or more of the following things:

- **An incorrectly addressed envelope**. You or your supervisor may want to call attention to this fact when replying to the correspondence.
- **A letter with no return address**. The envelope usually will have the return address.
- **An envelope that has a significantly different postmark from the date on the document**. The document date may be compared with the postmark date to determine the delay in receiving the document.
- **A letter specifying an enclosure that is not enclosed**. Write "no enclosure" on the letter and attach the envelope.
- **A letter containing a bid, an offer, or an acceptance of a contract**. The postmark date may be needed as legal evidence.
- **An envelope that appears to contain any suspicious substance or materials**. Follow your organization's procedures for handling suspicious mail.

In many organizations, incoming mail receives a hand stamp or a stamp from a small machine that imprints the date and time of receipt. This procedure can be an important step as it furnishes a record of when the correspondence was received. If mail arrives later than a predetermined deadline, the stamped

Handling incoming mail is an important duty for an administrative assistant.

Stokkete/Shutterstock

date of receipt is a recorded confirmation of the date the letter was received. If the letter has no date line, the received date stamped on the letter indicates approximately when the correspondence was mailed. Also, when an invoice is received, which, in a large organization may require several days to process as it travels from department to department obtaining appropriate coding and approvals, the received date stamped on the item can be very important to the accounts payable department.

Reviewing and Annotating

Busy executives appreciate help with the large amount of mail that crosses their desks each day. As an administrative professional, you can help by visually scanning all received mail and underlining the important words and phrases with a coloured pen, pencil, or highlighter. You should also check mathematical calculations and verify dates that appear in correspondence.

If an enclosure is missing from the letter, make a note of this omission. If an invoice is received, check the calculations. Indicate any discrepancies in a note. If the correspondence refers to a previous piece of correspondence, pull that item or the file and attach it to the new correspondence, noting the attachment.

Writing AT WORK

In addition to reviewing correspondence received in the mail, you may be asked to **annotate** it (write notes about previous action taken or facts that will assist the reader). You can annotate by writing notes in the margin of the correspondence or by attaching sticky notes. The advantage of sticky notes is that they can be removed when you and the executive are finished with them.

Annotations may also be used to remind the executive of a previous commitment. For example, the executive might have agreed to have lunch with the person who signed the correspondence. When answering the letter, the executive may want to refer to their lunch plans.

Organizing and Presenting

After you have completed the preliminary mail sorts and have opened, date- and time-stamped, read, and annotated the mail, you are ready to do a final sort and to place the items in their respective folders. Folders help maintain confidentiality; for example, someone walking into your supervisor's office will not be able to easily read the material. Colour-coding the folders also helps your supervisor to see at a glance which mail needs to be handled first. Here is one arrangement you might use:

- **Immediate action.** This mail must be handled on the day of receipt or shortly thereafter (red folder).
- **Routine correspondence.** Such mail would include memoranda and other types of non-urgent mail (blue folder).

- **Informational mail.** Included in this folder are periodicals, newspapers, advertisements, and other types of mail that do not require answering but are for informational reading (yellow folder).

If you have been working with your supervisor for some time, you may have learned that they do not want to see some mail, such as certain types of advertisements or catalogues. Also, you may be authorized to answer routine requests for information. Discuss with your supervisor where the mail should be placed and how frequently it should be presented. Depending on how often mail is delivered, your supervisor may ask that you organize and present it approximately 30 minutes after you receive it. Never destroy mail (even what you consider to be junk mail) unless your supervisor has given you the authority to make these decisions.

Routing

At times, more than one person may need to read a piece of correspondence or a publication. In the case of correspondence, if you feel it is urgent that all individuals immediately receive the information, scan or make photocopies of the correspondence and email or forward a hardcopy to each person on the list. If it is not urgent, route the actual correspondence, using a routing slip to save copying costs. A routing slip is also an effective method for circulating publications.

You can purchase routing slips or create your own (an example is shown in Figure 8-2). For example, if you regularly route correspondence to the same individuals, you can create a routing slip that already has the individuals' names printed on it. If you are circulating several publications to the same people at the same time, vary the order of the names on the list so that the documents do not always start their circulation with the same person.

FIGURE 8-2

A Routing Slip

ROUTING SLIP			
Description of Document:	Draft — Travel Policy and Procedures		
Date:	October 21, 20--		
Please circulate to:			
Order	Name	Date	Initial
	Guy Beauchamp		
2	Luyin Wu		
1	Keri-An Mahar		
3	Ryan Hughes		
	Return to:	Guy Beauchamp	

Capital Trust Company

9 St. Clair Avenue West, Toronto, ON M4 1K6
Telephone 416-368-8484

April 25, 20--

Mr. Arthur R. Channing, President
Astrolite, Limited
400 West Georgia Street
Vancouver, BC
V6B 1Z3

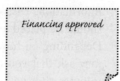
Financing approved

Dear Mr. Channing:

We have now received a final report on the financing of your proposed plant in Windsor, Ontario. It appears that no difficulty will be encountered in providing the amount you require on the terms you requested.

Mr. C. E. Cabot and Ms. R. R. Ashcroft have both signified their intention to serve on the Advisory Board of Capital Astrolite Ltd. The addition of these two prominent industrialists to your control body is a major achievement and should make much easier any further development plans you might have for operations in Canada.

Your interim account has been established at our main office in Montreal. Mr. Wells has been informed of this, and we have arranged a temporary credit for his use until such time as your account in placed on a formal basis. Please arrange to provide an opening deposit of $1,000.

Sincerely yours,

Names added to mailing list

I. A. Wilson

Cheque requisition attached for your signature.

I. A. Wilson, President

IA/ds

An annotated letter

Handling Email

Some executives expect the administrative professional to assist with their emails. If so, be certain that you understand how they want you to handle them. You might be expected to answer routine email; if so, your employer needs to know that you have done it. Here are some suggestions for handling your supervisor's email:

- Check email regularly not constantly. For example, you may check it at 9 a.m., 11 a.m., 2 p.m., and 4 p.m., or more frequently, depending on your supervisor's preference.
- Do not open email marked "Confidential" unless your employer instructs you to do so.
- Read the email, reply to the email (if appropriate), and forward it, if necessary, to appropriate individuals and copy your supervisor so that they are aware of the action you have taken.
- If the individual does not know that you routinely handle the email of your employer, be explicit in the email when you answer it. Say, for example, "Mrs. Florentine has asked that I respond to your email."
- If you cannot handle the email, send a note to your supervisor telling them. If your employer needs to handle it immediately, mark your email as urgent.

When your employer is out of town, handle the email as usual, assuming you have been authorized to do so. If not, forward the email to the appropriate person who is in charge during your employer's absence. In Chapter 10, you will be introduced to some suggestions for organizing your email.

Handling Mail in Your Supervisor's Absence

In Chapter 12, you will be introduced to some of the responsibilities of an administrative assistant while an executive is out of the office and travelling on behalf of the company. One of your responsibilities will be to handle the mail. Talk with your supervisor before they leave to understand your mail-handling responsibilities. Be specific with any questions so you have a clear understanding. Mistakes in handling mail can be costly to the company. Here are some general guidelines for handling mail:

- When you receive urgent mail (any mail, including email, that includes a matter that needs immediate handling), respond to the correspondence the same day. If you cannot answer the mail, send it to the appropriate person in your organization who can answer the correspondence. Your supervisor will usually have designated someone who is in charge in their absence. Make sure that person receives the urgent correspondence quickly.
- Promptly answer any mail that falls within your area of responsibility.
- File in a separate folder any mail that has been answered (with the answer attached); your supervisor may want to review it when they return. Create a folder in your email system named "Supervisor out of Office Sept 1–15" to hold copies of all email you dealt with in their absence. This folder can be shared with your supervisor while they are out of town or left to discuss upon their return.
- Keep in a separate folder any mail that can wait for your supervisor's return. Retrieve and add to the folder any previous correspondence that will be needed when reviewing the mail.

Outgoing Mail

While an administrative professional's responsibilities for handling outgoing mail will vary, the primary role is to ensure that mail leaves the office in a timely manner using the fastest service available. In a large organization, you would be responsible for preparing the mail for processing by mailroom employees. Mailroom employees may pick up the mail at various times during the day (when delivering incoming mail, for example), or you may be responsible for taking time-sensitive outgoing mail to the mailroom.

Mailrooms today are automated. Multi-functional equipment is used to fold, sort, label, and attach postage to outgoing mail, and software is used for maintaining mailing lists.

In large companies, the **outsourcing** of mail services may be implemented as a cost-saving measure. Firms that handle mail services for organizations include Kelly Management Services and Pitney Bowes Management Services Canada Inc.

The Internet is used extensively to gather information relating to post office services, to access related associations, and to track delivery status (Canada Post and express carriers, such as Purolator and others, provide detailed delivery tracking information online). More details on mail services and mail-processing equipment can be found at:

- www.neopost.ca
- www.francotyp.ca
- www.pitneybowes.ca

In the mailrooms of large companies, computer applications allow staff to easily record the **accountable items** (express items), including registered mail and items sent via private courier. To establish the sender's identity and enter the recipient's name, a bar code on incoming items is scanned. Mail can then be easily sorted by whatever delivery scheme is being used—by floor, building, department, or division. Mailrooms also use software to track mail expenditures by departments or divisions within the organization. Such tracking allows department managers to control their postal budgets more effectively.

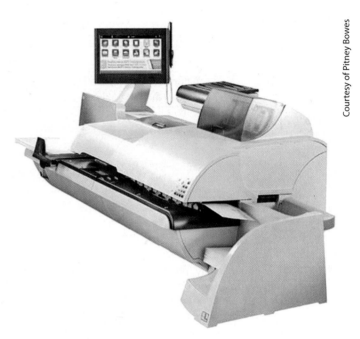

Courtesy of Pitney Bowes

Postal meter from Pitney Bowes

In a small company, the administrative professional usually has the responsibility of preparing and processing the mail, which may also involve taking it to the local postal office or calling the mailing service to arrange pickup. Whether you work in a large or a small company, your responsibilities may include preparing correspondence for mailing, adhering to automation requirements, sealing and stamping items not processed through the mailroom, and maintaining mailing lists.

Preparing the Mail

By following these procedures consistently and carefully, you can save your organization both time and money.

- Check that every letter is signed and that any enclosures noted are included. Your supervisor may require a file copy of the signed letter.

- If enclosures are too large to send with the letter and must be sent in a separate envelope, check to see that the address on the second envelope is correct. Mark it with the appropriate class of mail.
- Address envelopes carefully. Your word processing software can automatically generate a label or envelope based on the address you have keyed into the letter. As a result, you need only key and proofread the address once. Check the address against your records. When an organization's address changes, be sure to update your mailing list. Ensure you have chosen the correct envelope size so that the address placement will be correct. Figure 8-3 illustrates a correctly addressed standard envelope. Note the required blank space

that MUST appear at the bottom of the envelope to accommodate the electronic postal equipment. Review CPC's website to determine how to correctly address different envelopes (e.g., large envelopes and envelopes with graphics).
- Make sure any special mailing notations are included and correctly positioned on the envelope.
- If a mailroom employee seals your mail and applies postage, you may be requested to stack your envelopes with the flap up (piggyback style) to facilitate passing them through the postage meter.
- Insert all interoffice correspondence in appropriate envelopes (as shown in Figure 8-1) with the name and department of the addressee listed on the envelope.

FIGURE 8-3

A Correctly Addressed Standard Envelope

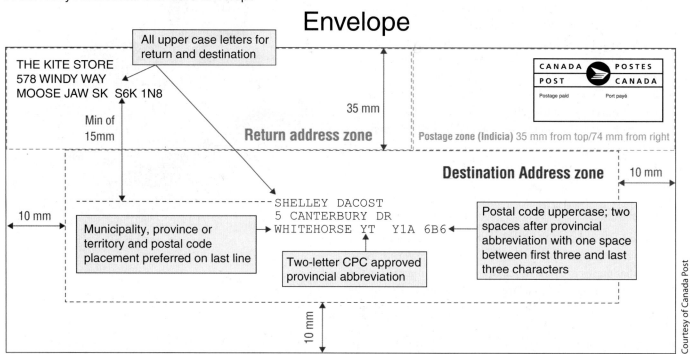

Adhering to Automation Requirements

As an administrative professional, you are responsible for properly preparing outgoing mail for the automated sorting equipment used by Canada Post and private services. Envelopes that are not legible or that do not show a postal code will require additional handling. Adhering to automation requirements ensures that mail is consistently delivered on time. In addition to being sorted by postal code, mail may also be scanned and sorted by bar code, using a **BCS** (bar code sorter). A bar code is similar to the UPC (Universal Product Code), which is found on everyday items such as groceries. When the bar code or UPC is scanned at the cashier, the price of the product is identified. When using Canada Post's Ship-in-a-click parcel

shipping service, a mailing label is generated, which includes a bar code. Private mail services, such as FedEx and UPS, also use bar codes to sort their large volumes of mail.

Dividing the country into 18 zones, Canada's six-character alphanumeric postal code system employs the following pattern: letter number letter (space) number letter number. The first letter represents the regional zone, usually an entire province or territory, with the exception of Ontario whose population size necessitates several major subzones. The two characters that follow, a number and a letter, provide additional division of the region by city, town, or municipality. The second group of characters identifies more specifically the location within a city, town, or municipality—whether

FIGURE 8-4
Canadian Geographic Postal Code Regions

The First letter in Canada's postal code system identifies each of the country's 18 regional zones.

the item is to be delivered to one side or the other of a street, or perhaps a specific building on a street or even a specific floor of a large building. In the case of CanAsian Airlines, the project company for this textbook, the postal code "T2P 4C4" represents the following:

- T designates Alberta.
- 2 designates Calgary.
- P designates an area within Calgary.

The next three-character group identifies the west tower of a large building known as the Bankers Hall. See Figure 8-4 for an illustration of Canadian geographic postal code regions.

The *Canadian Postal Code Directory* is no longer available for purchase. A postal code is quickly obtained by visiting the CPC site at www.canadapost.ca. Click on the Find a Postal Code link on the home page and you are provided with a blank field. Begin keying a business name, address, or postal code, and CPC's AddressComplete application will suggest results as the text is entered. If you require a postal

code for a new address not yet in the AddressComplete database, call Canada Post (1-900-565-2633 for service in English or 1-900-565-2634 for service in French) and, for a small fee, it will be provided. The option to locate an address when you know the postal code (formerly Reverse Search) is also available.

In addressing envelopes or packages, Canada Post requests the following:

- The address is keyed in ALL CAPITALS (using uppercase and lowercase letters is also acceptable).
- The attention line is keyed as the first line of the address.
- No punctuation is used unless it is part of a name.
- The CPC-approved two-letter provincial, territorial, or state abbreviations is used; see Figure 8-5 for approved Canadian abbreviations. A complete listing that includes U.S. abbreviations can be found in the Formatting Business Documents guide on the MindTap site for this textbook or the Addressing Guidelines on the CPC website.

FIGURE 8-5

CPC-Approved Two-Letter Provincial and Territorial Abbreviations

Province/Territory	Abbreviation	Province/Territory	Abbreviation
Alberta	AB	Nunavut	NU
British Columbia	BC	Ontario	ON
Manitoba	MB	Prince Edward Island	PE
New Brunswick	NB	Quebec	QC
Newfoundland and Labrador	NL	Saskatchewan	SK
Northwest Territories	NT	Yukon	YT
Nova Scotia	NS		

© Canada Post Corporation

- The municipality (city), province or territory, and postal code are keyed on the same line with one space between the municipality and province or territory, and two spaces before the postal code. If this line becomes too long, the postal code may be placed on the last line by itself.

More detailed information about addressing mailable items is available in the Addressing Guidelines section of the *Canada Postal Guide* provided by CPC; it can be downloaded from the CPC website. A link to this section can be found on the MindTap site for this textbook.

Here you will find examples for correctly keying the following:
- civic (street) addresses
- RR (rural route) and general delivery addresses
- post office box addresses
- bilingual addresses
- U.S. and international addresses

Technology AT WORK

The guide also provides other useful information, such as the following:
- correct abbreviations for street types, directions, and designators
- approved two-letter abbreviations for Canadian provinces and territories and for U.S. states
- English and French versions of country names

Bookmarking this handy guide will ensure you are doing all you can to expedite your company's mail. The CPC website also provides videos that show the automated processing of the mail and explain the importance of adhering to these guidelines.

Sealing and Stamping

If you work in a medium or large office, you may not be responsible for sealing and stamping the mail; the outgoing mail is likely sent to a mailroom where these tasks are done using automated equipment. Envelopes are fed into the meter and stacked, sealed, weighed, meter-stamped, and counted in one continuous operation. The all-in-one metered mail imprint serves as postage payment, a postmark, and a cancellation mark. A postage meter prints directly on letter-sized envelopes or on adhesive strips that are then affixed to larger envelopes or packages.

If you work in a small office, using a postage meter to seal and stamp envelopes saves time and ensures faster delivery since, unlike stamps, metered postage does not need to be cancelled during processing by Canada Post. Postage is cancelled when bars, the date, the time, and the location where the mail has been processed are printed over the stamps. This cancellation prevents the stamps from being reused. (See the photo of a cancelled stamp.)

Organizations can lease postage meters from one of the three approved private companies in Canada—Neopost Canada Ltd., Francotyp Postalia Canada Inc., or Pitney Bowes Canada. The **die** (an engraved metal stamp used for

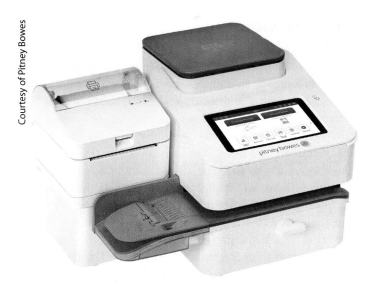

Postage meter suitable for a small office

Maintaining Mailing Lists

Most companies have correspondence they send to certain groups of individuals. As an administrative professional, your responsibility is to maintain a current mailing list. You must periodically update addresses and will occasionally add new names to the mailing list. By using the appropriate software, you can maintain mailing lists on your computer, updating them quickly and easily. You can print address labels and envelopes from your mailing lists.

Domestic Postal Services

The way we send and receive mail has changed with the advent of electronic technology. Canada Post, a Crown corporation, has committed to modernization, and in recent years has become more efficient. Reaching more than 15 million addresses through more than 6000 post offices nationally, Canada Post remains the main provider of a wide variety of mail services, only some of which are covered in detail here. Descriptions of these additional services can be located on the CPC website at www.canadapost.ca. The services offered and fees charged change periodically so it is important for administrative professionals to keep current and check the Canada Post website frequently.

impressing the postage) on the meter may include business logos or other messages that are printed concurrently and in addition to the postage. Once an account has been created with the meter supplier, either a specified amount is prepaid into the account or arrangements are made to receive a monthly statement so that the digital meters can be refilled online or over the telephone 24/7 through your meter supplier. You may be responsible for monitoring the amount remaining in the meter to determine when postage refilling is necessary. Depending on the terms of your contract with your meter supplier, another payment on the account may also be required. It is important also to consider the issue of security around the postage meter (also known as the **franking** machine). Designating one person to be the keyholder and sole operator for the machine is a proactive action in preventing possible theft of postage.

Stamps are cancelled to prevent reuse. The cancellation mark may be done by machine, hand stamp, or indelible pencil if missed by initial processing. A date, time, and location is usually included in the cancelling die.

Communicating AT WORK

Listen carefully when being given instructions for preparing mailings. The executive may not tell you whether to use Canada Post or a private carrier or which class of mail service to use. Instead you may simply be told, "This is routine," or "Be sure this contract gets to Ms. Martinez tomorrow."

You will be expected to make mailing decisions based on when the letter or package should arrive, the cost of delivery, and any special services that are needed. If you are not sure about the required delivery time or other special needs for mailing a letter or package, ask the executive for more details.

Domestic postal services (mail delivered within Canada) provided by Canada Post generally fit into one of the following three categories:

- transaction mail
- direct marketing
- parcel services

Transaction Mail

Lettermail 1

Lettermail refers to any type of mail that measures no more than 156 by 245 millimetres and weighs 50 grams or less. It includes letters, cards, postcards, financial reports, and other promotional or non-promotional mailable items partly keyed or handwritten.

Incentive Lettermail 2

Delivery of large volumes of lettermail at discounted prices can be arranged by signing an Incentive Lettermail Agreement with Canada Post. To be eligible for this rate, businesses must meet a required minimum number of items (1000 items), mail must be presorted when delivered to a CPC outlet, all items must be of the same size, and all items must meet the CPC established machineability and readability guidelines. Canada Post provides an online Do-it-Yourself Checklist to assist businesses in avoiding common errors in mail preparation that could result in unnecessary delays or additional charges.

Direct Marketing 3

Admail

Admail enables businesses to promote their products and services by delivering their message directly to specific customers, neighbourhoods, or prospects. Two types of direct mail are available from Canada Post:

- Addressed admail enables businesses to promote their products and services to specific delivery addresses.
- Unaddressed admail or householder mail does not contain any specific delivery address and is delivered to locations based on demographics, consumer purchasing behaviour, or geographic location.

Business Reply Mail 4

A self-addressed, postage-prepaid business reply card or envelope is used by businesses and other organizations to request information, raise funds, or receive payments or subscription renewals.

Publications Mail 5

Periodical publications produced in Canada may be eligible for distribution at the publications mail rate. The periodical must be published at least twice a year, be mailed in Canada for delivery in Canada, be either individually addressed or bundled and unaddressed, and contain less than 70 percent advertising in at least half the issues mailed in a year. The maximum allowable weight varies from 50 grams for individually addressed items to 22.7 kilograms for bundled unaddressed copies. Rates are based on the weight of the piece and the distance from origin to destination.

Parcel Services

Parcel services offered by Canada Post have grown to meet the evolving demands placed on businesses as a result of the exponential growth in online shopping. Offering a full spectrum of economical and timely services to urban and rural Canada, Canada Post provides delivery solutions, including delivery to a residential or business address, to a post office, or to a community mailbox. Canada Post's online tracking tool allows customers to go online or use their mobile device to determine where their shipment is at any time in the delivery sequence and, when returns are necessary, customers can access return labels from a business or the CPC website. For delivery of documents, packets, and parcels that do not exceed 30 kilograms or three metres in combined length and **girth** (a measurement around the thickest part) businesses can choose from among several CPC parcel services, including Priority™, Xpresspost™, Xpresspost™ Certified, Expedited Parcel™, and Regular Parcel™.

Priority™ 6

Priority™ is the fastest mail service for time-sensitive documents and parcels. Delivery times are guaranteed and online confirmation is available at www.canadapost.ca/track. The service operates 365 days a year. Prepaid envelopes, available in different sizes, may be purchased in advance and used at any time.

Xpresspost™ 7

Xpresspost™ offers next-business-day delivery to local and regional destinations, and two-day service between most major Canadian destinations. Xpresspost™ envelopes, labels, and boxes are available at Canada Post outlets. Pickup service is available for a fee to Canada Post account customers only.

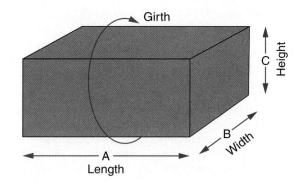

Total measurement of a package must not exceed three metres.

Xpresspost™ Certified 8

In addition to offering the same service as Xpressspost™, this service captures the recipient's signature upon delivery of the item, making it suitable for important notices or legal or court documents. If the receiver refuses to accept delivery, the item is returned to the sender.

SHIP FROM	Bill of Lading Number:
[Name] [Street Address] [City, ST ZIP Code] SID No.:	**BAR CODE SPACE**

SHIP TO	Carrier Name:
[Name] [Street Address] [City, ST ZIP Code] CID No.:	Trailer number: Serial number(s):

THIRD PARTY FREIGHT CHARGES BILL TO	SCAC:
[Name] [Street Address] [City, ST ZIP Code]	Pro Number: **BAR CODE SPACE**

Special Instructions:	**Freight Charge Terms** (Freight charges are prepaid unless marked otherwise): Prepaid ❑ Collect ❑ 3rd Party ❑ ❑ Master bill of lading with attached underlying bills of lading.

CUSTOMER ORDER INFORMATION					
Customer Order No.	# of Packages	Weight	Pallet/Slip (circle one)		Additional Shipper Information
			Y	N	
			Y	N	
			Y	N	
			Y	N	
Grand Total					

Bill of lading template in Microsoft Word

Expedited Parcel™ 9

Expedited Parcel™ is a cost-effective ground service that offers next-day local, three-day regional, and seven-day national delivery. Items are tracked, delivery is guaranteed, and status can be checked online.

Regular Parcel™ 10

Regular Parcel™ is the most economical shipping service offered by Canada Post. The standard delivery times are local delivery within two business days, up to five days regionally, and up to nine days between other Canadian destinations. Regular Parcel™ is used for mailing items such as books, circulars, catalogues, and other printed or non-printed matter that weighs no more than 30 kilograms.

Bill of Lading 11

A **bill of lading** is a document that itemizes a shipment's contents, quantity, and delivery destination. It accompanies items such as parcels or packages being shipped from a supplier to a customer. In addition to being a legal document between a supplier and a carrier, it also serves as receipt of the shipment when signed for by an authorized recipient.

Other Products and Services

Canada Post offers the following services that are beneficial in special situations: collect on delivery (COD), insured mail, and registered mail.

Collect on Delivery (COD) 12

COD, available for a fee, allows mailers to collect the price of goods or postage on merchandise from the addressee when the item is delivered. The amount to be collected from the recipient cannot exceed $1000.

Insured Mail 13

This service provides compensation to a mailer for loss or damage of mailable items. Coverage up to $1000 is available for lettermail; up to $100 on Regular Parcel™ when delivery confirmation is purchased; and up to $5000 on Xpresspost™. Items may not be insured for more than their value. To make a claim with Canada Post, a receipt or proof of value of the item being claimed is required. A detailed list of items not eligible for insured mail can be found in the *Canada Postal Guide*.

Registered Mail 14

Registered mail, which may include lettermail and non-document materials such as coins or jewellery, provides proof of mailing and proof of delivery. The sender is given a date-stamped official registration receipt, and a signature is secured, free, upon delivery. The sender can access, online and at no charge, a secured image of that signature usually by noon the following business day. A hardcopy of the signature is also available, for a fee, by contacting customer service.

Additional information, such as a list of items that are restricted or unacceptable for this service, is online at www.canadapost.ca.

U.S. and International Mail Service and Requirements

As organizations continue to expand into international markets, you may need to send documents and parcels to the United States and internationally. The principal categories of international mail provided by CPC are U.S.A. or International Letterpost, Xpresspost U.S.A. or Xpresspost International, and International Incentive Letterpost.

U.S.A. or International Letterpost 15

Items posted in Canada bearing a Canadian return address are shipped by air and can include letters, cards, postcards, and self-mailers (items without a cover) weighing no more than 50 grams and oversize items, no more than 500 grams.

Xpresspost U.S.A. or Xpresspost 16 International

This service provides fast, guaranteed on-time delivery, with signature confirmation, of documents, packets, and parcels to the United States and other participating countries at a cost much less than a courier.

Advice of Receipt 17

An *advice of receipt* is an option available for purchase when sending *registered mail—international*. The addressee's signature is obtained on the card at the time of delivery and then returned to the sender, thereby providing confirmation of delivery. *Registered mail—U.S.A.* is automatically delivered as Xpresspost, which includes a recipient signature at no additional cost. An advice of receipt card is no longer necessary and the signature can be tracked on the CPC website at www.canadapost.ca/track.

International Incentive Letterpost 18

Similar to incentive lettermail in Canada, this classification of international service caters to Canadian businesses that send a large volume of commercial mail to the U.S. and other international destinations. The three service options are premium, per item, and standard incentive service. *Standard incentive* is the lowest cost choice with the longest delivery times. Unlike premium or per item services, undelivered items are disposed of or recycled locally. *Premium* and *per item* services are airmail services that include, at no additional cost, the redirection of an item or the direct return of undeliverable mail.

Customs Requirements

All international mail is subject to the laws and customs regulations of both the originating and destination countries. Customs declaration forms must be completed for all international parcels but are not required for letterpost items. In the case of Xpresspost U.S.A. and Xpresspost International, the customs declaration form is included in the shipping label.

The Canada Post website contains a vast amount of detailed information regarding domestic and international mailing and shipping; only a limited amount of that information has been included here. Regulations, services, and rates change regularly—check the CPC site frequently to maintain currency.

Alternative Delivery Services

Private Delivery Services

Canada Post cannot handle everything that needs to be shipped domestically or internationally. Several private companies in both Canada and the United States offer local, national, and international delivery services. Four major companies—Purolator Courier Inc., FedEx, United Parcel Service (UPS), and DHL Canada—offer Canadian business customers shipping solutions, tools, and applications that can be tailored to their individual needs.

Some of the services offered by these companies include the following:
- overnight delivery of letters, documents, and packages
- daily pickup services
- online tools for selecting services, calculating rates, looking up addresses, validating and printing labels, creating a bill of lading, and tracking shipping history

You can find information about each of these companies and the many other services they provide at their websites:
- www.purolator.com
- www.fedex.com
- www.ups.com
- www.dhl.com

The UPS Store, which has many independently owned outlets across Canada, also provides packing and shipping services in addition to mailbox service. Stores pack the material, ship it through UPS, insure it, and make certain it reaches its final destination anywhere in the world. They will also stuff envelopes, meter mail, accept CODs, and hold and forward your mail while you are away.

Courier Services

When you require prompt local delivery of time-sensitive material, your best choice is likely a courier service. Within a matter of a few hours, courier services can have a messenger pick up the item and deliver it locally. Based on the size of the item and distance of delivery, the cost for this type of delivery service is generally higher than Canada Post. However, when rapid delivery is required, a courier service is your best option.

Ground Services

Some small rural communities in Canada may not have a postal outlet. Instead, bus, truck, or rail service, where available, can be used for parcel delivery. Most bus companies offer services every day of the week, and next-day delivery may be possible. Pickup service is also offered by some bus companies; check with their local offices for rates and delivery and pickup options.

Air Freight

Some of our most northern communities can be accessed only by air. The airlines that serve these locations have different rates depending on weight and the urgency of the delivery. Pickup and delivery options are also available with air services.

Managing Reprographic Equipment

Reprographics refers not only to the process of making copies but also to any piece of equipment that makes copies of an original. Most offices have digital multi-functional equipment that includes the features of a printer, scanner, fax machine, and copier. This equipment is available in different configurations and speed ratings. As an administrative professional, you may use this equipment to make copies of outgoing mail for filing or cross-referencing, to make copies of some incoming mail to route to others, or to make copies to use as working copies. It is important to make ethical decisions when doing so. Knowing the capabilities of copiers will help you understand the importance of ethical copying and avoid wasting resources by making unnecessary copies.

Copier Classifications

Copiers are classified into four basic categories, depending on their speed. The number of copies that are typically made each week or month will indicate whether you need a low-, mid-, or high-volume copier (see Figure 8-6). When purchasing or leasing a copier, you should consider the features you need; the cost of the copier, toner, and ink cartridges; and the availability and cost of maintenance and repairs.

FIGURE 8-6

Copier Classifications

Low-Volume Copiers	Produce copies in the range of 12 to 30 cpm (copies per minute) and 500 to 4000 ppm (pages per month)
Mid-Volume Copiers	Produce approximately 20 to 49 cpm and from 5000 to 80 000 ppm
High-Volume Copiers	Produce approximately 50 to 140 cpm and from 100 000 to 400 000 ppm
Copy/Duplicators	High-performance machines generally found in specialized copy/duplication centres or in print shops

© 2017 Cengage Learning

If you work for a small company, you may be asked to research and recommend a copier for purchase by the company. Consider the following questions:

- How many people will use the copier?
- How many copies will be made per month? What size of paper will be used? What are the potential costs of consumables such as toner?
- Do you expect the volume of copies produced to increase or decrease?
- What type of materials will be copied?
- What features are needed? Collating or stapling of multi-page documents? Colour copying?
- Are there space limitations for the copier? (If so, the size of the copier may be an issue.)
- Will it be used as a networked printer for a group or department?

Copier Features

Office copiers have several features that can be helpful in your work. Learn to use the features of your particular copier by reading the product manual, viewing videos provided by the manufacturer, or attending training sessions. The following features are relatively standard in all categories of copiers:

- **Reduction and enlargement.** This feature allows you to make the copy larger or smaller than the original. Reducing the size of large documents (from legal size to letter size) ensures all filed copies are a uniform size. Enlarging an original allows the document to be magnified so that fine details on an original can be made more legible.
- **Automatic document feeding.** The automatic document feeder allows you to copy multi-page documents without having to lift and lower the **platen cover** for every sheet.
- **Duplexing.** Copying on both sides of a sheet of paper is known as **duplexing**. On this setting, the copier automatically prints on both sides of the page, saving paper.
- **Editing.** Some copiers have built-in editing features. These features include border erasing, centring, colour adjusting, marker editing, and masking. Marker editing lets you change the colour of specific sections of a document to highlight these areas. Masking allows you to block out areas of sensitive or confidential information.
- **Collating and stapling. Collating** means creating multiple sets of documents that are preassembled in the desired order. Depending on your needs and the equipment being used, you can program copiers to collate only or to collate and staple sets of materials.
- **Automatic folding.** Some copiers include a feature that allows drawings and schematics to be folded into a convenient size for handling and distribution. The fold can also be **offset** (not folded to the edge of the paper) so that the folded materials can be placed in three-ring binders or envelopes.

- **Networking.** A digital copier that is routed through a network provides employees who are on the network with the capability to print, copy, fax, or scan directly from their workstation.

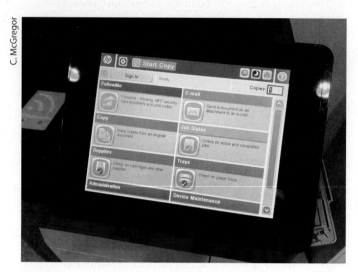

Sample copier interface

Multi-functional Digital Copiers

Installing a multi-functional digital copier can result in savings for an organization by reducing the required dedicated equipment—fax machines, printers, scanners, and copiers. This type of equipment provides an economical alternative for smaller firms. Larger firms can analyze the needs of different departments in their organization and install multi-functional copiers in areas where documents are being printed, scanned, copied, and faxed. Dedicated equipment can then be installed where only one function is required.

Cost Control

Conserving paper is **ecologically** important (important to the relationships between human groups and their physical and social environments). Many organizations monitor the use of copiers in an effort to avoid the waste that occurs when employees make more copies of a document than are actually needed. The extra copies are often made "just in case"; but, more often than not, they are eventually discarded.

To curb abuses, many organizations use copy control devices. Every system operates a little differently, but they share the same basic features. The user is provided with either an account number or some other physical device that is used to access the copier. The number of copies made and the person (or the department) is recorded, so that copying costs can be automatically charged back to the appropriate client, department, or division. This system allows managers to review the number of copies made by each person or department. If the copy count seems too high, appropriate action

can be taken to investigate whether unnecessary copies are being made.

Additional ways to control costs include selecting the proper supplies for the copying job and recycling used paper. In-house documents such as a department meeting agenda can be printed on less expensive paper, while documents going outside the organization may require higher-quality paper. Specialty papers—coloured paper, card stock, and glossy stock—may be used to create advertising brochures and flyers. These papers are more expensive than standard copy paper and should be used only when needed.

Many companies keep bins for used paper near the copier area. Pages that have smudges or do not copy properly can be put in the bins for reuse or recycling. Paper documents that are no longer needed can also be recycled. This paper may be sent to a recycling centre or shredded to use as packaging material for shipping items, representing one way that an office can go green. If your company does not have a workplace recycling program, check out the suggestions for creating such a system by visiting Earth911.com.

In addition to recycling paper, organizations need to purchase and use recycled paper products and to examine how they can reduce the use of paper in the office. In addition to using email for interoffice communication and creating electronic rather than hardcopies of documents, organizations can consider these suggestions:
- When appropriate, choose the duplexing feature.
- Reuse paper: create memo pads, telephone answering slips, and similar items or shred the paper and use it for packaging instead of plastic pellets.
- Print only the number of copies needed.
- Make hardcopies of emails only when documentation of the communication is necessary.

Ethical, Legal, and Privacy Considerations

Unfortunately, some employees use the office copier to copy materials for personal use without approval of the company. Such behaviour is clearly an ethical violation. Behave ethically by using the office copier for approved uses only. You should also be aware of the legal restrictions on the copying of certain documents. **Copyright** is the exclusive right granted to the author or creator of an original body of work to reproduce or authorize someone else to reproduce the material. Behaving ethically when copying means that you *do not* engage in the following activities:
- Copying documents for your personal use.
- Copying cartoons, jokes, and similar types of information to be distributed to your friends and co-workers.
- Copying documents you need for an outside professional group, such as a service club—unless your company

supports your work with this organization or you have approval to do so.

- Copying materials restricted by the Copyright Act, such as published works (e.g., textbooks), birth certificates, passports, driver's licences, and so on. Generally speaking, without the express, written consent of the author, the Act makes it illegal to reproduce copyright materials for commercial distribution. If you have questions about what is legal to copy, check with your organization's lawyer or check the Copyright Act.

Multi-functional digital printers and copiers scan into memory every document being copied before printing. With this "scan once/print many" feature, additional copies can be easily created without having to feed the original copy into the machine again. However, if confidential information has been copied, anyone may be able to retrieve it from the memory device in the copier. It is, therefore, important to clear the memory of the copier/printer after making the required copies to protect the privacy of individuals and the confidentiality of the document contents. Before disposing of a photocopier, scanner, or fax machine, ensure that the memory has been cleared.

Print Shops

Large organizations will generally dedicate space and specially trained personnel to handle the diverse and very large runs of copies they produce. Colleges and universities, for example, prepare a variety of documents, from graduation announcements or invitations to instructor handouts, annual reports, and calendars, all of which need special handling—special paper and binding. If your job description includes managing the production of special documents, you may need to provide original copy. It may also be possible to provide your copy to the print shop electronically as an attachment to an electronic print requisition.

In either case, the original copy should be clean, free of errors, well prepared for reproduction—handwritten copy in pencil does not reproduce well—and accompanied by a requisition that clearly spells out the final product to be returned to you. You will need to specify details such as whether you want duplexing, coloured paper, collating, stapling, and/or printing on three-hole-punched paper. When you require special details such as laminating or binding, you must factor in extra time for the completion of the job. Also, when you are preparing an important project such as a presentation to external business associates or company shareholders, allow extra time to proofread a copy before the final production begins. By immediately identifying potential errors such as a missing page or a page printed incorrectly, you can ensure that the job will be accurately and efficiently completed within the expected time frame, which will reflect positively on you,

your supervisor, and your company. Most print shops will guarantee turn around in a certain amount of time—24 or 48 hours. Be sure to consider all these factors when planning your print job.

Laminators

Laminators are used to provide a protective covering for documents such as certificates, signs, business cards, and ID badges for a conference. Cold laminators are best for heat-sensitive papers or documents printed with an ink-jet printer.

Binders

Professional-looking bound reports or presentations can be created in-house with a binding machine. The most common binding machine punches holes on the left side of a multi-page document and then binds the pages by inserting a plastic comb that comes in various sizes to accommodate a variety of projects. When preparing the original document, ensure that the text will not be caught up in the binding by offsetting the left margin of the document by approximately three centimetres or 1.25 inches.

Shredders

For those times when a copier malfunctions or copies must be destroyed, businesses often install a **shredder** near the copier. This machine cuts paper into either strips (a strip shredder) or confetti-like material (a cross-cut shredder). Over the past few years, the use of shredders at home and in the office has increased due to the impact of technology and the threat of identity theft. When documents containing confidential or sensitive information are tossed into the trash, people with unethical motives can use this information in some of the following ways:

- Social insurance numbers (SINs) and birthdates can be used to create false identity papers and open fake chequing accounts.
- Competitors can use information gathered from discarded papers to damage a company. For example, a company's bid on a project may get into the hands of a competitor who then underbids just enough to win the contract.
- Information about new technology being developed by the company may get into the hands of information criminals who use it to the detriment of society.

You can choose from among many shredder models, depending on the volume of paper or types of other media to be shredded and the level of security required after shredding. High-end shredders are capable of shredding large volumes of paper (up to 50 pages with one motion) as well as CDs and DVDs. Cross-cut shredders create the smallest pieces and therefore provide the highest level of security; strip shredders are the least secure because the strips could possibly be reassembled.

Some organizations may contract the services of a company that specializes in shredding documents and other media. During an annual purging of records, the volume of records needing to be shredded may exceed the capacity of the equipment in-house. A shredding company can either bring a shredding truck onsite to facilitate this task or can provide a locked shredding box that is picked up on a scheduled basis. Today, shredded paper is recycled by many businesses as packing material. Since mailrooms process a large amount of paper and often pack materials for shipping, they use shredders too.

Soft Skills — TEAMWORK

In Chapter 5 and again in Chapter 7 you were introduced to the importance of teamwork in collaborative writing and preparing presentations. *Employability Skills 2000+* identifies teamwork as one of the primary categories of skills that is vitally important to your success in almost all workplace situations. Review again the attributes listed there by accessing the brochure on the Conference Board of Canada's website.

In this chapter, you have learned the importance of working closely with your employer in processing incoming and outgoing mail. Understanding your employer's needs when processing mail—how it is to be sorted, organized, and routed—and working together to set parameters ensures clients or customers will receive prompt responses to their requests or inquiries. This example is merely one important team situation in the workplace; on a daily basis in various types of teams, you will work with numerous individuals—your workgroup, other administrative assistants, your supervisor, and your administrators.

A truly effective team consists of two or more people who need each other to accomplish the best results possible. Team members must complement each other's specialties. They must come together, concentrating on doing their best to win. This analogy holds true in the workplace. If you are to be an effective team member or leader, you must understand the qualities needed to make an effective team. Then you must work to build effective teams within the organization.

The effective workforce team is a group of people, each with their own special talents and skills, who work together to produce the best product or outcome. Characteristics of an effective team include the following:

- Team members are skillful in discussion. They pay attention not only to the words said but also to the tone of voice and what is not said.
- Team members have excellent inquiry skills. They ask appropriate questions of each other.
- The team encourages an atmosphere of openness and trust.
- Team members encourage new ideas.
- The team creates a safe haven for all participants to be honest in their statements and actions pertaining to the goals of the team.
- Team members actively listen to each other. They do not interrupt.
- Team members resist the temptation to criticize each other or each other's ideas.
- Each team member builds their own self-awareness. When a team member is frustrated or confused, they silently ask: What am I thinking? What am I feeling? What do I want at this moment?
- Team members explore impasses. They ask these questions of each other: What exactly has happened? What is our objective? What do the data reveal? What do we need to do? What is the best decision consistent with organizational goals?

Chapter Summary

The summary will help you remember the important points covered in this chapter.

- The administrative professional's responsibilities for incoming mail include sorting, opening, keeping selected envelopes, date- and time-stamping, reviewing and annotating, organizing, routing, and handling mail during the executive's absence.
- The administrative professional's responsibilities for outgoing mail include preparing the mail, adhering to automation requirements, sealing and stamping, using metered postage, and maintaining mailing lists.
- Canada Post classifications of mail include lettermail and incentive lettermail, admail, business reply mail, publications mail, Priority™, Xpresspost™, Expedited Parcel™, and Regular Parcel™.
- The principal categories of international mail provided by Canada Post are U.S.A. or International Letterpost, Xpresspost U.S.A. or Xpresspost International, and International Incentive Letterpost.

- Private mail services and courier services, such as Purolator, FedEx, UPS, and DHL Canada, offer fast and efficient delivery of mail.
- The administrative professional uses copiers daily and should be knowledgeable about the types of copiers and their basic features. Multi-functional digital copiers combine the capabilities of a fax, printer, scanner, and copier.
- When making copies, the administrative professional should be ethical—that is, they should avoid copying documents for personal use, cartoons and jokes to be distributed to friends and co-workers, and materials restricted by the Copyright Act.
- Shredding a document using strip or cross-cut shredders is important when the information is confidential or might be used to harm the organization.
- Recycling programs help businesses save costs and protect the environment.
- The effective administrative professional understands the importance of teamwork and is constantly developing team skills.

Key Terms

accountable items p. 135
annotate p. 133
BCS p. 136
bill of lading p. 141
Canada Post Corporation (CPC) p. 130
collating p. 143
copyright p. 144
die p. 138
duplexing p. 143
e-stamps p. 138
ecologically p. 144

epost p. 130
epost Connect p. 131
franking p. 139
girth p. 140
offset p. 143
outsourcing p. 135
platen cover p. 143
reprographics p. 143
shredder p. 145
Xpresspost p. 140

Discussion Items

These discussion items provide an opportunity to test your understanding of the chapter through written responses and discussion with your classmates and your instructor:

1. Why should you sort mail into categories before presenting it to the executive?
2. When reviewing incoming mail, what should you do when a letter lists an enclosure, but nothing is enclosed?
3. What is the purpose of annotating mail?

4. Identify the three categories of domestic postal services in Canada. Identify two of the mail classifications used by Canada Post in each of these categories.
5. Why might you select Regular Parcel for mailing a package with Canada Post rather than Priority?
6. What are two strategies a company might use to reduce copying costs?

Critical-Thinking Activity

Mr. Albertson was recently out of town for two weeks. While he was out, you became sick and had to take three days off. You called in and talked with Adelaide Stein, another administrative assistant, who agreed to handle Mr. Albertson's mail and other items. You came back two days before Mr. Albertson returned. You did not have a chance to talk with Adelaide about the mail that was received in your absence; however, she left you a note about a few things. Mr. Albertson did not understand some of Adelaide's notes to him and asked you to explain. You could not explain since you had not yet talked with Adelaide. Mr. Albertson was upset and asked you to get the information immediately. You did so, but you know that Mr. Albertson thinks you did not perform your job well. Explain what you can do now.

21st Century Skills

 Life and Career Skills
CAREER

 Learning and Innovation Skills
INNOVATION

 Information, Media, and Technology Skills
TECHNOLOGY

 Data
DATA FILE

Building Workplace Skills

Project 8-1 (Learning Outcome 1)

CAREER

You work for a small company and handle several types of outgoing mail. Individual business letters; bulk mailings of promotional letters, postcards, and brochures; confidential contracts; and small packages, catalogues, cheques, and invoices are examples of the materials you mail. Items are sent to recipients both locally and around the country. Some items require overnight delivery. For other items, two to three business days are acceptable for delivery. Promotional postcards and brochures can typically be mailed using less expensive options and with longer delivery times. Given that the items you mail have varied delivery times and cost considerations, you spend a considerable amount of time selecting mail services. What can you do to streamline the procedures you use in selecting the best services for outgoing mail? Describe the steps you could take to address the issue.

Project 8-2 (Learning Outcome 1)

CAREER

Below is a list of Mr. Albertson's incoming mail that you are to handle.

a) Explain how you would sort and place items in folders.

b) Prepare a list of the mail as it is to be arranged, listing the folder into which you would place each piece. If there are problems, explain how you would handle them. Submit your work to your instructor.

1. a confidential letter to Mr. Albertson
2. a copy of the *National Post*, a newspaper
3. a new product advertisement
4. a letter with enclosures
5. a letter sent by Xpresspost
6. a letter from China sent by courier
7. a catalogue of computer supplies
8. a letter with no letterhead address
9. a letter stating a cheque is enclosed; no cheque is enclosed
10. a letter referring to a letter written by Mr. Albertson two weeks ago
11. a copy of the magazine *Maclean's*
12. a letter sent by FedEx for next-day delivery

Project 8-3 (Learning Outcome 2)

TECHNOLOGY   DATA FILE

Access the MindTap site, using the printed access card on the inside cover of your textbook. Locate the Student Course Data file Project 8-3a, a form letter, and Project 8-3b, a mailing list. Make two changes to the letter:

1. The session has been moved to March 21.
2. The session will be held in CanAsian's Galaxy Room.
   Make the following three changes to addresses on the mailing list:

1. Luther Maston of Vitale Furniture has moved to 1915–14 Avenue NE, Calgary, AB T2E 1G8.
2. David Sam of VosDan Construction has moved to 39–22 Street NW, Calgary, AB T2N 4W7.
3. Tien Wang of S & G Imported Car Parts has moved to 108 Prestwick Avenue SE, Calgary, AB T2Z 3S6.

Look up the postal codes for the other eight names given below, and add them to the mailing list.

Once you have made the changes to the letter and the mailing list, prepare letters and envelopes for only those individuals whose postal codes start with T2E. Use the letterhead form file Project 8-3. Sign the letters for Mr. Albertson with your initials under the signature, fold the letters, and place them in the envelopes. Bundle the envelopes in alphabetical order; putting one copy of the revised letter on top. Print out a copy of the revised mailing list, sorted alphabetically by company name. Submit the package to your instructor. You may want to place a copy of the letter, the mailing list, and the merged documents in your e-portfolio.

- Mary Giovannetti, Hunt Manufacturing Corporation, 135 MacLaurin Drive, Calgary, AB
- Roxanne Florentine, Robinson Drugs, 3407–26 Avenue SW, Calgary, AB
- Brendan Mahar, The Roof Shop, 6032–5th Street SE, Calgary, AB
- Allan Argent, Kaczmarski Services Inc., 400–620 12th Avenue SW, Calgary, AB
- Janet McDonald, Soft Warehouse, 310–605 1st Street SW, Calgary, AB
- Bruce Milley, Western Business Systems, 3200–118th Avenue SE, Calgary, AB
- Tony Kwok, Stampede Organic Foods, 221–18th Street SE, Calgary, AB
- Addas Abbah, Computers Unlimited, 2807–36th Street SW, Calgary, AB

Project 8-4 (Learning Outcome 3)
Online Project

TECHNOLOGY

Using the Canada Post website (www.canadapost.ca), determine the appropriate class of mail and the mail services you would use to send the following items:

1. a package valued at $3000 and weighing three kilograms that must be at its Canadian destination within two days
2. a letter that must reach the addressee before noon on the date after it is written
3. three books that weigh a total of three kilograms
4. a package that weighs five kilograms, is worth $400, and must reach the addressee in the United States by the next day
5. a letter that must reach its Canadian destination the next day and for which you need evidence of delivery
6. a package weighing five kilograms that must be received in Japan within two days
7. valuables that are worth $5000
8. a letter that must reach China within three days

Project 8-5 (Learning Outcomes 4 and 5)
Collaborative Project

TECHNOLOGY

Work with two of your classmates on this task. Search the Web for the types of copiers available from two manufacturers; for example, copiers made by Hewlett-Packard and Canon. You work for CanAsian, and the copier is for your work area. Approximately 300 copies are made every week. It should print both colour and black-and-white copies and should have basic features such as reduction/enlargement, duplexing, and automatic document feeding. Recommend which copier the company should purchase and give your reasons. Submit your recommendations in memorandum form to your instructor, citing your Web references. Use the memorandum form file Project 8-5. As you work on this assignment, use the effective teamwork characteristics you learned in this chapter. In your memorandum to your instructor, include a statement describing how you worked together as an effective team.

Project 8-6 (Learning Outcome 5)

CAREER

Recently, your two assistants, Guy Beauchamp and Luyin Wu, have not been getting along well. Almost every day, one of them comes to you with a complaint about the other. You do not understand the problems; they seem to be petty and a waste of time. For example, Guy complained one day that Luyin was five minutes late getting back from lunch, which caused him to be five minutes late in taking his lunch. Luyin complained that Guy was pushing his work off on her. Your advice to both of them was to work together to handle the problem situations. However, the situation is getting worse, not better. You decide you need to help. You know they must work together as a team and with you as a team. What suggestions would you make to them? Submit your suggestions in a memorandum to your instructor. Use the memorandum from file Project 8-6.

Project 8-7 (Learning Outcome 4)

CAREER

You are friends with Josh Roland, another administrative assistant at your company. You have heard three people complain recently about Josh's behaviour. In one instance, he refused to let another person who needed to make only two copies interrupt his long copying job. Another time, he left the copier with a paper jam. Today, after Josh had finished using the copier, it was completely out of toner and paper, and he left it in that state. Since you are Josh's friend, you think you should approach him about his lack of courtesy regarding use of the copier. What can you say to Josh to encourage him to improve his behaviour while keeping his goodwill? Use the memorandum form file Project 8-7.

Make the Grade with MindTap

Stay organized and efficient with MindTap—a single destination with all the course material and study aids you need to succeed. Built-in apps leverage social media and the latest learning technology. For example:

- ReadSpeaker will read the text to you.
- Flashcards are pre-populated to provide you with a jump-start for review—or you can create your own.
- You can highlight text and make notes in your MindTap Reader. Your notes will flow into Evernote, the electronic notebook app that you can access anywhere when it's time to study for the exam.
- Self-quizzing allows you to access your understanding.

Visit nelson.com/student to start using **MindTap**. Enter the Online Access Code from the card included with your text. If a code card is not provided, you can purchase instant access at NELSONbrain.com.

Endnotes

1. "Parcel Services Customer Guide," Canada Post, November 15, 2013, with amendments up to August 30, 2018, http://www.postescanada. ca/cpo/mc/assets/pdf/business/parcelserviceguide_en.pdf, accessed July 2018.

CHAPTER 9

Maintaining Financial Records

Do I Qualify?

Accounting Assistant

Small company seeks responsible and motivated worker to assist management and accounting staff. Attention to detail and ability to multi-task is an asset. Duties include:

- using accounting software to enter sales and purchase transactions and prepare financial statements
- maintaining a petty cash fund and register
- preparing payroll and maintaining payroll accounting records
- ordering office supplies
- preparing daily deposits and reconciling bank accounts
- compiling monthly reports and preparing the monthly balance sheet

LEARNING OUTCOMES

After studying this chapter, you should be able to:

1. Identify and describe basic business financial services, procedures, and software support.
2. Use and maintain various financial forms and documents.
3. Reconcile a bank statement.
4. Describe the basic elements of preparing employee payroll.
5. Establish and maintain a petty cash fund and register.
6. Prepare basic financial statements, including income statements and balance sheets.
7. Demonstrate a commitment to community involvement.

Every organization—no matter how large or small—must keep financial records. While you are working as an administrative professional, the type and size of the organization you work for will determine how much responsibility you will have for maintaining financial records. The time you spend on these activities each day will vary with the size of the organization and the degree of automation in place.

A large organization may have an accounting firm or department that handles the payment of all bills, reconciliation of statements, and preparation of payroll. The role played by an accounting department or firm in maintaining financial integrity is highly specialized.

In a smaller firm, you may be expected to maintain records of financial transactions. You need to know how to invoice clients and collect on accounts, prepare a deposit slip, reconcile a bank statement, and maintain a petty cash fund. Part of your responsibilities may include preparing the payroll, which requires knowledge of federal and provincial or territorial labour standards; regulations regarding minimum wages and deductions at source for taxes; workers' compensation; and medical and employment insurance premiums.

This chapter introduces you to the types of basic financial information processed in the office and the procedures and terms related to maintaining financial records.

Banking Activities

Managing banking transactions is an important and exacting task for the administrative professional working in a smaller firm. You will need to know how to

- prepare currency and cheques for in-person and remote deposit
- process the payment of current accounts
- keep a register of all deposits made and payments processed
- understand a bank statement
- reconcile the bank statement with the register

Depositing Funds

A business chequing account is the type of bank account generally established and used by business organizations. Whether in-person or through remote capture, funds should be deposited regularly. To make an in-person deposit at your financial institution, you will need to prepare a **deposit slip** in duplicate listing all the items that are to be deposited—cash plus endorsed **cheques** (legal documents authorizing the bank to pay a specific sum to a designated payee). When a new business account is opened, your financial institution will provide a book of multiple-copy deposit slips encoded with your account number and company name.

When you present your deposit, the financial institution will remove and retain the original deposit slip and stamp the copy. The copy remains in the deposit book and serves as your record. Your organization may have numerous bank accounts, and each will have a separate deposit slip book. Figure 9-1 illustrates the most common elements of a deposit slip; the format will vary from one financial institution to another.

When preparing cheques for deposit, take care to ensure that the cheques are valid. If a cheque is **postdated** (i.e., the date on the cheque is in the future), it is not eligible for clearing. However, due to the large volume of cheques and the degree of automation, some postdated items may inadvertently be processed rather than returned. A cheque is considered to be **staledated** if it is dated more than six months earlier. Although the cheque may be returned for that reason, the institution accepting it may choose to contact the payer's financial institution to confirm whether the cheque will still be accepted. If so, it will be processed. See Figure 9-2 for some depositing guidelines.

FIGURE 9-1
Sample Deposit Slip

① The date of the deposit

② The name of the company making the deposit

③ The account that is to be credited

④ The amount of cash for deposit

⑤ A listing of cheques for deposit

⑥ The initials of the depositor and teller

⑦ The total of the deposit

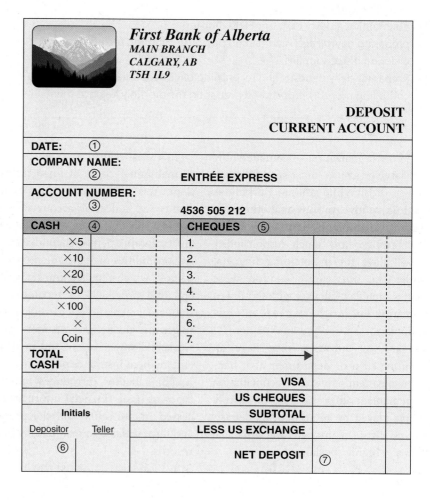

FIGURE 9-2

Guidelines for Preparing Cheques for Deposit

You should ensure
- the values expressed in words and figures are identical
- the cheque has been signed
- the cheque is not postdated or staledated
- the cheque has been written in ink
- all cheques are appropriately endorsed
- cheques are grouped together based on financial institution

Endorsing a cheque means signing it on the back. Endorsing is done by the **payee**, the organization or person to whom the cheque is written. Endorsement legally permits a financial institution to transfer monies to the payee; the institution is then able to collect the funds from the **drawer**, the organization or person who has written the cheque. Acceptable endorsement methods include handwritten endorsements in ink and a rubber endorsement stamp that shows the company name and account number.

Cheques can be endorsed in three ways (see Figure 9-3):
- **Blank endorsement** is the signature of the payee. Once a blank endorsement is made, the cheque can be cashed. This type of endorsement should be used only when the payee is at the bank and immediately before the cheque is presented to the teller.
- **Full endorsement** permits a cheque to be transferred from the original payee to another payee. The words "Pay to the order of" followed by the name of the new payee are written on the back of the cheque preceding the signature of the endorser (the original payee). Once endorsed in this way, only the second payee will be able to endorse it further for deposit or cash.

FIGURE 9-3

Blank, Full, and Restrictive Endorsements

Blank Endorsement	Full Endorsement	Restrictive Endorsement
Laura Genore	Pay to the order of Thomas Genore Laura Genore	For Deposit Only To the Account of Entrée Express 4536 505 212

- **Restrictive endorsement** requires no signature but provides the highest level of protection and "restricts" what can be done with the cheque by writing or stamping the words "For deposit only to" followed by the full account number on the back of the cheque. This endorsement specifies that the deposit must be placed in a designated account, and that it must be deposited in full—no cash can be paid out from the cheque itself. Restrictive endorsement is widely used in business, especially when deposits are made by mail, through a night depository, or through an automated teller machine (ATM).

Businesses that have a business chequing account at Canadian financial institution can access **e-deposit or remote capture deposit**. Cheques may be deposited quickly, easily, and securely anytime from anywhere with a secure Internet connection. After you have registered for online banking and downloaded and installed the app from your financial institution, it is possible to deposit individual or multiple cheques, either by taking a picture of the cheques with a smartphone or tablet or by using a compatible scanner connected to a computer. Images of the cheques appear on your computer screen, and the file can be saved for proof of deposit. Once the e-deposit is completed, identify these cheques with the words "Electronically deposited" (your institution may provide a stamp to use to do so). Store the cheques for the time required by your financial institution (usually 90 days) then destroy or store according to your organization's records management policy.

ATMs equipped with scanners can efficiently process individual or multiple cheques for in-person deposits. After an access card is inserted and the passcode entered, individual cheques can be stacked and fed into the scanner. Once processing is complete, the user may select to print a receipt with or without an image of each cheque.

Writing AT WORK

As an administrative professional, you may create documents, such as project bids or contracts, using standard text for such documents. You may write or change only certain terms that pertain to that particular project. Such documents typically contain numbers. Take extra care to make these numbers correct. Including an incorrect completion date for a project or an incorrect fee for services can result in lost money for your company.

Customers will not be happy if your company does not meet the terms of the bid. Always double-check any calculations you make from source numbers to generate numbers for the final document.

Some financial documents, such as contracts, often show numbers written in both words and figures, such as ten thousand dollars and $10,000. Using this procedure can help you identify some types of errors ($1000 rather than $10,000) when proofreading the document. Having another person check the amounts in a document while you read the numbers from another source can also be helpful when proofreading documents with numbers. After you have done general proofreading for the entire document, check the document again, focusing specifically on the numbers.

Accounts Payable

An **invoice** is a bill itemizing the goods or services bought and sold. The vendor or seller—the business organization that has supplied the service or product—presents the invoice to the purchaser. Figure 9-4 illustrates a typical invoice with common information.

A **monthly statement** documents the activities on an account—purchases as well as payments made during the month—and are usually due at the beginning of each month. The accuracy of these invoices and/or monthly statements must be verified prior to making payments. Check each invoice against the prices quoted or records detailing the prices previously paid for similar items. Verify the accuracy of monthly statements by comparing the items listed on the statement against invoices received, sales slips, and other records of account payments. When you are satisfied that the invoice or statement is accurate, initiate the payment.

Your organization may manage its accounting activities by using commercially available money management or accounting software such as Quicken or Sage 50 Accounting. These software programs include the capability of producing cheques and will post the amount directly to the cheque register. If you are not using accounting software to prepare

FIGURE 9-4

Completed Invoice for Computer Components

FIRST CLASS COMPUTERS
210 – 605 1st Street
Calgary, AB ①
T2P 3S9

INVOICE

| INVOICE TO: ② | Rasmussen Realty Services
6030 – 5th Street SE
Calgary, AB
T2H 1L4 | ③ INVOICE DATE:
④ INVOICE NO.:
⑤ TERMS: | June 23, 20--
1009932
Net 30 days |

QTY	DESCRIPTION	UNIT PRICE	AMOUNT
2	19" TFT Flat Panel Monitor	325.00	650.00
2	Internal DVD CDRW Combo Drive	150.00	300.00
2	Optical Cordless Mouse ⑥	35.00	70.00
1	Security Screen	201.33	201.33
			$1,221.33
	⑦	GST	61.07
		TOTAL	$1,282.40

① The name and address of the vendor

② The name and address of the purchaser

③ The invoice date

④ The invoice number

⑤ The terms of the sale

⑥ The details of what was sold

⑦ The total amount payable, including taxes

cheques, cheques can be written by hand or on your computer using single-solution cheque preparation software.

All cheques need the signature of someone authorized by the organization to sign on its behalf. Individuals authorized by the organization to sign cheques will have already provided appropriate documentation and signature samples to the financial institution.

Your organization's financial institution will provide you with a supply of cheques to be used for payment of invoices from companies for which the use of electronic funds transfer is not an option. Cheques are available in the following formats:

- A chequebook with a stub attached on which you record the details of the cheque being written. (See Figure 9-5.)
- A book with an accompanying register in which you record the details of each cheque written and deposits made. (See Figure 9-6.)

- A **voucher cheque**, which includes a form directly below the cheque for recording the details of the payment, can help both the company and the payee to identify the purpose of the cheque. (See Figure 9-7.)

Writing a cheque out to "Cash" is risky. Such an instrument can be cashed by anyone into whose hands it falls. Cheques should always be written as payable to a specific payee. Figure 9-8 offers some guidelines for the preparation of cheques.

Although many invoices will arrive by mail, Canada Post's epost includes a constantly growing list of companies from which you may receive invoice statements online. With epost, you can receive and pay bills and manage accounts online. You can also sign up to receive epost notifications via text message reminders and SMS text messages to your mobile

FIGURE 9-5

Completed Cheque with Stub

No. 156 $1,282.40	**Rasmussen Realty Services** 6030 – 5th Street SE Calgary, AB T2H 1L4 **No. 156**
Date July 1, **20--**	July 1, **20--**
To First Class Computers	**PAY TO THE ORDER OF** First Class Computers------ $1,282.40
For Computer Accessories	Twelve hundred eighty-two----------40/100 **DOLLARS**

Previous Balance	7,856	65
Amt. Deposited	750	00
Total	8,606	65
Amt. This Cheque	1,282	40
Balance	7,324	25

First Bank of Alberta
Main Branch
Calgary, AB
T5H 1L9

Memo: Computer Accessories   *Mark Rasmussen*

0004 123 456 987

FIGURE 9-6

Cheque Register Recording Deposit, Cheque, and Balance

CHEQUE REGISTER								
Cheque No.	Date	Description	Amount of Cheque		Amount of Deposit		Balance	
							7,856	65
	23/06	Deposit			750	00	8,606	65
156	01/07	Computer Accessories	1,282	40			7,324	25

FIGURE 9-7

Completed Voucher Cheque

Rasmussen Realty Services		156

Rasmussen Realty Services
6030 – 5th Street SE
Calgary, AB T2H 1L4

156

July 1, 20--

PAY Twelve hundred eighty-two-----40/100 DOLLARS $1,282.40

TO
THE
ORDER
OF

First Class Computers
210-605 – 1st Street SW
Calgary, AB T2P 3S9

Mark Rasmussen

0004 123 456 987   AUTHORIZED SIGNATURE

REMITTANCE ADVICE — PLEASE DETACH BEFORE DEPOSITING CHEQUE

DATE	DESCRIPTION	AMOUNT
June 23	Computer Accessories as follows:	
	2 - 19" TFT Flat Panel Monitor	650.00
	2 - Internal DVD CDRW Combo Drive	300.00
	2 - Optical Cordless Mouse	70.00
	1 - Security Screen	201.33
	GST	61.07
		$1,282.40

FIGURE 9-8

Cheque-Writing Guidelines and Tips

- Use ink to prepare all handwritten cheques.
- Date each cheque and stub.
- Using the fewest possible words, write out the amount of the cheque, starting at the extreme left of the line, putting an initial capital on the first word only.
- Write the amount in figures, starting close to the pre-printed dollar sign, and write the figures close together to prevent additional figures being added.
- If cheques and stubs are not already numbered, number them consecutively.
- Ensure that the values expressed in words and in figures are identical.
- If using cheques with a stub, first complete the stub, including details of all bills—if more than one—being covered by the cheque; then complete the cheque.
- Identify the purpose of the cheque in the bottom left corner. Some cheques include a memo line for this purpose (see Figure 9-5).

- If using a **cheque register**, enter the details of the transaction.
- Whenever space remains on a line, such as after the payee's name or in the words or figures area of the cheque, fill the space up with a line so that nothing else can be added.
- Ensure the individual name of the payee is correctly spelled. Courtesy titles (*Mr., Mrs.,* or *Dr.*) are unnecessary.
- Mistakes should not be erased or covered up with liquid paper. Write "VOID" in large letters across the face of the cheque and the stub and prepare a new cheque. Retain the cheque and stub in the files, or if using a register, record the cheque as void in the register and retain the cheque in the files.
- Obtain a signature from an authorized signatory. Ensure the signature is completed in ink.

device. You can find out more about the epost service by visiting the Canada Post website. A link to this site is available on the MindTap site for this textbook.

Business organizations generally use cheques rather than cash to pay invoices received from other businesses. Using **electronic funds transfer (EFT)**, a convenient method of managing your personal accounts payable, may not be an option for businesses. In the case of your personal account, you compile a list of payees by adding the company names and your account numbers with those companies. It is then a simple matter to select a company from the list, enter the amount of payment, and indicate the date on which the sum is to be withdrawn from your account and transferred to the account of the payee. Payments can be made for any amount up to the amount currently on deposit with your bank or financial institution.

The use of EFTs for business organizations is at the discretion of the financial institution and with the exception of Revenue Canada payments for source deductions and goods and services tax (GST) or harmonized sales tax (HST) remittance may not be permitted for security reasons. Cheques can be signed only by those persons who have signing authority, usually executives. Therefore, granting access to online banking for the purpose of making payments to those who do not have signing authority presents a security concern. Some banks are now taking measures to correct this loophole using a password protection system.

Reconcile the Bank Balance

In the previous section on writing cheques, you saw how the cheque register is used to record and track the cheques written. The cheque register is also used to record deposits to the account as they are made. You can see in Figure 9-6 that entering both cheques and deposits and then calculating the current balance after each entry maintains the currency of both your financial data and the information about the balance of your account.

At the end of each month, you will print out (or your financial institution will provide) a statement of all activities on your account for that one-month period. The balance in the cheque register will not be equal to the balance shown on the bank statement for several reasons:

- All deposits made and entered into the register may not yet have been recorded by the bank.
- All cheques you have written and entered into the register may not yet have been cleared for payment.
- Interest or other credits may have been added to your account by the bank.
- Service charges may have been deducted from your account by the bank.
- An entry or a calculation error may exist.

Accounting for the differences between the two figures is known as *reconciling the bank balance.*

If your financial institution sends you a hardcopy of the monthly bank statement, it may also include images of your cancelled cheques. These images are a record of the cheques you have written that have been cleared by the bank; that is, the amount has been deducted from your account and given to the payee. If you have hardcopy delivery, your online statement will include a link to the image of the cleared cheque, which can be downloaded and saved or printed for your file. Figure 9-9 shows the front page of a statement. You can see how the bank itemizes deposits made, cheques that have cleared, interest payable if any, and any fees charged for the month.

The back of the statement may include a form that you can use to reconcile the final balance on the statement with the balance showing in your records. An example of such a form is shown in Figure 9-10; the four steps outlined in the figure will result in identical final balances being recorded on both the cheque register and the bank statement. Your bank balance will be reconciled.

If your financial institution does not provide a reconciliation form, you can download one from the Internet or easily prepare one on your computer using Microsoft Excel. See Figure 9-11 for a sample reconciliation form.

After you have completed the monthly reconciliation, the **cancelled cheques** or the images you retrieve from your online statement will provide legal proof of payment and should be stored in accordance with company policy.

Technology AT WORK

The Conference Board of Canada has identified numeracy skills as a fundamental requirement in the workplace. Under the heading "Use Numbers," it lists
- decide what needs to be measured or calculated
- observe and record data using appropriate methods, tools, and technology
- make estimates and verify calculations

These skills can be developed at home, at work, at school, or in the community. Software programs such as Quicken or Sage 50 will reconcile the bank balance by prompting you to enter the amounts of the cancelled cheques, interest, and any fees that have been charged. Find a technology tool that is appropriate to assist in maintaining your specific type of financial records.

Electronic and Online Banking

Canadians are enthusiastic adopters of electronic banking technology, using their mobile devices and the Internet at an increasing rate to manage their personal financial records. In

FIGURE 9-9

Sample Monthly Bank Statement

**First Bank of Alberta
Main Branch
Calgary, AB T5H 1L9**

Rasmussen Realty Services
6030 – 5th Street SE
Calgary, AB T2H 1L4

STATEMENT OF ACCOUNT		ACCOUNT TYPE	STATEMENT FROM - TO	
Branch No.	**Account No.**	CURRENT CHEQUING	June 01, 20--	June 30, 20--
123	456 987		Page 1 of 1	

DESCRIPTION	WITHDRAWALS	DEPOSITS	DATE	BALANCE
BALANCE FORWARD				8,821.88
PAYMENT TO 00864501355	486.29		June 01	
AVIVA/CGU INSURANCE	57.33		June 01	
CHQ 155	114.36		June 01	8,163.90
TERASEN GAS	148.00		June 06	8,015.90
ALBERTA HYDRO	68.00		June 15	7,947.90
TELUS	91.25		June 23	
DEPOSIT		750.00	June 23	8,606.65
INTEREST		11.28	June 30	
SERVICE FEE	9.95			8,607.98
	975.18	761.28		

its October 2016 issue of *How Canadians Bank*, the Canadian Bankers Association determined that Canadians of all ages are using the new technologies available from their financial institution to make their personal banking experiences more convenient. Online banking is the preferred method of banking for 76 percent of Canadians; 44 percent do some banking using their mobile device,[1] and 40 percent expect to do so in the near future.[2]

Banks and other financial institutions are also making it easier for companies to maintain their financial records. EFT, remote deposit, and online banking access make the company's financial data instantly available.

ATMs (also known as ABMs—automated banking machines) are located throughout the world at banks and elsewhere. They enable you to obtain cash, make deposits (only at bank locations), and check your account balance any time, including when banks are not open for business. While ATM use is declining in popularity, it is still regarded as an important method of conducting a wide range of personal banking transactions—88 percent of Canadians use ATMs to make cash withdrawals[3]—most business organizations do not make use of them, unless they are sole proprietorships or small partnerships.

Preauthorized automated transfer is another method employed by both individuals and business organizations to make payments on accounts that are invoiced monthly. Preauthorized automated transfers can also be used to transfer funds from one account to another within a financial institution.

E-cheques, or email money transfers, can be used to send money directly from one bank account to another. After registering for the service, adding the name and email address to your recipient list, and creating an individual security question, you are ready to initiate a funds transfer request. An email is sent to your designated recipient with instructions on how to collect the money. A small fee may be charged for this service.

Computer or Internet banking is likely to keep growing as banks devote significant resources to developing and refining technology and security. Log on to the website of your personal bank to see what is current in personal and business online services.

FIGURE 9-10

Sample Reconciliation Form Found on Back of Monthly Statement

 First Bank of Alberta

Balancing Your Records

Follow the four steps listed below to balance your statement.

Step 1 Add to your cheque register, as a deposit, any interest paid. Subtract from your cheque register, as a withdrawal, service charges.

Step 2 Compare withdrawals and deposits on the statement with entries made in the cheque register.

Step 3 List in the columns below all withdrawals and deposits recorded in the cheque register that are not listed on this or previous statements.

DEPOSITS		
01/07	1151	25

Step 4

The Ending Statement Balance for your current account is shown on the reverse of this monthly statement.

Enter Ending Statement Balance   8607.98

Add total of outstanding deposits recorded in register   1151.25

Subtotal   9759.23

Subtract total of outstanding withdrawals recorded in register   1867.55

OUTSTANDING CHEQUES		
01/07	1282	40
05/07	585	15
	1867	55

Present account balance on your records should be   7891.68

The account is balanced when the amount above matches the last balance listed in the cheque register. If these two amounts do not agree:

- Review the above steps for entry or calculation errors.
- Check to ensure that all deposits and withdrawals shown on the statement are recorded in the cheque register.
- Check for calculation errors in the cheque register.

Notify the branch within 30 days regarding any errors or irregularities noted on this statement.

FIGURE 9-11

Bank Reconciliation Form

BANK RECONCILIATION
Rasmussen Realty Services
As of September 30, 20--

Cheque Register Balance		15,400.23	Bank Statement Balance		15,300.12
ADD:			**ADD:**		
Interest Earned		60.71	Deposit of 29/09		1,295.85
		15,460.94			16,595.97
DEDUCT:			**DEDUCT:**		
NSF Cheque—J.Lee	1,500.00		Outstanding Cheques:		
New Cheque Order	25.00		No. 206	1,272.10	
Service Charges	15.95	1,540.95	No. 207	1,403.88	2,675.98
Reconciled Balance		13,919.99	Reconciled Balance		13,919.99

Petty Cash Fund

In this chapter, you have learned that most business organizations commonly use cheques or EFTs to pay accounts and control their financial records. All business organizations—large and small—will also occasionally need to pay for small incidental items such as postage, taxi fares, specialty office supplies, or refreshments. However, it is both time-consuming and inefficient to requisition a cheque for a small amount of money if you are working in a large organization, or writing a small cheque if you are working in a smaller business firm. A **petty cash fund**—the name is derived from the French word *petit*, for "small"—is usually established to handle the payment of purchases of small incidental items required by the office in the normal course of conducting business.

You can establish a petty cash fund to cover these expenses by writing a cheque on the current account of the business. The cheque can be for any amount. Usually the amount is based on either the estimated value or the actual calculated value of previous incidental expenses over a specific period, such as one month. A member of the department or office—often the administrative professional—is designated to monitor the fund. If you are given this responsibility, follow these guidelines.

- Keep on hand only sufficient funds to cover expenses for a specific period—two weeks, a month, or a quarter.
- Complete or obtain a petty cash voucher (see Figure 9-12) indicating the amount, date, and purpose of each expenditure.

FIGURE 9-12

A Completed Petty Cash Voucher

No. 256		$50.75
PETTY CASH VOUCHER		
DATE:	May 30, 20--	
PAID TO:	First Class Computers	
EXPLANATION:	Graphics Tablet	
CHARGE ACCT:	Supplies	
APPROVED BY:		RECEIVED BY:
M.A. Albertson		*Keri-An Mahar*
Authorized Signature		Recipient Signature

- Retain receipts for all expenditures (attached to petty cash voucher).
- Record all transactions using a petty cash register (see Figure 9-13) or a spreadsheet.

FIGURE 9-13

Petty Cash Register Page

PETTY CASH REGISTER

DATE	VOUCHER NO.	DETAILS	CREDITS	PAYMENTS
May 1			250.00	
May 5	250	Postage		15.75
May 9	251	Taxi to Spence and Associates		35.00
May 12	252	Toner		49.25
May 22	253	Cleaning supplies		8.56
May 24	254	Courier		10.45
May 29	255	Disk labels		7.95
May 30	256	Graphics tablet		50.75
Totals			250.00	177.71
June 1		Cash on hand	72.29	
		Cheque No. 135 to replenish fund	177.71	

- Ensure you can account for all monies—cash on hand plus receipts and/or vouchers should equal the full value of the fund.
- Keep the cash and vouchers secure.
- Prepare a petty cash fund summary on a regular basis.
- Replenish the fund before it gets too low by requesting a cheque for the amount needed to restore the total to its original (see Figure 9-14).

FIGURE 9-14

Petty Cash Replenishment Request Form

RASMUSSEN REALTY SERVICES
Petty Cash Replenishment Request

Petty Cash Summary
May 1 – May 31, 20--

Postage and Delivery	26.20
Miscellaneous Office Supplies	107.95
Travel	35.00
Cleaning Supplies	8.56
Total Payments	177.71
Cash on Hand	72.29
Total Petty Cash Fund	250.00
Submitted by:	*Kaili Tanner*

Employee Payroll Procedures

Preparing employee payroll, a function of financial accounting, is usually handled by the accounting department of larger organizations. In smaller organizations, this service may be purchased from an accounting firm or a bank or may be assigned to the administrative professional. If it is your responsibility, you can prepare payroll by using a spreadsheet or purchase software written specifically for calculating employees' **net pay**—gross pay less required and voluntary deductions. Companies are required by law to keep payroll records and to provide employees with a statement of earnings and deductions. To do this, you must know the federal and provincial or territorial regulations regarding minimum wages and maximum hours of work, how to calculate the amount of compensation due each employee, and the amounts that are required by law and must be withheld and then remitted to the respective governments on behalf of each employee.

Taxes

Three compulsory deductions are required by law: personal income tax, employment insurance (EI), and Canada Pension Plan (CPP; or Quebec Pension Plan in Quebec). As an example, Figure 9-15 illustrates the gross pay, the required compulsory and voluntary amounts to be deducted, and the net pay for Guy LeBlanc, an employee at CanAsian Airlines. This example is based on the *payroll deductions online calculator* available on the Canada Revenue Agency (CRA) website. A link to this site can be found on the MindTap site that accompanies this textbook.

Each month, employers are generally required to remit to the federal government these amounts plus an additional amount that is equal to the employee's CPP contribution. Deductions for CPP are age dependent, and the employer contribution for EI may be adjusted if employees are provided with a short-term disability plan. Rates may change periodically or whenever new legislation is implemented, such as an increase to the minimum wage. In some provinces and territories, health insurance and workers' compensation premiums are also a compulsory provincial government deduction. In order to assist employers so that they properly process payroll, the CRA publishes a *Payroll Deductions Formula* and *Guide for Employers regarding Payroll Deductions and Remittances*. A link to these guides can be found on the MindTap site that accompanies this textbook.

Other Deductions

In addition to compulsory tax deductions, there are a variety of different deductions that may be compulsory for an organization or may be requested by the employee. Examples of these deductions are as follows:

- **Insurance premiums.** Insurance premiums include health insurance, life insurance, and disability coverage. If an employee elects to participate in these programs they may be responsible to cover a portion or the entire insurance premium.
- **Retirement savings.** Retirement savings can include RRSP programs, profit sharing, or company pension plans. Every organization will have different retirement saving options and payroll deductions will vary.
- **Garnishments.** If an employee has been given a court order to repay a debt, these repayments can be automatically deducted and directed to the appropriate court office.
- **Union dues.** In a unionized environment, employees will be subject to an automatic payroll deduction to collect compulsory union dues.
- **Other.** If an organization requires employees to pay for parking they may provide an opportunity for automatic payroll deductions. In addition, companies may

FIGURE 9-15

CRA Payroll Deductions Online Calculator

Payroll Deductions Online Calculator

Results

Employee's name:	Guy LeBlanc
Employer's name:	CanAsian Airlines
Pay period frequency:	Weekly (52 pay periods a year)
Date the employee is paid:	20---01-01
Province of employment:	Alberta
Federal amount from TD1	Minimum - 10,527.00
Provincial amount from TD1	Minimum - 16,977.00

Salary income		$ 1,350.00	
Vacation pay		$ 150.00	
Total Cash income			**$ 1,500.00**

Taxable income for the pay period		$ 1,475.00	
Pensionable earnings for the pay period		$ 1,500.00	
Insurable earnings for the pay period		$ 1,500.00	
Federal tax deduction	$ 226.47		
Provincial tax deduction	$ 109.07		
Additional tax deduction	$0.00		
Total tax deductions		$ 335.54	
CPP deductions		$ 70.92	
EI deductions		$ 26.70	
Amounts deducted at source		$ 25.00	
Total Deductions			**$ 458.16**
Net Amount			**$ 1,041.84**

Amounts deducted at source	
Union Dues	$ 25.00
Total	**$ 25.00**

Weekly Payroll for Guy LeBlanc of CanAsian Airlines

Source: Canada Revenue Agency. Reproduced with permission of the Minister of Public Works and Government Services Canada, 2018.

encourage employees to donate to charities such as United Way and provide an opportunity to enroll in automatic payroll deductions to support this initiative.

Processing Payroll

Using EFT to process payroll is much more efficient than writing individual paycheques at the end of each pay period. The bank is provided with a list of employees and the amount payable to each, and the bank then uses EFT to transfer these funds to the individual employee accounts. Employees then receive a statement showing their gross pay, an itemized list of deductions, and the net amount that has been deposited to their account. Payroll intervals will vary for every organization and can vary depending on the job position. The most common payroll intervals are daily, weekly, bi-weekly, or monthly. CRA also requires that an organization provide each employee with a T4 slip by the last day of February in each calendar year. A T4 slip outlines an employee's wages, taxable benefits or allowances, retiring allowances, deductions withheld, and any pension adjustments they require to file their annual income tax return with the CRA.

Communicating AT WORK

Administrative assistants often key or file documents that have sensitive information about employee salaries, performance evaluations, benefits, or health records. This information is considered confidential. Never discuss the information you may see or read with persons who are not authorized to know the information. Discuss confidential topics by phone only in an area where you will not be overheard by others. Be sure to have verified the identity of the caller before discussing any personal information.

Take precautions to protect confidential information while it is in your care. For example, do not leave a file with confidential information displayed on your computer screen when you leave your desk. Place hardcopy documents in a folder or drawer where they will be out of sight. Communications that contain sensitive information should be sent in a hardcopy document placed in an envelope—not by email. Communications sent by email are not secure or private. They may be accidentally sent to the wrong person or reviewed by personnel in the information technology department as part of routine checks.

Financial Statements

Although no two business organizations are identical in their operations, all managers, owners, creditors, and investors generally rely on the same two financial statements as accurately representing the company's financial viability: the balance sheet and the income statement.

A **balance sheet** shows three things:

- a list of what the company owns—its *assets*
- a list of what the company owes—its *liabilities*
- the difference between the two—its *net worth*

The balance sheet is important because it gives a picture of the financial state of the organization on a specific day. It documents the ongoing liabilities for accounts payable, source deductions, GST or HST, and the bank balance.

The **income statement** (also known as the profit and loss statement) summarizes an organization's income and expenses over a specific period of time—a month, a calendar quarter (three months), or a year. It shows the amount of money made (profit) or lost (loss) during that period. This information makes it possible to forecast future directions for the organization.

The Balance Sheet

A balance sheet provides information about an organization's **net worth** at a specific time of the year. The document itself has four main sections—the heading, the assets (current and capital), the liabilities (current and long-term), and the owner's equity. The assets section of the balance sheet should equal (i.e., should balance with) the liabilities plus owner's equity.

FIGURE 9-16

Example of a Balance Sheet

Rose Corporation
BALANCE SHEET
As of December 31, 20--
(Dollars in Thousands)

ASSETS

Current Assets	
Cash and Cash Equivalents	$200,012
Accounts Receivables	276,282
Inventories	399,026
Prepaid Expenses	52,380
Total Current Assets	927,700
Property and Equipment, Net	1,409,151
Total Assets	$2,336,851

Liabilities and Stockholders' Equity

Current Liabilities	
Notes Payable, Current	$9,559
Accounts Payable	246,920
Accrued Expenses	225,009
Total Current Liabilities	481,488
Notes Payable, Long Term	658,697
Total Liabilities	$1,140,185
Stockholders' Equity	
Common Stock	$56,587
Additional Paid-in Capital	520,989
Retained Earnings	619,090
Total Stockholders' Equity	$1,196,666
Total liabilities and Stockholders' Equity	$2,336,851

The *heading* identifies the who, what, and when of the statement. This information is displayed in three separate horizontally centred lines at the top of the page. The first line identifies the organization, the second the type of statement, and the last the period covered by the statement.

The **assets** include two types of assets of the organization—the current assets and fixed assets. **Current assets** are cash or items such as accounts receivable or inventory that can readily be converted into cash on short notice. **Fixed assets** comprise land, buildings, or equipment that will be used over the length of the life of the organization, and are virtually permanent. On a balance sheet, listing current assets before fixed assets is known as using the **liquidity order**.

Liabilities are the debts of the organization. The *liabilities section* follows the assets section, and, like it, is presented in two parts—current liabilities and long-term liabilities. Current liabilities shows the ongoing commitment for CRA trust account liabilities, such as GST or HST and source deductions, and will include items such as **accounts payable** and bank loans—items whose payment is expected to be made within the next 12 months or during current operations. Long-term or fixed liabilities include mortgages and other debts whose payments will continue over a period of time longer than one year. While the format and content of a typical balance sheet will vary from firm to firm, it should remain the same from year to year. Figure 9-16 provides a sample balance sheet for a firm called Rasmussen Realty Services.

The Income Statement

An income statement consists of two main sections—the heading and the body. The body of the income statement is divided into three subsections—the revenue section, the expenses section, and the profit or loss section. Typically, an income statement is prepared each month to show income and expenses for the month. A yearly income statement is prepared to show income and expenses for the fiscal year. A **fiscal year** is a 12-month period used for accounting purposes. A fiscal year might be from January 1 through December 31, from July 1 through June 30, or any other continuous 12-month period.

As in the balance sheet, the *heading* answers the question, *who*, *what*, and *when* by identifying the organization, the type of statement, and the period of time covered. The *when* is very important. It may be for a one-month period only or for a longer period such as a quarter or a year. The example shown in Figure 9-17 identifies the type of financial statement—"Income Statement"; the name of the company—"Rasmussen Realty Services"; and the period—one month.

FIGURE 9-17

Sample Income Statement for a One-Month Period

Rasmussen Realty Services
INCOME STATEMENT
For Month Ending January 31, 20--

Revenue:		
Commissions Earned — Residential Properties	$25,000.00	
Commercial Properties	10,000.00	
Total Revenue		$35,000.00
Expenses:		
Salaries	10,000.00	
Computer Lease	2,000.00	
Utilities — Gas and Electric	250.00	
Telephone	125.00	
Advertising	4,500.00	
Total Expenses		16,875.00
Net Income		$18,125.00

The *body* of the income statement is formatted in three vertical columns. The column at the left, the widest, is used to describe listed revenue and expense items. The second or middle column (the first money column) is used when a section has more than one item. These detailed amounts are totalled in this column, and the total is entered in the third column (the second money column). The third column at the right is the totals column. When the revenue or expense section has only one item, the middle column is not used and the amount is entered directly in the totals column. With the advent of computerized bookkeeping, the three offset columns are not as common as they once were, but the format depends on how the chart of accounts has been set up.

The first section in the body itemizes all sources of revenue under the heading "Revenue" or "Income." The next section of the body details all expenses under the heading "Expenses." Last is the net profit or net loss section. This amount is calculated by deducting total expenses from total revenues. A positive result in this calculation corresponds to a net profit; a negative result, a net loss.

Whether or not you are routinely involved in financial recordkeeping, as an administrative professional you need to understand the role played by the company's accounting department, recognize the importance of current financial information, and be able to interpret financial statements. Whatever role you play in maintaining financial records, remember that accuracy and confidentiality are critical.

People AT WORK

Careers in Accounting

The field of accounting is a highly respected and valued profession. Three former national accounting designations—chartered accountant (CA), certified general accountant (CGA), and certified management accountant (CMA)—have been united under a new single designation, chartered professional accountant (CPA). CPAs are valued for their financial and tax expertise, strategic thinking, business insight, management skills, and leadership. As your business experience grows, you may decide to develop accounting expertise and become a CPA.

You can become certified as a CPA after successful completion of a series of required courses offered at your local college or online through the CPA prerequisite education program (PREP) offered by CPA Canada plus practical experience.

You can learn more about the profession by talking to those in your organization who have earned this designation or by visiting the CPA website.

Soft Skills

COMMITTED TO THE COMMUNITY

In Chapter 3, you learned about business ethics and the characteristics of the ethical organization. Three high-profile situations illustrate what can happen when the procedures governing financial documentation are abused or ignored: the 2001 Enron scandal in the United States, the 2004 sponsorship scandal in Canada, and the Canadian Senate scandal over expense abuses, which began to be revealed in 2012 and went to trial in 2015.

In addition to ensuring that appropriate "checks and balances" are in place to protect financial integrity, the ethical organization understands that it has a social responsibility to the community. CIBC is one such organization that is "committed to investing in community initiatives that are important to our clients and employees through corporate donations and sponsorships. We support and encourage the passionate spirit of employees to volunteer."

CIBC does this through "three focus areas of Kids, Cures and Community" and "strive[s] to make a significant social impact on key national issues, such as poverty and homelessness, while still being responsive to local community needs."*

Three of its five priorities are
- supporting the charitable and not-for-profit sector in Canada
- linking its community investment program to tangible community needs
- enabling employees to contribute[4]

The ethical organization is cognizant of the needs of its community and encourages its employees to participate in community activities. For example, you and other employees of your organization might
- serve on local community boards and commissions
- participate in the local chamber of commerce
- provide leadership to solicit funds for worthy causes
- Participating in professional or community activities could give you the opportunity to practise the financial recordkeeping skills discussed in this chapter.

Courtesy of CIBC.

Chapter Summary

The summary will help you remember the important points covered in this chapter.

- Every organization, regardless of size, must keep financial records.
- As an administrative professional, you may be required to prepare or check financial forms such as petty cash, invoices, bank reconciliations, income statements, and balance sheets.

- Payroll may be prepared by the accounting department, as a service provided by an accounting firm or a bank, or by the administrative professional.
- Compulsory deductions to be remitted monthly to the government include income tax, CPP (Canada Pension Plan) premiums, and EI (employment insurance) premiums.

Key Terms

accounts payable p. 164
assets p. 164
balance sheet p. 163
blank endorsement p. 153
cancelled cheques p. 157
cheques p. 152
cheque register p. 156
current assets p. 164
deposit slip p. 152
drawer p. 153
e-cheques p. 158
e-deposit or remote capture deposit p. 153
electronic funds transfer (EFT) p. 157
endorsing a cheque p. 153
fiscal year p. 164
fixed assets p. 164

full endorsement p. 153
income statement p. 163
invoice p. 154
liabilities p. 164
liquidity order p. 164
monthly statement p. 154
net pay p. 161
net worth p. 163
payee p. 153
petty cash fund p. 160
postdated p. 152
preauthorized automated transfer p. 158
restrictive endorsement p. 153
staledated p. 152
voucher cheque p. 155

Discussion Items

These discussion items provide an opportunity to test your understanding of the chapter through written responses and discussion with your classmates and your instructor.

1. Explain how the role of an administrative professional might vary depending on the organization.
2. List and explain the purpose of each of the three different types of cheque endorsements.
3. What steps would you take to reconcile a bank statement with the cheque register? If the two are not equal, how would you try to resolve the issue?

4. List the three compulsory payroll deductions. What other payments must be remitted to the federal government?
5. Identify the major components of a petty cash fund and explain the steps you would take to establish such a fund.
6. Identify and explain the differences between an income statement and a balance sheet.

Critical-Thinking Activity

Each department of CanAsian Airlines operates and manages its own petty cash fund to cover the cost of incidental office-related expenses. In your department, Guy has been delegated the responsibility of maintaining this fund. As his supervisor, you are authorized to sign the requisition that is sent to the accounting department at the end of each month to replenish the fund.

Over the past few months, you have observed Guy opening the petty cash box and giving what appear to be small amounts to various individuals in the office. When you review the requests to replenish the fund, however, you notice that the requisition has no reference to these persons; nor are petty cash vouchers signed by these individuals included with the requisition. The policy and procedures manual, given to all new CanAsian employees, has a section on maintaining the fund. It states clearly that these monies are to be used only for office-related expenses.

While you have every confidence in Guy's ethics and integrity, and in his ability to maintain this fund, you suspect that Guy has been advancing monies to these individuals for personal use.

- How will you raise this issue with Guy?
- What questions will you ask him?
- What directions could you provide to help him resolve this issue?

21st Century Skills

 Life and Career Skills
CAREER

 Learning and Innovation Skills
INNOVATION

 Information, Media, and Technology Skills
TECHNOLOGY

 Data
DATA FILE

Building Workplace Skills

Project 9-1 (Learning Outcome 1)

Online Project

TECHNOLOGY

Using the Internet browser of your choice, search for information on computer accounting, payroll, or money management software. Many vendors of software will include an online demo highlighting the best features of the software. Run the demos and compare the features of two software programs. Prepare a summary of your comparisons and submit it to your instructor.

Project 9-2 (Learning Outcome 1)

Collaborative Project

INNOVATION

Work with two of your classmates on this task. Choose from one of the following:

a) Interview a bank manager to determine the automatic or electronic services the bank offers to its business clients. Prepare a presentation for your class.

b) Interview an administrative professional about their responsibilities for financial recordkeeping in their business organization. Prepare a presentation for your class.

c) Locate a business in your community where the administrative professional is responsible for preparing payroll. Interview them about this task and determine what software they use. Prepare a presentation for your class.

Background to Projects 9-3, 9-4, 9-5, and 9-7

CAREER

CanAsian Airlines considers itself to be a good corporate citizen. The company's mission and values statement encourage and support all company employees who wish to make a commitment to the community. CanAsian is a strong supporter of the United Way, which annually raises funds to support a variety of community health and social service providers. The annual United Way campaign is scheduled to begin soon, and you have volunteered to serve on the local CanAsian fundraising committee. You know that at the first meeting, a chairperson, a recording secretary, and a treasurer will need to be selected. You have decided to put your financial recordkeeping skills to use by volunteering to be the treasurer. At the meeting, your offer is accepted, and you will now begin to keep track of all income and expenses during the three-month campaign.

Complete Projects 9-3, 9-4, and 9-5 and submit them to your instructor.

Project 9-3 (Learning Outcome 2)

CAREER   DATA FILE

As a first step, you have opened a chequing account (215 331 789). You will deposit all funds received to this account and use it to make payments as necessary. The bank has provided you with a cheque register to document and record all transactions. The campaign officially begins the first week of October and in that week you receive several contributions. They included cheques as follows:

Martin Albertson	$1500	Luyin Wu	$120
Guy Beauchamp	$ 75	Keri-An Mahar	$500
James Robertson	$ 600	Greg Lee	$250

Each department at head office has held a 50/50 draw where the proceeds of ticket sales are divided equally between the winner and the fundraising campaign. At the end of the week, in addition to the cheques noted above, you also have the following cash to be readied for deposit: fifty $1 coins, thirty-five $2 coins, ten $5 bills, three $10 bills, and two $20 bills.

A cheque register, a deposit slip, and six cheques are available in files Project 9-3a, 9-3b, and 9-3c. Use the information provided to complete the deposit slip. Be sure to put a restrictive endorsement on the cheques and record the deposit in the cheque register.

Throughout the month you continue to receive direct contributions and cash funds from raffles and 50/50 draws. The weekly deposit totals are as follows:

Week 2	$5346 (cash $346; cheques $5000)
Week 3	$2894 (cash $594; cheques $2300)
Week 4	$1785 (cash $285; cheques $1500)

Assume that you have made these deposits at the end of each week and that you have entered them into the cheque register. (In an actual situation, you would also issue individual receipts for each contribution.)

Project 9-4 (Learning Outcome 2)

The fundraising committee had some interesting ideas to encourage the widest possible involvement of the employees at head office. Implementing these ideas required the purchase of some items. You have received several invoices. At the beginning of the last week of the month, you have set aside time to pay the invoices. As you are the person who opened the bank account, you are authorized to sign the cheques.

Cheque forms are contained in file Project 9-4. Use the following information to prepare these cheques. Be sure to also enter the amounts into the cheque register.

Lumiere Restaurant	$250	(raffle prize of a dinner for two)
Staples Office Supplies	$33.33	(raffle and 50/50 draw tickets)
The Casual Gourmet	$65.23	(fundraising committee lunch)
The Village Bouquet	$65.75	(floral arrangement—monthly raffle sales winner)
High River Rentals	$250	(rental of barbecue for luncheon)

Project 9-5 (Learning Outcome 3)

In the first week of November, you receive the first monthly statement from the bank (Project 9-5a). The balance as of the end of October is $10 977.76, which includes interest of $20.84 and processing fees of $2.85. You notice that the last deposit you made was too late to have been captured in this statement,

and that two of the cheques you wrote, for Staples and The Village Bouquet, do not appear on the list of cancelled cheques. Print a copy of the reconciliation form Project 9-5b. Reconcile the bank statement with the cheque register you have created based on the transactions recorded in Projects 9-3 and 9-4.

Project 9-6 (Learning Outcome 5)

Guy is taking an extended vacation and will be away from the office for the next month. Usually you would delegate the responsibility of maintaining the petty cash fund to another member of your staff, but because Luyin is still fairly new, you have decided to add this job to your other duties.

Guy has processed the replenishment request, so you will be starting a new petty cash register for this month. The balance is $150. Print out a copy of the petty cash register form Project 9-6a. Record the amount of $150 on the first line of the Credits column. (Use the current month of the year in completing this exercise.)

The following were the cash payments you made from the petty cash fund during this month:

Day	Voucher No.	Description	Amount
1	115	Whiteboard pens	$ 7.34
5	116	BlueLine Taxi to airport	$15.00
8	117	Floral arrangement	$21.39
15	118	Coffee supplies	$18.48
25	119	Courier	$13.65
30	120	Plant fertilizer	$ 6.41

Total the cash payments and calculate the balance as of the end of the month. Forward the balance to the beginning of the next month and, using the petty cash replenishment form Project 9-6b, summarize the month's expenses and prepare a request for funds.

Project 9-7 (Learning Outcome 6)

Fast-forward to the end of December and the conclusion of the United Way campaign at CanAsian's head office. It has been a very successful campaign, and employees at the head office location have been very generous in their direct contributions and participation in the various fundraising activities organized by the committee. It is now time to prepare a statement itemizing the revenues raised and the expenses incurred. As treasurer of the committee, you have this responsibility (see Figure 9-17 for an example).

Combine the information in Projects 9-3, 9-4, and 9-5 regarding revenues raised and expenses incurred in the first month of the campaign with the following data:

Month 3	
Cheques from various individuals	2210.00
Karaoke night—ticket sales	3000.00
50/50 draw and raffle sales	985.00
Purchase flowers—monthly prize winner	65.75
Printing charges	210.00
Bank interest	40.05
Bank service charges	1.25
Month 2	
Cheques from various individuals	1500.00
Barbecue lunch ticket sales	900.00
50/50 draw and raffle sales	1500.00
Purchase flowers—monthly prize winner	65.75
Paper napkins, etc.—barbecue	105.55
Bank interest	25.32
Bank service charges	1.25

Project 9-8 (Learning Outcome 4)

CAREER

One of the other administrative assistants at CanAsian is about to return to work after being on maternity leave for the past year. She will be employing a live-in nanny to care for her child and asks you to provide her with some information on preparing payroll for this person. Based on the minimum wage for 40 hours per week in your province or territory, use the online payroll calculator on the Canada Revenue Agency website to provide her with an example. She plans to pay her employee monthly and will include a portion of the amount required by your province or territory for vacation pay in each payroll. Print out a copy of the calculations and the employer remittance summary that show her the monthly amounts she will need to remit to the federal government for these three compulsory deductions.

Project 9-9 (Learning Outcome 6)

TECHNOLOGY   CAREER

Add to your e-portfolio by describing how you can demonstrate a commitment to community involvement. For example, if you have an interest in assisting with the education of young children, you might volunteer to help in an elementary school; or if you enjoy working with people who are ill or injured, you might volunteer to work in a hospital. The purpose of this project is to encourage you to think about your strengths and interests so you can assist your community. Remember, the ethical organization and individual seek to give back to the community in whatever way possible. Think futuristically and commit to working in your community in the future. You will not be engaging in this activity this semester unless you decide you want to. Save your reflections under an appropriate name in your e-portfolio folder.

Make the Grade with MindTap

Stay organized and efficient with MindTap—a single destination with all the course material and study aids you need to succeed. Built-in apps leverage social media and the latest learning technology. For example:

- ReadSpeaker will read the text to you.
- Flashcards are pre-populated to provide you with a jump-start for review—or you can create your own.
- You can highlight text and make notes in your MindTap Reader. Your notes will flow into Evernote, the electronic notebook app that you can access anywhere when it's time to study for the exam.
- Self-quizzing allows you to access your understanding.

Visit nelson.com/student to start using **MindTap**. Enter the Online Access Code from the card included with your text. If a code card is not provided, you can purchase instant access at NELSONbrain.com.

Endnotes

1. "How Canadians Bank," Canadian Bankers Association, https://www.cba.ca/Assets/CBA/Files/Article%20 Category/PDF/info-howCanadiansBank-poll-2016-en.pdf, accessed, July 30, 2018.
2. "How Canadians Bank."
3. "How Canadians Bank."
4. "Community Investment," CIBC 2014 Corporate Responsibility Report and Public Accountability Statement, http://corporateresponsibilityreport.cibc.com/pdfs/social.pdf, accessed May 16, 2015.

CHAPTER 10

Managing Physical and Electronic Records

LEARNING OUTCOMES

After studying this chapter, you should be able to:

1. Define records management and explain how it is used within an organization.
2. Describe equipment, supplies, and media for filing physical and electronic records.
3. Describe types of records storage systems.
4. Apply the rules for indexing records.
5. Apply filing procedures for physical and electronic records.
6. Demonstrate improved decision-making skills.

Do I Qualify?

Administrative Assistant—Corporate Records

Fast-paced law office is looking for a hard-working and reliable administrative assistant to perform the following duties:

- assist lawyers and paralegals with extended file searches
- open files and maintain a bring-forward system to ensure follow up and receipt of requested materials and documents
- maintain a filing system; store, and retrieve files at the request of lawyers and paralegals
- coordinate case transfers, including creating inventory lists for files
- process files for off-site storage
- independently review and process correspondence on a daily basis
- communicate filing backlog and any other file-room issues to the team leader
- Dependability, attention to details, effective decision-making skills, and the ability to follow and interpret procedures are required for success in this job

---

Technology has significantly impacted the handling of records within an organization. We have the ability to create, use, maintain, and store records electronically without ever making paper copies. However, we seem to want both, and as a result, we are seeing an explosion in the amount of paper records and electronic records being generated.

People will often read an email and then print out a paper copy even though an electronic copy can be easily maintained; or a document is scanned for electronic storage and also stored in a physical file. We seem to have difficulty giving up paper even when we have excellent technological records management capabilities.

What does this situation mean for the administrative professional in today's workplace? It means you need to be proficient in both physical (paper) and electronic records management systems. It is important that essential physical or electronic information be quickly retrievable when it is needed. Whenever a record cannot be located or quickly retrieved, it is both a frustrating and costly process. Any delay in record retrieval can

- cost the organization hundreds or possibly thousands of dollars
- require decisions to be made on the basis of incomplete information
- result in the loss of a valuable client

A record that cannot be found or is lost can have a more significant impact on an organization because it can

- result in a lawsuit
- negatively impact a legal case because of missing information

The administrative professional is the individual most often held responsible for locating a record and for doing so in a timely manner. An understanding of records management procedures and techniques can simplify the process for you and allow you to be known as the person who can locate needed materials instantly—a skill that can make you invaluable to your supervisor and the organization.

This chapter first covers records management in general and detailed coverage of the management of physical records. It concludes with records management techniques related to electronic records.

Records Management

Because records are so valuable, they must be properly managed. **Records management** is defined as the systematic control of records from the creation of the record to its final disposition. A **record** is any type of recorded information. This information may be a printed document, such as a letter or report, or an electronic file, such as an email message or spreadsheet table. In some organizations, sound recordings, movies, photographs, and images on a variety of media may also be considered records. Successful organizations use the information in records to make decisions, handle daily operations, and plan for the future.

Records Value and Life Cycle

Records are important because they provide a history of a business or an organization. Based on their content and purpose, records' value to a business or an organization may be administrative, legal, or historical. (See Figure 10-1.)

FIGURE 10-1

Records Values

Value of Records

Area	Examples
Legal	Articles of incorporation, contracts, deeds
Financial	Budgets, balance sheets, income statements, receipts for travel and equipment purchases, bank statements
Historical	Employee evaluations, payroll records, job termination records
Daily Operations	Policy and procedures manuals, organization charts, minutes of meetings, sales reports, production reports

© 2017 Cengage Learning

After records are created or received by an organization, they are distributed manually or electronically, internally or externally to the appropriate individual or individuals. They have value for a period of time. During this time, records are stored and may be retrieved for use. Eventually, most records are destroyed because they are no longer useful. The records life cycle has five phases (Figure 10-2):

1. creation or receipt of the record
2. distribution of the record internally or externally to people who use the information
3. use of the record (making decisions, locating information, etc.)
4. maintenance of the record (storing and retrieving as needed)
5. disposition of the record (retaining or destroying)

FIGURE 10-2

Life Cycle of a Record

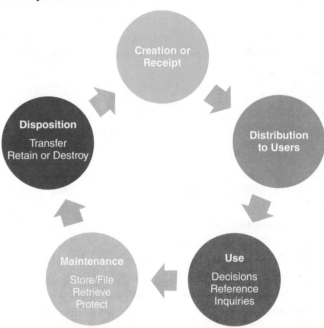

Records Management Components

The first step in establishing an effective records management system is the creation of a comprehensive set of organizational policies and procedures for managing the life cycle of a record.

The records management department, or the person in charge of records management, must clearly document the policies and procedures for managing the records, either in a manual or on the organization's intranet. This document should include how records are to be stored, how long they are to be kept active, and how inactive records are to be stored and destroyed. Without such guidelines, personnel in different departments may store records differently, which can result in confusion, mishandling of records, and loss of important records. Following is a list of the essential components of a records management system:

- an organizational set of policies and procedures for managing the life cycle of a record
- necessary equipment and media
- appropriate filing supplies
- record storage system or systems
- adherence to established indexing rules appropriate for the storage system
- retention schedules
- established procedures for moving files from active to inactive status, and guidelines governing their destruction
- procedures for maintaining and updating the records management system
- records management manuals and ongoing training for personnel

These components, explained in detail in the next sections, are necessary for a physical system, an electronic system, or a hybrid system that combines the two (prevalent in most organizations).

Legal Requirements for Managing Physical and Electronic Records

In Canada, it is important for organizations to comply with legal requirements related to the collection, distribution, storage, and destruction of physical and electronic records. Legal requirements will vary depending on the goods and services provided by each organization. The various legal requirements include the following:

- **The Personal Information Protection and Electronic Documents Act (PIPEDA).** PIPEDA applies to how organizations collect, use, and disclose personal information. The Office of the Privacy Commissioner of Canada's website outlines the organizations that are bound by this legislation and details how they can ensure compliance with the requirements. Different provinces have created similar legislation to PIPEDA, which is also available for review. A link to the site is available on the MindTap site for this textbook.
- **Legal records.** The Law Society of Ontario has established guidelines for lawyers with respect to file management practices. These guidelines as well as essential requirements are available on the Law Society's website. A link to the site is available on the MindTap site for this textbook.
- **Medical records.** The Canadian Medical Association has established a records management policy for medical

practitioners. This policy and related information is available on the Canadian Medical Association's website. A link to the site is available on the MindTap site for this textbook.

Managing Physical Records

Physical records include items such as traditional paper documents (forms, correspondence, contracts, reports, and hardcopy printouts of email or Web pages), microfilm rolls or microfiche sheets, films, videos, recordings, and photographs.

Equipment

Vertical files store physical records in traditional storage drawer cabinets, with the most common vertical file cabinets having four drawers. Lateral files are similar to vertical files except that the entire file drawer rolls out sideways, exposing the entire contents of the drawer at once. Less aisle space is needed for a lateral file cabinet than for a vertical file cabinet.

Movable-aisle systems consist of modular units of open-shelf files placed directly against each other. The cabinet has a wheel at the end of the unit that permits convenient and safe movement. In larger systems, wheels or rails permit the individual units to be moved manually or electrically on tracks in the floor. Safety features may include an infrared photoelectric beam that automatically resets itself when the person or object is no longer breaking the beam. A key-operated carriage lock or a pressure-sensitive strip running the length of the file cabinet at floor level is another safety measure that prevents the system from moving. To ensure the security of records, magnetic identity access fobs are swiped through a reader or a password code is entered, permitting only authorized personnel entrance to the system. These movable systems take up less space than standard files, making them a viable option for organizations with a high volume of active records. As many organizations have limited storage space, offsite storage can often be a good alternative. When implemented, it requires careful management by the administrative professional. A complete and accurate listing of all records stored offsite and the time required to retrieve these records must be kept onsite. Advance notice (often 48 hours) is typically required to access and retrieve offsite records.

Supplies

Basic filing supplies for physical records include file guides, file folders (manila, hanging, or suspension type), and file folder labels.

Lateral files use less space than vertical files.

File Guides

A file guide, usually made of heavy pressboard, is used to separate the file drawer into sections. Each guide has a tab on which is printed a name, a number, or a letter representing a section of the file drawer in accordance with the filing system. Guides with hollow tabs in which labels are inserted are also available. The filing designation (known as the **caption**) is keyed on the label and inserted in the tab. Figure 10-3 illustrates one type of file guide. Guides are always placed in *front* of the folders.

FIGURE 10-3
File Guide

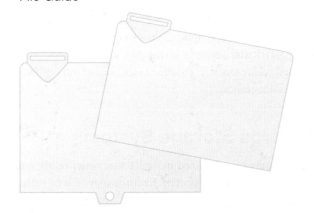

File Folders

A file folder is generally made of manila (strong paper or thin cardboard) in one of two sizes—either letter size (8-1/2 × 11 inches, or 216 × 279 mm) or legal size (8-1/2 × 14 inches, or 216 × 356 mm). Folders are also available in a variety of colours.

The filing designation for the correspondence placed in the folder is keyed on a file folder label, which is then affixed to the tab of the folder. The tab may be at the top of the folder for traditional drawer files or on the side of the folder for open-shelf filing. Folders are made with tabs of various widths, called **cuts**, designated straight cut, one-half cut, one-third cut, and one-fifth cut. File folders may be purchased with these cuts in various positions. For example, if you are buying folders of one-third cut, you may want to have all the tabs in first position (on the left). Or you may want to also have the tabs in the second (in the centre) and third (on the right) positions. By choosing tabs in all three positions, you are able to see the file captions on three folders at once. Figure 10-4 illustrates the cuts in various positions.

Movable-aisle systems save space.

FIGURE 10-4
Folder Cuts

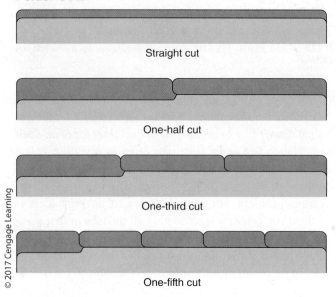

Straight cut

One-half cut

One-third cut

One-fifth cut

© 2017 Cengage Learning

As the number of sheets in a folder increases, the records will tend to ride up in the folder and may begin to cover the label. To prevent this, use the score lines along the bottom edge of the folder to refold the folder, giving it a flat base on which the documents can rest. Each score line accommodates approximately 25 sheets of paper. A file folder can store a maximum of 100 sheets of paper, at which point it should be subdivided into two folders. Figure 10-5 illustrates the score lines and the flat base that is created when they are used.

FIGURE 10-5
Score Lines

© 2017 Cengage Learning

Hanging or suspension folders are another choice in storage equipment. Small metal rods attached to the folders allow them to hang on the frame, which is placed in the file drawer. Using the precut slots on the folder, plastic tabs and insertable labels may be placed in any position on the folder. One or more standard folders can be placed in the hanging folder to group similar files together. Similar to score lines on standard folders, box-bottom hanging folders

have cardboard inserts that fit into the bottom of the folder to expand the base of the folder (Figure 10-6). These are used for storing larger records (binders) or groups of manila folders.

FIGURE 10-6
Box-Bottom Suspension Folders

Photo by Dick Hemingway

Score lines on folders or box-bottom folders provide a flat base for record storage.

File Folder Labels

File folder labels can be purchased as pressure-sensitive adhesive paper in continuous strips or sheets. Your computer software programs have features to format standard label sizes. Using the software features makes it easy to create and print labels.

Labels are available in white, a variety of colours, or white with a coloured strip at the top. Using colour on labels can speed up the process of filing and finding records, and can help to eliminate misfiling. Coloured labels may be used to designate a particular subject (green for budget items; blue for personnel items), to identify a project that extends past one year, to indicate geographic divisions of the country, or to designate particular sections of the file. It is then easy to spot a misfiled folder since its coloured label will stand out from the surrounding labels.

Records Storage Systems

Records may be organized in alphabetic order using a name, subject, or geographic system. Records may also be organized in numerical order. The organization used should be the one best suited to the needs of the organization.

Alphabetic Storage Method

The alphabetic storage method uses the letters of the alphabet to determine the order in which a record is filed. This is the most common method used and is found in one form or another in every organization. An alphabetic system has many advantages:

- It is a **direct access** system. There is no need to refer to anything except the file to find the name.
- The dictionary arrangement is simple to understand.
- Misfiling is easily detected by alphabetic sequence.

Figure 10-7 illustrates an alphabetic file for physical records. Records are filed according to the basic alphabetic filing rules, which are introduced in the next section of this chapter.

In this example, the primary guides are placed in first position (at the left). Special guides, used to lead the eye quickly to a specific area of the file, are in second position (in the middle). Individual folders, such as ARNOUX GERALD, hold only records related to that individual or company.

A general folder (also known as a miscellaneous folder) holds records for names that do not have enough records (usually three to five records) to warrant an individual folder. The general/miscellaneous folder is always placed at the end of each section.

FIGURE 10-7
Alphabetic File

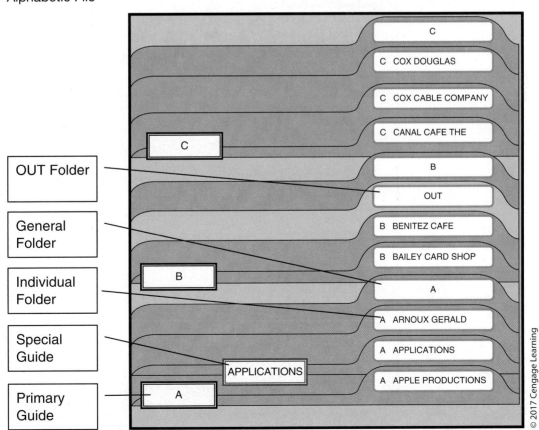

© 2017 Cengage Learning

The Out Folder indicates that a folder normally stored in that location has been removed. Working with out guides, out folders, and out sheets is covered later in this chapter.

Variations of the alphabetic storage method include the **subject storage method** (arranging records by their subject) and the **geographic storage method** (arranging records by geographic location).

Subject Storage Method

Subject storage method filing is widely used in most organizations. Although subject order is useful and necessary in certain situations, it is the most difficult classification to maintain. Every record must be read completely to determine the subject—a time-consuming process. Determining the subject is difficult to control, since one person may read a record and decide the subject to be one thing and another person may read the record and decide the subject is something entirely different. For example, one person classifying records about "advertising promotions" may decide that the subject is *Advertising* while another may decide that the subject is *Promotions*.

Figure 10-8 shows a subject file. The main subjects are indicated by the primary guides in the first position. Secondary guides indicate subdivisions of the main subjects. A subject folder holds records for each secondary guide. A general/miscellaneous folder holds other records on that subject that do not have enough records for a separate subject folder. For example, records for customer services that are not related to discount cards would be in the customer services general/miscellaneous folder.

A permanent cross-reference guide directs filers to look for records related to *advertising* under *promotions*.

A subject system can be a direct or indirect access system. When the system is direct, the subject file is simple (with only a few subjects), and access can be obtained directly through its alphabetic title. Keeping the subjects in alphabetic order is necessary. Most subject systems, however, are more complex and locating records is indirect—requiring some type of index. An **index** is a listing of the names or titles used in a filing system. Without an index, it is almost impossible for the subject storage method to function satisfactorily. This index may include several levels, and terms for cross-referencing can

FIGURE 10-8
Subject File

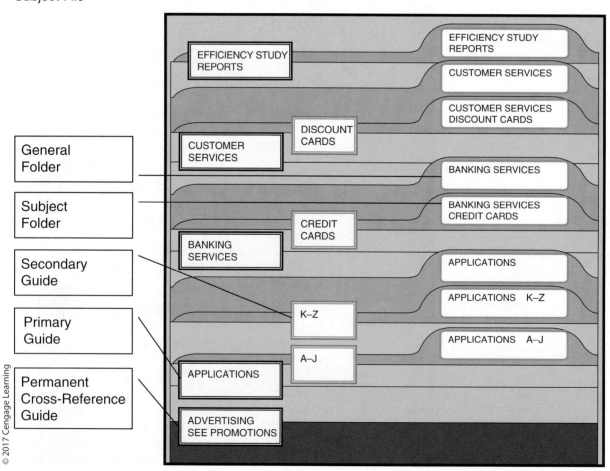

FIGURE 10-9
Three-Level Subject Index

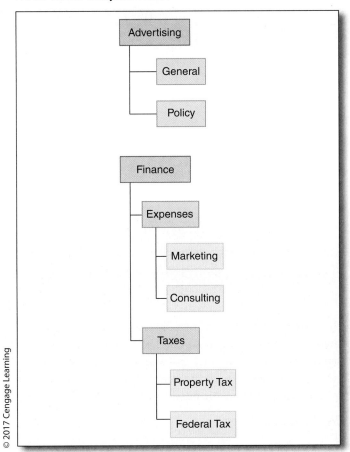

Advertising Art & Layout Service
See Artists—Commercial; Graphic Designers

Doctors
See Chiropractic Physicians; Clinics; Dentists; Hospitals; Optometry, Physicians & Surgeons—MD; Physicians & Surgeons—DO; Physicians & Surgeons—Podiatrists

© 2017 Cengage Learning

also be incorporated. Figure 10-9 illustrates a three-level subject index. The index should be kept up to date as new subjects are added and old subjects are eliminated. When new subjects are added, the index provides guidance, and helps to avoid the duplication of subjects.

Notice above that all dentists are grouped together, all hospitals are grouped together, and so on. If this information were filed using a straight alphabetic method, each dentist would be listed by their name and each hospital would be listed by its name. If arranged in straight alphabetic order, finding information without knowing the specific name of a hospital or a dentist could be impossible.

Geographic Storage Method

Geographic storage method is another variation of an alphabetic system in which related records are grouped by place or location. Geographic filing is considered a direct method if you know the location of the business or individual. When you do not, it is an indirect system and requires a separate geographic index file in a physical system or the appropriate

keywords (unique identifiers) set up for an electronic system so you can query the system in a variety of ways.

Figure 10-10 illustrates a geographic arrangement. Geographic filing is particularly useful for

- utility companies—street names and numbers are of primary importance in troubleshooting
- real estate firms—they organize listings according to city, district, or municipality
- sales organizations—they track the geographic location of their customers
- government agencies—they file records by province or territory, municipality, or other geographic division

FIGURE 10-10
Geographic File

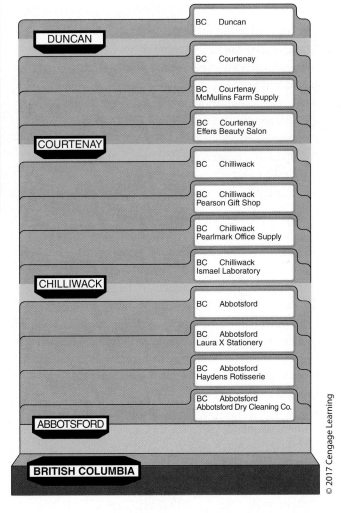

© 2017 Cengage Learning

In a physical geographic system, you file records by province or territory and city; file guides are used to indicate the province or territory and city. File folders are arranged alphabetically behind the guides, with labels on tabs identifying the company or individual. Folders are divided into three types: individual folders, city folders, and a general provincial or territorial folder (not illustrated but would be placed at the end of the provincial or territorial section in the drawer). Individual folders hold records for one person or company. City folders hold other records for that city. General provincial or territorial folders hold records for that province or territory that do not relate to one of the individual or city folders.

Numeric Storage Methods

The system that provides the highest level of security is the numeric system. This type of system maintains confidentiality because names do not appear on the guides or folder labels. With the *numeric storage method*, records are assigned numbers and then arranged in a numeric sequence when stored. The numeric method is particularly useful to the following businesses:

- insurance companies that maintain records according to policy numbers
- law firms that assign a case number to each client
- real estate agencies that list properties by code numbers

The physical numeric file has four basic parts:

1. The **accession log** (a document that records the numbers that have been assigned), which *must* be accurately maintained and printed out regularly.
2. An alphabetic index (a file containing the names of individuals, organizations, and companies and the numbers they have been assigned)
3. An alphabetic general file (for records that are not assigned a number)
4. a numeric file

In practice, here is how the numeric method works:

1. When a document is ready to be filed, the alphabetic index is consulted to determine the number that has been assigned to that particular client or customer.
2. The assigned number is placed on the document; the document is placed in the numeric file.
3. If the filing name is new and no number has been assigned, the document may be placed in the alphabetic file until the client or customer has enough documents (a minimum of three to five) to open an individual numeric file.
4. If it is necessary to establish a new numeric file, the accession log is consulted and the next number in numeric sequence is assigned.

Three variations of numeric filing are described below:

- consecutive number filing
- terminal-digit filing
- alphanumeric filing

Consecutive Number Filing

Figure 10-11 illustrates the numeric method with records arranged in consecutive order. In the *consecutive storage method*, also called *serial* or *straight-number* filing, each digit is an indexing unit. The first digits of a number are compared to determine the filing order. Similar to an alphabetic system where units or characters in units are compared to determine

© 2017 Cengage Learning

FIGURE 10-11
Numeric File

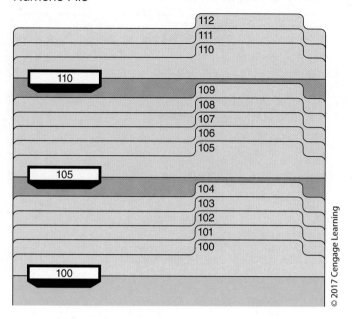

the correct order, when the first digits are the same, the second digits are compared, and so on. The numbers used may be part of the record itself, such as a number on an invoice, or the number may be written on the record. As each new numeric file is added to the system, the number assigned becomes higher.

Terminal-Digit Filing

Terminal-digit filing is another variation of the numeric storage system. In the consecutive numeric method, as the files increase, the numbers, assigned to new files in numeric sequence, become higher or longer. Each new file needs to be placed behind all the lower-numbered files. A disadvantage of this system occurs when the numbers become several digits long; filing items correctly becomes difficult, as all new files tend to congregate disproportionately in one location of the system.

One remedy is to use terminal-digit filing, in which the digits are separated into groups of two or three digits with either a space or hyphen separating the groups of numbers (Figure 10-12). For example, assume that you are setting up a file, and the file number is 129845. That number would be indexed in two-digit groups (12-98-45). By adding zeros to the left of a smaller number, three groups are created (the number 69845 becomes 06-98-45). The last two or three digits of a six- or nine-digit number, respectively, are used to identify the primary division for storing the records, and the numbers are coded from right to left rather than left to right.

The document with file number 129845 would be indexed first by the last two digits, 45. The next digits indexed would be 98, then 12. The document would be stored in a drawer labelled 45, behind a guide labelled 98, in a folder labelled 12 directly behind the one labelled 11. The next number assigned in chronological order would be 12-98-46. The primary unit would be 46, so the file would be placed in a different drawer,

FIGURE 10-12
Terminal-Digit System

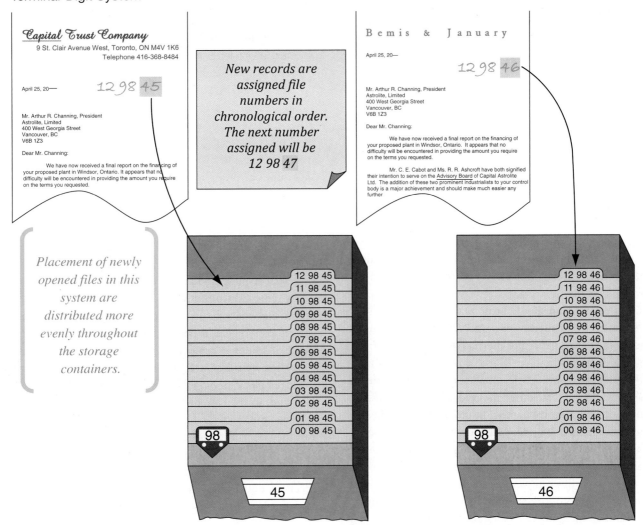

labelled 46 behind guide 98 and after file 11. In this system, when sequentially numbered records such as these are added to terminal-digit storage, these new and typically more active records are filed in different locations, thereby distributing new records more evenly throughout the storage system. New records, therefore, do not accumulate in one location as they do in the straight numeric system.

Alphanumeric Filing
Alphanumeric filing combines alphabetic and numeric characters. For example, RM-01 Records Management may be the main directory, with the subdirectories being RM-01-01 Physical Filing Methods and RM-01-02 Electronic Filing Methods.

Chronological Filing
Chronological filing is a variation of numeric filing. The physical records are arranged by reverse date order within a file folder. This arrangement places the oldest records at the back of the file and the newest records at the front. The files may be divided by year or month, depending on the number of records.

Filing Procedures for Physical Records

Storing records is an important step in processing physical records. Misfiling is easy to do and can make it almost impossible to locate the record at a later date. The following procedures should be followed before placing the record in the folder:

- **Inspecting** is checking to see that the correspondence is ready to be filed. A release mark (such as the supervisor's initials, a file stamp, or some other agreed-upon designation such as PA [put away] or BF [bring forward]) informs you that an incoming record is ready to be filed. A copy of an outgoing record is generally considered ready to be stored but may also contain a release mark as confirmation. If you are unclear, check with the originator before storing. When a BF notation is placed on a record, make a note in your follow-up system for the specified BF date. Your notation should include the name of the requisitioner and a description or location of the record to be retrieved.

- **Indexing** is the thought process of determining the caption (the name) by which the record is to be stored and by which it may later be requested, and is accomplished in conjunction with coding.
- **Coding** is the physical marking of the record that breaks the caption into separate **indexing units**. This marking is usually done by placing a forward slash (/) between each unit, and by underlining the **key unit** and placing a number above the balance of the units in the caption.

2	3
Eva / Kellie / Rianna	

When determining the caption on incoming correspondence, use the company name as shown in the letterhead if it is a business organization and the individual name as shown in the closing if it is an individual. When determining the caption in an outgoing communication, look to the individual or company name shown in the letter address (or in the "To" line in a memorandum).

- **Cross-referencing** should be done when a record could be requested by an alternative name. The original document is indexed and coded; the alternative name is underlined in the document and an "X" or "x-ref" is placed in the margin. A photocopy is made or a cross-reference sheet prepared that is then indexed, coded, and stored under the alternative name. The cross-reference sheet includes the name under which the original document has been stored. If the record is later requested under the alternative name, the location of the original document is easily found. Examples of personal and business names and rules for cross-referencing are presented after the section on indexing rules. Figure 10-13 illustrates a cross-reference sheet that accompanies a letter that is coded and ready for storage.
- **Sorting** is placing the records in order for storage. Sorting records before going to the file cabinet or other storage container speeds the storage process. **Alphabetizing** is the comparison of units in a caption, unit by unit and letter by letter, to determine a difference.
- **Storing** is the placing of a record into storage containers—file folders, drawers, or shelves. The copy of any outgoing correspondence created should be stapled to the front of incoming correspondence then placed in the individual folder in reverse date order—the most recent document at the front of (or on top of) all records in the folder. Place the top of the document to the left side of the folder so that when a folder is later removed from the cabinet, placed on a desk and opened, it is ready to read like the pages of a book. If no individual folder exists, the records are placed in the general/miscellaneous folder for that section and arranged within the folder in alphabetic order based on the indexing units. When three to five records

for the same caption have accumulated in the general/miscellaneous folder, an individual folder is prepared and placed in correct alphabetic order in the drawer.

Figure 10-13 illustrates the cross-reference sheet that accompanies a letter that has been released for filing and that contains both a BF and a cross-reference notation.

The documents easiest to retrieve are those that have been stored. Often a business document contains a deadline or other time-sensitive information that requires future action, days or even weeks later. Rather than leaving such a document unfiled, adding a "BF" notation (which includes the date it should be "brought forward") will release it for filing and simultaneously flag it for attention at a later date. In this way, the document is stored and easily accessible as a reference for others in the office but will be retrieved and distributed to the requisitioner on the follow-up (BF) date.

Retrieving records as a result of a BF notation or a written or verbal request results in a document or a complete folder being removed from physical storage. It is important to both record its whereabouts in the office and ensure its prompt return to storage. It is possible that during the time the document or folder is removed from physical storage it may be requested by other staff members. Replacing it with an *out sheet, out guide,* or *out folder* serves to identify its current location and, in the case of the out folder, provides a temporary storage container for newly received records. These records can then be placed in the original folder on its return. In electronic records, when multiple people have access to the same records, and someone has a file open, the other people will receive a notification that the file is open and can request an update when the file has been closed and is ready for use.

Communicating AT WORK

As you manage records, you may see confidential information contained in the records. Confidential information is data that should be kept private or secret from those who are not authorized to have access to this information. Discuss confidential information with co-workers or others only if you are sure they are authorized to know the information and only for business purposes.

Reasonable protection must also be exercised to keep records that contain confidential information secure. Users should follow company policies for handling confidential information.

In some offices, a written request bearing the signature of a designated person is required for release of classified or confidential records.

In an electronic system, access to confidential records is limited to those users who know the password or have been given access through a security system.

In other instances, confidentiality of records may preclude users from removing the records from the storage room.

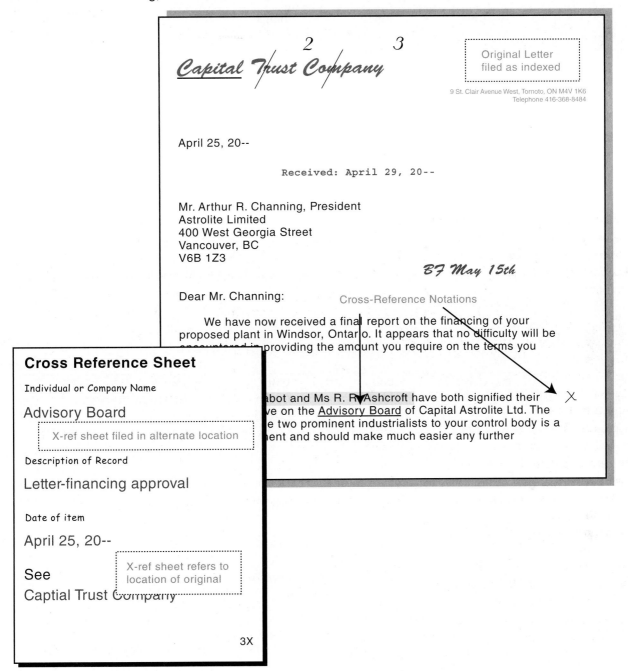

Alphabetic Indexing Rules

The rules for filing are an important component of any effective records management system. While they may vary slightly from organization to organization according to specific needs, most will be based on the rules published by ARMA International. The rules in this chapter are compatible with ARMA's Alphabetic Filing Rules.

Rule 1: Indexing Order of Units

A. *Personal names.* A personal name is indexed in this manner:
- The surname (last name) is the key unit. If determining the surname is difficult, consider the last name written as the surname.
- The given name (first name) or initial is the second unit.
- The middle name or initial is the third unit.

A unit consisting of just an initial (as in the following example) precedes a unit that consists of a complete name beginning with the same letter—*nothing comes before something*. Punctuation is omitted.

Name	Key Unit	Unit 2	Unit 3
Carlos Almeida	ALMEIDA	CARLOS	
Carlos A. Almeida	ALMEIDA	CARLOS	A
Carlos Anthony Almeida	ALMEIDA	CARLOS	ANTHONY

B. *Business names.* Business names are indexed as written, using letterheads or trademarks as guides. Each word in a business name is a separate unit. Business names containing personal names are indexed as written.

Name	Key Unit	Unit 2	Unit 3	Unit 4
Beaumont Health Centre	BEAUMONT	HEALTH	CENTRE	
Beaver Creek Golf Club	BEAVER	CREEK	GOLF	CLUB
Chuck Beaver Pharmacy	CHUCK	BEAVER	PHARMACY	

Rule 2: Minor Words and Symbols in Business Names

Articles, prepositions, conjunctions, and symbols are considered separate indexing units. Symbols are considered as spelled in full. When the word *the* appears as the first word of a business name, it is considered the last unit.

Examples of articles, prepositions, conjunctions, and symbols that are commonly found in business names are given here.

Articles	a, an, the
Prepositions	at, by, for, in, of, off, on, out, over, to, with
Conjunctions	and, but, or, nor
Symbol	&, ¢, $, #, % (and, cent or cents, dollar or dollars, number or pound, percent)

Name	Key Unit	Unit 2	Unit 3	Unit 4	Unit 5
A Bit of Honey	A	BIT	OF	HONEY	
At Home Laundry	AT	HOME	LAUNDRY		
The $ and ¢ Shop	DOLLARS	AND	CENTS	SHOP	THE

Rule 3: Punctuation and Possessives

All punctuation is disregarded when indexing personal and business names. Commas, periods, hyphens, apostrophes, dashes, exclamation points, question marks, quotation marks, underscores, and diagonals are disregarded, and names are indexed as written.

Name	Key Unit	Unit 2	Unit 3	Unit 4
Ahmad's Grooming	AHMADS	GROOMING		
A-Z Video Company	AZ	VIDEO	COMPANY	
North/South Printing	NORTHSOUTH	PRINTING		

Rule 4: Single Letters and Abbreviations

A. *Personal names.* Initials in personal names are considered separate indexing units. Abbreviations of personal names (*Wm., Jos., Thos.*) and nicknames (*Liz, Bill*) are indexed as written.

B. *Business names.* Single letters in business and organization names are indexed as written. If single letters are separated by spaces, index each letter as a separate unit. An acronym (a word formed from the first letter, or first few letters, of several words) is indexed as one unit regardless of punctuation or spacing. Abbreviated words (*Mfg., Corp., Inc.*) and names (IBM, GM) are indexed as one unit regardless of punctuation or spacing. Radio and television station call letters are indexed as one unit.

Name	Key Unit	Unit 2	Unit 3	Unit 4
CTV Television	CTV	TELEVISION		
G.M. MOTORS	GM	MOTORS		
J. V. Hildebrand	HILDEBRAND	J	V	
Jas. W. Hildebrand	HILDEBRAND	JAS	W	
Wm. R. Hildebrand	HILDEBRAND	WM	R	
J K of Toronto	J	K	OF	TORONTO

Rule 5: Titles and Suffixes

A. *Personal names.* A title before a name (*Dr., Miss, Mr., Mrs., Ms., Professor, Sir, Sister*), a seniority suffix (II, III, *Jr., Sr.*), or a professional suffix (CRM, DDS, MD, *PhD*) after a name is the last indexing unit. Numeric suffixes (II, III); are filed before alphabetic suffixes (*Jr.*, Mayor, Senator, *Sr.*). If a name contains a title and a suffix (Ms. Riley Mahar, DVM), the title *Ms.* is the last unit. Royal and religious titles followed by either a given name or a surname only (*Father John, Princess Diana*) are indexed and filed as written.

Name	Key Unit	Unit 2	Unit 3	Unit 4
Princess Charlotte	PRINCESS	CHARLOTTE		
S. R. Fitzgerald II	FITZGERALD	S	R	II
S. R. Fitzgerald III	FITZGERALD	S	R	III
S. R. Fitzgerald, Jr.	FITZGERALD	S	R	JR
S. R. Fitzgerald, Sr.	FITZGERALD	S	R	SR
Ms. Helen Johns, CPA	JOHNS	HELEN	CPA	MS
Dr. Helen Johns	JOHNS	HELEN	DR	

B. *Business names.* Titles in business names are filed as written. Remember, the word *The* is considered the last indexing unit when it appears as the first word of a business name.

Name	Key Unit	Unit 2	Unit 3
Doctors' Hospital	DOCTORS	HOSPITAL	
Dr. Atkins Bakery	DR	ATKINS	BAKERY

Do Self-Check A.

SELF-CHECK Ⓐ

Complete the table below to check your understanding of the first five indexing rules. Determine the following: key unit, second unit, third unit, and fourth unit. Check your answers with those at the end of the chapter.

Unit			
	Key Unit	*Unit 2*	*Unit 3*	*Unit 4*
Henry Hubert Bowers, Jr.	_____	_____	_____	_____
Roger Alan Driver	_____	_____	_____	_____
Elite Autobody Shop	_____	_____	_____	_____
The $ Store	_____	_____	_____	_____
Z. T. Glasier, III	_____	_____	_____	_____
U-R Rental Company	_____	_____	_____	_____
CBC Television	_____	_____	_____	_____
Sister Mary Vanetta	_____	_____	_____	_____
Physicians' Hospital	_____	_____	_____	_____

Rule 6: Prefixes—Articles and Particles

A foreign article or particle in a personal or business name is combined with the part of the name following it to form a single indexing unit. The indexing order is not affected by a space between or within a prefix and the rest of the name, and the space is disregarded when indexing.

Examples of articles and particles are à la, D', Da, De, Del, De la, Della, Den, Des, Di, Dos, Du, E', El, Fitz, Il, L', La, Las, Le, Les, Lo, Los, M', Mac, Mc, O', Per, Saint, San, Santa, Santo, St., Ste., Re, Ten, Ter, Van, Vande, Van der, Von, and Von der.

Name	Key Unit	Unit 2	Unit 3	Unit 4
Paul Alan LaFaver	LAFAVER	PAUL	ALAN	
MacDugal's Meat Market	MACDUGALS	MEAT	MARKET	
McDouglas & Edwards	MCDOUGLAS	AND	EDWARDS	
Mary Lou St. Marie	STMARIE	MARY	LOU	
Alex P. von der Platz	VONDERPLATZ	ALEX	P	

Rule 7: Numbers in Business Names

Numbers spelled out in business names (*Seven Seas Restaurant*) are filed alphabetically. Numbers written in digits are filed before alphabetic letters or words (*B4 Photographers* comes before *Beleau Building Co.*). Names with numbers written in digits in the first units are filed in ascending order (lowest to highest) before alphabetic names (*229 Club, 534 Shop, First Settlers Bank*). Arabic numerals (*2, 3*) are filed before Roman numerals (II, III). Names containing Roman numerals are filed in ascending order according to their Arabic number equivalents.

Names with inclusive numbers (*33–37*) are arranged by the first digit(s) only (*33*). When hyphens separate three or more numbers written as digits, remove the hyphens as you would when hyphens separate words. (1-2-3 Markets would be coded as 123/Markets.) Names with numbers appearing in other than the first position (*Pier 36 Café*) are filed alphabetically and immediately before a similar name without a number (*Pier and Port Café*).

When indexing names with numbers written in digit form that contain *st, d, nd, rd,* and *th* (*lst, 2d, 2nd, 3d, 3rd, 4th*), ignore the letter endings and consider only the digits (*1, 2, 3, 4*).

When indexing names with a number (in figures or words) linked by a hyphen to a letter or word, ignore the hyphen and treat it as a single unit. When indexing a name with a number plus a symbol, treat it as a single unit.

Name	Key Unit	Unit 2	Unit 3	Unit 4
4 Cent Copy Centre	4	CENT	COPY	CENTRE
4th Street Garage	4	STREET	GARAGE	
400–410 Daniels Court	400	DANIELS	COURT	
Four Seasons Health Spa	FOUR	SEASONS	HEALTH	SPA
Highway 30 Café	HIGHWAY	30	CAFÉ	
Highway Service Station	HIGHWAY	SERVICE	STATION	
10-Minute Photo	10MINUTE	PHOTO		
55+ Games	55PLUS	GAMES		

Rule 8: Organizations and Institutions

Banks and other financial institutions, clubs, colleges, hospitals, hotels, lodges, magazines, motels, museums, newspapers, religious institutions, schools, unions, universities, and other organizations and institutions are indexed and filed according to the names written on their letterheads.

Name	Key Unit	Unit 2	Unit 3	Unit 4
Bank of Montreal	BANK	OF	MONTREAL	
First United Church	FIRST	UNITED	CHURCH	
Winston Churchill Elementary School	WINSTON	CHURCHILL	ELEMENTARY	SCHOOL

Rule 9: Identical Names

When personal names and names of businesses, institutions, and organizations are identical (including titles as explained in Rule 5), the filing order is determined by the addresses. Compare addresses in the following order:

- city names
- province, territory, or state names spelled in full—not abbreviated (if city names are identical)
- street names, including *Avenue, Boulevard, Drive, Street* (if city and province, territory, or state names are identical):
  a. When the first units of street names are written in digits (*18th Street*), the names are considered in ascending numeric order and placed together before alphabetic street names.
  b. Street names written as digits are filed before street names written as words.
  c. Street names with compass directions are considered as written (*South Park Avenue*).
  d. Street names with numbers written in digits after compass directions are considered before alphabetic names (*East 8th, East Main, SE Eighth, Southeast Eighth*).
- house or building numbers (if city, province, territory, or state, and street names are identical):
  a. House and building numbers written as digits (*912 Riverside Terrace*) are considered in ascending numeric order and placed together before spelled-out building names (*The Riverside Terrace*).
  b. House and building numbers written as words are filed after house and building numbers written as digits.
  c. If a street address and a building name are included in an address, disregard the building name.
  Postal codes are not considered in determining filing order.

Name	Key Unit	Unit 2	Unit 3	Unit 4	Unit 5	Unit 6	Unit 7
Liz Bowman 212 Luther Saint John, New Brunswick	BOWMAN	LIZ	SAINT JOHN	NEW BRUNSWICK			
Liz Bowman 818 Oak Vancouver, British Columbia	BOWMAN	LIZ	VANCOUVER	BRITISH COLUMBIA			
Brother's Pizza 11120–114 Street Edmonton, Alberta	BROTHERS	PIZZA	EDMONTON	ALBERTA	114		
Brother's Pizza 10510 Jasper Avenue Edmonton, Alberta	BROTHERS	PIZZA	EDMONTON	ALBERTA	JASPER		
Brown Computers 500 Columbia Building Edmonton, Alberta	BROWN	COMPUTERS	EDMONTON	ALBERTA	500	COLUMBIA	
Brown Computers Five Hundred Building Edmonton, Alberta	BROWN	COMPUTERS	EDMONTON	ALBERTA	FIVE	HUNDRED	
Elder Market 213 Clendenan Street Toronto, Ontario	ELDER	MARKET	TORONTO	ONTARIO	CLENDENAN	STREET	213
Elder Market 944 Clendenan Street Toronto, Ontario	ELDER	MARKET	TORONTO	ONTARIO	CLENDENAN	STREET	944

Rule 10: Government Names

Government names are indexed first by the name of the governmental unit—federal, provincial or territorial, municipal, or city. Next, index the distinctive name of the institution (department, bureau, office, or board). The words *Office of, Bureau of,* etc., when they occur, are retained for clarity and are considered separate indexing units if they are part of the official name. *Note:* If *of* is not part of the office name as written, it is not added as an indexing unit.

A. *Federal.* Use three indexing "levels" (rather than units) for Canadian government names. Use *Canada Government* as the first level. The second level is the name of the institution (department or top-level agency). Level three is the next most distinctive name. If necessary, invert the names to file by the distinctive name. The Government of Canada has adopted a streamlined naming convention that has eliminated the use of the words *Department* and *Department of* at the beginning and added *Canada* to the end of institutional names (see www.Canada.ca for a complete listing). The words *of* and *of the* are considered extraneous and when they occur should not be considered when indexing. They may be placed in parentheses for clarity. In the following examples the first level of a Canadian (federal) government institutional name is understood to be *Canada Government.*

Name	Level 2	Level 3	Unit 1
Violation Reporting Recreational Fishing Fisheries and Oceans Canada	FISHERIES AND OCEANS	RECREATIONAL FISHING	VIOLATION REPORTING
Pacific Environmental Science Centre Environment Canada	ENVIRONMENT	PACIFIC ENVIRONMENTAL SCIENCE CENTRE	
Income Tax Department Customs and Revenue Agency	CUSTOMS AND REVENUE	INCOME TAX DEPARTMENT	

B. *Provincial/territorial and local.* The first indexing units are the names of the province/territory, municipality, or city/town. Next, index the most distinctive name of the department, board, bureau, office, or government/political division. The words *Province of* or *Territory of, City of, Department of, Board of,* and so on are added only if needed for clarity and only if they are in the official name. They are considered separate indexing units.

Name	Key Unit	Unit 2	Unit 3	Unit 4	Unit 5	Unit 6	Unit 7
Ministry of Municipal Affairs							
Province of British Columbia							
Victoria, British Columbia	BRITISH	COLUMBIA	PROVINCE	OF	MUNICIPAL	AFFAIRS	MINISTRY
Kings County							
Department of Public Works							
Campbell's Cove, Prince Edward Island	KINGS	COUNTY	PUBLIC	WORKS	DEPARTMENT	OF	

Foreign. The names of a foreign government and its agencies are often written in a foreign language. When indexing foreign names, begin by writing the English translation of the government name on the document. Use this English translation for indexing. The most distinctive part of the English name is the first unit. Then index the balance of the formal name of the government, if needed or if it is the official name. Branches, departments, and divisions follow in order by their distinctive names. States, colonies, provinces, cities, and other divisions of foreign governments are followed by their distinctive or official names as spelled in English.

Name	Key Unit	Unit 2	Unit 3	Unit 4
United States of America	UNITED	STATES	OF	AMERICA
Polska Rzeczpospolita Ludowa	POLISH	PEOPLES	REPUBLIC	
Estados Unidos Mexicanos	UNITED	MEXICAN	STATES	

Do Self-Check B.

Self-Check Ⓑ

Check your knowledge of Rules 6–10 by completing the table below. Determine the key, second, third, and fourth units. Check your answers with those given at the end of the chapter.

	Unit			
	Key Unit	Unit 2	Unit 3	Unit 4
Moncton Cleaners	_____	_____	_____	_____
3rd Street Movie	_____	_____	_____	_____
43–47 Rogers Road Materials	_____	_____	_____	_____
7 Seas Restaurant	_____	_____	_____	_____
Etienne Laberge, 712 Royale, St. Augustine Quebec	_____	_____	_____	_____
Ministry of Health and Welfare	_____	_____	_____	_____
Health Canada	_____	_____	_____	_____
Department of Skills Training, Province of Saskatchewan	_____	_____	_____	_____

Cross-Referencing Personal and Business Names

Cross-references should be prepared for the following types of personal names:

1. **Unusual names.** When determining the last name is difficult, use the name that *appears last as the key unit on the original record*. Then prepare a cross-reference using the *first-appearing* name indexed as the key unit.

Original	Cross-Reference
Tam / Tran	Tran / Tam
	See Tam Tran

2. **Hyphenated surnames.** Deal with hyphenated surnames as shown below.

Original	Cross-Reference
Sue / Loaring-Clark	Clark / Sue / Loaring
	See Loaringclark Sue

3. **Similar names.** "See also" cross-references are prepared for all possible spellings.

Baier	Bauer	Bayer
See also	See also	See also
Bauer, Bayer	Bayer, Baier	Baier, Bauer

Cross-references should be prepared for the following types of business names:

1. **Compound names.** When a business name includes two or more individual surnames, prepare a cross-reference for each surname other than the first.

Original	Cross-Reference
Peat Marwick and Main	Marwick Main and Peat
	See Peat Marwick and Main
	Main Peat and Marwick
	See Peat Marwick and Main

2. **Abbreviations and acronyms.** When a business is commonly known by an abbreviation or an acronym, a cross-reference is prepared for the full name.

Original	Cross-Reference
IBM	International Business Machines
	See IBM

3. **Changed names.** When a business changes its name, a cross-reference is prepared for the old name and all records are filed under the new name.

Original	Cross-Reference
DaimlerChrysler	Chrysler
	See DaimlerChrysler

4. **Foreign business names.** The name of a foreign business is often spelled in the foreign language on the original. The English translation should be written on the document and the document stored *under the English spelling*. A cross-reference should be placed under the foreign spelling.

Original	Cross-Reference
French Republic	République Française
	See French Republic

Records Retention, Transfer, and Disposal

Retention Schedules

In both electronic and physical systems, it is important to know how long records should be retained by the organization. Knowing the various categories of records shown in Figure 10-14 will help you determine and understand records retention schedules.

The retention schedule should identify the period of time a record should be retained by determining:

- the length of time that a record should be retained in active storage
- the length of time that a record should be retained in inactive storage
- the process for destroying records that no longer need to be retained in inactive storage

FIGURE 10-14

Records Categories

Category	Description and Examples
Vital records	Records that are essential for the continuation of the business and that are usually irreplaceable—copyrights, property titles, and mortgage documents—should never be destroyed.
Important records	Records that support the continuing operations of the business that could be replaced at considerable cost in time and money—personnel files, inventories, and financial statements—may be transferred to inactive storage but should not be destroyed.
Useful records	These records—letters, emails, and memos—are used in daily business and are replaceable with some delay or inconvenience.
Nonessential records	These records—announcements and meeting agendas—have no useful value after their use. They are usually not considered to be a record.

As an administrative professional, you generally will not make decisions regarding the retention schedule. If your organization does not have a records retention schedule, check with your supervisor before making any decisions about how, when, and whether documents should be transferred or destroyed. You may need to consult with the legal counsel of the organization—or, if you are working in a small organization, an outside legal firm—before developing appropriate schedules for specific types of documents. A sample retention schedule is shown in Figure 10-15.

FIGURE 10-15

Retention Schedule

Record Category	Retention Period	Retained in Active File	Retained in Inactive File
Employee personnel records (after termination)	6 years	2 years	4 years
Payroll records	6 years	2 years	4 years
Patents	Indefinitely	Indefinitely	—

The Canadian government provides its employees with guidelines regarding records/information management, which are also relevant to a wide variety of other environments. Links to this site can be found on the MindTap site for this textbook.

Records Transfer

At some point in the life of an electronic or physical record, on the basis of records retention information, you will decide to destroy it, transfer it to inactive storage, or retain it permanently. When distinguishing between active and inactive records, use the following categories:

- **Active records.** These are used three or more times a month and should be kept in an accessible area.
- **Inactive records.** These are used fewer than 15 times a year and may be stored in less accessible areas than active records.
- **Archive records.** Have historical value to the organization and are preserved permanently.

Two common methods of transfer are perpetual and periodic.

Perpetual Transfer

With the **perpetual transfer**, records are continuously transferred from the active to the inactive files. The advantage of this method is that all files are kept current, since any inactive material is immediately transferred to storage. The perpetual transfer method works well in offices where projects or tasks are completed. For example, when a lawyer finishes a case, the file is complete and probably will not need to be referred to at all or certainly not frequently. Therefore, it can be transferred to the inactive files.

Periodic Transfer

With **periodic transfer**, active records are transferred to inactive status at the end of a stated time. For example, you may transfer records that are more than six months old to the inactive file and maintain records that are less than six months old in the active file. You would carry out this transferring procedure every six months.

Records Disposal

In physical storage systems, the cost of maintaining documents that are no longer of any use can be significant, mainly because of the floor space necessary for the file cabinets.

When physical records have reached the end of their life cycle, they should be destroyed in accordance with organizational policies. If they are not confidential, they can be recycled; if they are confidential, they should be destroyed beyond any possible recognition.

Writing AT WORK

If you work for a large organization, filing procedures may be standardized across your department or the organization. In some organizations, especially small companies, procedures used for filing records may vary by department or even by employee. If you work in such a situation, you should write a list of procedures that you or your department uses for filing records.

The procedures should contain enough details so that a temporary employee or someone from another department can easily follow them to file and retrieve records in your absence.

Maintaining and Updating the File Management System

The records management needs of an organization change over time. Additionally, new physical and electronic systems, equipment, and storage possibilities become available. Organizations must keep current on what is available and change their systems as appropriate. Although changing systems can be expensive in the short term, new systems often save money in the long term by offering improved speed and accuracy and requiring less staff time to operate.

People AT WORK

Records Manager

If the organization is large, generally at least one person in a management position is responsible for the ongoing maintenance and updating of the system. This person may have acquired certification through courses and programs of study available at local colleges and then maintained currency through attendance at ARMA International conferences. Changes in records management systems and new equipment necessitate ongoing training for all those involved in records management. The organizational person in charge of records management generally provides this training. The MindTap site to this textbook includes a link to the ARMA International website where you can find information on the CRM (certified records manager) designation, publications on records management available from their bookstore, career placement services, and regular publications such as *The Information Management Journal* and *InfoPro*.

Managing Electronic Records

The computer has become a major electronic records management component, with records moving from computer to computer without ever being printed. Electronic records are document files created in specific software applications—word processing, spreadsheet, database, email, and others. These files are stored on computer storage devices where they can be easily accessed or changed. As the number of computer files increases, the need to organize and manage electronic records has become an important priority for businesses. As an administrative professional, you need to develop an effective and efficient method of storing and retrieving electronic documents.

Types of Electronic Records

Electronic records may be part of an electronic database or automated system. For example, customer names, addresses, and telephone numbers may be recorded in a database. Electronic records may also consist of individual word processing files (letters, reports, and contracts), spreadsheet files (budgets and cost analysis reports), and graphics files (presentations, drawings, and photos).

Automated Records

Electronic records are often created automatically. For example, when a customer enters an online order, the automated order system creates and stores a record of the order. The customer's contact and payment information are added to a customer database. When the customer orders from the company again, that information can be accessed by the order system so that the customer does not need to enter it again. An email order confirmation is automatically sent to the customer, and the order information is automatically sent to the warehouse. Once the items have been shipped, tracking information is available from the company's records or the delivery company's records.

Individual Records

Creating and receiving electronic records are routine processes for an administrative assistant. You will key letters, memos, and reports, and receive many email messages. Not all electronic documents that you create or receive should be treated as a record. Only those items that have continuing value for the organization should be considered records. An email from a co-worker reminding you about tomorrow's brown-bag lunch does not have continuing value and is not considered a record.

Database Records

A database is a collection of records about one topic or related topics. The records can be updated, copied, or deleted as needed. You can use queries and filters to find particular subsets of information and to create reports using the information. An electronic database may be made available to many users in an organization via a network or an intranet, or it may be stored on a single computer for use by a few people. A database is often used to create an index or an accession log for a physical records system. While Microsoft Access is an example of a popular database program with many sophisticated features, you may also choose to use the database feature of a spreadsheet program to create a mini database. An Access database file with just a few records will consume significantly more storage space than a database file created using an Excel workbook.

Electronic Record's Life Cycle

An electronic record has a life cycle similar to that of a physical record. The life cycle has the following steps:

1. creation and storage
2. use and distribution
3. retention and maintenance
4. disposition

Creation and Storage

Electronic files are created using specific application software. These files can be stored on your hard drive (the C drive), on a network drive that might be designated by any letter of the alphabet from G to Z, or some other storage media.

Whatever storage device is being used, a unique file name must be determined—no two files in the folder can have an identical name.

The space available on the media being used can be quite large. Unless the files are organized in some way, it would soon be impossible to locate and retrieve anything—the files would be much like pieces of paper tossed randomly into a drawer. Organization is mostly achieved by creating electronic folders or libraries for storing related files. To further organize your files, you can also create folders (known as sub-folders) within these folders. While it is possible to create folders within folders within folders, it is best to keep the organization shallow (many folders at the same level) rather than deep (folders within folders within folders).

Many administrative professionals create a file-naming system for electronic files that parallels the physical records system. It might be alphabetic, subjective, or numeric, or a combination of these systems. The most important aspect of electronic file management is to create a system that makes retrieval quick and easy. Chose meaningful names for the files and folders you create, and be consistent in your naming procedure.

In addition to using a consistent naming procedure, many programs allow you to enter **metadata** (information about data) for records you create. Metadata can include such details such as title, author name, subject, and keywords that identify the document's properties—its topics or contents, as shown in Figure 10-16. These properties can be used to search for the document when you cannot locate it by name.

In a networked environment, the file server is divided into directories. You will be allocated a section of the network on which to store your files, similar to having a file cabinet by your desk. Within the networked environment, you will be granted access rights to this section of the network and to certain other directories/libraries; in some directories, you may be able only to read, and not modify or delete the file content. Often, master documents—documents that will be used by

FIGURE 10-16
Document Properties

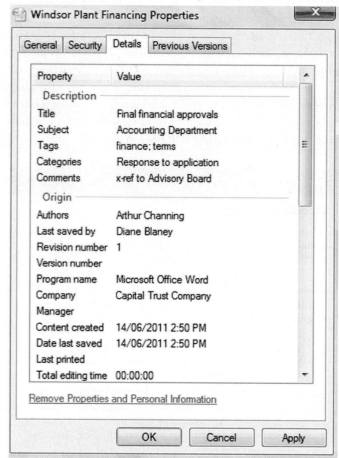

Used with permission from Microsoft.

all employees of a department or organization—are placed in these restricted locations. They can be copied into your dedicated area and from there you can personalize and save them within your own file system, leaving the original unchanged. Figure 10-17 illustrates the file structure of network drives.

FIGURE 10-17
File Structure of Network Drives

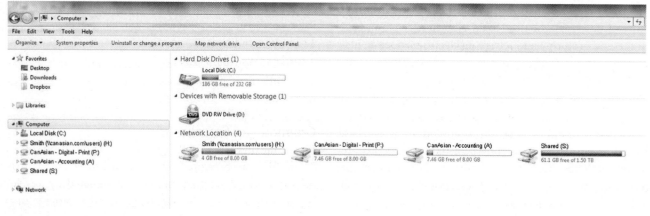

Used with permission from Microsoft.

Use and Distribution

The use of electronic records is as varied as the use of physical records. You or the recipients of the record may use the information it contains to answer questions, make decisions, compile data, or complete other activities. Distribution may be accomplished through electronic channels such as email or shared folders on a network. In addition to printing and distributing through non-electronic channels such as mail or fax, files can be copied and distributed on removable storage devices—flash drives, CDs, or DVDs. When the record is sent as an attachment to an email, users can create folders in the email program where received files can be saved, organized, and managed.

Electronic records, like physical records, can inadvertently be stored in or moved to an incorrect folder, making them difficult to locate. When this happens, the search feature of your operating system can be used to help locate the file on any drive on the computer or on any drive to which the computer connects. You can search by filename, date, or specific text within a document file. Email programs also have a search component. You can use it to search by the name of the sender or recipient, by the approximate date, by the subject, or by message text.

Automated records are created and distributed automatically. Knowing how to access, use, and maintain these records is important. For example, to answer a customer's questions, a customer order may be retrieved by searching for the customer's name, phone number, or order number.

Retention and Maintenance

While electronic storage is not nearly as space-intensive as physical record storage, some cost is involved in maintaining unneeded documents. Establishing a retention schedule for your electronic files and moving them from one folder to another or to a removable storage device (a process known as data migration) can help ensure storage space is occupied by files that have no continuing value to the organization. By using data migration to copy or move files and folders onto new media, and in new formats as they become available, you can ensure that today's electronic storage can be read with devices used in the future. Keeping your file structure clean by regularly deleting unnecessary files ensures more active files are easier to locate. Figure 10-18 provides suggested procedures you may wish to adopt.

FIGURE 10-18
Procedures for Electronic File Retention

File Type	Retention Period	Tips
Daily correspondence	Five (or ten) days	Create five (or ten folders) named Day 1 to Day 5 (or to Day 10 for a two-week system). Store all correspondence in Day 1 on Monday of the first week, in Day 2 on Tuesday of the first week, etc. Once the designated period is over, return to the Day 1 folder and delete the documents that were created and stored one (or two) week(s) previously. You can then reuse the folder. This system will help to keep your directory active.
Weekly, monthly, quarterly, or annual reports	Retain until the next report is created	You may be able to use the format or some text of the previous document in the preparation of the current report.
Meeting agenda	Use the previous agenda to create the current agenda for a meeting	Updating the previous document is quicker than beginning from scratch every time you require an agenda for a regularly scheduled meeting.
Proposals and special reports	Retain until printed and distributed	Use the versions capability of your word processing software so you can return to a previous version of a document if necessary. Once the file is printed and distributed, delete it or archive it.

In a large organization, maintenance of electronic files will likely be handled by your computer services department. Those staff will have an incremental and a full backup schedule in place. With *incremental backup*, new or changed documents are backed up daily. Complete network backups are usually scheduled at weekly, monthly, or quarterly intervals; this network backup is known as *full backup*. This protection does not include your own hard drive; you will need to develop a similar backup schedule yourself if you are storing important files locally.

Disposition

Generally, the disposition of records you create or receive will be at your discretion. When records are no longer needed, they should be deleted, or the storage medium should be destroyed.

For electronic records such as automated records, someone in the company will be responsible for transferring the records to offline storage and eventually destroying them or placing them in permanent storage in accordance with company policy.

Whether electronic records are stored on your hard drive, the office network, or other media, they should be managed through the four phases of the electronic records life cycle: creation and storage, use and distribution, retention and maintenance, and disposition.

Storage Media

Physical records are stored in file cabinets; electronic records are stored on electronic media. In addition to the hard drive of a computer, a variety of external storage media can be used for storage of electronic records, including external hard drives, CDs, DVDs, flash drives, and online file servers.

- Using an external hard drive, files can be saved, retrieved, copied, and deleted. The drive connects to a computer using a USB port, making the device and the files stored on it easily portable from one computer or office to another. External hard drives are useful for
  - freeing up and providing additional storage space for an internal drive
  - long-term storage of files
  - backing up of files from a computer
  - storage of sensitive material that can be secured in a safe
- *CD (compact disc)* technology has become popular in digital archiving because information can be read any number of times but cannot be modified or erased. If information to be stored on a CD will need to be revised, then choose to use CD-RW (CD, rewritable) technology.
- *DVD (digital versatile disc)* technology is a popular choice for file storage. A DVD can contain video and sound files, as well as data files, such as a word processing document. Unlike the CD-RW that records on only one side of the disc, a DVD disc may have one or two sides and one or two layers of data per side. The number of sides and layers determines the disc capacity.
- A *flash drive* is a storage device that contains a memory chip for storing data. Flash drives, also known as jump drives, thumb drives, and memory sticks, can hold anywhere from several megabytes to several gigabytes of data. They connect to a computer via a USB port. Once files are saved on the device, no power source is required for the device to continue to store files. Flash drives offer users the same options as external drives.
- Online storage options, or *cloud computing*, facilitate collaboration between employees while providing access to an organization's records from any Internet-connected desktop, laptop, tablet, or smartphone. One consideration facing many organizations in Canada is the location of cloud-based servers. Many cloud-based servers are physically situated in the United States, making them subject to the U.S. Patriot Act. Storage of personal data such as medical records and credit card transactions protected in Canada by PIPEDA could be vulnerable to interception by U.S. authorities. For privacy considerations regarding electronic records, as well as commercial implications, many Canadian firms have chosen to not use cloud servers.

Microform is a general term for microimage media such as microfilm and microfiche. Most applications of microform storage are for inactive or infrequently accessed records such as personnel records of former employees and newspapers stored in libraries. Microforms were once the only way to store records in a compact way, but microfilm, microfiche, and the magnification equipment needed to read them now take up too much room and have all but been replaced by file conversion to digital formats.

Working with Database Records

As an administrative professional, you will be expected to work with existing databases by adding, deleting, or editing records; answering questions; and preparing reports. While you may not be required to design and create databases, knowing the basics steps in doing so will help you understand how to use them.

A database contains tables of data. Data in each table are organized in fields—name, address, city, and province or territory. All fields related to one person make up a record, and a group of records related to one subject is stored in a table as illustrated in Figure 10-19. Additional tables with related data can be created and linked to one another.

Storing data in related tables eliminates the duplication of fields and allows you to create queries and reports based on data from several related tables.

When deciding which fields to use in a database table, consider the smallest unit of information you might use separately from the other information. For example, to create personalized letters using mail merge, only a person's last name is used in the salutation of a letter. This field would not be available in a database that allocates only one field for the customer name. By creating separate fields for the customer title, customer first name, and customer last name, you can easily create personalized salutations that correctly include only the customer's title and last name.

Word processing and spreadsheet software both contain features for creating simple database tables that are similar to the tables created in database programs. Whenever a document is created based on a database format, sorting on any field is possible. Fields can be sorted alphabetically or numerically, or, in ascending or descending order. It is possible to search and find an individual record or to apply filters to show only those records that match a specific criterion.

Electronic Document Management Systems

Electronic document management systems (EDMS) are also increasingly being used by organizations to manage electronic records. These programs can help to automate many of the manual processes in records management. Rather than using word processing or database programs to create searchable databases, EDMS software provides options for automating electronic records throughout the life cycle. EDMS software can provide the electronic tools needed to access your organization's information quickly and efficiently. Some systems are geared to specific industries, such as medical offices and law firms, to provide appropriate solutions unique to those practice areas.

FIGURE 10-19

Database Table

	Title ▾	First Name ▾	Last Name ▾	Address ▾	City ▾	State ▾
	Ms.	Margaret	Balli	224 Grandview Dr.	Newport	KY
	Mr.	Scott	Barkley	4100 North Bend	Cincinnati	OH
	Ms.	Sue	Coates	691 Meadow Lane	Cincinnati	OH
	Mrs.	Dineen	Ebert	27 Main	Indianapolis	IN
	Ms.	Jenna	Ericksen	34 Emerson	Covington	KY
	Mr.	Mike	Goldstein	321 Asbury Dr.	Cincinnati	OH
	Ms.	Linda	Hartley	2570 Foxfield	Naperville	IL
	Ms.	Melissa	Hefferin	2300 Johns St.	Kankakee	IL
	Ms.	Patti	Jachowicz	302 North Lake	Cincinnati	OH
	Mrs.	Petrina	Jackson	120 Western	Naperville	IL
	Mrs.	Barbara	Johnson	764 Prairie	Henderson	KY
	Ms.	Rachael	Johnson	421 Capitol	Springfield	IL
	Mr.	Steve	Johnson	660 Washington	Dayton	OH
	Mr.	Stephen	Joyner	4563 Findley Ave.	Lawrenceburg	IN

Used with permission from Microsoft.

The features of EDMS include the following:

- faster retrieval of documents
- reduction in the labour costs involved in processing files
- ability to view, print, fax, email, or annotate any document from your PC
- recovery and repurpose of space previously used for manual filing and storage
- safe storage of backup copies of all files
- generation of activity reports by department and user
- generation of guidelines for records retention and disposal
- increased security and control of who can view documents

The Future of Records Management

The field of records management is becoming increasingly complex. Emerging technologies affect our access to information and the speed and accuracy with which this access is possible. Increasing the security and protection of your organization's vital records will be critical for both physical and electronic records. As an administrative professional, you will want to monitor these changes and adapt your system to meet these challenges.

Soft Skills

EFFECTIVE DECISION MAKING

Effective decision making is important in all areas of your work as an administrative professional, including records management, which is more than just arranging items in alphabetic order—it is an exercise in making decisions.

A *decision* is the outcome or product of a problem, a concern, or an issue that must be addressed and solved. The process by which a decision is reached includes five steps, which are shown in Figure 10-20. You should systematically follow these steps when making a decision.

FIGURE 10-20

Effective Decision-Making Steps

- Evaluate the Decision
- Test the Alternatives and Make the Decision
- Generate Alternatives or Possible Solutions
- Establish the Criteria
- Define the Problem or the Purpose

Chapter Summary

The summary will help you remember the important points covered in this chapter.

- Records management is the systematic control of records from the creation of the record to its final disposition.
- A *record* is any type of recorded information including emails, letters, reports, spreadsheets, personnel records, or any other type of organizational record.
- Records are considered to have administrative, legal or legislative, or historical value.
- The record life cycle has five phases: creation or receipt, distribution, use, maintenance, and disposition.
- An effective records management system has the following components:
- an organization-wide records structure
- necessary equipment and media
- appropriate filing supplies
- records storage system or systems
- adherence to established indexing rules appropriate for the storage system
- retention schedules
- established procedures for moving files from active to inactive file status and guidelines governing their destruction
- procedures for updating the management system
- records management manuals and ongoing training for personnel
- Records in a physical or an electronic system may be organized in alphabetic order, numerical order, or a combination of both.
- Procedures for filing physical records include inspecting, indexing, coding, sorting, storing, and preparing cross-references as needed.
- Cross-referencing is necessary when a record may be sought under more than one name.
- Alphabetic indexing rules based on those developed by ARMA International are used for indexing and coding physical records in an alphabetic filing system.
- The computer is a major electronic records management component. Electronic records may be stored online or on a variety of external storage media, such as external hard drives, CDs, DVDs, and flash drives.
- Retention schedules (indicating the length of time a record should be maintained) are essential to effective records management systems.
- Records and information management systems may be manual, electronic, or a combination of the two.

Key Terms

accession log p. 178
alphabetizing p. 180
caption p. 173
coding p. 180
cross-referencing p. 180
cuts p. 173
direct access p. 175
geographic storage method p. 176
important records p. 187
index p. 176
indexing p. 180
indexing units p. 180
inspecting p. 179
key unit p. 180

keywords p. 177
metadata p. 190
nonessential records p. 187
periodic transfer p. 188
perpetual transfer p. 188
record p. 171
records management p. 171
retrieving p. 180
sorting p. 180
storing p. 180
subject storage method p. 176
useful records p. 187
vital records p. 187

Responses to Self-Check A

Name	Key Unit	Second Unit	Third Unit	Fourth Unit
Henry Hubert Bowers, Jr.	Bowers	Henry	Hubert	Jr
Roger Alan Driver	Driver	Roger	Alan	
Elite Autobody Shop	Elite	Autobody	Shop	
The $ Store.	Dollar	Store	The	
Z. T. Glasier, III	Glasier	Z	T	III
U-R Rental Company	UR	Rental	Company	
CBC Television	CBC	Television		
Sister Mary Vanetta	Vanetta	Mary	Sister	
Physicians' Hospita	Physicians	Hospital		

Responses to Self-Check B

Name	Key Unit	Second Unit	Third Unit	Fourth Unit
Moncton Cleaners	Moncton	Cleaners		
3rd Street Movie	3rd	Street	Movie	
43–47 Rogers Road Materials	43	Rogers	Road	Materials
7 Seas Restaurant	7	Seas	Restaurant	
Etienne Laberge, 712 Royale, St. Augustin, Quebec	Laberge	Etienne	Saint Augustin	Quebec
Ministry of Health and Welfare	Canada	Government	Health	
Department of Skills Training, Province of Saskatchewan	Saskatchewan	Province	of	Skills

Discussion Items

These discussion items provide an opportunity to test your understanding of the chapter through written responses and discussion with your classmates and your instructor.

1. List the essential components of a records management system.
2. Identify and explain records storage methods.
3. What is the difference between the indexing and coding filing procedures?
4. What is the purpose of a cross-reference?
5. How does the terminal-digit numeric storage method differ from the consecutive numeric storage method?
6. What is the advantage of entering metadata for electronic records that you create?

Critical-Thinking Activity

CanAsian has a relatively good company-wide records management program. Both physical and electronic management systems are maintained, with individual offices filing their records manually as long as they are active and then moving their records to electronic storage after the active period has passed. CanAsian has not produced a company-wide records management manual. The records manager has encouraged individual offices to move to electronic filing for most active records; however, most offices have not followed the recommendation. You have moved to electronic filing for almost all the records you oversee. Several of the other administrative professionals have seen your system and have asked for your help in transferring their files to an electronic system. Mr. Albertson has given his permission for you to work with them.

Using the decision-making model presented in this chapter, describe the problem and the steps you would take to assist the others in filing and managing their records. What suggestions, if any, would you make to the records manager?

Building Workplace Skills

Project 10-1 (Learning Outcomes 1, 2, and 3)
Collaborative Project

CAREER

Team up with three of your classmates on this task. Interview one administrative professional concerning records management; your interview may be done by email. Ask the following questions. Report your findings orally to the class.

1. What records management system(s) do you use (manual, electronic, or a combination of these systems)?
2. What storage methods do you use (alphabetic, numeric, or alphanumeric)?
3. If you use an alphabetic method, do you also use subject and geographic methods?
4. What is your role in document management?
5. Does your company have a records retention schedule? If so, may I have a copy?
6. What aspect of records management is the most difficult for you?
7. What suggestions do you have for the beginning administrative professional in terms of how to handle records management?

Project 10-2 (Learning Outcomes 4 and 5)

CAREER   DATA FILE

Access Project 10-2. For each group of names, indicate the indexing units and sort the names in correct alphabetic order. The correct response is given for the first group as an example. Using the form provided, key your responses; submit your work to your instructor.

Project 10-3 (Learning Outcomes 4 and 5)

CAREER   DATA FILE

Access Project 10-3a. Print out the document and cut on the cut lines to create index cards. Index and code the units on each card. Arrange the cards in correct alphabetic sequence. Access Project 10-3b. Use or print out the document to record

the number printed in the top right corner of each card as they appear from top to bottom (front to back) when arranged in alphabetic order. Submit a copy of your work to your instructor.

Project 10-4 (Learning Outcomes 4 and 5)

CAREER   DATA FILE

Access Project 10-4a. Print out the document and cut on the cut lines to create index cards. Index and code the units on each card for a geographic classification system. Arrange the cards in correct order for a geographic system. Access Project 10-4b. Use or print out the document to record the number printed in the top right corner of each card as they appear from top to bottom (front to back) when arranged in geographic order. Submit a copy of your work to your instructor.

Project 10-5 (Learning Outcomes 4 and 5)

CAREER   DATA FILE

Access Project 10-5. Indicate the subject you would use for storing the correspondence listed. Mark your answer to the right of each item. Print out and hand in your answers to your instructor.

Project 10-6 (Learning Outcome 5)

CAREER   TECHNOLOGY

Using the index cards from Project 10-4, create a database. Enter the customer information. Also add a field for the customer number. (The number is in the top left corner of the card.) Retrieve the list by province and territory; print out a copy of the list. Next, retrieve the list by customer number; then print out a copy of the list. Turn in both printouts to your instructor and, if you wish, place one copy in your e-portfolio.

Project 10-7 (Learning Outcome 4)

CAREER   DATA FILE

Physical records that you are to store in a terminal-digit numeric filing system have been assigned the numbers listed below. Using Project 10-7, code the numbers in the form provided for Part A. Then, in preparation for placing the records in the files, determine the correct sort order. Use the form provided for Part B to enter the numbers that you have determined would be the correct order for storage.

06 24 79	06 75 23
06 25 79	06 75 22
08 19 45	06 24 78
07 02 98	08 92 15
08 54 79	08 93 15
08 19 23	07 01 14

Project 10-8 (Learning Outcome 5)

Online Projects

Several companies provide file hosting and backup services for personal or business files via the Internet. Search the Internet using a search term such as "online storage." Access

several links on the search results list and read the information provided. Access Project 10-8a; write a memorandum to your instructor describing the services provided by one company. Identify the Web sources you used.

Electronic Document Management Systems (EDMS) is introduced in this chapter. Search the Internet using this search term or the term "document management software." Read about the features of the software. Select one of the features and write a brief paragraph summarizing the information provided. Access Project 10-8b and submit your findings in a memo to your instructor.

Project 10-9 (Learning Outcome 6)

Add to your e-portfolio by determining how you will continue to increase your decision-making skills. File your plan under an appropriate name in your e-portfolio folder.

Make the Grade with MindTap

MINDTAP

Stay organized and efficient with MindTap—a single destination with all the course material and study aids you need to succeed. Built-in apps leverage social media and the latest learning technology. For example:
- ReadSpeaker will read the text to you.
- Flashcards are pre-populated to provide you with a jump-start for review—or you can create your own.
- You can highlight text and make notes in your MindTap Reader. Your notes will flow into Evernote, the electronic

notebook app that you can access anywhere when it's time to study for the exam.
- Self-quizzing allows you to access your understanding.

Visit nelson.com/student to start using MindTap. Enter the Online Access Code from the card included with your text. If a code card is not provided, you can purchase instant access at NELSONbrain.com.

CHAPTER 11

Planning and Organizing Meetings and Other Events

LEARNING OUTCOMES

After studying this chapter, you should be able to:

1. Describe types of business meetings and appropriate formats for various situations.

2. Describe the roles and responsibilities of the meeting leader, the administrative professional, and participants for meetings and conferences.

3. Identify types of virtual meetings—teleconferences, video conferences, and web conferences.

4. Plan meetings and prepare related materials.

5. Prepare agendas and minutes.

Do I Qualify?

Administrative Assistant

Growing company seeks an administrative assistant with good planning and organizational skills. The successful candidate will possess strong communication and listening skills and will be able to think outside the box, multi-task, and troubleshoot when problems arise. Job duties include:

- handling telephone and written communications
- working collaboratively with co-workers and managers
- planning meetings and handling related tasks
- doing research and creating documents and presentations
- delegating responsibilities as appropriate and providing direction to co-workers when organizing meetings and other events

Meetings in the Workplace

Meetings are a way of life in the workplace. In an environment where businesses are downsizing, you might expect fewer meetings; however, the opposite is actually closer to reality. Resolving issues and making decisions by working collaboratively in teams has become more common. This collaborative approach has effectively increased rather than decreased the number of meetings that are being held. Even estimating conservatively, administrative professionals could spend an average of four hours a week in meetings; managers could possibly spend 50 to 80 percent of their workweek in meetings. Since time is money, these meetings can be very costly to business.

Meetings can be a good means of generating ideas, sharing information, and making decisions. However, it is imperative that meetings be both effective and necessary, and that meeting time be spent as productively as possible. Unfortunately, many meetings are unnecessary or unproductive, thereby wasting the time of both the individual participants and the organization. Unnecessary meetings generally occur when no clear purpose or agenda has been defined or when no follow-up action has been identified. You may have attended a meeting where it seemed as if the major purpose was to avoid making a decision or to engage in small talk with other participants. Such occasions often result in participants wondering why the meeting was called in the first place. Consider

FIGURE 11-1
Criteria for Determining When a Meeting is Necessary or Unnecessary

A Meeting Is *Necessary*	A Meeting Is *Unnecessary*
• Advice is needed from a group of people. • A group needs to be involved in solving a problem or making a decision. • An issue needs clarification. • A group needs to receive information that may be difficult or confusing and may require discussion. • A problem exists but it is not clear what the problem is or who is responsible for dealing with it. • Quick communication is necessary with a large number of people.	• The purpose of the meeting and/or the appropriate people to attend are not clearly identified. • Confidential or sensitive personnel matters need to be addressed. • There is inadequate data for the meeting. • There is insufficient time to prepare for the meeting. • Group members feel considerable anger or hostility among themselves, and need time to calm down before coming together. • One-way information needs to be shared.

the criteria in Figure 11-1 when determining whether a meeting is necessary or unnecessary.

This chapter will help you develop the knowledge and skills needed to assist your supervisor in planning, organizing, and facilitating meetings that are effective and productive for all. This chapter will also help you develop the skills to be a productive team member and to run an effective meeting.

Types of Meetings

A variety of informal meetings are regularly held within an organization, such as *staff meetings* or meetings with customers and clients of the business; some meetings may be more formal in nature, such as *board of directors meetings*, *committee* or *task force meetings*, *project team meetings*, and *customer/client meetings*. As businesses become increasingly multinational, you may also be responsible for organizing *international meetings*. As an administrative professional, you need to understand these different types of meetings.

Staff Meetings

An executive may meet informally with the staff who report to them. The purpose of staff meetings may be to review directions, plans, or assignments, or to handle routine issues. These meetings may be scheduled on a regular basis or arranged as needed. Informal meetings with customers or clients are generally small, including only two or three people.

Board of Directors Meetings

Most large corporations and organizations operate with a board of directors that meet once a month or less often. The chairperson of the board leads the meeting, and the conduct of these formal meetings is defined by procedures outlined in the **bylaws**—the organization's written policies and procedures. If the organization is a public entity required by law to hold meetings that are open to the public, a notice of the meeting is posted according to legal procedures. An agenda indicating the items to be discussed is distributed before the

meeting and participants generally follow parliamentary procedures documented in *Robert's Rules of Order*.

Staff meetings are held regularly in many companies.

Committee and Task Force Meetings

In most organizations, an **ad hoc committee** (also known as a *task force* may be formed to deal with a specific issue or problem. Established for a specific purpose or project (such as planning, producing, and marketing a new product) the committee is disbanded once the purpose has been accomplished or the project has been completed. A **standing committee** is generally established for an ongoing purpose. For example, one standing committee may be a safety committee that meets regularly (perhaps every month) to identify and address safety concerns. While the standing committee continues to function from year to year, its members may change periodically.

Project Team Meetings

Project teams are frequently used in organizations. For example, a project team might be formed to plan, produce, and market a new product. The team may include people in product research and design who will create a new product, people in manufacturing who will oversee production of the product, and people in sales and marketing who will plan or oversee the advertising and sales of the product. Although team members are from different departments, they work together on the project. This type of project team may also be called a cross-functional team.

Customer/Client Meetings

Some employers hold meetings with customers or clients. These meetings are generally small, including only two or three people. For example, a lawyer may meet with a client to discuss the evidence in a case. An engineer may meet with a customer to discuss the design of a product.

International Meetings

In international organizations, upper-level managers commonly meet with staff in locations outside Canada. Also, as organizations in Canada continue to broaden their international scope, meetings to pursue international opportunities are held with business leaders in many other countries. You may be involved in setting up or participating in electronic meetings with individuals from other countries, or the meetings may be held in other countries. In international meetings, remember that cultural differences exist, and these differences must be understood and respected. Otherwise, you may be dealing with an international incident rather than achieving a resolution on an important contract or issue. It is important that you do your homework before the meeting.

Find out as much as you can about the culture or cultures that will be represented. Then, be sensitive to the needs of the individuals in the meeting. Remember to consider the differences in time zones; for example, when it is noon in Halifax, it is the following day in Beijing. Use the time zone calculators on the Internet to help you find a suitable time when everyone can meet electronically.

International meetings are typically more formal in nature than local meetings. Learn and use the proper greetings. Follow accepted practices for exchanging business cards and giving (or not giving) gifts or other amenities.

International meetings are typically more formal in nature than local meetings.

Communicating AT WORK

Etiquette for International Meetings

- Learn and use proper greetings in all meetings. Greetings become doubly important in a virtual meeting so do not ignore them in such a situation.
- Do not use first names of participants. Even though using first names is common in North American meetings, it can be considered inappropriate in other countries.
- Acknowledge the leader of the other group(s). For example, if the presidents of companies are involved, they should be recognized first and should speak first.
- Remember the hierarchical nature of the international participants and show respect for everyone but especially for those in positions of authority.
- Disagree agreeably; in some cultures, it is offensive to be contradictory.
- Avoid gesturing with your hands. In another cultural context, such gestures may mean something you do not intend. Also, some people are offended by gestures.
- Watch your body language; remember that body language has different meanings in different cultures.
- Do not mistake a courteous answer for the truth. Yes does not always mean yes, and no may not mean no.
- Understand the concept of time; in some cultures, it is precise, while in others it is more fluid.

Meeting Formats

The meeting format is typically face to face. Organizations will continue to have numerous face-to-face meetings because of the increase in teamwork within organization and the need for these teams to share information in person. Audio conferencing (although an older technology) remains a viable type of meeting format. The use of video conferencing and web conferencing is growing.

Face-to-Face Meetings

Even with the variety of technology that is available today, the traditional face-to-face meeting format where participants gather at a common location is an important means of conducting business. Advantages of face-to-face meetings include the following:

- A creative, interactive group discussion is more likely to take place when people are together in the same room; the participants can see and hear all group members.
- People can observe and respond to body language of participants.
- People generally feel more relaxed in this type of session because its format is more familiar.
- The atmosphere generally allows people to deal more effectively with difficult items.
- More group members are likely to participate in a face-to-face meeting.

Although face-to-face meetings can be effective, they have some disadvantages. Travel to and from the meeting can be costly, particularly to another city, province, or country. Costs include not only transportation and possibly overnight hotel rooms but also the productive work time lost in travel. The meeting rooms may be expensive. If the meeting is held at the company, finding a vacant room or a room that is used for multiple purposes can be a problem. Socializing can consume part of the meeting time if it is not controlled by the leader. People (particularly those who work together daily) may tend to rely on their colleagues' suggestions or solutions, reducing creative contributions.

Virtual Meetings

An alternative to face-to-face meetings, virtual meetings use telecommunication technology so that individuals at different locations can participate in a meeting as if they were in the same room. Through a variety of technology-assisted, two-way (interactive) communications, participants can choose from teleconferencing, videoconferencing, or web conferencing, each one of which provides a different communication advantage.

Teleconferences

A **teleconference**, also known as a **conference call**, is a meeting in which more than two individuals at different locations attend and communicate with each other via a telecommunications network. The communication device may be as simple as a standard telephone or a speakerphone around which a small group may gather. A small group conference call can be easily arranged by pressing the appropriate button on your telephone and following the instructions provided by your service provider to connect all participants. For larger groups, you can arrange for a meeting room with microphones, speakers, and bridging technology. Bridging services,

Bridging equipment is used to connect participants at multiple locations through dial-in access to a single phone number.

supplied by telecommunication service companies, provide individuals or groups of participants in multiple locations with access to a single phone number that is used to dial in and connect with one another.

In addition to local telecommunications providers, several teleconference service providers can also assist you in arranging a conference call. Using the key term *teleconference service providers Canada*, search the web to locate companies that provide these services in Canada and review some of the services they provide by accessing their websites.

One of the main advantages of a teleconference is the ability to gather participants on short notice (assuming their schedules allow). Other advantages include

- connecting individuals at any location
- using familiar, readily available, and inexpensive telephone technology
- reducing expenses related to travel and administrative support
- increasing the number of meeting participants
- receiving digital recordings of meetings

Although a very effective method of group communication and collaboration, the conference call has some disadvantages. The primary disadvantage is the lack of visual input. Because participants miss the visual clues that come from body language, misunderstandings can arise over something that has been said. It can be difficult to determine who is speaking, especially when some group members are not known to one another. During the call, the following guidelines will help make conference calls more effective:

- Identify yourself whenever you speak.
- Take turns speaking; ask whether anyone else wants to speak.
- When sharing the site with others,
  - pace the microphone as close to the speaker as possible
  - avoid side conversations—these sounds can be picked up by the microphone and are distracting to all
- Mute the microphone when you or others at your site are not speaking.

Video Conferences

A **video conference,** similar to a teleconference, is a meeting in which two or more people at different locations use telecommunication technology—computers, video or web cameras, and microphones—to participate in a virtual face-to-face meeting where they can *see* and *hear* one other in real time. Small group video conferences can be easily arranged using a computer or mobile device that has video-conferencing software such as Skype, IBM Sametime, or Google Hangouts. On a larger scale, groups of participants may gather together in dedicated video-conferencing rooms where audio and video connections are provided for several people at different locations.

Video conferences allow for individuals at distant locations to hear and see one another while discussing issues.

Web Conferences

Web conferences include three types of virtual meetings: the web meeting, the webinar, and the webcast. Using text, audio, and/or video, interactive communication happens in real time over the Internet. As with other types of virtual meetings, web conferences save the time and expense of travelling. A web conference can be between just two people but is usually held with numerous participants. It can have either a two-way video component—commonly known as a web meeting—or a one-way video component, known as a webinar or webcast.

A **web meeting** is a meeting where groups of people anywhere in the world connect to exchange ideas and information via computers and an Internet or a local area network connection. This technology provides people the opportunity to work collaboratively and productively in **real time**, simultaneously creating documents such as presentations, spreadsheets, reports, and proposals. Microsoft Skype for Business is a cloud-based instant messaging and meeting service (see Figure 11-2). Participants can move quickly and easily from instant messaging to online meetings with audio-, video-, and screen-sharing capabilities.

In a **webinar,** a presenter can share information and conduct question-and-answer sessions with participants. A webinar does not, however, provide the same level of interactive possibilities as a web meeting.

A **webcast** is primarily a presentation tool; because it is broadcast simultaneously to hundreds of recipients, it can be compared to a television broadcast except it takes place over the Internet. The one-way nature of this type of conferencing means that there is little opportunity for the presenter and the audience members to interact.

Advantages and Disadvantages of Virtual Meetings

As in face-to-face meetings, all types of virtual meetings have advantages and disadvantages.

Advantages include the following:

- Individuals can participate in a meeting or conference anytime from anywhere.
- Participants save time and the costs of meals and accommodation.

FIGURE 11-2

Skype for Business See, talk, and share information with Microsoft Skype for Business.

- A considerable amount of information can be presented concisely through the use of sophisticated audio and video technology.
- People who have expertise in a number of different areas can be brought together.
- A recording of the meeting can be provided to individuals who were not in attendance.

Disadvantages include the following:
- Participants have less opportunity for effectively brainstorming ideas.
- The structured environment leads to less spontaneity between individuals.
- Small nuances of body language are less likely to be picked up over the monitor.
- Participants have less opportunity for interaction before or after the meeting, which is a benefit in face-to-face meetings.

VIDEOCONFERENCING TIPS

The following guidelines will help make any video conference an effective and productive experience for all.

Be prepared:
- Designate a central contact person to be responsible for organizing the video conference.
- Develop a plan to handle any technical issues that may arise.
- Prepare an agenda, a list of attendees, and an outline of the meeting objective(s); distribute these and other relevant materials before the meeting.

During the meeting, do the following:
- Begin and end on time. Introduce all participants (consider using name tents) and use their names when directing questions to specific people. Announce when participants enter or leave the meeting.
- When speaking, make eye contact with the camera and allow for transmission delays. (Pause at the end of comments to allow other participants to respond, pose a question, or make a comment.)
- Practise standard meeting etiquette:
  - Be on time, courteous, and professional.
  - Turn off cellphones, beepers, and watch alarms.
  - Be present—when your microphone is on, avoid side conversations, shuffling papers, or other distracting activities that can be picked up; mute the microphone when not speaking.
  - Dress professionally—as if you are attending a face-to-face meeting; avoid jewellery and bright or boldly patterned clothing that could cause audio or visual distraction.

Whether the meeting is face-to-face or virtual, in the office with employees or colleagues, or on the road with clients and prospects, the same principles apply—be respectful of people's time, have an agenda, focus on what needs to be achieved, begin and end on time, and conclude with action items. Carefully analyze the meeting's purpose and the outcomes expected. This will help to determine the most appropriate meeting format. By following the guidelines presented here, you can ensure the meeting is effective.

Participating in Web Meetings

Leaders and participants have the same basic responsibilities during web meetings as for face-to-face meetings. However, web meetings will be more effective if participants follow these guidelines:
- Install any software needed for the meeting on your computer and test it, if possible, before the meeting.
- If you will be using webcams and the computer's microphone and speakers to take part in an online video meeting, make sure the camera, microphone, and speakers are working and are adjusted properly.
- When using a webcam is not an option, you may want to show a photo of yourself briefly during the meeting introduction.
- Use the mute button on your microphone or telephone when you are not speaking to avoid transmitting background sounds.
- Log on using the information provided by the leader a few minutes before the meeting time.
- If you will be speaking by telephone, call the number given a few minutes before the meeting time.
- If attendees cannot see one another and there are several people in the meeting, identify yourself by name when you make comments or ask questions.
- If a chat feature is part of the meeting software, use it to make a private comment to another attendee or to make comments to the entire group in response to questions or instructions from the meeting leader.
- Give your full attention to the meeting. Resist the urge to check emails or do other tasks while the meeting is in progress.

Leaders should be familiar with the equipment and software that will be used in the meeting. Leaders may want to hold a brief practice session with one or two co-workers. It is important to know exactly what attendees will see on their screens when you use various features of the meeting software. Remember that some people may be attending the meeting using a device such as a smartphone or tablet, which has a smaller screen than a laptop computer. Take this into account when considering the size of images and text fonts to display.

Some programs allow the leader to turn over control of the screen to a participant. If a leader plans to ask one or more participants to share their screens during the meeting, the participants should be told this ahead of time so they can be prepared. If attendees are to appear on screen as part of live video, the leader should let attendees know ahead of time. If the video will be recorded, attendees should also be given that information.

For some meetings, there may be several people attending in person in one room and one or more people attending online. If cameras will be used to show attendees, try to have one camera that can show individuals as they speak and another that can show all or most of the group at once. If an electronic whiteboard will be used in the meeting room, be sure the camera will show the images from the whiteboard clearly to the online attendees.

The leader can use the agenda to keep the meeting discussion on track. The agenda should be shown at the beginning of the meeting and again each time the discussion moves on to the next item. As with in-person meetings, the leader should ask for feedback from attendees regarding the effectiveness of the meeting and ways to improve future meetings.

Before the Meeting—Roles and Responsibilities

As you help plan and organize a meeting, remember that before, during, and after a meeting, everyone has a role to play: the person who initiates and usually leads or facilitates the meeting; the administrative professional who assists in planning for the meeting, making the necessary arrangements, and preparing the required materials; and the meeting participants. Each individual or group has specific roles and responsibilities that help ensure an effective and productive meeting.

The Meeting Leader's Responsibilities

The meeting leader is responsible for determining the purpose of the meeting, setting the objectives and planning the agenda, deciding who should attend, and determining the number of attendees. They may work closely with the administrative professional in accomplishing these tasks.

Determine the Purpose and Objectives

Every meeting must have a purpose; without it, there is no need for a meeting. Generally, your supervisor will call the meeting, so it is their role to state the purpose. Unless you as the administrative professional are calling the meeting, it is generally not your responsibility to determine the purpose of the meeting. However, you do need to understand the purpose of the meeting to make appropriate arrangements. If your supervisor does not tell you the purpose of the meeting, ask. Your asking may help your supervisor define the purpose; in other words, it may help crystallize their thinking regarding the meeting.

Every meeting should also have specific written objectives. Objectives should clearly define the purpose and state what is to be accomplished. For example, if the purpose is to establish a strategic plan for the following year, the objectives might be

- to evaluate the accomplishment of objectives for the current year
- to establish objectives and timelines for the following year, based on the organization's three-year strategic plan
- to determine the resources needed to meet these objectives
- to determine the responsibility for carrying out all objectives

When meeting notices clearly state both the purpose and the objective of the meeting, all participants will understand why the meeting is being called. Sharing the objectives with the participants beforehand allows them to be prepared for the meeting. If they have questions about the purpose, they will have an opportunity to ask their questions before the meeting.

Plan the Agenda

The meeting leader's role is to plan the agenda. The **agenda**, which should be distributed before the meeting, is a document that lists the topics to be discussed at a meeting (see Figure 11-3). The agenda should include the following information:

- name of the group, department, or committee
- date and time of the meeting
- location of the meeting
- the items to be discussed, in order of presentation
- the individual responsible for presenting each agenda item
- background materials (if needed)

A well-planned agenda saves time and increases productivity in a meeting. Be realistic in planning times to discuss each agenda item. If some attendees may not be able to stay for the entire meeting, place the most important agenda items before

FIGURE 11-3

Meeting Agenda

MEETING AGENDA			
Board of Directors			
Delbrook Centre – Cedar Room			
9–11 a.m. November 22, 20--			
1. Welcome and Introduction Adoption of Agenda Approval of Minutes-October Meeting and Business arising	(20 minutes)		Martin Albertson
2. Plans for Key Volunteer Rally	(45 minutes)	ACTION	Keri-An Mahar
3. Sports and Venue Report	(30 minutes)		Ryan Hughes
4. Director Updates	(15 minutes)	ACTION	Martin Albertson

less important ones. Send the agenda to the people invited to attend the meeting at least two days before the meeting. By providing participants with the proper information before a meeting, the leader can use the time in the meeting effectively, and decisions can be made in a timely manner.

Identify Participants

People invited to the meeting should be those who can contribute to accomplishing the objectives, who will be responsible for implementing the decisions made, or who represent a group affected by the decisions. In the previous situation where the purpose is to establish a strategic plan for the next year, all managers in the department should be invited to the meeting.

Now, assume that another meeting is being called. The objective is to brainstorm ideas for international expansion in three or four new countries. The people who should attend are the officers of the company since this decision will eventually be presented to the board of directors for approval.

In determining who should attend a meeting, consideration should always be given to the purpose of the meeting and who is most affected by the issue or problem that is to be discussed. Consideration should also be given to the background of the individuals being invited. For example, the diversity found in a **heterogeneous group** (a group having dissimilar backgrounds and experiences) can often solve problems more satisfactorily than a **homogeneous group** (a group with similar backgrounds and experiences). A heterogeneous group often brings varying points of view to the problem. Creative thinking through the diversity of participants present is more likely to occur than with a homogenous group. However, a more heterogeneous group may require a skilled facilitator in order to make the meeting productive.

In the two examples given previously, the participants have been selected based on their expertise in the matter being discussed. Now, assume a very different type of meeting will take place. This meeting is one in which the group is to determine new product lines for the company to pursue. An extremely creative group is needed to brainstorm ideas. One way to accomplish the goal is to include individuals from a cross section of the company with different backgrounds, education, and experiences. Generally, a heterogeneous group will bring varying views to an issue or problem.

The ideal number of participants is based on the purpose of the meeting and the number of people who can best achieve that purpose. A good size for a problem-solving and decision-making group is from 7 to 15 people. This size group allows for creative **synergy** (the ideas and products of a group of people developed through interaction with each other). There are enough people to generate divergent points of view and to challenge each other's thinking.

Small groups of six people or fewer may be necessary at times. For example, if the purpose of the meeting is to discuss a personnel matter, only the human resources director and the supervisor may be in attendance. If the purpose of the meeting is to discuss a faulty product design, only the product engineer, the manager of the engineering department, and the line technician may be present. Having only a few people in a meeting has advantages:

- Participants may be assembled more quickly.
- The meeting can be informal, resulting in more spontaneity and creativity.
- Group dynamics are easier to manage.

The disadvantages of a small group include the following:
- Points of view are limited.
- The participants may not generate enough ideas to create the best solution to the problem.
- Participants may not be willing to challenge one another's point of view, especially if they are a close-knit group.
- Participants may lack some of the details surrounding the issue.

Establish the Time and Place

The meeting leader is responsible for suggesting or establishing the approximate time of the meeting and identifying its general location. The administrative professional will check with participants to determine the most appropriate time for the meeting and select a location or reserve a meeting room. If a meeting is the first of a series of routine meetings, a recurring booking should be made for subsequent meetings. Doing so eliminates work for the administrative professional and also helps the participants avoid future schedule conflicts.

The Administrative Professional's Responsibilities

As an administrative professional, you have several responsibilities before, during, and after any meeting—face-to-face or virtual. Working closely with your supervisor, you will determine the purpose of the meeting, the agenda items, the attendees, and the responsibilities you are expected to perform. Some responsibilities you will be expected to handle on your own; however, you must understand your supervisor's preferences. When you first join an organization or begin to work with a supervisor, take time before each meeting to learn their needs and preferences. Once you have spent time with a particular supervisor, you will have less need to discuss the details. However, continue to discuss the purpose of the meeting and general expectations with your supervisor each time; otherwise, you may make decisions that could cause problems.

Confirm the Meeting Date and Time

At times, your supervisor will require a specific date and time for a meeting; at other times, only a general timeframe will be given, leaving date and time details to the administrative professional to arrange based on the availability of all participants. If you are responsible for establishing the date and time of the meeting, you will need to consider the schedules of the other participants. Check with them (or their administrative assistants) to determine their availability. If you have access to employees' individual online calendars, you can determine yourself whether and when participants are available. If not, you may wish to use scheduling or polling software such as Doodle to survey the group.

Each member of the group has input into determining a preferred meeting time. It is a good idea to avoid scheduling meetings immediately after lunch, at the end of the day, or on Monday mornings or Friday afternoons. Monday mornings are often used to get an overview of the week and handle any pressing items that may have occurred over the weekend. Friday afternoons are often used to complete projects and plan for the next week.

Meetings should generally last no longer than two hours. When people sit for longer than two hours, they become restless and lose interest. If a meeting must run two hours or longer, schedule short five- to ten-minute breaks every 40 or 45 minutes to allow people to move around.

Select and Prepare the Room

As soon as you have confirmed the date and time of the meeting and the number of attendees, room arrangements should be made. Most organizations will have conference rooms of different sizes that may be reserved. Select a room that is appropriate for the size of the group. In a room that is too large, participants may feel lost in all the empty space. In a room that is too small, participants will feel crowded, and the group may even be in violation of local fire department regulations. You can make a large room seem smaller by setting up chairs or tables in one corner of the room or, if movable partitions are available, by arranging them around the actual space that will be used for the meeting.

It is a good idea to locate the temperature controls before a meeting and determine how to change the temperature yourself if the room becomes too hot or too cold during the meeting. A hot and stuffy room or one that is ice-cold is a distraction when participants are trying to make important decisions. Maintenance personnel may be available to assist

Courtesy of Doodle

| Table view | Calendar view | Administration |

Most popular date: Wed 28/01/15 10:00 AM | Close poll ▼

6 of 6 invitees

Who is missing?

| | January 2015 | | | | | |
| | Fri 23 | Tue 27 | | Wed 28 | | |
	3:00 PM	3:00 PM	7:00 PM	10:00 AM	3:00 PM	7:00 PM
Diana	✓	✓	✓	✓	✓	✓
Dianne		✓		✓	✓	
Naomi		✓	✓	✓		
Gail		✓		✓		
Mike	✓			✓	✓	
Lynn	✓	✓		✓		
	3	5	3	6	2	1

Use a polling program to help determine the best time for a meeting.

but it may take them a while to get to the room, and usually the task is a simple one. Since bodies give off heat, the room generally will be warmer with people in it.

If you are selecting a room for a virtual meeting, be certain the room is large enough to accommodate the equipment needed and that the necessary connections are available. Check the electrical outlets in the room. Are there enough? Are they positioned so you do not have to string extension cords across the room? (Doing so can be hazardous.) The seating arrangement must allow all individuals to see the monitors, electronic whiteboards, or whatever other device is used. If possible, book the room for 30 minutes before the meeting so that you can check the equipment connections and perhaps even conduct a test meeting to ensure the equipment is working properly. Having a technical support person on standby in the event of technical issues helps to ensure meeting time is not interrupted.

A room can affect what happens during a meeting. Room inadequacies can start a meeting off on the wrong foot. The arrangements should allow for maximum effectiveness from the participants. If you carefully plan the room arrangements, you can help the meeting begin on a positive note.

Technology AT WORK

The administrative assistant may have access to an online calendar of meetings scheduled in the organization. Such a calendar saves time and effort if it is kept up-to-date because you can see times when people are already committed to other meetings.

Employees may make their online calendars accessible to members of their work group or to their supervisors and the group's administrative assistant. Before sending a meeting notice, you can check the online calendar of each person you plan to invite to find a time when everyone can attend.

Several programs are available online for scheduling meetings. Some of the programs are free or have a free level; others charge a fee for use and require you to register. Scheduling programs allow the user to select a range of dates on a calendar and send them to attendees. The attendees pick the dates and times that work best for them and reply. The user can view the responses and select the best time for the meeting. Some programs suggest one or more meeting times for you. If you are interested in learning more about this type of software, investigate websites for programs such as Doodle, Time Bridge, or When Is Good. You can also search the Internet using the terms *apps for scheduling a meeting*.

Determine Seating Arrangements

Choosing the seating arrangement of a room depends on the objectives of the meeting and the number of participants. The four basic seating arrangements are rectangular, circular (or oval), semicircular, and U-shaped. Figure 11-4 illustrates these arrangements.

FIGURE 11-4
Seating Arrangements for Meetings

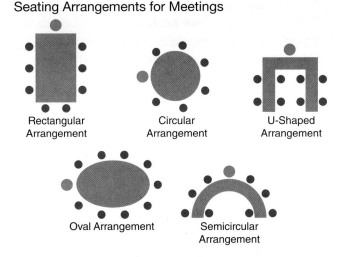

Rectangular Arrangement

Circular Arrangement

U-Shaped Arrangement

Oval Arrangement

Semicircular Arrangement

The **rectangular arrangement** allows the chairperson or leader to maintain control since they sit at the head of the table. This arrangement is best suited to formal meetings and is also appropriate when the purpose is to have individuals talk in groups of twos or threes. Individuals seated next to or opposite each other are able to discuss issues as they arise. If discussion is an important aspect of the meeting, the table should not be too long. A long table may make communication difficult because of the inability to hear clearly or see the nonverbal behaviour of all participants. A long table can also prevent the chairperson from taking part in discussions if they are at a distance from participants.

The **circular and oval arrangements** work best when the purpose of the meeting is to generate ideas and discussion in a relatively informal meeting. These arrangements encourage interaction and participation. Participants can make direct eye contact with everyone else in the group. Communication channels are considered equal among all participants because no one person is in a dominant position.

The **semicircular or U-shaped arrangements** work well for informal meetings of small groups (from six to eight people). The chair or leader has moderate control, since they can sit in a fairly dominant position. These two arrangements work well for presentations because the visuals can be set up at the front.

Prepare and Distribute the Notice of Meeting

A notice of meeting is just that—a notice. It should include the following:

- purpose and objectives of the meeting
- location, date, and time
- name of the person to whom participants should respond if it is someone other than the sender of the notice of meeting and a deadline to do so
- if available, background information and other materials to be considered before the meeting

A notice of meeting does not list the topics for discussion; that is the purpose of the agenda. An agenda may form part of the notice of meeting or may be attached to it. Since the two documents contain common elements, if the agenda topics have been determined, distributing an agenda to the participants can serve as both the notice of a meeting and the agenda.

The most effective way to notify participants of a meeting is to email them or use Microsoft Outlook, Google Calendar, or another online scheduler to deliver an electronic invitation. An online meeting request can be sent to potential participants with the subject of the meeting and then "save the date." The message area can contain a description of the purpose of the meeting and a note of "details to follow." If, however, details about the meeting, such as links to documents for discussion and other information useful to participants, are available, they can be attached or included in the message area. Recipients can then use their computer or mobile device to respond to the invitation—accepting or declining—and the meeting information will be automatically added to their own online calendar. This way, the meeting date has been added to the calendars of all attendees, and any reminders, changes, updates, or further information or instructions regarding the meeting are saved in one place for easy retrieval.

A list of the invitees and their individual responses are available for the organizer to see. See Figure 11-5 for an example of an electronic notice of meeting with a hyperlink to materials and an agenda attached.

FIGURE 11-5

Electronic Meeting Notification Response and Attendance Tracked

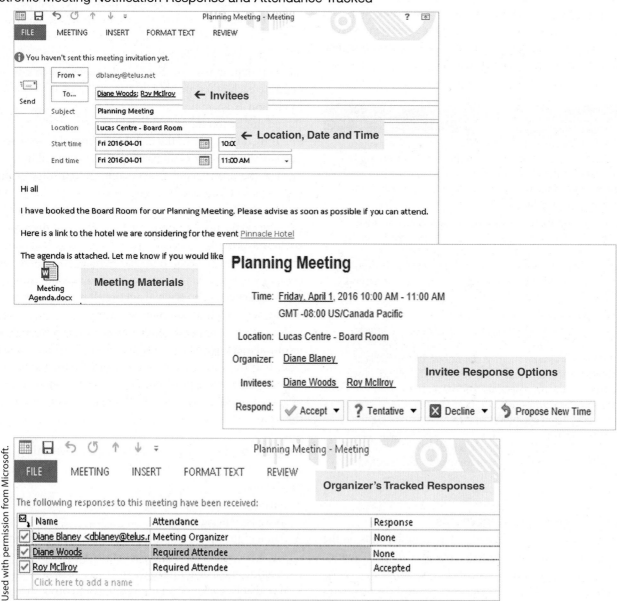

Responses to electronic meeting invitations can be automatically tracked.

You may be responsible for following up to confirm participant attendance. As a reminder, email or telephone those who have not yet responded or their administrative professional. Let your supervisor know who will and will not be attending and who might be late. Prepare a list of all invitees, indicating those participants who plan to attend so that your supervisor can see potential attendance at a glance and can record participant attendance during the meeting. If many of the invitees are unable to attend, it may be necessary to cancel or reschedule. Although not generally a good idea, cancelling or rescheduling a meeting is best if key individuals are unable to attend.

Prepare and Distribute the Agenda

Participants have a responsibility before coming to a meeting to be prepared but unless they know what to expect, being prepared is difficult. Participants need and should receive a detailed agenda and any supporting materials at least a day or two (preferably a week) beforehand. The meeting leader is responsible for determining the specific items for consideration at the meeting; the administrative professional is responsible for preparing and distributing it. The agenda should include the following information:

- name of the meeting or the group
- date of the meeting
- start and end times
- location
- order of topics and activities of the meeting, which could also include the anticipated time (e.g., Budget Report at 2:30 p.m.)
- person responsible for presenting each topic or activity
- action expected on each item
- background materials (if needed and not already distributed with a meeting notice)

Ask your supervisor or the meeting leader whether a time span should be included for individual agenda items. Although not essential, including time spans reminds people of the importance of time and adhering to a schedule. If time frames are not listed, the facilitator of the meeting will need to keep an eye on the time and move the discussion along.

The order of agenda items can vary. Some people think the most difficult items should be presented first so participants can deal with them while they are fresh. Others think the difficult items should be presented last. Review previous agendas to determine past practice or check with the meeting leader to find out the preferred order.

Formatting the document varies across companies and sometimes even across departments within an organization. Once you have established a format for the agenda of a particular type of meeting, use it to create a new template to be used in the future. Word processing programs include a variety of templates that simplify the production of preparing an agenda. Figure 11-3 illustrates an agenda.

In this example, the word "Action" is listed after certain agenda items to indicate that a decision should be made during this meeting. Such an approach helps participants know what is expected of them. If they are to make a decision, they can come prepared to do so. If a decision will not be made on an item, the meeting leader should let the group know what will happen. Will the item be discussed again at a later date? Will it be referred to another group? Participants can contribute more completely when they understand what is expected of them.

Use email or, if hardcopies of background materials need to be sent, interoffice or external mail to distribute the agenda and additional materials to participants. Keep meeting materials as concise as possible; most people will not take the time to read lengthy documents.

Prepare Meeting Materials

Assemble a folder for each meeting your supervisor will attend or lead. The folder should include several items:

- the meeting notice and/or the agenda with a list of the people who will be in attendance
- materials that have been sent out beforehand and notes that are needed at the meeting
- presentations or additional handouts

If the meeting is offsite, you may need to provide directions to it. The Global Positioning System (GPS) capability of smartphones and navigational aids in most new cars can provide driving directions, and even traffic reports. However, your supervisor may prefer that you use an online site such as MapQuest, Google Maps, or Yahoo! Maps to obtain and print out hardcopies of maps and driving instructions to place in the meeting folder.

Materials should be sent to all participants well in advance of the meeting. These materials can be attached to the email notice of meeting or made available to all through shared access to a secure online drop box. If several pages are to be distributed during the meeting, place them in folders—one folder for each individual. Sometimes participants are expected to take notes. Demonstrate your initiative and professionalism by providing pen and paper in the folder.

Order Equipment and Other Items

Determine what equipment, if any, is needed for the meeting. Will an electronic presentation be made? If so, you will need to ensure that a projection device is available that is compatible with the laptop or tablet to be used by the presenter; you may also need to ensure that a screen is present. Prepare a list of equipment needed and document the arrangements that have been made and who is responsible for each. If something is your responsibility, note that. Before the meeting begins, take your list to the meeting room and check that the necessary items are all present and in working order.

Providing beverages is not mandatory but water should usually be available. For a morning meeting, coffee, tea, and juice along with muffins or Danish would be appropriate, and for an afternoon meeting, consider tea, coffee, or pop and cookies. Check the company policy (e.g., refreshments may only be required for meetings longer than two hours) and with your supervisor to see what they prefer to do.

For a luncheon meeting, you may have the responsibility of calling the caterer, selecting the menu, and arranging for the meal to be served. Avoid a heavy lunch, especially if you are expecting people to work afterward. A salad or light entree is more appropriate for a working lunch. Also, if people will likely take notes, soup would not be a good choice. It is also important to select items that are easy to eat and with a variety of vegetarian and protein choices. If the room is small, choose food items that generate as little clutter and use as few dishes as possible.

For a dinner meeting, you may have the responsibility of working with an outside caterer. Provide a menu that meets the health, religious, or dietary needs of most participants. If you do know the participants, provide food that meets their individual needs. If you do not know them, ask the caterer to recommend dishes for specific circumstances (e.g., vegan, non-dairy). Be certain to ask your supervisor the budget allocation for the meal.

For a dinner meeting at a hotel, you can expect assistance from the hotel staff. You will usually be responsible for selecting the menu. If the event is formal, you might wish to have table decorations and place cards. When selecting the seating arrangement, you should be familiar with the group; your supervisor can help you with this task. You want to avoid seating people next to each other who do not get along.

The Participants' Responsibilities

It is not enough for participants to simply attend the meeting. They have been asked to the meeting because the chairperson believes they have something to offer. Participants' responsibilities begin before the meeting, when they should read and respond promptly to the meeting notice and review any related materials received beforehand. Being prepared means understanding the purpose of the meeting, analytically evaluating the materials in relation to the purpose of the meeting, and taking seriously the responsibility to contribute to the success of the meeting. No one appreciates the person who comes to a meeting late and opens up the pack of materials for the first time, clearly not having read the material beforehand.

During the Meeting—Roles and Responsibilities

The Meeting Leader's Responsibilities

When you are assisting at a meeting in your role as an administrative professional, the leader (also known as the *chairperson* or *chair*) is usually your supervisor. If your organization uses a team approach to resolve issues or accomplish specific tasks, you, as an administrative professional, may be the team leader or co-leader (one member of a team of two) responsible to chair or lead a meeting. In both situations, it is important to know the following roles and responsibilities of a meeting leader:

- Keep the participants focused on the agenda.
- Encourage participation from everyone in the meeting.
- Limit the domination of any one person in the meeting.
- Positively reinforce the contributions of all individuals.
- Keep the discussions moving toward the determined outcomes.

Follow the Agenda

At the beginning of the meeting, the chairperson should state the purpose of the meeting and let participants generally know the outcomes that are expected and whether any special procedures such as *Robert's Rules of Order* will be followed. For example, if the purpose of a meeting is to establish a direction for the department for the next two years, the expected outcomes of the meeting may be to determine at least two departmental objectives. If it appears several participants wish to speak and discussions may become lengthy, the chairperson could indicate that a **speaker's list** will be kept. Adopting this procedure ensures that everyone will have an equal opportunity, in an orderly fashion, to contribute.

If participants stray from the agenda, the chairperson is responsible for sensitively but firmly bringing them back to the topic being discussed. For example, the chair might say, "Thank you for your comments. We can put that issue on the agenda for a future meeting. Now let's continue discussing the departmental objectives we must set."

Determine the Procedures

Formal meetings, such as of the board of directors of a corporation or the annual business meetings of a professional organization, are generally highly structured, with procedures in place that govern the actions of participants. It may be necessary for the chairperson to adhere to **Robert's Rules of Order** (first published 1876; now in its 11th edition). These guidelines for *parliamentary procedure* cover the conduct of participants. Such rules are not strictly adhered to or necessarily appropriate for informal meetings such as small committee meetings, departmental meetings, or informational meetings. You should, however, become familiar with them and with the

FIGURE 11-6

Meeting Terminology

- **Ad hoc (special) committee.** A committee, also known as a task force, created to deal with a specific task or issue. It is typically dissolved once the task is complete.
- **Amendment.** A change in the wording of a motion that has been made.
- **Bylaws.** The rules and procedures that govern the operation of an organization.
- **Minutes.** A written record of the meeting.
- **Motion.** A formal expression of a proposal or an action to be undertaken. It must be recorded verbatim (that is, in the exact words spoken by the mover) in the minutes. It requires a mover (the presenter of the motion) and a seconder (a person who may or not support the motion but is in favour of the motion being discussed). After the motion has been debated, it is voted on by the meeting participants.
- **Parliamentary procedures.** The procedural rules that ensure all participants have an opportunity to participate in the decision-making process.
- **Quorum.** The minimum number of participants required to be present at a meeting before decisions can officially be made.
- **Resolution.** A formal expression of opinion or direction of an organization (similar to a motion).
- **Standing committee.** A committee created to deal with ongoing matters.

terminology given in Figure 11-6. Understanding these basic guidelines can help the chairperson to maintain control of discussions, keep participants focused on the agenda and task at hand, and ensure that all those in attendance have an equal opportunity to participate fully.

Robert's Rules of Order is available in full or simplified versions, which are often adapted by individual organizations. Some organizations choose to post on their websites those aspects of the rules that will be adopted in whole or in part at all meetings within the organization.

Check your local bookstore or library for more information; you will find several books available. The MindTap site for this textbook contains links to the *Robert's Rules of Order* official website and other websites that provide additional information on chairing successful meetings and meeting planning.

Manage Time

The leader is responsible for beginning meetings on time, even if several people are late in arriving. If the meeting notice or agenda indicates a 9 a.m. start, the meeting should begin sharply at 9. Do not wait for latecomers; doing so is unfair to those who have made the effort to be on time. Time frames—the beginning and ending times—were established when the meeting notice was sent out, and some participants may have made commitments based on this information. People will soon get the message that meetings start on time, and they will

be more prompt in the future. Be prepared with phone numbers for all participants so that if the meeting leader needs you to contact someone who has not arrived, you can do so.

The same holds true for ending meetings; the meeting leader is responsible for monitoring the end time of the meeting. Starting and ending on time can help the group accomplish its objectives in the allocated time. Allowing a meeting to run over significantly from the time scheduled is poor management and insensitive to the needs of the participants. Calendars are generally tightly scheduled and to permit one meeting to go longer than scheduled may make participants late for other commitments. People will appreciate your being respectful of their time constraints.

Encourage Participation

Once the meeting begins, the meeting leader is responsible for encouraging all individuals to participate. They should help individuals feel secure enough to say what they really think. If, as the meeting gets under way, several people have not spoken, the chairperson may encourage them by saying:

- "Glenda, what direction do you think we should take?"
- "Guy, we haven't heard from you on this issue. What are your thoughts?"

It is important to let each participant know that their opinion is valued. To encourage everyone to contribute and to demonstrate respect for participants and the comments they make, the chairperson might make one of the following statements:

- "Thank you for that contribution."
- "That's a great idea."
- "Thanks. Your idea has some real possibilities for us. Can you expand on it a bit more?"

The chair is also responsible for seeing that no one person dominates the conversation, even if that person's contributions are beneficial. The chairperson can use one of the following statements:

- "Azmeena, that is an excellent idea. Eduardo, how could it be implemented in your area?"
- "Thanks, Azmeena; Eduardo, what do you think about the direction?"

The meeting leader needs to keep the participants focused on the agenda, positively reinforce all individuals for their contributions, and keep the discussion moving to accomplish the desired outcomes.

Facilitate Decision Making

The chairperson is responsible for helping the participants reach a decision about the issue or problem, or for providing direction if a decision is needed. The chair must carefully assess whether all alternatives have been discussed and can then summarize the discussions and state what they believe to be the solution before moving the group toward a decision. For example, the chair might say, "We seem to have identified each issue and the possible solutions. Does anyone have anything more to add?" Then the chair can move to resolution by saying "Now let's determine which solution will work best in our present situation." Once a resolution is reached, the chair can check to see if all participants agree by asking, "Now that we have reached a resolution, is everyone in the room comfortable with it? Are we overlooking anything? Are there problems we haven't addressed?"

One of the responsibilities of the meeting leader in a meeting is to encourage participation by all those present.

The Administrative Professional's Responsibilities

Greeting participants and introducing them to one another may be part of your responsibilities at the beginning of a meeting. Your courteousness, warmth, and friendliness can go a long way toward making people feel comfortable and getting the meeting off to a good start. During the meeting your main responsibility will probably be to take the minutes (a record of the meeting).

Taking the Minutes

The minutes are a concise record of the discussions that occurred and decisions that were made during the meeting. With the exception of motions, minutes do not need to be recorded **verbatim** (word for word). When recording discussions, you should summarize and record all pertinent information; for motions, include the name of the person who made the motion, the name of the person who seconded the motion, the exact (verbatim) wording of the motion, and whether the motion passed or failed. Figure 11-7 lists items that should be included in the minutes.

Taking meeting notes is not as easy as it sounds. You may feel anxious the first time you are assigned the responsibility of taking notes and preparing the minutes of a meeting.

FIGURE 11-7

Items to Include in the Minutes of a Meeting

- The name of the group
- The type of meeting (regular, special, monthly)
- The date, time, and place of the meeting, and the time the meeting started
- The name of the person leading the meeting
- The name of the person acting as recorder
- The names of participants present and absent
- Approval or correction of the minutes from the previous meeting
- Reports of committees, officers, or individuals
- Actions taken and/or motions made
- Items on which action needs to be taken and the person responsible for taking the action
- The date and time of the next meeting (if one has been scheduled)
- Time of adjournment
- The signature of the chairperson of the meeting (not required for informal meetings)
- The signature of the secretary for the group (not required for informal meetings)

However, with practice you will gain confidence in doing so. Adopting some of the following tips will help you feel comfortable and competent when taking notes at a meeting.

- Determine how you will take your notes.
  - Will you use a laptop or tablet? If so, create a template for the minutes that includes the agenda heading and the standard identifying information (name of group, date, time the meeting began, place, etc.). Then you can focus on and perhaps participate in the discussions while making your notes. (To be prepared in the event of a technical failure, have a backup available—paper and pen.)
  - Will you use pen and paper? If so, write rather than print your notes—writing is faster. Develop a set of abbreviations that can be used to reduce the amount of writing required. Review your notes as soon as possible after the meeting.
- Review the agenda, previous minutes, and related materials beforehand—know what the meeting is expected to accomplish.
- Prepare a list with the names of individuals expected to attend and use it to record participants as they arrive. This list is particularly useful when determining whether a quorum is present. If you have not met all attendees, circulate the list at the beginning of the meeting so they can initial beside their name. Names of attendees and those who are absent often form part of the minutes.
- Make sure you know who everyone is so that you are able to correctly identify them in the minutes. If necessary, draw a seating plan that identifies each participant.
- If previous minutes need to be corrected, make the correction by hand on the original and include a description of this correction in the current minutes.

- Sit near the chairperson so you can hear clearly what they say.
- If you need assistance to clarify details at any time during the meeting, let the chair know! It is better to communicate your need for clarification than to miss an important detail. Decide beforehand on a method to signal the chair.
- Record the name of the mover (and perhaps a seconder) of any motions made.
- Record motions verbatim. If the motion is lengthy, pass a piece of paper to the mover of the motion and ask that person to write out the motion for you. This approach will ensure the motion is recorded accurately. You may, as the meeting recorder, be asked to repeat the motion for the group before a vote is taken.
- Listen to the discussions and attempt to gain an overall sense of what is being discussed. Create brief notes that capture the essence of the discussion—you can use these notes to fill in the details later. Include in the written record the specific details about who will do what, when, and how. Write "Action" or "Agreed" beside items when discussion concludes or after the vote has been taken.
- If a committee is being created or officers elected, record their names and positions.
- Record the date, time, and place for the next meeting, and the time that the meeting ends or adjourns.

If you have used a tablet or laptop, you need only read over your notes, make necessary changes to the file, format the file, and distribute the document. Such an approach is faster than taking notes by hand or making an audio recording of the meeting and then having to key everything after the meeting.

Writing AT WORK

You may be asked to record notes for minutes during a meeting and to write the minutes after the meeting. Minutes should include the following information:
- name of the group
- date, time, and place of the meeting
- name of the presiding officer
- members present and absent
- approval or correction of the minutes from the previous meeting
- reports of committees, officers, or individuals
- complete information for motions made
- items on which action needs to be taken and the people responsible for taking the action
- a concise summary of the important points of discussion
- the date and time of the next meeting (if one is scheduled)
- the name and title of the person who will be signing the minutes, along with space to sign their name

The Participants' Responsibilities

Participants are responsible for arriving on time and contributing thoughtful, well-considered, or well-researched comments. Participants should demonstrate appropriate meeting etiquette by
- respecting the chair's role
- giving their full attention to the meeting
- being courteous to other participants
- listening non-judgmentally to others
- participating in discussions without dominating them
- turning off pagers and cellphones so that text messages, emails, and phone calls cannot be answered during that time
- taking notes

Participating in a meeting may sound simpler to do than it actually is—your mind may wander and you could find yourself focusing on other work-related tasks or on personal issues. However, your positive contributions could provide the perspective that brings the meeting back on track when discussions stray, or they could help the chairperson keep the meeting focused.

If a meeting does go longer than scheduled, it is perfectly acceptable as a participant to excuse yourself and leave the meeting. In doing so, let the meeting leader and others know you have a previous commitment but that you will review the minutes and be prepared for the next meeting. This comment demonstrates your desire to fulfill your commitments and lets the other participants know you are being responsible, not inconsiderate or rude—but rather that you are fulfilling another obligation.

After the Meeting—Roles and Responsibilities

The Meeting Leader's Responsibilities

Evaluate the Meeting
Generally, with informal meetings within an organization, no formal evaluation is necessary. However, an informal evaluation can be done by the chairperson (and possibly by the participants). If attendees are forthright, they may tell the chairperson they found the meeting to be a waste of time. When attendees make such a statement, the chair should seek clarification on exactly what they meant. The chair may also want to ask two or three individual participants how the meeting went. In either case, the chair will also want to consider the following questions to help evaluate the meeting:
- Did everyone in attendance take part in the meeting?
- Was the nonverbal behaviour positive?
- Were participants creative problem-solvers?

- Did participants exhibit a high energy level?
- Was the purpose of the meeting satisfied?
- Were appropriate decisions made?
- Can I improve the way I handled the issues, the people, or the meeting?

If the meeting is relatively formal, the chairperson may ask participants to complete an evaluation form. See Figure 11-8 for a sample.

FIGURE 11-8
A Meeting Evaluation Form

Meeting Evaluation
Place a check mark in the "Yes" or "No" column. Attach any additional comments you may have to this form.

1. Was the purpose of the meeting accomplished?
   Yes ☐ No ☐

2. Was the agenda received in time to prepare for the meeting?
   Yes ☐ No ☐

3. Was the room arrangement satisfactory?
   Yes ☐ No ☐

4. Did the chairperson help the group accomplish the goals of the meeting?
   Yes ☐ No ☐

5. Did the chairperson adhere to the agenda?
   Yes ☐ No ☐

6. Were the appropriate people included in the meeting?
   Yes ☐ No ☐

7. Did all attendees participate in the discussion?
   Yes ☐ No ☐

8. Did attendees listen to each other?
   Yes ☐ No ☐

9. Did the chairperson encourage participation?
   Yes ☐ No ☐

10. Did the meeting begin on time?
    Yes ☐ No ☐

11. Did the meeting end on time?
    Yes ☐ No ☐

12. Were decisions that were made consistent with the purpose of the meeting?
    Yes ☐ No ☐

The Administrative Professional's Responsibilities

After a meeting, review with the meeting chairperson what did and did not go well. Such a review helps you plan more effectively for the next meeting. Your duties after the meeting include ensuring that the meeting room is left in order, preparing the minutes, and handling other details.

Routine Tasks

These routine tasks are essential after a meeting:

- Return all equipment. See that additional tables and chairs are removed or returned to their proper location.
- Clean up any food or beverage leftovers, or notify the cleaning staff if the room needs a general cleaning.
- On your task list or calendar, make a note of items that require future attention by you or your supervisor.
- Send out any necessary follow-up correspondence.
- Evaluate the meeting. Review what happened and consider how you might improve the arrangements for the next meeting; if you used a caterer, was the quality of the food acceptable? Were the staff helpful?
- Keep notes on meetings for an appropriate length of time so that you are able to refer to them when planning the next similar meeting. Keep the names and telephone numbers of contact people. These notes will help ensure future success.
- If the chair has decided on a formal evaluation, you may be expected to prepare and administer the evaluation and summarize the results.

Prepare the Minutes

Minutes are not necessary for all meetings; however, the record they provide reminds participants of the discussion that occurred and the responsibilities they may have agreed to as a result of the meeting. The overview of discussions, decisions, and action items provides the information needed so that non-attendees, too, can be well informed prior to the next meeting.

Minutes are required in the following situations:

- when decisions are made that affect a large number of people
- for formal meetings, such as board of directors' meetings
- when participants act upon a list of different topics and a record is necessary to recall the events
- when the same type of meeting is held on a regular basis and a record is needed of the group's continuing activities
- when meeting results need to be reported to the president or other officers of the organization

If minutes are necessary, they should be prepared and distributed within 24 to 48 hours of a meeting. Prompt preparation and distribution of minutes reminds participants of their responsibilities before the next meeting and gives those who were unable to attend a sense of what occurred and what decisions have been reached. Non-participants (those who are not members of the group but who are interested or affected) may also receive a copy of the meeting minutes. For example, minutes from a company board meeting may be made available to all executives within a company.

Although there is no set format for writing minutes, checking previous minutes of the group will provide you with a sense of the format followed in your organization. Your word processing program will have a variety of templates from which you can choose, or your organization may use templates that include the preferred formatting and the standard information common to all minutes. Minutes generally include the following information:

- The title *Minutes*, the group's name and type of meeting, and the date.
- The names of the meeting leader, members present and absent, and, optionally, those who arrived late and whether or not a quorum was established.
- Minutes are usually single-spaced. Margins should be at least 1 inch (about 2.5 cm). If the minutes are to be placed in a bound book, the left margin should be 1-1/2 inches (about 3.75 cm).
- Numbered paragraphs or subject captions that usually correspond to the agenda items can be used as paragraph headings.
- Motions made, names of the mover and the seconder (if there is one), and the outcome of the motion—whether it passed or failed.
- A concise summary of the important discussion points, the items on which action needs to be taken, and the name(s) of those responsible.
- The date and time of the next meeting if one has been scheduled.
- The time the meeting adjourned or ended.
- Minutes of informal meetings do not require signatures; the minutes of board meetings and professional organizations are generally signed. When minutes are to be signed, a signature line should be provided.

Store minutes electronically or in hardcopy form in a binder or notebook. Retain them for future reference with the agenda and all pertinent materials that were presented. Minutes from a meeting are shown in Figure 11-9.

The Participants' Responsibilities

Your responsibilities as a participant do not necessarily end once the meeting is over. For example, you may be responsible for undertaking some research or other action before the next meeting; or you may have been asked to work with one or two other people to bring back a recommendation to the next meeting. Whatever the task, it must be completed in a timely manner; others are depending on it.

Conferences and Other Events

Executives may belong to a professional organization in a particular field of expertise, such as accounting, engineering, or human resources. Many of these organizations hold at least one major conference each year. Most companies encourage their executives to participate in conferences as a means of broadening their knowledge. As a member of a professional organization such as the International Association of Administrative Professionals (IAAP), ARMA International, the Canadian Information Processing Society (CIPS), or some local organization, you too may attend or perhaps help to plan some of their conferences. While a conference, convention, or special event is much larger in scope and has more participants than a meeting, many of the principles of organizing effective meetings can be applied to organizing these larger events. Event planning is a skill that many employers seek in their administrative professionals. Your program of study may include a complete course devoted to this topic.

Your role as an administrative professional may be to assist your supervisor in planning a conference. Similar to planning for a meeting, you will have a variety of responsibilities before, during, and after the event. In doing so, you may use event planning software. You may also work with a professional meeting or event planner.

Before the Event

Preparing for a regional or national conference takes months of work. Good planning ensures a smooth, successful event. Poor planning can result in a disorganized, ineffective event. Event management software such as Smartsheet, a spreadsheet, or Microsoft OneNote can help you to keep the details organized and ensure important arrangements are not overlooked.

Similar to planning a meeting, when planning a conference, one of the major responsibilities is to determine the location and meeting facilities. Contact the chamber of commerce in the city being considered. Ask for information about the city and appropriate conference facilities. Request conference planning guides from the hotels and conference centres that give floor plans of the facilities, dining and catering services, price list of rooms, and layout of meeting rooms. Once the city and hotel have been selected, detailed arrangements need to be made for meeting rooms, guest rooms, meals, and so on.

Your task will not be to invite someone to speak unless you are working on a conference where you are a member and assisting with the planning (an IAAP conference, for example). However, you may contact presenters to make travel and lodging arrangements before the conference. If you are responsible for making hotel arrangements for a presenter, you should determine the types of accommodations the presenter would prefer (within the cost limitations of the budget), as presenters' expenses are usually covered, at least in part, by the host organization. For example, does the presenter need an accessible room? If the conference is not at a hotel, you might give the presenter a choice of two or three area hotels (within your price range). If you are making flight reservations, you need to know the person's desired arrival and departure times and any other transportation needs.

FIGURE 11-9
Meeting Minutes

MINUTES

Summer Games Association

MONTHLY MEETING - BOARD OF DIRECTORS

Delbrook Centre – Cedar Room
November 22, 20--

PRESENT: Martin Albertson (Chairperson), Keri-An Mahar (Recorder), Sabina Burrell, Sarah Chung, Ryan Hughes, Dean Kvanstrom, Dianne Lyons, Annika Strilchuk

ABSENT : Mae Michaluk, Jeremy Siu

1.   The meeting was called to order at 9:00 a.m. Attendees were asked to introduce themselves, Chairperson Albertson welcomed new members Sabina Burrell and Dianne Lyons.

The agenda was approved by consensus with the following addition:

➢   Approval of Logo; added as item 5

Minutes of the October meeting were approved as circulated with one amendment. Under item 7, the prizes donated for the Key Volunteer Rally were from "Towne and Country Sports" and not from "Country Sports".

Business Arising

Sabina confirmed the process for registering as a Non-Profit Society has been completed. As a result a bank account has been opened and funds can now be deposited.

Dean indicated that confirmation for a location for the Opening Ceremonies has been received from the hotel at Lonsdale Quay.

2.   Keri-An reported on the plans for the Key Volunteer Rally, Since she does not have a Chair for the Reception Committee, she will assume responsibility for this function but will need help from other Directors. Martin volunteered to help with beverage purchases, Sarah with name badges and Dianne with equipment rentals. Martin indicated he would need a projector for a video he will be presenting. Keri-An asked other Directors to contact her if there was anything else she needed to arrange.   **ACTION ALL**

3.   Ryan reported on the determination of the sports to be involved. To date 23 of the 28 of the activities have been confirmed with 5 sport specific associations still to reply. He is arranging for a sport venue tour sometime early in the spring, Date TBD. All Directors will be expected to attend.   **ACTION RYAN**

4.   All Directors reported on their progress in recruiting chairs for their various directorates. Still needed a Director of Communications and Director of Promotions. Names of any potential candidates should be forwarded to Martin to contact.   **ACTION ALL**

5.   Three examples of a logo for the games were circulated. Considerable discussion produced no consensus Item tabled to next meeting.

Next meeting December 20, 20-- in the Committee Room at City Hall.

The meeting adjourned at 11:00 a.m.

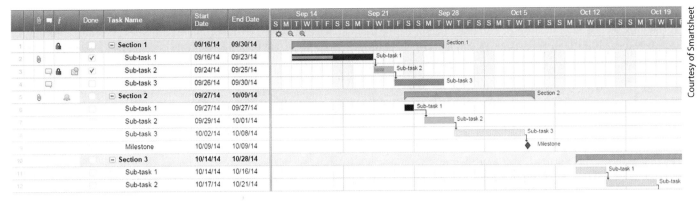

		i	Done	Task Name	Start Date	End Date	
1	🔒		☐	⊟ Section 1	09/16/14	09/30/14	
2	📎		✓	Sub-task 1	09/16/14	09/23/14	
3	💬🔒	📷	✓	Sub-task 2	09/24/14	09/25/14	
4	💬		☐	Sub-task 3	09/26/14	09/30/14	
5	📎		👤	⊟ Section 2	09/27/14	10/09/14	
6				Sub-task 1	09/27/14	09/27/14	
7				Sub-task 2	09/29/14	10/01/14	
8				Sub-task 3	10/02/14	10/08/14	
9				Milestone	10/09/14	10/09/14	
10				⊟ Section 3	10/14/14	10/28/14	
11				Sub-task 1	10/14/14	10/16/14	
12				Sub-task 2	10/17/14	10/21/14	

Courtesy of Smartsheet

Event planning software provides a visual timeline that helps keep event details organized and ensures important arrangements are not overlooked.

Preregistration is typically held before the conference; you may be involved in setting up the preregistration in addition to actually registering individuals. Most registration is now done online, and your role may be to design the online registration process and post the appropriate information online. Also, you may be involved in preparing packets of information for the registrants. Registration packets often include program information, a list of participants, and a small gift or two.

You may want to have the speakers post their presentations, handouts, or other materials to a website before the conference. Before the conference, add templates, logos, or other formatting to give all the information a coordinated look. You can distribute this information online after the conference, or you might provide conference attendees with a USB drive that contains the materials. You may need to work with your company's IT personnel or a service provider to share the materials with attendees. You may also be responsible for making sure all presenters have posted their material by a certain date after the conference has taken place.

During the Event

Your responsibilities during the conference may include running errands, delivering messages to participants, and solving any problems that may occur. Other responsibilities may include checking the room arrangements, equipment needs, meal arrangements, and a multitude of other last-minute details as they arise. Since you are a representative of the company for which you work or the organization of which you are a member, it is imperative that you present a positive image at all times. Keep a smile on your face, and handle even the most difficult situations with poise and confidence.

After the Event

After the conference, your basic duties involve cleaning up and following up. These responsibilities include seeing that all equipment is returned, presenters are assisted with transportation to the airport, letters of appreciation are sent to presenters and others, expense reports are completed, and bills are paid. You may also be responsible for seeing that the proceedings of the conference are published and made available to participants. You may not be responsible for writing the report, but you may be responsible for working with the conference reporters in assembling and distributing it. At many conferences, the sessions are recorded and made available to participants on the conference website. You may be responsible for assembling presentations from different presenters, and uploading them to the website.

A post-conference evaluation session should be held with all individuals who worked on the conference. At this meeting, you will need to review the areas that were successful and those that were not. The participants may have completed a formal evaluation of the conference. If so, the evaluations need to be tallied and summarized in the post-conference evaluation session.

People AT WORK

Meeting or Event Planner

Meeting or event planners coordinate the details of a meeting or conference as requested by a client. The client may be a business, an organization, or an individual. A meeting planner typically handles tasks such as these:

- determining and arranging for the meeting location at a hotel or convention centre
- handling lodging arrangements and coordinating transportation requirements for participants
- arranging for meals and other food and beverage services, possibly in conjunction with a caterer
- arranging for necessary telecommunication services
- arranging for any necessary audiovisual equipment
- assigning exhibit space and working with exhibitors to resolve any issues related to the exhibits

Your company may hire a meeting planner to coordinate the details of a large meeting or conference. You may work with the planner to explore ways to meet your company's needs and stay within your budget.

Take note of all issues and problems, which should be passed on to the appropriate organization or company personnel so that people involved in the next conference will have the benefit of your experiences. No one ever wants to make the same mistake twice. A record of the problems or issues and their solutions or outcomes will help the next group avoid some mistakes.

Soft Skills

VALUE CLARIFICATION

Values are ideas or qualities that we view as important. They determine how we live on a day-to-day basis. For example, knowledge is a value. We may or may not spend much time thinking about what we value, but the decisions we make each day are influenced by the values we have.

Our early values are learned from significant people in our immediate environment—our parents or guardians and other family members—and from educational, social, and religious institutions, such as our schools and places of worship. Our values are not static; that is, as we grow and change, our values may change. As you study the material in this course and perform the tasks given, you should come to understand your own value system. Your value system shapes what you believe, how you live and work, and how you relate to others.

Values are not inherently good or bad. However, the way in which you live your values may involve behaviours that are either acceptable or unacceptable in a particular society. Such a statement is incorrect; everyone has values. The values a person holds simply may not match our values.

Chapter Summary

The summary will help you remember the important points covered in this chapter.

- Meetings can be a good means of generating ideas, sharing information, and making decisions. Unnecessary and unproductive meetings waste the time of both the individual and the organization.
- A meeting is considered unnecessary when its purpose or the appropriate people to attend have not been clearly identified, when there is inadequate data or insufficient time to prepare, when one-way information could be better communicated by other means, when there is a need to discuss confidential or sensitive personnel matters, or when a considerable amount of anger or hostility exists.
- Meetings may be informal, such as staff or customer/client meetings, or formal, such as a board, committee, or project/task force meeting.
- Meeting formats may be face-to-face or virtual. Teleconferences, video conferences, or web conferences—web meetings, webinars, and webcasts—are examples of virtual meeting formats.
- The meeting leader is responsible for determining the purpose and objectives of the meeting, planning the agenda, determining the participants, and establishing the time and place. The administrative professional may assist with these tasks.

- The administrative professional is responsible, in consultation with the meeting leader, to select, reserve, and prepare the meeting room; determine the seating arrangement; prepare and distribute the meeting notice, agenda, and meeting materials; order equipment and food and beverages; handle duties during the meeting; and follow up after the meeting.
- During the meeting, the chairperson is responsible for determining the procedures, adhering to the agenda, managing time, encouraging participation, and reaching decisions.
- The participant's responsibilities include reading material before the meeting, being on time, adhering to the agenda, making contributions, listening thoughtfully to other participants, and carrying out any responsibilities assigned during the meeting.
- Compared with meetings, conferences are much larger in scope and have more participants. The administrative professional may be involved in planning a conference; carrying out duties during the conference, such as solving problems, running errands, and assisting with registration; and follow-up activities such as writing letters of appreciation, filling out expense reports, and paying bills after the conference.

Key Terms

ad hoc committee p. 199
agenda p. 204
amendment p. 211
bylaws p. 199
circular and oval arrangements p. 207
conference call p. 201
heterogeneous group p. 205
homogeneous group p. 205
minutes p. 211
motion p. 211
parliamentary procedures p. 211
quorum p. 211
real time p. 202
rectangular arrangement p. 207

resolution p. 211
robert's rules of order p. 210
semicircular or U-shaped arrangements p. 207
speaker's list p. 210
standing committee p. 199
synergy p. 205
teleconference p. 201
values p. 218
verbatim p. 212
video conference p. 201
web meeting p. 202
webcast p. 202
webinar p. 202

Discussion Items

These discussion items provide an opportunity to test your understanding of the chapter through written responses and discussion with your classmates and your instructor.

1. When is a meeting unnecessary?
2. Identify and describe three types of virtual meetings.

3. What are the responsibilities of an administrative professional when preparing for meetings?
4. What is considered good etiquette when participating in an international meeting?
5. From the board of directors to the office staff, meetings are commonplace in companies and other organizations.

For each of the following situations discuss the type of meeting described and the format(s) that could be used for the meeting.

a. The persons responsible for the overall direction of a company are meeting to discuss long-range plans and policies.

b. A group of employees from one location are meeting to discuss the ongoing issue of office safety.

c. A group of employees from locations around the country are meeting to write a recommendation for a new flextime work policy for the company.

d. The manager of the human resources department is meeting with people who work in that department to discuss the progress of work assignments.

e. Company representatives and customers from the United States, Germany, and India are meeting to learn about new products the company will introduce next quarter.

f. A new flextime work policy has been approved by the board. Employees need to be informed.

Critical-Thinking Activity

CanAsian Airlines is planning an online conference for its Calgary and Beijing executives. The meeting is being held to begin discussion of the strategic direction of the airlines for the next five years. You have been asked to coordinate with the various offices on agenda items. Once you receive the agenda items, you will be working with Mr. Albertson to send out the necessary materials and the agenda. You have contacted the appropriate administrative professional in each office to discuss these details. To date, you have received agenda items from two of the three executives in the Calgary office and one of the three executives in the Beijing office. You have emailed a reminder to the administrative professional in each office, asking for the executive's agenda; you have received no response. The meeting is only a month away, and you are becoming anxious. You know you must get the agenda out soon. You do not want to go to Mr. Albertson with the situation, but you do not know how to handle it. What should you do?

 21st Century Skills

 Life and Career Skills — CAREER

 Learning and Innovation Skills — INNOVATION

 Information, Media, and Technology Skills — TECHNOLOGY

Data — DATA FILE

Building Workplace Skills

Project 11-1 (Learning Outcomes 1, 2, 3, 4, and 5)

Collaborative Project

 INNOVATION CAREER

Mr. Albertson is planning a meeting with not-for-profit groups and several large businesses within the Calgary community to consider ways in which the organizations might work together on these major issues affecting the city: transportation, crime, inner-city housing, and public education. The not-for-profit groups involved in this meeting are the Department of Social Services, the Calgary Foundation, the Chamber of Commerce, the Asian-Pacific Coalition, the Junior League, and the First Nations Council. The businesses are Talisman International, MDS Health Care, Clark Associates Inc., Godwin Tools, and Lowell Granite. The group's work will take approximately one year; recommendations from this group after one year of operation will go to the mayor for action.

The first meeting will be an organizational one to develop a mission statement and to establish goals for the group. Mr. Albertson has already contacted the community leaders, and they have agreed to serve on the task force. Mr. Albertson has asked you to handle several of the arrangements for him. Since this project is fairly extensive, you ask your two assistants to work with you. (Assemble a group of three for this project—you and two of your classmates.) Mr. Albertson is considering a virtual meeting. He asks you to research the advantages and disadvantages of teleconferencing and web conferencing. Prepare a memorandum to Mr. Albertson, using the memorandum form Project 11-1 on the MindTap site (access to which is provided with the printed access card on the inside cover of your textbook), summarizing the results of your findings; include copies of the articles you found. Then draft a letter for Mr. Albertson, inviting participants to the first meeting; use the letterhead in Project 11-1a on the MindTap site. The meeting will be held two days—Thursday, November 15, beginning with lunch at noon and ending at 4 p.m., and Friday, November 16, beginning with breakfast at 8:30 a.m. and ending at 11 a.m.

Prepare an agenda. The agenda on November 15 should include a welcome to the group from Mr. Albertson; lunch; an introduction of the participants; and a video conference with Dr. Peter Sigman, who has been working with inner-city issues for over 15 years. Dr. Sigman will be in Toronto; the participants at the meeting will have a chance to interact with him after his presentation. The remainder of Thursday afternoon will be devoted to writing a mission statement for the group. On Friday morning, the group will begin to develop their goals. Mr. Albertson will facilitate both sessions.

Plan a team meeting with your two classmates to determine who will be responsible for each task. (Optional: Use Doodle or some other evite application to poll your classmates to determine when you can meet.)

At your meeting determine how you will work together as a team. Use the team evaluation form Project 11-1c from the MindTap site. Discuss it with your teammates so everyone understands what evaluation criteria are being used. Once you have completed the project, each member of your team should complete the evaluation form.

1. Refer to the section in this chapter that discusses the administrative professional's responsibilities in assisting with meetings. Make a list of the things your group must do. Include menus for lunch and breakfast.

2. Write a memorandum to Mr. Albertson summarizing these details using the memo form Project 11-1.

3. Prepare a draft of a letter inviting the not-for-profit groups and the businesses to the meeting. Include an agenda. Give the draft to your supervisor for approval. (In this case, the supervisor will be your instructor.) The meeting will be held in the Board Room at CanAsian. Once your instructor has approved the letter and the agenda, prepare letters and envelopes for the invitees. Include the agenda for the two days. Addresses are given in Project 11-1b.

4. Complete the team evaluation form separately, and then discuss your evaluation with your team members. Next, prepare a team evaluation that consolidates the opinions given by each team member. Submit it to your instructor. Use the form file Project 11-1c. (Provide each member of your team with a copy for your collective evaluation.)

Project 11-2 (Learning Outcome 5)

CAREER

Attend or view on television a meeting of a local club, governmental body, or civic organization. For example, municipal council meetings are often broadcast on local television channels. YouTube also has meeting videos that can be used for this activity. Take notes as the meeting is conducted. Prepare minutes of the meeting. As a guide, you can use the minutes in Figure 11-9 or some other style suggested by your instructor. Write a short report that describes the behaviour and comments of the meeting leader and the participants. Evaluate the success of the meeting and the effectiveness of the leader and the participants.

Project 11-3 (Learning Outcome 4)

INNOVATION

You belong to a professional association for administrative assistants in Calgary and have been asked to work on a committee planning a conference. You have been asked to create a flyer that will be posted on the conference website. Preliminary details for the flyer can be found in file Project 11-3. Use graphics, different fonts, and any other design elements you feel appropriately represent the activities. Place a copy of this flyer in your e-portfolio.

Project 11-4 (Learning Outcome 4)

TECHNOLOGY

Online templates for agendas and other meeting documents are available that can assist you in creating these typical meeting documents. Access these templates and download several different styles of documents that you think might be useful. Save these templates as part of your e-portfolio.

Project 11-5 (Learning Outcome 3)

TECHNOLOGY

Many software programs are available for purchase or free trial download that can be very useful for administrative professionals when planning/conducting meetings and other events. Some of the following programs offer an opportunity for a free demo or a video demonstrating the features of the program. Search the Internet for these and other programs. Choose one to download and try it or view the demo provided. Discuss these features with your classmates. Some suggestions follow:

Meetings

WebEx, GoToMeeting, or Skype for Business are three software programs that make it possible for business people to meet from any location using a tablet, laptop, or smartphone with a camera, headset, and microphone.

Scheduling

Doodle has a feature that makes it possible to survey a group of people that may not be on the same calendar or network to obtain individual input on selecting an appropriate date and time for a meeting. For example, you can use Doodle to set up a meeting with members of your IAAP executive who work for various organizations. Invitations to respond to a poll can be sent to their respective email addresses.

Event Planning

Smartsheet provides templates for all the activities needed in organizing and planning events, tracking projects, and maintaining marketing reports.

Make the Grade with MindTap

Stay organized and efficient with **MindTap**—a single destination with all the course material and study aids you need to succeed. Built-in apps leverage social media and the latest learning technology. For example:

- ReadSpeaker will read the text to you.
- Flashcards are pre-populated to provide you with a jump-start for review—or you can create your own.
- You can highlight text and make notes in your MindTap Reader. Your notes will flow into Evernote, the electronic notebook app that you can access anywhere when it's time to study for the exam.
- Self-quizzing allows you to access your understanding.

Visit nelson.com/student to start using **MindTap**. Enter the Online Access Code from the card included with your text. If a code card is not provided, you can purchase instant access at NELSONbrain.com.

Coordinating Business Travel

Do I Qualify?

Travel Administrative Assistant

The ideal candidate will have at least three years of office experience and the ability to work in a fast-paced team environment. Duties include:

- reviewing travel request forms prior to booking travel
- making travel arrangements for air, hotel, and rental cars using approved lists and websites
- handling revisions to travel arrangements
- following company guidelines for securing the best rates
- preparing travel expense forms in accordance with company policies, coding expenses in accordance with company guidelines, and obtaining appropriate approval of expenses before submitting to accounting

LEARNING OUTCOMES

After studying this chapter, you should be able to:

1. Plan domestic and international travel arrangements.
2. Prepare a detailed itinerary.
3. Describe the responsibilities of an administrative professional regarding a supervisor's trip.
4. Complete an expense report.
5. Maintain a positive attitude.

Travel is a way of life for many business executives, and with the growth of our global economy, the amount of international travel has increased dramatically. Many North American businesses are now multinational, having locations both within Canada and abroad; and many international companies now have locations in Canada. The car industry is a good example of international locations. Ford, Honda, Mazda, Toyota, Mitsubishi, and Nissan are some of the car manufacturers from abroad who have manufacturing or assembly plants in North America. The United States and other countries make the most of land, labour, and technical expertise available in other parts of the world to decide where to produce and assemble a product.

Having offices or subsidiaries in other cities may require the company's executives to travel. Executives, and possibly you and other administrative professionals, are often members of professional organizations that conduct provincial, territorial, or national conventions at least once each year. As an administrative professional, you too may occasionally need to travel. To handle travel arrangements effectively, you need to become familiar with the types of services available. This chapter will first introduce you to this variety of services and help you to understand your options and will then focus on making travel arrangements and helping you understand your responsibilities while the executive is out of the office.

Domestic Travel

Air Travel

Time is an extremely important commodity for busy executives. As a result, travelling by air rather than car or rail is generally preferable.

A traveller can fly from Toronto to Vancouver in approximately five hours or from Winnipeg to Dublin in approximately seven hours. During a flight, travellers can use their time productively by reading newspapers, journals, or periodicals. During the flight, travellers can also use their laptops, tablets, or smartphones to communicate with coworkers or clients and to complete work tasks.

Flight Classifications

While different airlines may use slightly different names for their flight classes, all airlines offer essentially three broad classes—first class, business class, and economy class. International flights generally offer all three classes. Longer national and some international flights offer business class and economy class. Since 1991, when EVA Air first introduced the premium economy class category, this new flight class has grown in popularity and is now available from many carriers.

In an effort to stay competitive and provide customers with a variety of options, low-cost carriers have entered the market. A low-cost carrier offers lower fares in exchange for minimizing or eliminating services found on traditional flights or requiring customers to be additional fees for select services and accommodations onboard. These services may include baggage allowances, food and beverage services, as well as overall comfort and legroom onboard. In Canada, these carriers include Air Canada Rouge, Canada Jetlines, Swoop, and Wow. Internationally and in North America, popular low-cost carriers include RyanAir, Wizz Air, JetBlue, and Southwest.

First-class accommodations are the most expensive of the three classes and the most luxurious. First-class travellers typically have individual pods where they can lie down and get a restful sleep. The quality of food, choice of entrees, and service time are personalized. Meal presentation may include cloth napkins, tablecloths, silverware, and china dinnerware. Complimentary alcoholic beverages and headsets for listening to music or viewing movies are provided. There are more flight attendants per passenger than in the other classes, which means greater attention is given to each flyer. First-class customers have access to a private lounge in the terminal while waiting for their flight departure. They exit the aircraft first and board at any time during the boarding process. All first-class travellers have no-cost access to individual power ports, Wi-Fi access to the Internet, and the airline entertainment app for personal mobile devices.

Business-class accommodations provide a level of service between first class and economy. The business-class section is located in front of the economy class—either directly behind

Tablets, smartphones, and laptops allow us to continue to be productive as we travel regionally, nationally, and internationally.

first class or at the front of the plane if first class is not offered. Designed especially for passengers travelling for business purposes, business class is not available on all aircraft or on all flights. Typically, this class is offered on international and long-distance domestic flights such as those between Toronto and Vancouver. Services provided include many of those offered to first-class travellers, such as complimentary Wi-Fi and entertainment app access for personal mobile devices, more spacious and comfortable seating or pods, more legroom than economy class, complimentary alcoholic beverages, and, when offered, better food than economy class. Like first-class travellers, business-class travellers also have access to a lounge in the terminal while waiting for their flight departure and are allowed to exit first and board at any time during the boarding process.

Many companies recognize the effects of **jet lag** (the feeling of exhaustion following a flight through several time zones) on the international traveller. For example, many companies have implemented policies that approve first-class or business-class travel for executives who travel long distances so that they can sleep while travelling. This means business travellers are often able to be productive immediately upon arrival at their destination.

Economy-class accommodations are typically the lowest-priced seats on the airplane. Also known as coach or tourist class in other countries, seats are closer together than either business or first class, and fewer flight attendants are available to serve the needs of the travellers. Some airlines may offer complimentary snacks; some will charge a fee. Complimentary beverages usually include pop, fruit juice, water, tea, and coffee. Many airlines also provide economy-class travellers with Wi-Fi access to the Internet and entertainment apps for use with personal mobile devices. Customers may be required to pay a fee for this access, and they can buy or rent a headset if they have not brought one with them. When available, premium economy offers the flyer some benefits similar to business class, including larger more comfortable seats, complimentary refreshments, increased baggage allowance, and priority boarding.

Company-Owned and Chartered Planes

Large corporations may lease their own plane or fleet of planes if the amount of travel by company employees makes it advantageous to do so. Smaller businesses may contract with one of the small airlines that specialize in privately chartered jet service, renting an entire airplane rather than purchasing individual seats on a commercial flight. Generally small in size, chartered planes are usually located adjacent to regular airports and use the same runways as the major airlines. Food may be available on these jets for an additional cost; flight attendants are generally not available.

Relatively new to the scene is Ubair, whose goal is to bridge the divide between private and commercial aviation using an app to make chartering a private plane as simple as requesting a taxi. Available in Canada, the United States, and the Caribbean, Ubair has access to a significant number of planes through a variety of aircraft management companies. As an option, when compared with commercial flights, chartering through Ubair may prove to be both surprisingly affordable and much more convenient for the business traveller.

Airline Loyalty Programs

For the frequent business traveller, membership in a frequent traveller program may be worthwhile. Loyalty programs provide customers with the opportunity to collect points to redeem for future flights, upgrade their flight, and/or provide them with complimentary or reduced-cost access to lounge areas in the airport. Membership is available through individual airlines and each program is unique. A variety of services are available in the lounges, including

- high-speed and wireless Internet access for mobile devices; and equipment to print, fax, and scan documents
- conference rooms, lounge space, and showers
- reading material
- complimentary alcoholic beverages, pop, juice, and coffee
- hot and cold refreshments
- assistance with airline reservations

Ticketing

Reservations for air travel can be made online or by telephoning the airline directly. Once the reservation is completed, a trip confirmation email message is sent to the traveller. This document contains the basic information needed—the confirmation or receipt number and the departure and arrival times. Using this information, travellers are able to access their reservation on the airline website within 24 hours of a flight. Once they have checked in, they can choose to print a hardcopy of their boarding pass or have it sent electronically to a tablet or smartphone. Some airlines have apps for mobile devices. These apps allow users to access various services such as the following:

- find, compare, and book flights
- check flight status
- receive notification of flight changes
- update travel preferences
- obtain an e-boarding pass
- pay for checked bags
- view in-flight entertainment options
- access airline club membership data

Use a touchscreen check-in kiosk to print your boarding pass.

It is also possible to check in at the airport. Travellers present their e-ticket to the ticket agent at the airline ticket counter, where a boarding pass is printed and checked baggage can be dropped off. Alternatively, travellers can use a touch-screen check-in kiosk at the airport, by inserting a travel document such as a passport or entering the confirmation/receipt number onto the screen. The e-reservation information is retrieved from the airline database and a boarding pass is printed. Travellers can then proceed directly through security and on to the departure gate, with just a short stop to drop any tagged checked baggage onto a conveyor belt. Most airlines have implemented a charge for checked baggage for travellers in economy class. This fee can be paid during the online check-in.

On occasion, it may be necessary to cancel or change a flight reservation. It is a good idea when booking a flight to confirm the airline policy for cancelling or changing the reservation. The policy for cancellations, which varies depending on the class of flight booked, is described on the airline's website and may include a charge. If the ticket is non-refundable or non-transferable, it can usually be used at a later date to travel to either the same or a different destination. These airline policies may influence an organization's policy regarding the preferred flight class to be used when arranging business travel. For example, your organization's policy may recommend booking only travel that is flexible, even though doing so may not result in the least expensive fare. Another option is to purchase flight passes that can be used by a pool of travellers; cancelled bookings simply go back into the pool and are used as required by any traveller.

An Air Canada electronic boarding pass sent to a mobile device enables a traveller to board a flight paper free.

When mechanical problems or other issues cause a flight to be changed or cancelled, passengers are not charged. The airline tries to make the situation as painless as possible. To help offset the inconvenience being experienced by their passengers, airlines may provide vouchers for food or a hotel room if the change involves an overnight stay.

Parking Services

Large airports generally provide a free shuttle service from a parking lot or rental car location to the airport gate. However, you are charged for parking your car, with the fee based on how long your car is parked. Since parking at an airport for an extended period of time can become expensive, large cities generally provide frequent private shuttle services to the airport from various locations around the city. Paying for a shuttle to and from the airport may be cheaper than paying for parking at the airport for an extended time.

Airline Security

Everyone who travels by air must go through airport security checkpoints. Carry-on baggage, and in some cases checked baggage, must also go through security checkpoints. These checkpoints were developed after 9/11 to help prevent passengers from bringing anything on a plane that would enable them to take over or damage the plane. A variety of security precautions such as full-body scanners are currently in place at airports around the world. As new incidents of potential terrorism occur, these security precautions will continue to be constantly revised. Being knowledgeable about current security measures is important for business travellers; check for changes before travelling. The following general suggestions will help business travellers expedite their security clearance and cope with the security procedures at airports:

- Arrive early. Most airlines advise arriving at the airport up to two hours, and in some cases three hours, before the scheduled departure. Travellers who have special needs or concerns may be advised to arrive even earlier.
- Carry proper identification. Acceptable government-issued photo identification such as a passport is required for all international travel and when crossing the U.S.–Canada border by air.
- When possible, check in and print a boarding pass or request an electronic confirmation sent to your mobile device before arriving at the airport. By taking this step and having only a carry-on bag, you can proceed directly to security, bypassing the queue at the ticket counter.
- Inspect your bags and remove any prohibited items. A list of currently prohibited items is available on the airline website.
- Follow the screening guidelines. Keep your identification and boarding pass in a location that is easy to access; wear shoes that can be easily removed. If you are travelling with a laptop computer, you may need to take it out of the carrying case for screening. No two airport security areas process travellers in exactly the same way. Be prepared to adjust to what is required.

Relaxed security measures, dedicated lanes, and kiosks are available in some airports for travellers with membership in

Trusted Traveller Programs such as Nexus and TSA Pre✓. Details can be found at www.cbsa-asfc.gc.ca/prog/nexus/menu-eng.html and www.dhs.gov/trusted-traveler-programs. Low-risk travellers who qualify are not required to remove their coats or shoes, or to present their toiletry bag at security.

Checked Bags

Travellers may need more clothing and other items than the amount that will fit in a carry-on bag. Airlines have regulations about the size and types of bags that can be checked in to the airplane's storage areas. Check the airline's website for information about checked bag sizes, the number of bags allowed, and fees for checking additional bags. A list of prohibited items can be found at the Canadian Air Transport Security Authority (CATSA) website and may also be listed on the airline's website. A Breeze Through Security CATSA mobile app is also available. This app allows users to enter the name of an item to see whether it is prohibited. A similar tool is available on the CATSA website.

Checked bags should have a tag attached that can be used to identify the owner of the bag. Because anyone in the baggage claim area can see the tag, security concerns are an issue. If you place your name and home address or home phone number on the tag, you could be more likely to be targeted for a home robbery while you are away. Placing your name and cellphone number on the tag is a safer option. You could also place the phone number of your destination hotel on the tag so you can be contacted there if your luggage is lost. As an added precaution, print on paper the same information that is on the tag and place it inside the bag. This information will allow the airline to contact you if the tag is lost from the bag. It is a good idea for carry-on bags to have the same tags as checked bags.

Smart luggage tags are another option for labelling bags. A smart tag may have a barcode that can be scanned or a code that can be entered online to identify the owner of the luggage. Some smart tag companies allow travelers to enter a travel itinerary online so airlines can forward lost luggage.

Ground Transportation

Once executives arrive at their destination, they may need some type of ground transportation to their hotel. That transportation may be a taxi or shuttle bus. When making arrangements, check taxi costs and the availability of shuttle services to the destination hotel. Some hotels provide a free shuttle service to and from the airport. Shuttle services are also available from private vendors, which may be less expensive than taxi service. Limousine service is also available at many airports, the cost being approximately the same as taxi service.

If executives must attend meetings at several locations during their stay, renting a car may be the most economical and convenient method of ground transportation. Car rental agencies are available at most airports. Car rental apps, which are available for mobile devices, allow users to search rental car locations and book a vehicle. Cars may also be rented through airlines or travel agents or on the Internet. When renting a car, specify the make and model preferred; the date, time, and location the car will be picked up and returned; and always request a vehicle navigation system—Global Positioning System (GPS). Most car rental agencies have age restrictions; depending on the agency, the person renting the car must be at least 21 or 25.

Hotel Reservations

Hotel reservations can be made by telephone, through travel agents, and online through hotel and travel websites. Always check for booking fees or cancellation restrictions when making reservations. The lowest room rate may require immediate payment and may not be refundable if the reservation must be cancelled. Some hotels provide breakfast at no additional charge, and most have business centres with computers, copiers, and other equipment for use by business travellers. Tablets, smartphones, and other mobile devices are standard equipment for travelling executives. Wireless Internet access from a traveller's room is generally available in most hotels. Meeting rooms are also available in many hotels. If you are making hotel reservations directly with the hotel, let the reservations clerk know the equipment and meeting rooms that are needed and whether the traveller will arrive late. You can simply ask the hotel to guarantee the room for late arrival; this procedure ensures that the hotel room is not released to someone else. You will, however, be charged for the room should the traveller not arrive or not call the hotel to cancel within the time permitted in its cancellation policy guidelines.

Car Travel

If an executive is travelling only a few hundred kilometres, they may prefer to travel by car. Some executives use cars furnished by the company; the company pays gasoline expenses. Other executives are reimbursed on a per-kilometre basis for any job-related car travel. Your responsibilities for a trip by car may include determining the best route to follow, making hotel reservations, and identifying restaurants along the way. You can find this information yourself on the Internet by using Google Earth, Google Maps, or Yahoo Maps. Smartphones with a navigational application installed can be used to locate information related to restaurants, tourist sites, and other attractions within the proximity of the mobile device. Members of the local affiliate of the Canadian Automobile Association (CAA) can choose to obtain maps and hotel and restaurant information from the association rather than from the Internet.

Rail Travel

Long-distance rail travel is a seldom-used option in most parts of Canada, as it can potentially take more time than travelling by air. Travelling short distances by rail, such as the Via Rail run between Montreal and Toronto or the Amtrak service in the United States, may be faster than flying when you factor in the extra time required to drive to the airport and pass through security. Train stations are generally located close to the city centre, and their fares are usually less expensive than airfares. Travel by train allows the executive the freedom to work during a trip using a mobile device. First-class and sleeping accommodations are available on trains, along with coach accommodations for more economical travel. Reservations and information on routes, schedules, and rates are available on the Via Rail Canada site for Canada and the Amtrak site for the United States.

International Travel

Because of the increasingly global nature of business, executives must sometimes make trips abroad. As an administrative professional, you need to know how to make arrangements for international travel. You should also know something about the business culture of the country the traveller is visiting.

Flights and Appointments

We covered various flight classifications earlier in this chapter; however, travellers should be aware that on international flights, weight and size restrictions for luggage may vary from one airline to another. International travellers must arrive at the airport earlier than domestic travellers; most airlines suggest arriving two to three hours before the flight to allow sufficient time for check-in, which can be more involved for international flights.

If you are setting up appointments or meetings for the executive, remember the time zone differences. Jet lag can limit an executive's effectiveness. Since it takes the body about a day to adapt to the new environment for each time zone crossed, try to give the traveller an extra day to recover from the trip before scheduling meetings.

If possible, you should not schedule appointments in the office for the day before the executive leaves on a trip or for the day the executive returns. The day before a trip is usually busy in preparation for the trip, and when the executive returns from a trip, they must again contend with time zone changes.

Travel Documents and Currency

International travellers need a passport. Travellers may also need a visa, health-related documents, and local currency.

Passports

A Canadian **passport** is an official travel document issued by the Government of Canada that facilitates travel abroad and certifies the identity and citizenship of an individual. A passport is required to enter most countries; even if a country does not explicitly require a passport, having one in your possession when you cross any border is a good idea because it shows proof of your identity and citizenship. Since the events of 9/11, border security procedures have become more rigorous. Official government identification is required of citizens who are crossing the Canada–U.S. border by car. A passport, a Nexus identification card, or an enhanced driver's licence (which is currently available in British Columbia, Manitoba, Ontario, and Quebec) is acceptable when crossing the Canada–U.S. border by land or sea. Possession of a Nexus card gives the holder access to designated priority crossing lanes at many Canada–U.S. border crossings. When all occupants of a car have a Nexus card, the vehicle occupants can often bypass a long queue of waiting vehicles at busy border crossings.

Passport application forms can be obtained from a regional passport office or a designated Service Canada receiving agent location. However, it is recommended that you visit Canada.ca/passport for the most updated version of the passport application forms; there, you can open and complete online a PDF-fillable form to download, print, and submit. Applications submitted in person before an agent can be processed within two weeks (10 business days); applications submitted by mail or through a designated receiving agent can be processed within four weeks (20 working days). Canada.ca/passport has more information on the complete passport application process. Figure 12-1 details the simplified renewal application process.

FIGURE 12-1

Simplified Renewal Application Process

When you use the simplified renewal application process, you do not need to submit your proof of Canadian citizenship, supporting identification, or guarantor information, as you would have required in the general application process. However, you must submit your previous passport with your Simplified Renewal Application. To be eligible for simplified renewal you must have been 16 years of age or older at the time of your previous application, and the name on the form must be exactly the same as it appears on page 2 of the submitted passport. Along with your application form, the required fee, and two photos (taken within six months of the date the application is submitted with the name and address of the photographer and date the photos were taken stamped on the back), you must submit a previous Canadian passport that

- was/is valid for 5 or 10 years
- is not damaged
- was never reported lost or stolen
- is still valid or expired for no more than one year

Courtesy of Citizenship and Immigration Canada

Travellers are responsible for ensuring that their passport is valid for travel. Many countries require that your passport be valid for several months after the date you plan to leave; otherwise, the traveller may be refused entry. Each country sets its own rules, so you should consult the travel advice and advisories at travel.gc.ca/advice to confirm the requirements of each of your destination countries.

Adult applicants can choose to apply for a passport that is valid for five or ten years from the date of issue. As soon as it is received, sign it to render it valid and enter your personal information and emergency contacts. Keep the passport with you while travelling in foreign countries; do not leave it unattended in your luggage, vehicle, hotel room, or elsewhere. It is also a good idea to photocopy page 2 of your passport to carry separately from your passport. You can also email it and other important travel documents to yourself, send it to your epost account if you have one, or upload it to your cloud storage so that you can access the documents quickly if they are lost or stolen while you are travelling.

Since 2013, all Canadian passports have been issued as 36-page electronic passports, or e-passports. These e-passports reduce the risk of tampering and identity fraud by including a digital facial image and other digital security features unique to the Government of Canada. Details about the passport holder appear in multiple places that can be scanned and compared with the personal data stored on the e-passport chip. Extra security features reduce processing times at border crossings and other Canadian entry points by enabling machine-assisted verification, where available. This technology helps border officials determine that the passport is authentic and confirms the identity of the holder.

A link to Canada's passport program site is provided on the MindTap site that accompanies this textbook.

Visas

A **visa** is a document granted by a foreign government that permits a traveller to enter and travel within a particular country. It is usually in the form of a stamped notation on a passport, indicating that the bearer may enter the country for a certain period. Rules and restrictions for visas vary from country to country. Some countries require the traveller to apply for and obtain a visa prior to the trip. Be sure to check with the consulate of the country in question sufficiently in advance of the executive's trip. To assist you, Passport Canada provides links to consulates (diplomatic missions) on its website.

Health-Related Documents and Precautions

Some countries require people entering the country to have had specific vaccinations or health tests, such as testing for contagious diseases. Records documenting these tests or vaccinations may be required for travel to the country. The entry requirements for a particular country should be checked before every trip in case of changes; for example, many countries have enacted specific practices in response to the 2014 Ebola outbreak or the 2015 Zika virus outbreak. The Passport Canada website provides current travel reports on safety and security, local laws and customs, entry requirements, health conditions, and other travel warnings. A travel agency or the website of the country to be visited can also supply information about required vaccinations or tests.

Before leaving for a foreign country, the traveller should check with a physician concerning any medical issues. Travellers who take prescription medicine should order enough medicine to cover their needs while they are away and take some extra medicine as a backup in case some of the medicine is lost or the trip lasts longer than planned. Do not pack prescription medicine in checked baggage; use your carry-on luggage for your medication, written prescriptions, and the contact information for the doctors who prescribed the medication and the pharmacists who filled the prescriptions.

The environmental factors in foreign countries can differ from those in Canada, and it is easy to develop some type of illness as a result of another country's food, water, or climate. A physician can prescribe medications for colds or stomach-related illnesses.

Tap water in another country may be safe for local residents; however, it may contain different microbes from the water in Canada, thus causing possible digestive problems. To be safe, use purified water at all times, even when brushing your teeth, washing your hands, or rinsing raw foods. For the same reasons, you may want to avoid consuming ice served in drinks. Many restaurants and markets serve and sell purified water.

Currency

Before leaving Canada, money can be exchanged at banks and currency exchange offices for the currency of the country being visited. If tipping is expected in the destination country, it is useful to have a supply of small-denomination notes in the appropriate currency. More money can be exchanged as needed upon arrival at the destination country. Any currency left over at the end of a trip can be exchanged back into Canadian currency. The rate of exchange for various countries

---

Technology AT WORK

An e-passport (Canada electronic passport) is the same as a traditional passport with the addition of a small electronic chip (integrated circuit) embedded in the back cover. The chip stores the following information:

- the same data shown on the data page of the passport
- a digital image of the passport photograph
- the unique chip identification number
- a digital signature to protect the stored data from alteration

Since 2013, Canada has been issuing only e-passports. Passports without chips can be used until they expire.

is published in the newspaper and is available online. Several websites provide currency converter utilities that show equivalent amounts in two or more currencies. To find such a website, search the Internet using the term "currency converter." It is always a good idea to be aware of the exchange rates before travelling to another country and, once in the destination country, to pay attention to the exchange rates, which can change daily. Exchange rates are not always the same; for example, the rate at a bank may be more favourable than at an airport or less favourable than at a money exchange.

The proliferation of **ATMs** (automated teller machines) throughout the world has made it much easier to obtain funds while travelling. Cash in the currency of the country is dispensed from the ATM. The exchange rate is automatically calculated, and the traveller's account is debited in Canadian currency. Many companies establish accounts for executives to use while travelling on business. When you use a credit card to make purchases quoted in a foreign currency, the credit card company will automatically apply the current daily exchange rate to the charge on your account.

Transportation Arrangements

You may need to make local travel arrangements within a country. Hotel and rail arrangements should be made before arriving. Car arrangements may be made after arriving.

International Car Rental

Travel agencies can arrange for car rentals before executives arrive in a country, or cars can be rented after travellers have arrived. In most countries, a Canadian driver's licence is sufficient. You may obtain an international driving permit from a local CAA office. Travellers must have appropriate insurance. They should also familiarize themselves with the driving regulations of the country they are visiting. Driving conditions are often quite different in other countries. For example, the steering wheel may be mounted on the right side of the car, or the country's custom may be to drive on the left side of the road.

International Rail Travel

Many countries, particularly those in Europe, have excellent rail service. Service is frequent, relatively inexpensive, and a traveller can get from one European city to another in a relatively short time with limited inconvenience. The trains are clean, and the accommodations are comfortable. Underground rail and bus transportation are also convenient and are inexpensive ways to travel in many European countries.

Cultural Differences

Travellers need to be knowledgeable about and sensitive to the customs and culture of the country they are visiting. Business practices can differ greatly from country to country. For example, in some countries, business gifts are expected.

In others, business gifts are not particularly welcomed. If a gift is given it should be small: a nice pen or a memento representative of Canada. Executives must be aware of customs and taboos when giving gifts to avoid inadvertently offending someone. Figure 12-2 lists some gift taboos.

FIGURE 12-2

Understanding Gift Etiquette

- In English-speaking countries, including Britain, Ireland, and Australia, gifts are not expected and might even be considered inappropriate. Business gifts are also rarely exchanged in Spain and France.
- Gift giving is important in China, Japan, the Philippines, Russia, and Eastern European countries.
- When visiting China, present your gift to the Chinese official at your first meeting.
- In Korea, it is rude to open a gift in front of the giver.
- When giving gifts, be certain the gift is made in Canada. For example, it would be inappropriate to give a gift made in that country to someone from China.
- Appropriate gifts include pens, pen-and-pencil sets, or other desktop items such as a small box or paperweight. Items from your home province or territory and books of historical areas of your province or territory are also appropriate.
- Photo albums containing pictures of the people you met on your trip are appropriate gifts.
- Flowers are *not* a universally acceptable gift to take to someone who is hosting you in their home. If flowers *are* acceptable, the colour and type of flower are important. For example, in Italy, chrysanthemums are displayed mainly at funerals. In Brazil, purple flowers signify death.
- In France, it is appropriate to take flowers to a dinner host. Chrysanthemums (primarily funeral flowers) or red roses (indicating romantic intent) should not be sent. Chocolates are also an acceptable gift for the French dinner host.

A basic understanding of the culture of the people in the country where the executive is travelling will help you make appropriate travel arrangements. Information about other countries may be obtained from a variety of sources:

- *Consulates of the country to be visited.* (A **consulate** is an office of a government in a foreign city that acts to assist and protect citizens of the consul's country.) These offices usually have printed materials and information available on their websites. They are also willing to answer questions about local customs and culture.
- *Travel books.* These books, available at libraries and bookstores, generally contain information about local customs and business practices.

Books about doing business with a particular country being visited. These books are also available at libraries and bookstores.

- *Seminars and short courses.* The company may arrange for consultants to assist personnel in understanding the culture abroad. Local colleges and universities often provide short courses or one-day seminars on the culture of various countries and tips on doing business with particular countries.

- *The Internet.* Numerous articles are available that review cultural differences internationally. It is also a good source for finding books concerning cultural differences.

Here are some general rules that apply to international travel:

- Learn the appropriate greeting for the country you will be visiting.
- Learn how to say please and thank you in the language of the country.
- Have business cards printed with your name and your company name in both English and the language of the country you are visiting.
- Do not criticize the people or customs of the country you are visiting. Show appreciation for the music, art, and culture of the country.
- Remember that business generally is more formal in other countries than it is in North America.
- Dress appropriately: business suits for men and conservative dresses or suits for women. Although dress in North America has become more casual than in the past, you cannot assume that the same is true for international organizations. Casual business dress generally does not impart a professional image. It may be seen as sloppy dress. It is also important to be well groomed.
- Eat the food that is offered you; do not ask what you are being served; show appreciation to your host. (If you do have allergies or religious limitations, try to communicate your restrictions to your host in advance or politely inform them of foods you cannot eat but suggest that you could try other items.)
- Be courteous and respectful at all times.

Travel Procedures

How travel arrangements are made depends on the company where you work. Large organizations may have a travel department that follows administrative guidelines to organize and book travel for all employees. Smaller firms may expect that individuals will make their own travel arrangements, while others will use a travel agency to schedule all company travel. This agency becomes knowledgeable about the needs of the company, thereby providing the unique services the company requires. Whether you contact the travel agency on your supervisor's behalf or make the arrangements yourself, as an administrative professional you will likely have a role in making travel arrangements.

If an executive is travelling by air, you need to know the name of the preferred airline (if the executive has a preference) along with the frequent flyer number. A **frequent flyer program**

is an incentive program offered by most airlines that provides a variety of awards after the accumulation of a certain number of mileage points. Awards may include upgrades from economy to first class and free airline tickets.

You should also determine whether the flight is to be direct (if possible) or whether the executive is willing to change planes. Budget may be a consideration and less expensive flights are sometimes available if the executive is willing to change planes. The downside of changing planes is the hassle of getting from one flight to another and the increase in travel time. If the change occurs in the United States, it may mean collecting baggage, clearing customs, and repeating the boarding security check once again.

You should also know the seating preference of the executive—aisle or window—as well as the preferred class of flight—first class, business class, premium economy, or economy—which may be dictated by company policy.

If you are making arrangements for more than one top-level executive to travel to the same location at the same time, company policy may dictate that the executives fly on separate airlines. In case of a serious accident, both executives would not be lost to the company.

If an executive is travelling by rail, you need to know similar information: type of accommodations (coach or first

Communicating AT WORK

The first time you help to plan a trip for an executive, talk with the person about their travel preferences. If you are to be an effective agent, you must have the following information:

- flight preferences—class of accommodations, seating, meals
- hotel preferences—price range, number of nights, single or double room, size of bed (full, queen, king)
- car rental preferences—type of car, size, make, model, number of days of usage, and pickup and drop-off locations
- reimbursement policies of the company—whether a **per diem** rate (daily food allowance for which no receipts are required) is in effect or receipts are required for meals and other travel expenses
- arrangements for transportation to airport or train station
- appointments to be made—where, when, and with whom
- materials—business cards, smartphone, laptop, and so on
- person in charge while the executive is away
- correspondence and calls—how they will be handled in the executive's absence
- the executive's credit card number or company account number for charging tickets, hotel, car rental, and so on

When you are first made aware of an upcoming trip, open a file folder where you can store notes and other information relating to the trip. Create an electronic folder for documents or open a new section in OneNote to track your preparations. Details of the trip are then available for instant referral when needed.

class), sleeping accommodations (if travelling on the train for more than one day), and ticket delivery (whether tickets will be picked up at the train station, mailed, or delivered).

Arrangements by a Travel Agency or Travel Department

Travel agencies are companies that offer travel advice and make travel arrangements for clients. They book flights and arrange for online delivery of confirmations, make hotel reservations, arrange car rentals, and perform specialized services that the executives may need (such as obtaining workspace or meeting space at the destination). They prepare an itinerary, which lists airlines, flight numbers, departure and arrival times, hotel reservations, and car rental arrangements. Travel agencies invoice the company directly for the cost of tickets and any other expenses that they may have incurred on a behalf of a client, such as a deposit to guarantee a hotel reservation for late arrival. Since they no longer receive commissions from airlines, a fee will be charged if the service provided is limited to making flight arrangements. Commissions received by travel agencies from hotels and other service industries when services are booked may help to minimize charges to the client. Travel agencies may also provide 24-hour assistance to travellers who encounter problems such as cancelled or delayed flights.

In a large organization, a travel department will provide many of the same services. They do not usually offer travel advice but will have an in-depth knowledge of organizational policy and traveller preferences.

Arrangements by the Assistant

Regardless of how travel arrangements are made, you as an administrative assistant will have a role. It is a good idea to set up a folder when you learn about an upcoming trip. Place all notes and information relating to the trip in the folder. It is then available for instant referral when needed.

Making these arrangements online is the most efficient method of doing so, although in some instances, you may find it necessary to telephone the airlines, hotels, and car rental agencies directly. All major airlines have a website where you can check flight availability and compare costs. One-stop online travel-booking sites such as Expedia and Travelocity can be used to compare not only costs but also the airlines offering the most direct route for a particular trip.

Both sites negotiate and consolidate fares directly with major airlines and offer below-market deals to consumers. Before confirming arrangements, ensure that you are familiar with any limitations linked to these special fares. Can they be changed or upgraded at a later date? Are they valid for standby on other flights? Can points on a frequent flyer program be accumulated?

You may assist executives with travel arrangements by determining passport and visa requirements, checking on currency needs, researching health issues in the country to be visited, making hotel reservations, arranging car rental, and arranging rail transportation. You may also be responsible for the following:

- preparing a complete itinerary
- completing a travel advance fund form to obtain funds in advance of the trip
- preparing and assembling materials for the trip
- checking the calendar
- confirming appointments
- determining how matters are to be handled while the executive is away

Prepare an Itinerary

Once you have determined where and when the executive is to travel and after you have made the appropriate travel arrangements, you need to prepare an itinerary. The itinerary is a must for you and your employer. The **itinerary**, a detailed outline of the trip, is a record of all trip arrangements for you and the executive. An itinerary should include flight numbers, airport names, departure and arrival times, hotel arrangements, car rental information, appointments, and any other pertinent information. If you are working with a travel agency, it will provide an itinerary that includes flight, hotel, and car information. However, an agency does not have the information on appointments and other special information. The executive needs an itinerary that reflects *all* the activities on the trip. You are responsible for compiling all the details into one document. It is a good idea to prepare multiple copies of the itinerary:

- one for the executive
- one for the executive's family
- one for the person who will be in charge while the executive is away
- one for your files

Figure 12-3 shows an itinerary prepared by the administrative professional. If the executive is travelling from one time zone to another, time zones should be included on the itinerary; otherwise, they are not necessary.

Another option for creating an itinerary is to use software applications like TripIt and Flight Tracker to consolidate all travel details. TripIt automatically creates an itinerary, provides links to maps for hotels, and when used with Flight Tracker, advises the traveller of flight interruptions or delays. The itinerary can be shared with other people, and as the travel organizer, you can make changes that are automatically communicated to the traveller. You can also print out a hardcopy of the itinerary as backup for the mobile application. Check it out. A link to Tripit.com is on the MindTap site accompanying this textbook.

FIGURE 12-3

Detailed Itinerary Prepared by the Administrative Professional

Itinerary for Andrea Robichaud	
April 1 to April 3, 20-- **Vancouver, British Columbia**	
Monday, April 1	**(Regina, Saskatchewan to Vancouver, British Columbia)**
9:30 a.m. CST	Leave Regina International Airport on Air Canada flight AC 106 (e-ticket confirmation in briefcase)
2:00 p.m. PST	Arrive Vancouver International Airport
	Take shuttle bus to Four Seasons Hotel Vancouver, telephone 604.555.0124 (confirmation 454038)
	Hotel reservations at the Four Seasons Hotel Vancouver, 791 W Georgia St., telephone 604.555.0156 (confirmation 828382)
3:30 p.m. PST	Meeting with Alex Wright, Steve Roche, and Bryan Law, Room 212, Ranier Building, telephone 604.555.0129, blue folder contains papers for meeting
Tuesday, April 2	**(Vancouver, British Columbia)**
10:00 a.m. PST	Meeting with Alice Snell and Andrei Taylor, Conference Room A, Temple Building, telephone 616.555.0165, manila folder contains papers for meeting
	Lunch with Alice and Andrei follows the meeting; they are making arrangements for lunch
3:00 p.m. PST	Meeting with Jenna MacPhee and Kale Graham, Conference Room C, Temple Building, telephone 616.555.0166, red folder contains meeting notes
Wednesday, April 3	**(Vancouver, British Columbia to Regina, Saskatchewan)**
9:30 a.m. PST	Meeting with Lisa, Rachel, and Steven Genore of Genore & Associates, Room 220, Thurston Building, telephone 616.555.0138, yellow folder contains proposed contract
1:30 p.m. PST	Leave Vancouver International Airport on Air Canada Flight AC 127 (e-ticket confirmation in briefcase)
5:00 p.m. CST	Arrive Regina International Airport

© Cengage Learning

Obtain Travel Funds

Companies differ in how they handle funds for trips. Airline tickets may be charged directly to the company, or the traveller may pay for the tickets and be reimbursed later. Hotel, meals, and car rental may be charged on a credit card provided by the company. Another practice is for the individual to be given a cash advance to cover all expenses of the trip. To do so, the individual fills out a travel fund advance form or requisition before leaving, indicating how much money they will need for lodging, meals, and so on. The company advances the money to the employee before they leave on the trip. Another practice is for the executive to use a credit card or, when they need cash, an ATM to pay the expenses; reimbursement is then arranged by the company upon returning from the trip. Most company policies require employees to turn in a receipt for an expense above a certain amount.

Prepare and Organize Materials

Several items may be needed for a trip. If it is an international trip, items such as passports, medications, business cards, and small gifts may be necessary. Whether the trip is domestic or international, several items usually must be prepared, such as reports for meetings and presentation materials.

Once the materials are prepared, the administrative professional assembles the appropriate number of copies and gives

www.tripit.com

●●●○○ CARRIER 📶 8:21 AM 📶 22% 🔋

Palm Springs or Bust
Fri, Jul 11 – Mon, Jul 14, 2014

✈ **FRI, JUL 11**

SFO – PSP
Virgin America 1592

2 45 PDT PM | **Depart SFO** San Francisco

4 08 PDT PM | **Arrive PSP** Palm Springs

DURATION: 1H 23M

| Confirmation **HUXTBL** | Terminal **2** | Gate ... |

| Seat **6A** | Get **Seat Advice** |

View
Airline & Booking Info

Note:
Take a cab from the airport, it's easier

Use TripIt to organize all trip details into one comprehensive itinerary.

them to the executive. The traveller needs items such as the following:

- e-ticket confirmation and possibly a boarding pass
- passport and visa if travelling to a country where a visa is required
- itinerary
- hotel and car rental confirmation
- credit cards and currency
- business cards

- special materials, reports, or contacts for appointments
- presentation materials
- laptop, tablet, or smartphone and the necessary accessories:
  - charging cables and voltage adapter for destination country if its voltage is different
  - updated data plans to cover the period and destination of travel
  - SIM card(s)—advise relevant parties of new phone numbers
  - research on how the traveller can quickly and easily obtain necessary data plans/SIM cards in the destination country or top up the account balances
- reading materials

Check Appointments

Check both your supervisor's calendar and your calendar, to see whether any in-office appointments have been scheduled when your supervisor will be away. If so, find out whether they are to be cancelled or whether someone else in the company will handle them. Then, notify the people involved. Also check other files, such as reminder files or pending files, to see whether any matters need to be handled before the executive leaves.

Email or call people the executive plans to see during the trip to confirm the appointments. Obtain or verify addresses and make a note of these addresses on the itinerary. Update your supervisor's electronic calendar to include any additional information, such as addresses that might be needed for each out-of-town appointment. If the executive will be driving, prepare maps with driving directions from the hotel to the location of all meetings. Then, if the GPS navigational aids are not installed in the rental car, the executive will have no difficulties determining the appointment location.

Duties During the Executive's Absence

During the executive's absence, you have the responsibility of making wise decisions within the scope of your responsibility. You should know which items to refer to someone else in the company and which items to refer directly to the executive through an email or a telephone call. You do not want to put an excessive number of calls through to the executive while they are away, but certain matters may require informing the executive immediately.

Find out who will be in charge during your employer's absence. Check to see whether your employer is expecting any important papers that should be forwarded. Knowing how to handle all incoming mail during your supervisor's absence was discussed in Chapter 9. You may want to refer to that section now.

Handle Messages

While executives are away, they may choose to email or call the office daily. If the executive prefers to call, determine the approximate time of day for the call so you can have all messages and items of importance ready to discuss with them. Always keep urgent messages and correspondence in a specific place on your desk so you can refer to them quickly. To ensure nothing is missed, keep a log of all items that need to be discussed with your supervisor, either when they call or on their return.

Handle Appointments

You may need to set up appointments for people who want to see your supervisor after they return. Remember that the executive will probably already have a full day of work to handle on the first day back so it is not a good idea to schedule appointments for that day. If you must, schedule as few appointments as possible and make them for later in the afternoon. Avoiding early morning appointments is also a good idea in case of delayed return flights.

Handle Correspondence

Answer all correspondence and emails, and handle all visitors and telephone callers in a timely manner. You may be responsible for seeing that all mail is given to the person in charge; you also may be required to assist the person in answering the mail. You may have the responsibility for answering routine correspondence. If so, copy your supervisor on emails and keep a copy of the correspondence and response for your employer to review after they return.

Post-Trip Activities

When the executive returns, you must brief them on what occurred in the office during the trip, providing all necessary information. You should also inform the executive of the appointments you set up, the telephone calls and correspondence you received, and other items that require their attention.

Follow-Up Correspondence

The executive may need to write several follow-up letters as a result of the trip. For example, thank-you letters are often sent, and information on products or services may need to be sent to customers. The executive may tell you what needs to be said and ask that you write or draft the correspondence.

The executive may also need to answer correspondence that accumulated during their absence; they may ask that you do the answering.

Tracking and Reporting Business Expenses

Keeping track of business expenses while travelling can be a hassle. Expense tracking apps can assist executives in the tedious chore of collecting receipts in an envelope for submission at the end of the trip. The applications, which are often free for a single user, are available for all smartphones. They can be used to quickly and easily record details of expenses; scanned or photographed images of these receipts can be stored along with this brief detailed record of the transaction. Once the trip is over, these expense details can be exported as Excel or PDF reports and shared via email or uploaded to a cloud-sharing application such as Dropbox or Google Docs.

Following a trip, some large organizations require employees to prepare an expense report and submit receipts for expenses above a certain amount. The company provides expense forms, and while the format of the forms will vary from company to company, they should be filled in accurately with the amounts totalled. A template form created in a spreadsheet program contains formulas that will automatically calculate the amount of money to be reimbursed to the traveller. In addition to recording flight and hotel expenses, you may be handed numerous receipts (meals and incidental expenses) to be included on the expense report. If the executive uses an expense-tracking app, these details may be provided in a format that is compatible with the expense form. Using this process streamlines the preparation of the expense report. Even in a small office, travel expenses must be documented. A simple spreadsheet can be created to record all expenses and calculate a total; the relevant receipts can then be attached.

Complete the report carefully, double-checking all figures and totals. Be sure that the necessary receipts are attached and that your figures match those on the receipts. Figure 12-4 shows a sample expense report prepared in *Microsoft* Excel. Here are some tips for completing an expense report:

- Identify the employee, providing name, department, and address.
- Date the form.
- Enter the expenses for each day, providing as much detail as possible for
  - transportation costs
  - meals with receipts
  - per diem claims (no receipts required)
  - charges for accommodation
  - cost of company entertainment, such as lunch with a client (include the names of the parties at the meal; some business expenses are disallowed depending on who attends—e.g., two business associates cannot claim for the same meal)

FIGURE 12-4
Expense Report

CanAsian Airlines
Expense Report

For the Week Ending	1/21/--			Destination	Charlottetown, PEI	
Employee Name	Milena Habjan					
Department	Customer Services			Purpose	Spring Sales Conference	

	Monday	Tuesday	Wednesday	Thursday	Friday	Saturday	Sunday	
Date	1/15/--	1/16/--	1/17/--	1/18/--	1/18/--	1/20/--	1/21/--	Total
Airfare								
Car Rental								
Local Transporation								
Tolls/Parking	12.50	12.50	12.50					37.50
Miles	242.00	5.00	242.00					
Mileage Amount	133.10	2.75	133.10					268.95
Lodging	165.50	165.50						331.00
Subtotal	311.10	180.75	145.60					637.45
Breakfast		13.00	13.00					26.00
Lunch	15.00	16.75	12.00					43.75
Dinner	34.58							34.58
Subtotal	49.58	29.75	25.00					104.33
Business Meals*		175.85						175.85
Other Entertainment								
Subtotal		175.85						175.85
Gifts	25.00							25.00
Other*								
Subtotal	25.00							25.00
Grand Total	385.68	386.35	170.60					942.63

| Employee Signature | *Milena Habjan* | Date | 1/23/- - |
| Supervisor Signature | *Robert Miller* | Date | 1/24/- - |

Comments:
*Explanation Required   Dinner on 1/16 with Standards Review Committee members: Joan Roberts, Tom Chung and Maria Gonzales

- Total the column.
- Obtain signatures—the traveller and the authorized manager if necessary.
- Attach all relevant receipts. Double-check that the receipted values are correctly recorded on the form. (Some organizations do not require receipts if a corporate credit card is used or if the expense is below a certain dollar amount.)
- Calculate the grand total.
- Deduct any monies advanced from the total.
- Calculate a net total.

All organizations expect their employees to perform their duties in an ethical manner. They also expect them to report instances of unethical behaviour when recognized. It is possible that you might be asked by your supervisor to include items on an expense report that are not listed as approved in the company travel policy guidelines. Gifts purchased overseas may be disallowed as there is no way to ensure they meet company guidelines, have actually been given, and have not been used as bribes. Many Canadian companies have strict guidelines on bribery.

Receipts for meals may include the costs of alcoholic beverages; however, most organizational policies prohibit including these in travel expenses. If you find yourself in a position of preparing an expense report for your supervisor that includes prohibited items, it is your responsibility to bring this to their attention. If the individual persists in including such items for reimbursement, you should report the activity to the person in your organization responsible for overseeing ethical activities.

Soft Skills

MAINTAINING A POSITIVE ATTITUDE

Sometimes when a manager is away and we are not sure how to handle something, we find ourselves thinking we cannot do the job. We may even become frustrated and negative about our abilities. Soft skills have been stressed throughout this book. We know that people lose their jobs more often because of a lack of soft skills rather than a lack of knowledge or technological skills. We also know from research that one of the most significant differences between high and low achievers is their attitude. High achievers maintain a positive attitude. They believe they can perform their job well, make a difference on the job, and solve problems. People with a negative attitude often believe they cannot perform their job well so they do not really try. People who have a positive attitude do not see everything in life as wonderful. However, they do see ways to change a bad situation.

Think now about your attitude. Is it generally positive or generally negative?

Assuming you accept the importance of achieving and maintaining a positive attitude, answer the following questions:

- What is a positive attitude?
- How do you go about achieving and maintaining a positive attitude?

Attitude is defined as "a state of mind or feeling with regard to some matter or position." A positive attitude merely means that you believe in yourself; you believe that you have the power to make positive things happen in your life. Even though you might believe you have a positive attitude, consider these situations:

- Do you procrastinate in your coursework, putting off homework to the last minute and then doing a poor job?
- Do you engage in activities harmful to your health even though research shows the behaviour to be harmful?
- Are you extremely critical of everyone, including yourself?

If you answered yes to any of these questions, chances are your actions do not always reflect what you believe is a positive attitude. So how do you go about achieving and maintaining a positive attitude? Here are some suggestions:

- Practise visualization. Picture yourself in positive situations where you are achieving your goals and solving your problems.
- Listen to yourself talk. Do you often say, "I don't think I can do that" or "I know I won't be successful on that job"? Control your inner voice. Say to yourself—silently or out loud—"I didn't mean that. I know I can do the job well and be successful, and here is how I will be successful." Then think through the ways that will make you successful in the particular situation you are confronting.
- Remind yourself often of your past successes.
- Surround yourself with positive people and ideas. Do not spend time with negative people. They can sap your energy and positive resolve.
- Continue trying to achieve whatever is important to you until you are successful.

Chapter Summary

The summary will help you remember the important points covered in this chapter.

- Airlines offer three broad flight classifications—first class, business class, and economy (or coach).
- In addition to flying, the executive may also travel by car or by rail. A local affiliate of the CAA can provide information for car travel, and the appropriate railroad can provide information about rail travel.
- When travelling internationally, the executive needs to be sensitive to different customs and cultures. The executive should take business cards with their name and the company name printed in both English and the language of the country being visited.
- A passport is necessary when travelling by air to the United States and anywhere internationally. Rail and bus transportation are other alternatives to renting a car when travelling internationally.
- In helping the executive to schedule travel, the administrative professional must know the dates and times of travel, the cities to be visited, hotel preferences, car rental preferences, appointments to be scheduled, materials needed, and so on.
- Arrangements for travel can be made through travel agencies or by the administrative professional by calling the airline, hotel, and car rental agency directly or by booking online on airline websites or one-stop travel-booking sites.
- The administrative professional has several responsibilities before the trip, including preparing an itinerary, obtaining travel funds, preparing materials for the trip, checking the calendar, confirming appointments, and understanding how matters are to be handled while the executive is away.
- While the executive is away, the administrative professional should handle messages, appointments, and correspondence; make the appropriate decisions; maintain a positive attitude; and use time wisely.
- When the executive returns, the administrative professional must bring the executive up to date on significant happenings and assist with any correspondence and reports that need to be prepared as a result of the trip.
- Expense-tracking apps for smartphones can assist the executive in the tedious chore of collecting receipts.
- When completing the expense report, verify all receipts and ensure prohibited items such as alcoholic beverages are not included in the request for reimbursement.

Key Terms

ATMs p. 230
attitude p. 237
business-class accommodations p. 224
consulate p. 230
economy-class accommodations p. 224
first-class accommodations p. 224

frequent flyer program p. 231
itinerary p. 232
jet lag p. 224
passport p. 228
per diem p. 231
visa p. 229

Discussion Items

These discussion items provide an opportunity to test your understanding of the chapter through written responses and discussion with your classmates and your instructor.

1. Why do many business travellers travel by air? List and describe the three broad classes of airline flights.
2. Describe how an e-ticket for air travel works.
3. List eight general rules that apply to travelling internationally.
4. What are five guidelines that will help business travellers cope with the security procedures at airports?
5. List four responsibilities of the administrative professional during trip preparation.

Critical-Thinking Activity

Numerous groups of Chinese administrators from the Beijing office of CanAsian visit the Calgary office, and Mr. Albertson often serves as a host for these groups.

Mr. Albertson has asked you to visit China with Keri-An Mahar, who has recently been made vice-president of human resources, to learn more about the Chinese culture so you can be of greater assistance to him when he hosts these groups. You will be in the Beijing office for one week. In preparation for your trip, you do some reading about culture and talk with one of the administrative professionals (who was born in China) about the culture. You think you are fairly well prepared. However, during the trip, some situations occur that make you feel embarrassed about your lack of preparation:

- The Chinese officials always offer you their business cards. You notice immediately that the cards have their names, addresses, and so on, in Chinese on one side and English on the other. You do have business cards, but your name and pertinent information are in English only.
- Small gifts are given to you in each office but you have nothing to offer in return.
- The Chinese officials take many photos of your visit; as you leave, they present both you and Ms. Mahar with photo albums.
- Since the trip was one week long, you took three bags with you. However, you were embarrassed as you went from the airport to the hotel because the Chinese host who met you insisted on carrying your bags.

- In the first meeting at the Beijing CanAsian office, you immediately extended your hand in greeting to each member of the Chinese group. Although they were very polite, you felt you had done something wrong.
- In an effort to show your friendliness, you immediately made small talk with the Chinese. An interpreter was present at all sessions. People were polite to you, but you sensed you had said or done something inappropriate.
- The Chinese hosts provided you with all lunches and dinners. The tables were filled with food, but you were not familiar with many of the dishes; the food was very different from Chinese food you had eaten in Canada. You politely refused several of the dishes offered. You wonder whether you made an error.

Respond to the following questions. Before you do, read the information in Critical Thinking Activity-12, found on the MindTap site (access to which is provided with the printed access card on the inside cover of your textbook). Additionally, discuss your answers with your classmates.

- What errors did you make, and what should have been done?
- What could you have done to prevent these errors?

21st Century Skills

 Life and Career Skills
CAREER

 Learning and Innovation Skills
INNOVATION

 Information, Media, and Technology Skills
TECHNOLOGY

 Data
DATA FILE

Building Workplace Skills

Project 12-1 (Learning Outcomes 1 and 2)
Online Project

TECHNOLOGY   CAREER

Mr. Albertson is visiting CanAsian's China office in Beijing from November 11 through November 16. Determine flight times and hotel arrangements by checking a website. The executive vice-president of the Beijing office, Pai Ying, will pick Mr. Albertson up at the airport. He will not need a car. He wants to leave the morning of Monday, November 11 and return the afternoon or evening of Saturday, November 16. He will fly first class and prefers low-calorie meals. He wants a nice hotel that includes a queen-size bed, a room for non-smokers, and exercise facilities. Mr. Albertson does not speak Chinese. His appointments while in China include the following:

November 14, 9 a.m., appointment with Chan Yi
November 14, 2 p.m., appointment with Sheng Mo

November 15, 10 a.m., appointment with Kuo Lu
November 15, 1 p.m., appointment with Niu Chih

Use a one-stop travel booking site such as Travelocity, Expedia, or your favourite booking site to determine the most appropriate flight times and hotel. Prepare an itinerary incorporating all details including the appointments. Note the number of hours on the itinerary for travel time; also note the time difference from Calgary to China. Submit the itinerary to your instructor.

Project 12-2 (Learning Outcome 3)

INNOVATION   DATA FILE

Mr. Albertson has returned from a recent trip to B.C., during which he met with several people. He has asked you to write a follow-up letter to a potential client, Mr. Cai, who lives in North Vancouver.

CHAPTER 12: Coordinating Business Travel

- Use Project 12-2 to prepare the letter.
- Writing as Mr. Albertson, thank Mr. Cai for meeting with you and indicate that you thought the meeting was very productive. Tell the client that the information he requested is provided in an enclosed brochure. Invite him to call you if he has any questions about the information. Indicate that you will call next week to discuss the information further.
- The client's name and address are shown below

  Mr. Raymond Cai

  Cai Inc.

  1501 Eastern Avenue

  North Vancouver, BC V7L 3G2

Project 12-3 (Learning Outcomes 1 and 3)

INNOVATION TECHNOLOGY

Select a country from the list below or ask your instructor for approval to research a different country. Use the Internet and other resources to research business customs and practices for this country. Write a report that details your findings. Include complete source information for the references used in writing the report. The report should address (but not be limited to) issues such as those listed below:

- attitudes toward time and appointments
- formality appropriate for business meetings and related events
- language spoken and possible need for an interpreter
- personal space comfort zones and nonverbal behaviour
- exchanging of business cards and gifts
- appropriate dress for business meetings
- travel alerts or warnings for this country
- health-related concerns for travel to this country
- currency of this country
- travel documents needed for a Canadian traveller (passport, visa, health documents)

Countries:	
Albania	Iran
Brazil	Italy
China	Japan
Egypt	Russia
France	Spain
Germany	India

Project 12-4 (Learning Outcome 1 and 3)

INNOVATION

Your supervisor will be travelling to the country you researched in Project 12-3 to meet with clients. The trip will begin one month from today and last for seven days, including travel time.

a) Select a city to which your supervisor will travel. Research flights to that city.

b) Select a flight itinerary for the trip and print/record this information.

c) Select a hotel where your supervisor will stay. Record the hotel name and address, reservation dates, and room rates as you would when booking the hotel.

d) Research the best way for your supervisor to get from the airport to the hotel and record those arrangements.

Project 12-5 (Learning Outcome 2)

INNOVATION TECHNOLOGY

Create an itinerary for your supervisor for the trip you planned in Project 12-4. Include the travel arrangements you planned earlier. Schedule three meetings with clients (choose names for the clients and appointment times) to be held at the hotel where your supervisor is staying.

Project 12-6 (Learning Outcome 4)

INNOVATION TECHNOLOGY DATA FILE

Open the Microsoft Excel Project 12-6 Expense Report from the data files. Edit the expense report to correct errors in spelling, capitalization, formulas, and numbers. Attach a comment about any missing information.

Project 12-7 (Learning Outcome 5)

TECHNOLOGY

Add to your e-portfolio by describing how you will continue to work on developing a positive attitude. File your reflections using an appropriate name in your e-portfolio folder.

Make the Grade with MindTap

Stay organized and efficient with **MindTap**—a single destination with all the course material and study aids you need to succeed. Built-in apps leverage social media and the latest learning technology. For example:

- ReadSpeaker will read the text to you.
- Flashcards are pre-populated to provide you with a jump-start for review—or you can create your own.
- You can highlight text and make notes in your MindTap Reader. Your notes will flow into Evernote, the electronic notebook app that you can access anywhere when it's time to study for the exam.
- Self-quizzing allows you to access your understanding.

Visit nelson.com/student to start using **MindTap**. Enter the Online Access Code from the card included with your text. If a code card is not provided, you can purchase instant access at NELSONbrain.com.

PART 4

Planning Your Future

Now that you have acquired the knowledge, developed the necessary fundamental skills, and reflected on the qualities of a successful administrative professional, you are ready to begin to seek employment and consider your working future. You can start the search at your local college or university placement office; by looking through newspaper advertisements or postings on the Internet; by using employment agencies, both public or government and private; by making direct contact with companies and other organizations; and by networking. Once you have researched an organization, getting that job interview requires a well-written letter of application and a professional résumé or e-portfolio. Practising your interview skills will help you feel comfortable at your first interview and when opportunities arise for job advancement or to change jobs.

This is also a time when you might want to consider how your future work life might look. You may decide at some point to consider other options, such as becoming an entrepreneur and working for yourself as a virtual assistant or as a teleworker for an organization; or having developed your leadership abilities—being responsible for and motivating others, resolving conflict, delegating and evaluating other employees—you may decide you want to take on more responsibility and look for opportunities where you can do so. Whatever you decide, these last chapters will help you polish your job search skills, identify and improve your leadership and management skills, and develop strategies that enable you to move forward.

Courtesy of Durham College

Amanda Quintal

Legal Assistant

My name is Amanda Quintal and I work as a legal administrative professional with a local law firm in Oshawa, Ontario.

I enjoyed my law class in high school and decided to pursue it further in my higher education. After graduation from high school, I took the law clerk/legal administration program at Durham College. It was a three-year program that involved a placement with a local, well-respected firm.

I was lucky enough that this placement turned into a job opportunity which led me to my current role today. I have been at the firm for six years and find it very rewarding.

What I enjoy about my job is that I am constantly learning. I get to interact with all levels of law enforcement as well as the court system in my region. I like knowing that I am doing something productive that contributes to society in a meaningful way.

Another thing I appreciate about my job is that there is never any shortage of work to do! I like being busy so this is an aspect of the job that really appeals to me.

My current position has allowed me to have many connections within the legal community and the court system. This ensures that I have many doors open to me for advancement in the future.

Courtesy of Eastern College

Christina Saunders

Medical receptionist/clerk, Horizon Health Network

My name is Christina Saunders and I graduated from the medical administrative specialist program at Eastern College in 2017. I am currently a medical receptionist/clerk for Gibson Health Clinic and the Fredericton Downtown Community Health Centre, which are both a part of the Horizon Health Network.

The decision to attend Eastern College was not an easy one for me. I had been working in the childcare profession for 22 years, and I wasn't sure about going back to school after so many years. My fears quickly subsided. What made the difference was knowing that I was working toward a career and not just a job.

In my current position, I feel privileged to work with patients and their families. I get to know them on a personal level and have the responsibility of keeping their medical records private and up to date. I enjoy being the go-to person between patients and their doctors.

I find the scheduling aspect of my job challenging at times. Patients can become frustrated when there are no appointments available. For me, the key is not to take their frustration personally, but instead to work with them to get them an appointment.

Going back to school was one of the best decisions I have made in my life. There are so many career paths that are open to me now that weren't there before.

CHAPTER 13

Seeking Employment

LEARNING OUTCOMES

After studying this chapter, you should be able to:

1. Identify sources of job information.
2. Research organizations and prepare a cover letter and a résumé.
3. Describe how to prepare for a job interview.
4. Identify skills for job advancement and job changes.
5. Commit to living your values in the workplace.

Do I Qualify?

Administrative Assistant

Property management firm seeks responsible workers to interact with tenants and handle administrative duties such as:

- documenting tenants' property concerns
- sending email announcements
- inputting data into Microsoft Excel
- answering a steady volume of incoming calls
- creating and publishing memos and other communications
- managing the schedule for conference rooms

An achievement-oriented demeanour, professional dress, and experience in property management are required.

You have almost completed this course. It is time now to stop and reflect on your abilities and the skills you have acquired—the knowledge you have learned in this and other courses and your ability to apply your skills effectively as you seek employment and advance in your chosen profession. As you reflect on the hard and soft skills employers consider most important in new hires, you may want to review the *Employability Skills 2000+* profile in Chapter 1. These and other soft skills—value clarification, self-management, ethical behaviours, decision making, positive attitudes, creativity, continual learning, conflict resolution, and anger and stress management—have been identified as extremely important in the workplace. You need to analyze what all of this means for you and your career path. What type of organization interests you? Where do you think your hard skills and soft skills will fit best? Where do you want your career path to go?

The workplace you are entering or may already be in is not the workforce of your parents, and it is certainly not the workforce of your grandparents. Unlike them, you probably will not work for one organization your entire career. Also, the days when an organization took care of its employees' career development are over. You will be responsible for your own growth and career path; sometimes, changing jobs is a part of that growth.

Now you are ready to begin thinking about the steps you need to take to identify a job that fits your skills and interests, apply for that job, and succeed at that job.

Sources of Job Information

One of the first things to do as you look for a job is to gather all the information you can about available job opportunities. Information is available through

- the Internet
- networking
- college or university placement offices
- newspaper advertisements
- employment and recruitment agencies—public, private, and temporary
- professional organizations
- direct contact

The Internet

A variety of resources for job seekers are available on the Internet. In addition to job listings, you will find tips for résumé and cover letter preparation and for interviewing. You are also able to research companies in which you have an interest and actually post your résumé on the Internet for employers' review. Check out some of the best-known big Canadian online job boards:

- WowJobs (www.wowjobs.ca) consolidates job postings from other job boards, classified ads, and company sites across Canada and around the world.
- Indeed (www.indeed.ca) will post your résumé for review by prospective employers.
- WorkBC (www.workbc.ca) lists job opportunities in British Columbia. Similar sites exist for each province and territory in Canada.
- Public Service Commission of Canada (www.jobs-emplois.gc.ca) hosts a job board that posts positions available in the federal public service and provides information on procedures about their regularly scheduled testing.
- Job Bank (jobbank.gc.ca) is Canada's one-stop online job board for employers, businesses, and job seekers. It provides listings of current job openings from coast to coast.
- Monster.ca (www.monster.ca) offers a career centre where you can access career advice and tips on preparing a résumé and interviewing; you can also view job openings and employer profiles, and post your résumé online. Use the mobile app to search for jobs anytime, anywhere.
- Workopolis (www.workopolis.ca) allows you to post your résumé, save job searches, and receive job notices by email for positions in a variety of job categories. The online resource centre offers advice on résumé writing, interviewing, and networking
- CanadianCareers.com (www.canadiancareers.com) provides information on marketing yourself, exploring careers, and finding work.

- Government of Canada Jobs (www.canada.ca/en/services/jobs) lists jobs available in the federal public service and also provides information on the latest government initiatives and programs to enhance employment opportunities.

These job boards provide some very useful job-search information and can be used to jump-start your job search by providing information on the kinds of jobs available and the skill sets employers are seeking. Using these big job boards, you can continue your search for jobs on individual corporate websites, on professional association websites, and on specialty sites such as CareerMBA.com.

Networking

Networking is making contacts with people who may help you in an activity, such as your job search or career growth. Most of us already have an extensive social network, including our relatives, friends, and others. As you begin looking for a job, you will want to develop a job-related network. How do you do that? Here are some suggested steps:

- Let people know that you are searching for a job. Contact individuals you know who work for firms where you would like to work. Ask for leads and referrals.
- Contact professional organizations. For example, you may contact the local chapter of IAAP. Contact administrative professionals who are already employed. Contact managers you know; ask for referrals for any job openings that exist. Try to obtain at least three or four names from each person with whom you speak.
- Join a professional social media network, such as LinkedIn. Professional social media sites allow you to meet other professionals in your career area and exchange information, such as job postings.
- Ask administrative professionals who are employed in the field how they obtained their positions and what they like or dislike about their jobs.
- Keep a record of every person with whom you talk, including their email or telephone number and any comments.

As part of your networking activities, evaluate your online presence on social media or other websites and apps. Material that can compromise your online image may include embarrassing party pictures; references to illegal activities, substance use, or alcohol consumption; or rude or politically insensitive comments. These representations can hinder a job search or be grounds for dismissal. Search the internet using your name to locate information about you that may have been posted by others. Review your credit score and credit report. Revise or remove, if possible, information that does not contribute to the professional image you want to project.

During your job search and interviews you will often be asked to introduce yourself. In order to make yourself stand out and to capture someone's attention, it is recommended to prepare and practise answering this question. This type of introduction is often called an elevator pitch or 30-second introduction. Your introduction should include the following information:

- a personal introduction that outlines what type of position you are looking for and why
- an explanation of what your career or educational history has been
- three or four key competencies and skills

Networking is an excellent way to obtain job information.

College or University Placement Offices

Most post-secondary schools maintain a placement office to assist students with job searches. Visit this office to orient yourself with the services that are available to you as a student, as well as the services available to you when you graduate. Your school may not receive enough calls from employers to provide positions for all students, but counsellors are usually well informed about job opportunities in the community. They know the employers who need entry-level workers, and they can match a job to your qualifications and abilities. Many placement offices also provide assistance with cover letter and résumé writing, as well as assistance with enhancing your interview skills.

Newspaper Advertisements

Employers and employment agencies list available positions in local newspapers. As many newspapers are moving to an online format, you can search for these ads on the newspaper's Web page or in the print copy. These ads describe the positions and the qualifications required and may provide information about the salaries offered.

Employment Agencies

There are two types of employment agencies: public and private. **Employment and Social Development Canada** is the national public employment agency. You can visit their local office to speak with a counsellor in person or access their job postings online. An advantage of this federally funded government agency is that its services are provided free to Canadian job seekers.

Private employment agencies charge either you or the employing firm a fee. The employer pays the fee when an applicant is hired. When you are responsible for the fee, you will be asked to sign a contract with the employment agency. Ensure you understand how the fee is calculated (usually 5 to 10 percent of your first year's salary) and how it is to be paid.

Private employment agencies will generally administer standard tests on behalf of employers. Be prepared to demonstrate your abilities and skills with the following:

- specific software packages, such as Microsoft Word, Excel, and PowerPoint
- keyboarding speed and accuracy
- grammar, punctuation, and proofreading
- mathematical operations and problem solving

A **temporary agency** (one that offers temporary work) is not a source of job information in the usual sense. A temporary agency can place you in numerous different companies. Some organizations also use temporary agencies in a similar manner. Without either party having any long-term commitment, you can gain an understanding of where you want to work as a full-time employee, and potential employers get first-hand knowledge of prospective employees. Often, full-time employment can result from a temporary placement—a win-win situation.

Professional Organizations

If you are a member of a professional organization, in addition to networking at meetings and other functions, check whether the organization maintains a listing of jobs in your area. You can also ask other members whether they are aware of any openings.

Technology AT WORK

Many online job boards allow users to create search agents, also called job scouts or job search agents. **Job search agents** are programs that automatically search job listings and retrieve job postings that match criteria you set. For example, you might request jobs in a certain geographic area. The results are sent to you by email at an interval you select, such as daily or weekly. You can review the job listing and respond to jobs that interest you.

Direct Contact

If you are interested in obtaining a position with a certain company or in a particular type of business, the **direct contact** or **cold call** (going directly to an organization without having an appointment, or sending a letter and résumé without knowing whether a job is available) is sometimes successful. Especially if you have a gift for selling yourself, you might find this approach beneficial. However, before you engage in the direct-contact approach, find out as much as you can about the company.

Never restrict your job search to walk-ins only. It can be time-consuming, and often has little likelihood of success. If you do use direct contact as one of your approaches, be sure to dress professionally and take several copies of your résumé when you visit a company to complete an employment application. Prepare to make a professional impression even on visits when you only plan to drop off an application.

Researching and Applying for Jobs

Once you have identified sources of information about jobs, you are ready to research the organizations and apply for jobs. Having information about an organization will help you tailor your résumé and cover letter to illustrate how your qualifications meet their expectations. Do not focus your research on just one organization; rather, select several organizations that interest you.

Researching Organizations

Before applying for any job, spend some time learning about the organization—its mission and vision, its financial history, its products or services, its reputation, the length of time it has been in business, and how it treats its employees. How do you do this? There are several possibilities.

Since many organizations have websites, that is probably the best place to start your research. Review everything on the site—read about the history of the organization, its philosophy, its mission and values, its strategic direction, and information about its products or services (Figure 13-1). You can also follow these suggestions:

- Read business journals, such as the *Canadian Business Journal*, which often profile some of the largest businesses in the country.
- Ask friends, relatives, and acquaintances what they know about the organization.
- Review an annual report of the company; most companies' annual reports are available online.
- Consult your local chamber of commerce or Better Business Bureau.
- Ask your college or university placement office for information.
- Check online to view the listing of Canada's Top 100 Employers—a link to this site can be found on the MindTap site for this textbook.

- Access Glassdoor (www.glassdoor.com) and LinkedIn to find out more about companies and the people who work at these companies.
- Use informal channels such as association blog sites or topic-specific blog sites to research an organization and its culture (i.e., the culture that organizations typically don't advertise).

FIGURE 13-1
Evaluating Possible Employers

When evaluating an organization as a possible employer, you will want to find answers to questions such as these:

- What are the organization's services or products?
- Is the organization multinational? Does the organization have branches in other provinces or territories?
- What has been the profit picture of the organization for the last several years?
- Is the organization financially secure?
- Is the organization growing?
- What is the reputation of its chief executive officer?
- Does the organization have a good reputation in the community?
- Is there a good relationship between the employer and the employees?
- Is the organization an equal opportunity employer?
- Are there opportunities for advancement?

Preparing a Cover Letter

The **cover letter** is a document sent to a potential employer to state your interest in a job and to transmit your résumé. This letter is generally the first contact you make with an organization and is the key to obtaining an interview.

The letter must sell your abilities to the employer. The person reading your letter gets a favourable or unfavourable impression of you from the content of your letter, your writing skills, and the format of the letter. This letter must be free of typos or spelling errors. If you make mistakes in the letter, you have little chance of getting an interview. Think of this letter as your chance to say to a prospective employer, "I am the person who can do the job; my work is always well written and free of errors." Conversely, a poorly written letter with errors suggests that you are disorganized, sloppy, unfocused, and ill-suited for employment.

The basic goals of a cover letter are as follows:

- State your interest in the position.
- Provide general information about your skills (specific information appears in your résumé) and sell your skills (let the reader know you have something to offer the organization).
- Transmit your résumé.
- Request an interview, providing your contact information.

Use Proper Format

Block style is a commonly used style for a cover letter; however, modified block style is also appropriate. Both mixed punctuation, with a colon after the salutation and a comma after the complimentary close, and open punctuation are appropriate. If you need to review letter and punctuation styles, refer to the Reference Guide available in MindTap.

You may be posting your letter and résumé online. This possibility will be discussed later in this chapter.

Writing AT WORK

Follow these tips for writing cover letters:
- Personalize each letter by reading and writing to the job notice published by the organization. Do not assume one letter is appropriate for all organizations.
- Address the letter to a specific person. If you do not have a name, call the company or check with the placement office, agency, or person who told you about the job.
- Use three paragraphs—an opening paragraph in which you provide a brief statement of your interest, a middle paragraph in which you describe your abilities, and a closing paragraph in which you request an interview, providing your contact information. You should mention in the second or third paragraph that your résumé is enclosed.
- Keep the letter short; put details in the résumé.
- Use correct spelling, punctuation, capitalization, and grammar. Use the spell and grammar check on your computer.
- Key the letter in proper form using an acceptable letter style.
- Print your letter on high-quality bond paper. If you do not own a printer that produces quality work, have your cover letter and résumé professionally printed.
- Send an original cover letter for each application. Do not send photocopies.

Address the Letter Appropriately

Be certain that you address the letter appropriately. Reread the address several times and proof the address that you have keyed against the position advertisement. You do not want to key the wrong title, misspell the recipient's name, or even send the letter to the wrong person. Never use "To Whom It May Concern" as a salutation. If a name is not given in the job vacancy notice, contact the organization to determine the name of the individual that your cover letter should be directed to.

Figure 13-2 provides an example of a cover letter. Notice that the four basic goals of a letter of application are followed carefully in the three paragraphs of the letter. Notice that the top of the letter includes the sender's address, telephone number, and email. A résumé will also include this information; however, if the letter and résumé are separated, this approach allows the organization to contact the sender.

Preparing a Résumé

The **résumé**, a concise statement of your background, education, skills, and experience, is an important part of your job application packet. Just as a cover letter is a sales letter, so is the résumé. It represents a very important product—you. The sections of a résumé may vary; there is no one perfect model. How you set up your résumé depends on your situation and how you want to present your qualifications. The following sections are common to most résumés though their placement may vary depending on the format you choose to use. Figure 13-3 outlines guidelines to keep in mind when preparing a résumé.

Heading

The heading, much like a letterhead, is at the top of your résumé and contains your full name and contact information—address, personal telephone number, email, and social network profile if appropriate. Enhance the formatting of your name with a different typeface or font size; possibly use a graphic line to separate it from the next sections.

Objective

The objective section informs the reader of the position you are seeking. Some career experts and industry professionals believe an objective is not necessary but this section can still be very useful. If you choose to use an objective, it should be concise and give your résumé focus, and can be labelled Career Objective, Job Objective, or simply Objective. See the following example.

> **Career Objective:** Detail-oriented administrative assistant seeking a challenging position with opportunities to use my technology and human relations skills.

Relevant Skills

In the skills section, identify your skill strengths. For example, list your computer skills, including your keyboarding skills and the various software packages in which you are proficient.

Education

List the schools you have attended and, if pertinent, the qualifications you have acquired. You might also list the specific courses, workshops, or programs of study you have taken, which pertain to the position you are applying for.

Employment History

List the companies where you have worked, the dates of employment, and your duties. You may want to reverse the order in which you present the education and experience sections on your résumé, presenting your most recent education

FIGURE 13-2
Cover Letter

Colette Soros

416-321-3100
Email: csoros@hotmail.com
Linkedin.com/in/colettesoros

1415 Kennedy Road
Scarborough, ON M1P 2L6

May 21, 20--

Ms. Keri-An Mahar
Human Resources Department
Delaware Accounting Services
300 Bay Street
Toronto, ON M5H 2S8

Four Goals of the Cover Letter

- Introduce yourself in the opening paragraph.
- Describe your abilities in the next paragraph.
- Indicate your résumé is enclosed.
- Request the interview in the closing paragraph.

Dear Ms. Mahar:

As demonstrated in my résumé, my experience and formal education makes me a strong candidate for the Administrative Assistant position posted on your organization's website. My Office Administration diploma from Centennial College and my one year of work experience have given me the skills and knowledge required to succeed in this position.

During my studies, I took courses in business communications, organizational behavior, accounting, administrative procedures and computer software. Additionally, I gained valuable practical experience through a work placement where I worked for 20 hours a week in the Registrar's Office at the College. During this placement, I prepared spreadsheets using Excel, keyed correspondence using Word, and handled student inquiries concerning admissions. Prior to beginning my studies, I also worked as a receptionist which enhanced my interpersonal skills as I was the first point of contact when dealing with a variety of customer inquiries.

You will find a résumé enclosed, which provides further details concerning my qualifications and experience. Please feel free to contact me to arrange a convenient time to further explore how my professional and educational experience will be an asset to your organization.

Thank you for your time and consideration.

Sincerely,

Colette Soros

Colette Soros

Enclosure

---

and job experience first. When you have experience that directly relates to the job for which you are applying, list it first. Remember that the résumé is a sales piece. You want to call attention to your bestselling features first.

Accomplishments

An accomplishments section allows you to detail your leadership and interpersonal skills, and provides evidence to future employers that you are a well-rounded person. If you have participated in special activities, maintained memberships in professional organizations, or achieved specific honours, list them here.

References

A reference is a person who can verify your academic ability and/or your work skills and habits, and is both willing and available to recommend you to employers. Choose your references carefully. Select those individuals who know your

FIGURE 13-3
Professional Résumé Writing Guidelines

Whichever style of résumé you prepare, keep these guidelines in mind.

- Always be accurate and honest when listing information on your résumé.
- Keep the résumé short—preferably one or two pages. If your résumé is longer than one page, be sure to include your name at the top of each page.
- Target your résumé to each job. Highlight those areas of your background or work experience that fit the position you are applying for.
- If you are a recent graduate and have held only part-time jobs, list them.
- If you have not had any paid work experience, list volunteer jobs or leadership positions you have held.
- Do not use personal pronouns (I, me, you). They are unnecessary and detract from the impact of the résumé.
- Describe your qualifications and skills in specific terms using action verbs; avoid vague language.
- Check your spelling and grammar usage. Read and reread the résumé several times. Ask someone who is a good proofreader and grammarian to review it.
- Avoid using abbreviations, with the exception of a degree designation.
- Use keywords in your résumé. Your document may be scanned by a computer that has been programmed to pick up on certain words that have been used in the advertisement; review the job ad for keywords and ensure you use them in your résumé. An administrative assistant should list specific software programs such as Microsoft Word, Corel Draw. Use "collaborative" or "team player" as keywords in your résumé; employers often seek people who work well with others.
- Take advantage of professional help when writing your résumé. Check Web sources, talk with your college or university placement representatives, and visit a bookstore or library for materials on résumé preparation.
- Avoid the use of résumé templates. Sell yourself and your skills by creating your own personalized templates with matching letterhead and résumé headings.
- Use high-quality, white, letter-sized paper for your résumé. Print on one side of the paper only. Do not fold or staple.
- Use a professional, neutral email address, such as rlsmith@yahoo.com. Never use an email address such as fungirl@me.com, partyhappy@look.com, or some equally unprofessional address.
- Include a link to your social networking site, especially when you know that the contents will present you in a positive light.

qualifications well and will take the time to respond to a reference request. It is inappropriate to include names of close relatives or personal friends.

Generally you should not list references on your résumé; the résumé is a place to highlight work experiences and skills. However, you may choose to include the heading References and the statement "References will be provided on request."

Be sure to contact your references before beginning a job search. Let them know what you are doing and ask whether you can use them as a reference. Verify the addresses and phone numbers of your references, their current employment, and their job titles and duties. Keep your list of references current by contacting them periodically, especially when changing jobs, addresses, or your surname. An accurate list of references can be a determining factor in the hiring of one applicant over another.

While you may carefully select your references and confirm they are available to support your job application, remember that job recruiters may research Internet user groups and join discussions, google your name, search for you on Facebook, and check out your LinkedIn profile to see what others say about you.

Depending on the type of job you seek and your employment history, you will likely choose one of three commonly used résumé formats—the chronological résumé, the functional résumé, or the combination-style résumé. Once your résumé has been created, you can publish it in a hardcopy or electronic format. In determining the format to use for your résumé, consider your purpose and background, and the requirements of the potential employer.

Chronological Résumé

A **chronological résumé** is a document that gives an applicant's work experience in order with the most recent experience listed first. This type of résumé is the most common and most preferred format for a résumé. It works well for showing progress and growth if the jobs listed reflect increasing responsibility. Figure 13-4 illustrates the format of a typical printed résumé in chronological order.

Functional Résumé

The **functional résumé** works well for individuals who have good educational backgrounds and skills but little or no work experience. Rather than focusing on work experience, the functional résumé documents those skills and abilities that are most applicable to the specific job you are seeking. While the information included is the same as in a chronological résumé, the organization of content is different—your education, experiences, and activities are clustered into categories that support your career goals. This format is usually

FIGURE 13-4
Chronological Résumé

Colette Soros

1415 Kennedy Road
Scarborough, ON M1P 2L6

416-321-3100
Email: csoros@hotmail.com
Linkedin.com/in/colettesoros

CAREER OBJECTIVE

Detail-oriented Administrative Assistant seeking a position to utilize my technology, communication, and human relation skills.

COMPUTER SKILLS

- Keyboarding speed of 90 nwpm
- Microsoft Office 365 (PowerPoint, Excel, Word, Access, and Outlook)
- Web page design
- Internet research

EDUCATION

Office Administration Executive Diploma
Centennial College
Scarborough, ON

September 20--to April 20--

Courses of Study: Business communications, organizational behaviour, accounting, administrative procedures, and computer software

WORK EXPERIENCE

Administrative Assistant (Work Placement)
Office of the Registrar, Centennial College
Scarborough, ON

September 20--to April 20—

- Prepared spreadsheets using Excel to track student enrollments
- Produced letters using Word to confirm students' acceptance to the College
- Filed correspondence electronically on College's network
- Handled a variety of student inquiries
- Assisted in designing class timetable

> **Arrange jobs in reverse chronological order and format job titles in bold for readability.**

Receptionist
Arthur Paper Company
Toronto, ON

June 20--to August 20--

- Greeted customers and visitors and answered the telephone
- Created correspondence

> **Use bulleted lists to make résumé easier to read.**

ACTIVITIES/HONOURS

- Recipient of the Lieutenant Governor's Silver Medal
- Member of the International Association of Administrative Professionals

appropriate when you have developed skills that are more relevant to the job than to the heading labels, or when you have had periods of time when you did not work; for example, you took a break from your career to have or care for a child or to travel. The functional résumé allows you to de-emphasize these gaps and emphasize your skill sets. A functional résumé is shown in Figure 13-5.

Combination-Style Résumé

The **combination-style résumé** works best for the experienced worker who has held several different jobs and when skills, titles, and heading labels are equally impressive. The chronological format with functional subheadings allows you to present your experiences in reverse chronological skill set order. This format is not the best choice when you do not

FIGURE 13-5
Functional Résumé

Colette Soros

1415 Kennedy Road
Scarborough, ON M1P 2L6

416-321-3100
Email: csoros@hotmail.com
Linkedin.com/in/colettesoros

OBJECTIVE

Secure a position as an Administrative Assistant to utilize my technology, communication and interpersonal skills.

COMPUTER AND COMMUNICATION SKILLS

- Conducted Internet research, analyzed findings, and presented a report on implementing green practice in an office environment
- Proficient in Microsoft Office (Word, Excel, PowerPoint, Access) to record, tabulate and present a variety of information
- Created and amended Web pages
- Worked in a team environment using workplace collaboration tools to produce class schedules
- Used Excel to prepare student enrollment numbers each semester; determined increases or decreases from previous semesters
- Conducted telephone surveys of past graduates

INTERPERSONAL SKILLS

- Successfully resolved student complaints on a variety of scheduling issues
- Trained student volunteers for campus tours

> Use action verbs and bullets to describe skills.

EDUCATION

Centennial College, Office A

Colette Soros   ← Header when subsequent pages needed →   Page 2

EMPLOYMENT HISTORY

Administrative Assistant (Work Placement)   September 20--to May 20--
Office of the Registrar, Centennial College

Receptionist, Arthur Paper Company   June 20-- to August 20—

ACTIVITIES/HONOURS

- Recipient of the Lieutenant Governor's Silver Medal
- Member of the International Association of Administrative Professionals

have numerous experiences that match a number of skills, or when you have multiple skills but a small number of different experiences (job titles or organizations for which you have worked).

Targeted Résumé

A **targeted résumé** is a résumé created specifically to the job that you are applying for. It takes more effort to create a targeted résumé but the effort is well worth it. It is advisable to write a targeted résumé for every job that you apply for. An employer can easily determine that you submitted a generic résumé rather than taking the time to provide one that highlights your qualifications and skills specific to the position they are trying to fill.

People AT WORK

Recruiter

A recruiter works in the human resources department of a company. Recruiters search for job candidates to fill positions at their company. They may travel to college or university campuses and to job fairs to talk with job seekers.

Recruiters may also screen, interview, and test applicants, deciding whether to recommend them for jobs. Recruiters must be knowledgeable about the company's personnel needs as well as the company's employment policies, wages, and benefits. They must also stay informed about laws and regulations related to hiring practices. If you apply for a job with a large organization, you may have contact with a recruiter.

Electronic Résumés

Human resources departments and recruiters use a variety of methods to process résumés. In addition to receiving hardcopy, print-based résumés, they, like job seekers, are using technology extensively. Not only do you need a traditional résumé with its bullets, bold headings, different font styles, and graphics to take with you to interviews, but you also need to prepare a version that can be submitted electronically to prospective employers. Many organizations have added sections to their home page that allow you to submit your résumé online. The content of your **electronic résumé** (statement of background and experiences submitted online) should be based on your hardcopy version. Electronic résumés are often scanned by a computer program for keywords that match words found in the related job listing. Because the résumé is scanned, the format of the document should be simple, and it should contain keywords that relate to the job listing. This process helps the organization to narrow its search to the most suitable candidates.

Your attachment can also be formatted in Microsoft Word or converted to a PDF (portable document format) file.

Converting it to a PDF file ensures that all the formatting enhancements you have used will be viewed by the reader just as you intended. PDF files cannot, however, be scanned by résumé software. When submitting your résumé and cover letter by email, check with the employer to determine which of these formats is preferred. It is possible that the employer will not open attachments because of the risk of a virus being present. If this is the case, use the job title in the subject line of the message and submit only one email message that contains both your cover letter and résumé in plain text format embedded in the body of the email.

You can also post your electronic résumé online to job boards or directly to the website of a specific organization, where you will find instructions for completing an online application form and uploading your résumé. Follow the guidelines for preparing a professional résumé and adapt it as follows for your electronic version. Remember, you are not creating a different résumé, merely altering the formatting of the print version. Follow these guidelines when preparing an electronic résumé:

- Use a single-column format with a maximum of 65 characters to each line.
- Be sure your name is the first line on your résumé.
- Use standard address format for the balance of your contact information (street, city, province or territory, postal code) placed on separate lines.
- If you have more than one telephone number, use a separate line for each.
- Use a basic, plain font (Times New Roman or Arial) and a font size of 11 to 12 points for the body.
- Use all caps for headings with a maximum size of 14 points rather than italics, bold, script, or underlining.
- Use well-known abbreviations; minimize the use of unfamiliar ones.
- Use keyboard characters such as asterisks (*), equal signs (=), tildes (~), and vertical separators (|) rather than bullets, graphic lines, shading, or boxes.

All these techniques will mean that your résumé will be entered into the company's system in the cleanest format possible. The résumé software will then read the text to identify and extract important information about you such as your name, address, phone number, work history, years of experience, education, and skills. See the example in Figure 13-6.

Completing an Employment Application

You may be asked to complete an **employment application** (a form used by organizations to obtain information about prospective employees) either before or after being interviewed. In some organizations, all applicants are required to fill out a form. Other firms ask only those people who are seriously being considered for a position to fill out a form.

FIGURE 13-6
Electronic Résumé

```
================================================================

COLETTE SOROS

1415 Kennedy Road
Scarborough, ON  M1P 2L6

Phone:  416-321-3100

Email:  csoros@hotmail.com
Linkedin.com/in/colettesoros

================================================================
OBJECTIVE

Secure a position as an Administrative Assistant to utilize my technology, communication, and
interpersonal skills.
~~~~~~~~~~~~~~~~~~~~~~~~~~~~~~~~~~~~~~~~~~~~~~~~~
COMPUTER AND COMMUNICATION SKILLS
~~~~~~~~~~~~~~~~~~~~~~~~~~~~~~~~~~~~~~~~~~~~~~~~~
Conducted internet research, analyzed findings, and presented a report on implementing green practice in
an office environment

Proficient in Microsoft Office (Word, Excel, PowerPoint, Access) to record, tabulate, and present a variety
of information

Created and amended Web pages

Worked in a team environment using workplace collaboration tools to produce class schedules

Used Excel to prepare student enrollment numbers each semester; determined increases or decreases from
previous semesters

Conducted telephone surveys of past graduates
~~~~~~~~~~~~~~~~~~~~~~~~~~~~~~~~~~~~~~~~~~~~~~~~~
INTERPERSONAL SKILLS
~~~~~~~~~~~~~~~~~~~~~~~~~~~~~~~~~~~~~~~~~~~~~~~~~
Successfully resolved student complaints on a variety of scheduling issues

Trained student volunteers for campus tours
```

If you are asked to do so, you should do the following:

- Read the entire application before starting to complete it.
- Print legibly.
- Spell correctly. Carry a pocket dictionary in case you need to look up a word.
- Answer every question completely and honestly. Be certain that the information you provide is consistent with the information on your résumé. If a question does not apply to you, put N/A (for "not applicable") in the blank so that it does not look like you overlooked the question.
- Be sure to have all the information with you that you need, such as your social insurance number, dates you attended schools, dates of employment, and complete addresses of previous employers and references.
- Answer all questions truthfully. A standard question included on the application is the reason for leaving your last position. If you were fired from your job you must say so, but you can make it positive by saying that your skills did not match those needed by the organization.

- The form usually concludes with a statement that the information you provided is accurate and that any misrepresentation is grounds for immediate dismissal. Some firms may discharge you, even after months of satisfactory work, if they discover you were untruthful on the application.
- Sign and date the form.

Job Interview Skills

A **job interview** is a meeting between a job applicant and a potential employer to discuss a job and the applicant's qualifications. In the interview, the employer will judge your appearance, personality, human relations skills, self-confidence, and other traits. The interviewer will question you about your experience and abilities, as identified in your cover letter and résumé. The interview is an opportunity for the prospective employer to get to know you and for you to get to know the interviewer and to learn more about the organization and the job you are applying for.

Employment Portfolio

You may want to prepare a portfolio of your work to take with you to the interview. A *portfolio* is a compilation of samples of your work and other career-related information. To be representative of your professionalism, it should be organized in a binder with tabs separating the various sections or stored on a thumb drive that can be left with the interviewer.

Consider including the following items in the binder:

- your business card
- your résumé
- awards or honours received
- education, training, or certifications
- letters you have written that demonstrate your writing style and document-formatting abilities
- reports you have produced that demonstrate your ability to conduct research and present the research in an attractive format
- spreadsheets, graphics, and slides you have created to demonstrate your knowledge of software

Your portfolio can also be prepared in electronic format as Web pages—known as an e-portfolio. A link in your electronic résumé can provide easy access to your e-portfolio for the interviewer. Preparing and presenting a portfolio during the job interview allows you to *show* what you can do, rather than merely talk about it.

Pre-interview Nervousness

Feeling nervous before an interview is natural. However, you want to control your nervousness. View each interview as a learning experience. After the interview, write notes about what went right and what went wrong. Concentrate on the positives; try not to make the same mistakes a second time. The more interview experiences you have, the more you will learn. Here are several suggestions that will help:

- Research the organization.
- Research national and local salaries for administrative professionals. Knowing about typical salaries will help you feel confident when responding to questions about salary. Check the Internet for national salaries and your local newspaper or placement office for local salary information.
- Practise interviewing by having a friend ask you questions (Figure 13-7 gives some typical interview questions you might use for your practice session).
- Plan something to do the night before the interview so you do not spend your time worrying about the interview. Go to a movie or dinner with a friend. Use some stress-reduction techniques—go for a walk, engage in positive self-talk, and get a good night's rest so you will be calm and alert.

Be certain you know the exact time and location of the interview. When travelling to the interview location, allow time for unexpected delays.

Helpful Interview Hints

Observe the following suggestions in this section to help you prepare for an interview and to make a good impression during the interview.

Before the Interview

Get a good night's rest so that you will be alert during the interview. Determine what you need to take with you: your portfolio, extra copies of your résumé in the event the interviewer has misplaced the one you sent, a list of your references (three to five are likely to be requested), and a pad and pen so that you can make notes or complete an application. Place these items in an orderly manner in your briefcase so that you are able to access them quickly and easily if required. Turn off or mute your cellphone and set it to go to voicemail before you enter for the interview. Store the phone out of sight during the interview so it will not be a distraction.

Dress and Grooming

Dress appropriately, which means dressing conservatively, even if you are applying for a position in a creative line of work. For both men and women, a suit is appropriate attire; wear a colour that not only looks good on you but also makes you feel good. Be well groomed. Women should keep jewellery to a minimum, and both men and women should avoid the use of fragrance. If you wear an overcoat, hang it in the reception area. Do not take it into the office where you are being interviewed. Women should try to do without a handbag; carry only a briefcase—it's one less item to juggle. You do not want to be burdened with numerous belongings.

Greetings

Greetings are your initial personal contact with the organization and are very important. Greet the receptionist with a friendly smile. Tell them your name, the name of the person you are meeting with, and the purpose of your visit. If you have to wait for the interviewer, do so patiently. Once in the interviewer's office, make appropriate eye contact and shake the interviewer's hand with a firm (but not tight) grip and use their name. When invited to do so, sit down.

During the Interview

Show genuine interest in what the interviewer says; be alert to all questions. Try to understand your prospective employer's needs and describe how you can fill them. Follow these suggestions:

- Be prepared to tell the interviewer about yourself, as it is a commonly asked question at the beginning of the interview.
- Be enthusiastic and positive; demonstrate pride in your skills and abilities.

FIGURE 13-7

Commonly Asked Interview Questions

Questions Relating to Your Interest in the Company and the Job

- How did you learn about this position?
- Are you familiar with our company?
- What interests you about our products/services?
- Why do you want to work for our company?
- Why do you want this job?
- Why do you think you are qualified for the position?
- Why should we give this job to you rather than another who is equally qualified?
- How would you describe your ideal job?

Questions Regarding Your Ability to Do the Job

- What are your greatest strengths?
- What is your major weakness?
- Why should I hire you?
- If I talked to your former employer, what would the person say about you?
- What in your past job did you enjoy the most? Why?
- What in your past job did you enjoy the least? Why?
- If I talked with your former colleagues, what would they say about you?
- What can you tell me about yourself?

Questions Regarding Education

- Why did you choose your major area of study?
- What was your academic average in school?
- What honours did you earn?
- In what extracurricular activities were you involved?
- Which courses did you like best? Least? Why?
- Do you feel you did the best work that you were capable of doing at school?
- How have the classes you completed as part of your major helped you prepare for your career?

Questions Regarding Your Ability to Fit into the Organization

- If you disagreed with something your supervisor asked you to do, what would you do?
- What type of work atmosphere do you prefer?
- How do you feel about working overtime?
- Is a sense of humour important at work? Why or why not?

- Tell me about a conflict you have had with someone. How did you handle that conflict?
- What is your definition of diversity?
- How do you handle pressure?
- How would your previous employers and co-workers describe you?
- Have you ever had trouble with other people on the job/ at school?
- What do you think determines a person's progress with a company?

Questions Regarding Experience

- Have you ever been fired or asked to resign from a position?
- Why did you leave your previous job?
- Have you had any problems with previous supervisors?
- What two accomplishments have given you the most satisfaction?
- What do you not do well?
- Why should I hire you?
- What salary do you expect?

Note on salary: You should have an idea of an appropriate salary before going to an interview. If you do not already know, ask the interviewer the starting rate for the company. If that amount seems appropriate, indicate that it is satisfactory; if not, you can reply that you had hoped for a higher salary rate but that you are interested in having an opportunity to show what you can do and in taking advantage of opportunities for advancement. If you are not interested in the position at the salary offered, say so. Be certain before you respond that you are really not interested, as your chances of being offered a higher salary may not be good and you may well lose out on a job offer.

Many interviewers will look for more than information on your qualifications; some of the questions presented here go beyond providing a concise summary of your skills, abilities, and interests, in an attempt to determine your work ethic, your personality, and whether you will be a good fit in their organization. Organizations look to hire people who are self-starters and good team players—people with a strong work ethic who are both adaptable and flexible. Be confident not boastful and ready with an answer to the most important question: What you can do for them.

- Answer questions thoroughly and concisely; do not talk too much.
- Express yourself clearly, with a well-modulated voice.
- Do not criticize former employers, instructors, schools, or colleagues.
- Try not to act nervous; avoid nervous gestures such as playing with your hair or jewellery.
- Do not tell jokes, argue with the interviewer, or brag about yourself.

At the Close of the Interview

The interviewer will usually give you a chance at the end of the interview to ask some questions; be prepared to do so. Figure 13-8 gives some examples. Listen carefully to the answers to your questions. Attempt to determine what the next step will be. Will there be another interview? When can you expect to hear the results of the interview? Does the salary seem appropriate? If it does not, will you consider accepting the position if it is offered? Reiterate your interest in the job (that is, if you are still interested). Smile pleasantly and thank the interviewer for their time. Smile and thank the receptionist as you leave.

FIGURE 13-8
Questions You Might Ask

If given the opportunity by the interviewer, you might ask a couple of these questions:

- Can you describe the specific duties of the job?
- Can you tell me about the people with whom I will be working if I am the successful candidate?
- I read on your Web page that your organization has grown tremendously over the last few years. To what do you attribute this growth? Do you expect it to continue?
- Can you tell me about advancement opportunities in your organization?
- What is the starting salary for this position?
- When will you make a decision about hiring?

Take a few minutes to read the questions in Figure 13-7, then formulate answers to the questions in Self-Check A. If you have concerns about the appropriateness of your answers, read the suggested responses provided at the end of the chapter.

Employment Testing

Be prepared to take tests. Expect to take tests pertaining to basic skills, such as keyboarding, spelling, math, proofreading, vocabulary, and reasoning ability. The law demands that any test given must relate to the job for which you are applying. Many employment tests are administered to determine your knowledge and evaluate your level of accuracy. Ensure that you listen carefully to test instructions. Do not hesitate to ask for clarification on any instructions you do not understand.

Self-Check Ⓐ

Answer these frequently asked interview questions.

1. What can you tell me about yourself?
2. How would your previous employers and co-workers describe you?
3. How have the classes you completed as part of your major helped you prepare for your career?
4. How would you describe your personality?
5. What skills do you possess that will help you excel in this position?

Multiple and Team Interviews

You may have more than one interview for a particular position. For example, a human resources professional may interview you first. Next, you may interview with your prospective supervisor. Finally, you may have a group interview with your prospective team members.

A team interview may be with two or three or even five or six people. Although this type of interview sounds intimidating, it need not be. Follow these additional tips specifically for a successful team interview:

- When introductions are made, pay careful attention to the individuals' names—if you can do so unnoticed, jot down their names or initials to assist you during the interview.
- Focus on each individual as the person asks a question.
- Listen carefully to the question, jot down a few notes to remind yourself of key points, and answer the question succinctly.
- Make eye contact with people and, if possible, use their name when responding to a question.
- When you ask a question, ask it of the group. If one member of the group has asked a question or said something that you need clarified, address that individual.
- If you find yourself getting nervous, glance occasionally at people who have given you positive feedback—those with a friendly face, open body language, and positive reactions to your responses. Say to yourself, "This person likes me; I am doing well."
- Thank the group when the interview is completed. Use their names, if possible; it shows you were paying attention.

Telephone and Online Interviews

Occasionally organizations will conduct a virtual interview (using telephone or videoconferencing tools, a candidate is interviewed by an interviewer at a distant location). If you are applying for a job in another city or for a national firm with its head office in a city other than yours, it is not necessary for you or the interviewer to meet in the same city for an interview. A telephone conference call or computer conferencing with WebEx or Skype can easily be arranged. You can be interviewed by one or more interviewers via the telephone or participate in a virtual video interview from any location in the world.

If you are scheduled for a virtual interview, you need to be well prepared. When a camera is involved, most people get a little nervous. However, your goal is to relax and treat the situation as if the person interviewing you is in the same room.

You may be interviewed by a team.

Virtual interviews require similar preparation to face-to-face interviews. In addition to the previous hints, consider the following additional suggestions when participating in a virtual interview:

- Make sure the technology is working properly and that you know how to use it. If possible, do a test conversation with a friend or adviser using the computer and software you will use for the interview.
- Take steps to control your environment. For example, if there is a phone in the room where you will be during the interview, unplug it or turn off the ringer. You do not want a ringing phone to interrupt the conversation.
- Close any software programs that may give you audible alerts or open windows on your screen before you begin the interview.
- Greet the interviewer warmly and with a smile, just as you would in person, and use the interviewer's name.
- Dress appropriately for the interview just as you would if you were meeting the interviewer in person.
- Try to forget the camera is there; do not concentrate on it. Concentrate on the interviewer and the questions you are asked.
- Dress in colours that look good on you and on camera. Black or grey generally does not come across well on camera. Do not wear jewellery that jingles. The noise on camera is even more noticeable than in person.
- Pay attention to body language and small nuances of the interviewer. Do not spend an inordinate amount of time answering any one question. Be warm and informative but also be concise.
- Enunciate carefully. Poor enunciation is more pronounced on camera than in person.
- Once the interview is over, thank the person and terminate the program.

Interview Follow-Up

After an interview, you should complete follow-up activities. You should write a thank you letter to the interviewer(s) and do a self-evaluation of how you performed during the interview. You should also make a record of the date of the interview; the company name and address; the names, positions, and contact information of the persons with whom you spoke; and other details that will help you remember the interview. You may find this information useful if you interview with the company for a different job at some point in the future.

Thank You Letter

Promptly after the interview, follow up by writing a letter or email thanking the employer for the interview and reviewing points of special interest. Figure 13-9 is an example **follow-up letter**. Adapt the content if you are sending an email. Use your judgment regarding whether an email or a formal letter would be best for each organization at which you interview.

When in doubt, send a letter. If you speak with two or more people during the interview, send a personalized message to each person. The letter or message should include information such as

- a thank you for the opportunity to interview
- a recap of your skills and abilities
- a statement of your continued interest in the job (if this is true)
- a reminder of the next steps you agreed on in the interview, such as when the decision is going to be made

If you have heard nothing about your application, a second follow-up message may be advisable a week or two after the first one. The second message should merely remind the employer of your continued interest in the job and express a willingness to return for another interview if necessary. Depending on the situation, you may want to make a third contact with the organization. Being persistent shows your interest in the job, and the organization may view it as a plus. You do not want to risk annoying the employer, so use good judgment in determining how many follow-ups are appropriate in each job situation.

After an interview, you may decide you are not interested in the position. In this case, you should promptly send a courteous message expressing your appreciation for having been considered and explaining why you do not want to remain a candidate. Although you are not interested in the present position, you may be interested in the future in another position within the company. If so, the courteous way you decline the first position may help when being considered a second time. You always want to keep the doors open.

Interview Evaluation

You may feel you did very well in the interview but not get the job. There simply may have been someone more qualified or with more experience than you. Organizations will usually provide you with a generic reason why this is so; most do not give exact reasons because of legal problems that may occur.

In any case, do not lose confidence in your skills and abilities. Play back the experience in your mind. Note the questions you had trouble answering, questionable reactions from the interviewer, and any errors that you believe you made. Think also about what went well and about how you can correct errors before the next interview. Review these thoughts with a trusted adviser and ask for some suggestions. Maintain a positive attitude, learn from each interview situation, and turn a job rejection into a positive learning opportunity.

Evaluating a Job Offer

Your goal is to find the right position for you. You will spend the major part of each week on a job, so you need to choose a position where you feel happy and productive.

FIGURE 13-9
Follow-Up Message

Colette Soros

416-321-3100
Email: csoros@hotmail.com
Linkedin.com/in/colettesoros

1415 Kennedy Road
Scarborough, ON M1P 2L6

June 15, 20--

Ms. Keri-An Mahar
Human Resources Department
Delaware Accounting Services
300 Bay Street
Toronto, ON M5H 2S8

> Begin by thanking the interviewer.
>
> Follow up with a recap of your skills and abilities, and indicate your continuing interest in the position.
>
> Close with a reminder of the next steps you agreed to at the conclusion of the interview.

Dear Ms. Mahar:

Thank you for giving me the opportunity to interview for the administrative assistant position with your organization. I appreciate the time you spent with me, and I enjoyed learning more about Delaware Accounting Services.

Because of my education and experience, I am confident I can be an asset to Delaware Accounting Services. My skills in technology, communications, and human relations will help me perform at a high level. The interview today reinforced my interest in joining your team; I was extremely impressed with what I heard from you about Delaware Accounting Service's philosophy of management and the directions the company is taking. I welcome the chance to become a part of the organization.

You may reach me at home by calling 416-321-3100 or by e-mail at csoros@hotmail.com.

Thank you again for your kindness, and I look forward to hearing from you within the next two weeks.

Sincerely,

Colette Soros

Colette Soros

Enclosure

Job Duties and Co-workers

When deciding whether or not to accept a job offer, you need to ask yourself whether the organization lived up to your expectations. Ask yourself the following questions:

- Do my skills and the position match?
- Is the work environment one in which I will be happy and will have an opportunity to grow?
- Will I have a chance to work with people I can respect and admire?
- Will the work be interesting?
- Will I be able to learn from the job duties and the people?
- Are the benefits and compensation packages acceptable?

You will be spending a major part of each week on the job—be certain you have found a position that will make you feel happy and productive.

Employee Benefits

In addition to your salary or wages, many organizations offer benefits to employees. When considering taking a job, you should consider the benefits offered, along with other factors about the job. These benefits can be a large part of the overall compensation received. Typical benefits include paid time off (vacation, holidays, and sick days), group insurance plans, retirement plans, and stock option plans. Once employed, you should be aware of the benefits offered by your company and how vacation days and holidays may affect work schedules.

Paid Time Off

Paid time off for business employees typically includes vacation days, statutory holidays, and sick days. Having time away from work for statutory holidays and vacations helps employees relax and return to work with a positive outlook and desire to perform well.

In Canada, the minimum number of days for paid time off provided by employers is legislated both on a federal and provincial or territorial level. Federally, the Canada Labour Standards Regulations outlines this information, and on a provincial or territorial level each province and territorial has their respective Employment Standards Act, which sets out the minimum requirements. Employers may choose to provide additional paid time off over and above those outlined in the legislation.

Group Insurance

Many companies offer health care insurance plans to employees. Insurance costs for members of a group plan are lower than when individuals purchase health care insurance on their own, making this a valuable employee benefit.

Some companies pay a portion of the insurance plan costs; others require employees to pay a portion of the cost. Insurance plan benefits will vary but some common options include coverage for dental, eye care, and paramedical expense reimbursement.

Retirement Plans

Most workers need to establish a savings and investment plan for their working years that will generate the income needed in retirement. Tax-deferred retirement plans and defined benefit plans are two options offered by some employers that can contribute to an individual's plan.

Many companies and organizations offer employees an option to enroll in a RRSP (registered retirement savings plan) program. The employee sets aside money through a pre-tax payroll reduction. The employer may also contribute money to the account. Sometimes employers match a certain percentage of employee contributions. Employees choose investments for their RRSP based on their willingness to take risks.

Some employers offer defined contribution or defined benefit pension plans. The amount contributed to the plan on your behalf increases as you continue to work for the company. Your benefits during retirement depend on the number of years worked, your salary, and other factors. These types of pension plans are costly for the company and complex to administrate. For these reasons, they are offered by fewer companies than in the past.

Job Advancement and Changes

Once you have successfully completed the interviewing process and accepted the job offer, your task is to perform the job well by applying your skills and knowledge. Listen to what co-workers and supervisors tell you. Observe and learn what is expected and accepted in the office. Make sure you have a clear understanding of your job duties and how you will be evaluated. Most companies provide job descriptions that detail the responsibilities of particular jobs. If you are not given one, ask for it. If a job description does not exist, ask your supervisor to review your duties with you.

Performing Successfully

Listen to what your supervisor and co-workers tell you. Pay attention to what is happening in the organization and learn daily from the people with whom you work and your supervisors within the organization.

It is your responsibility to know what your job is and not wait for your employer to describe every aspect of it. Do your job with commitment and professionalism. As a professional, you are responsible to not only meet but also exceed expectations and consistently produce quality work in a timely manner. You may want to review the section on professionalism in Chapter 1.

Growing from the Performance Appraisal

The frequency of **performance appraisals** varies from company to company and even from position to position. For a new employee, this appraisal may occur during the first three to six months and then annually or semi-annually thereafter. Some organizations provide information on evaluation procedures during the orientation for new employees. If you do not receive information concerning evaluation procedures, ask your supervisor. Your employer may also use the same performance appraisal form for all employees in your classification. If a form is used, ask for a copy. Another method of evaluation may be meeting with your supervisor to discuss your work performance, which is followed by a formal written evaluation document that becomes part of your personnel file.

A fairly common procedure during the performance evaluation is to ask you to evaluate yourself, paying attention to the job description that you were provided when you first took the job and any planning documents of the company that detail the goals that need to be accomplished. For example, if your unit has a planning document, you and your supervisor may have used it as a basis to determine your job responsibilities and establish your goals. Then, during the evaluation period, the planning document is used to determine whether you have accomplished your goals. Review the

Communicating at Work box for tips on how to handle a performance appraisal.

Advancing on the Job

Advancing on the job may mean doing your present job more effectively and efficiently. Learn your job well, work well with others, and learn new ways of doing your job better. Remain current on new equipment, software, and procedures related to your job. Work on improving your verbal, nonverbal, and written communication skills. Remember that you gain valuable work experience from whatever job you are assigned. Concentrate on doing each task of your job to the best of your ability.

Advancing on the job may also mean taking advantage of promotional opportunities that come your way. Remember that promotions usually come to those individuals who have performed well at their position in the company. Be ready for a promotion should the opportunity present itself. Learn as much as you can about other jobs in the company. Know how your present position fits into the organizational structure of the company. Stay informed about job openings in the company. Review Chapter 1, which outlined various certifications and job advancement opportunities available to administrative professionals.

Leaving a Job

You may decide to leave a job voluntarily, or you may be given no choice. Whatever your reasons for leaving (being unhappy with a position and deciding to leave on your own, looking for greater opportunities, or being forced to leave), you must handle your departure in a professional manner.

The Exit Interview

Most companies conduct an **exit interview**—a meeting between the departing employee and a company representative who is usually a staff member in the human resources department, not your immediate supervisor.

The purpose of the meeting is for the company to learn the departing employee's impressions of the company and possibly the reason why the employee is leaving. It is not a time for you to get even, to make derogatory remarks about your supervisor, or to unduly criticize the company. Regardless of your reason for leaving, you will probably need a reference from the company. Be honest and professional, not vindictive. For example, if you are leaving for a job that has greater opportunities for growth, you can say, "I've decided to accept a position with greater responsibility." You do not need to give all the reasons for your move. Keep in mind the adage about not burning your bridges. If you are leaving of your own choice, you may want to return some day.

A Layoff or Termination

At some time in your career, you may be laid off or fired. A layoff may be a downsizing of the company where other jobs are being eliminated in addition to your own. Keep in mind that you did not cause the situation. Even though the situation is difficult, the skills, abilities, and experience you gained from your job will help you to find another one. Remain positive and begin to think about what you want to do next.

What if you have been fired? Your feelings of fear, rejection, and insecurity are normal. However, it is no time to blame or feel sorry for yourself. It is time to take a hard look at your skills. Listen to what your employer tells you about your performance. What can you learn for the future? What steps do you need to take to ensure that you do not find yourself in the same situation again? In what areas do you need to improve? Talk with family, friends, and your closest advisers. Realize that the job may not have been the best one for you. Commit to finding a job that will better match your skills and abilities.

Soft Skills

LIVING YOUR VALUES

In Chapter 11, you spent some time clarifying your values. Think back now to the values you identified as most important to you. Ask yourself this question: How can I live my values in the job I have now or in a future job? For example, assume you identified *dependability* as one of your values. How do you live *dependability* on the job? You report to work on time. If your job requires eight hours of work each day, you work all of those eight hours. You do not spend an hour and a half for lunch every day when the organization allows an hour. You complete all projects in the time frame given you. If you know you will have trouble completing a project on time, you immediately let your supervisor know. You establish a plan for getting the work done when it is needed.

Consider two more values you may have identified—perhaps *cooperation* and *tolerance*. How do you live *cooperation* at work? You cooperate with your supervisor and your co-workers. If an assignment requires overtime, you put in the hours graciously. You do not complain or look for excuses. How do you live *tolerance* at work? You do not judge other people. You listen openly to what they have to say. You do not evaluate people based on their gender, age, or ethnicity.

Think about your own values and how you will live them on the job.

Chapter Summary

The summary will help you remember the important points covered in this chapter.

- Seek employment opportunities through networking, professional organizations, direct contact, the Internet, placement offices, and employment agencies.
- Research and learn as much as you can about the organization before applying for a job.
- The résumé is a concise statement of your background, education, skills, and experience arranged in chronological or functional order and prepared in either hardcopy or electronic form, or both.
- The four goals of a cover letter are to introduce you to the organization, to describe your skills and background, to transmit your résumé, and to request an interview.
- The interview is extremely important. Most interviews are in person but they can also be conducted via teleconference or Web conference. Prepare carefully and present yourself to the best of your ability.
- Read an employment application form completely before filling in each blank. Be truthful; state your background and experience accurately.

- After a job interview, send a follow-up message thanking the employer for the interview and reviewing points of special interest.
- To advance on the job, you must combine your skills and knowledge, listen to what co-workers and supervisors tell you, and observe and learn from performance appraisals and informal feedback.
- Formal performance appraisals are usually done within three to six months after you begin work. After that time, appraisals are done annually or semi-annually.
- If you decide to leave a job (either on your own or because of a layoff or termination), handle the situation professionally. Do not make negative comments about your supervisor, the job, or the company.
- If you are fired, remember that feelings of fear, rejection, and insecurity are normal. Take some time to analyze your skills. Listen to what your employer tells you about your performance. Learn from your mistakes.

Key Terms

chronological résumé p. 250
combination-style résumé p. 252
cover letter p. 247
direct contact or cold call p. 246
electronic résumé p. 253
Employment and Social Development Canada p. 246
employment application p. 253
exit interview p. 261
follow-up letter p. 258

functional résumé p. 250
job interview p. 254
job search agents p. 246
networking p. 245
performance appraisals p. 260
private employment agencies p. 246
résumé p. 248
targeted résumé p. 253
temporary agency p. 246

Discussion Items

These discussion items provide an opportunity to test your understanding of the chapter through written responses and discussion with your classmates and your instructor.

1. What are some common sources of information about job openings?
2. What is the purpose of a résumé? What different styles are used? What should be included in a résumé?

3. What is the goal of a cover letter?
4. List five hints for making a good impression during the interview.
5. What is the purpose of a follow-up message?
6. What is the purpose of performance appraisals? What might you be evaluated on in a performance evaluation?

Responses to Self-Check A

1. Briefly talk about your education and job experiences. Do not spend more than a minute or two on your answer. Be concise; this question should not take up much time in the interview process.

2. Make several positive statements, such as "My previous employer would say I am a hard worker and I complete my tasks in a timely manner. My co-workers would say I am easy to work with and I care about them."

3. Briefly describe the computer courses you took and the software packages in which you are proficient. Talk about how your English and communication courses improved your writing skills and your ability to interact with others.

Critical-Thinking Activity

Arturo Herrera has just finished a two-year business course in college. He has done well in school. He is proficient in Microsoft Word, Excel, and PowerPoint. His math and English skills are good, and he works well with people. He has applied at five different companies for administrative assistant positions, but he has been turned down for all of them. Arturo knows he has the skills necessary to handle the jobs; he does not understand why he has not been hired. Here is what happened on his last job interview.

Arturo was 10 minutes late for the interview. He left home in time to get to the interview, but he had trouble finding a parking space. When he went in, he told the receptionist he was sorry he was late but he could not find a parking space.

4. You might say you have an outgoing personality and you enjoy working with people.
5. You might mention your computer skills, writing skills, human relations skills, critical-thinking skills, and problem-solving skills.

The first question the interviewer asked him was "Could you tell me a little about yourself?" Arturo thought he did a thorough job with the question. He spent 10 minutes telling the interviewer about his life, starting from grade school. When the interviewer asked him if he had worked before, he said he had only had summer jobs. He told the interviewer he had recently been on five interviews and he believed the interviewers were unfair when they did not offer him the job.

What mistakes did Arturo make? How can he correct these mistakes in the future? How should he prepare for the next job interview?

21st Century Skills

 Life and Career Skills
CAREER

 Learning and Innovation Skills
INNOVATION

 Information, Media, and Technology Skills
TECHNOLOGY

 Data
DATA FILE

Building Workplace Skills

Project 13-1 (Learning Outcome 1)

Online Project

TECHNOLOGY   DATA FILE

Using the Internet, identify three sources of job information; at least one site should include jobs available for administrative assistants. Report your findings, including your sources, in a memorandum to your instructor. Include the information available on each website. List details for several administrative assistant job openings, including the city, province or territory, company, and salary (if given). Use the memorandum from Project 13-1 to report your findings to your instructor.

Project 13-2 (Learning Outcome 2)

CAREER

Identify a company or other organization for which you would like to work. Research the organization to find answers to questions such as those listed below. Write a summary of the information you find.

- What are the organization's services or products?
- Is the organization multinational? Does it have branches in other states?
- What has been the profit picture of the organization for the last several years?
- Is the organization financially secure?
- Is the organization growing?
- Does the organization have a good reputation in the community?
- Are there opportunities for advancement?
- To what name and address should a letter of application be sent?

Project 13-3 (Learning Outcome 2)

CAREER

Assume the organization you researched earlier has an opening for an administrative assistant. Write a cover letter and résumé for the position, assuming the position was posted on the organization's website. Use a résumé format that will best present your qualifications and experience.

Project 13-4 (Learning Outcome 3)

CAREER

Figure 13-7 outlines typical interview questions. Write an answer to five questions for each category of possible questions. Assume that you are interviewing for an administrative position at the organization you researched earlier.

Project 13-5 (Learning Outcome 4)

Collaborative Project

CAREER

As a team of three or four, interview an employed administrative professional. The interview may take place by email rather than in person. Ask the individual these questions:

- To what do you attribute your success in this position?
- What advancement opportunities are available in your company?
- What skills do you believe are necessary to earn a promotion?
- Report your findings to the class.

Project 13-6 (Learning Outcome 5)

TECHNOLOGY

Take some time to list your values. From this list, identify your major values and explain how you will commit to living those values in the workplace. Save the file.

Make the Grade with MindTap

Stay organized and efficient with **MindTap**—a single destination with all the course material and study aids you need to succeed. Built-in apps leverage social media and the latest learning technology. For example:

- ReadSpeaker will read the text to you.
- Flashcards are pre-populated to provide you with a jump-start for review—or you can create your own.
- You can highlight text and make notes in your MindTap Reader. Your notes will flow into Evernote, the electronic notebook app that you can access anywhere when it's time to study for the exam.
- Self-quizzing allows you to access your understanding.

Visit nelson.com/student to start using **MindTap**. Enter the Online Access Code from the card included with your text. If a code card is not provided, you can purchase instant access at NELSONbrain.com.

CHAPTER 14

Becoming a Virtual Assistant

LEARNING OUTCOMES

After studying this chapter, you should be able to:

1. Define telework, teleworkers, and virtual assistants.
2. Identify the advantages and disadvantages of working remotely.
3. Describe the individual qualities and skills necessary for success as a virtual worker.
4. Determine and practise the qualities and behaviours necessary in self-management.
5. Describe an effective workspace for a virtual assistant or teleworker.

Do I Qualify?

Medical Transcriptionist

A leading health care facility is seeking a transcriptionist to transcribe a variety of medical documentation. All work will be completed remotely and hours will vary depending on the needs of the health care facility. The successful applicant will have the following qualifications:

- diploma in office administration
- excellent typing skills with a minimum of 50 wpm
- knowledge of medical terminology, anatomy, physiology, and pharmacology
- proficiency with computers and ability to download various types of files and install software programs

---

Telework and the Virtual Assistant

A growing number of today's organizations and their workforce are choosing to make arrangements that encourage or permit work in remote locations outside of the traditional office.

Teleworkers, those individuals employed full- or part-time by an organization, use telecommunications technology to work from home or some other mobile work environment for part or all of the workweek. Several websites where you can learn more about telework can be found on the MindTap site for this textbook.

Telecommunications technologies have also created a niche for entrepreneurial freelance administrative assistants, known as **virtual assistants**. These self-employed administrative assistants work from a home office to provide off-site administrative or personal assistance to clients. This arrangement is popular with individuals and small start-up companies that may not require the services of a full-time administrative assistant.

Advantages and Disadvantages to Telework

Telework has both many advantages and many disadvantages for the employee and the organization. Before an organization decides to support telework, or before an individual decides to become a part of the rapidly growing teleworker group, a careful analysis should be made of the advantages

iStock/Thinkstock

An increasing number of Canadians are working remotely.

and disadvantages. The website for the Canadian Centre for Occupational Health and Safety (CCOHS) lists some of these (see Figure 14-1).

If you know someone who is a teleworker, or if you have done telework, you may know some advantages and disadvantages in addition to those identified by CCOHS. Working from home can provide access to family. It can also provide flexibility for couples to work for employers situated many kilometres apart or even in different cities. The opportunity to remain with an employer despite moving from one part of the country to another can be a valid reason for choosing telework.

As you can see from Figure 14-1, just as working in the traditional office has its downsides, so does the telework environment. Teleworkers can lose fringe benefits, such as paid vacations and insurance coverage, and may incur additional costs in purchasing supplies and equipment not supplied by the employer. Each individual considering telework must determine his or her goals, career directions, priorities, and needs—each person's set of values will determine whether they will find telework attractive.

FIGURE 14-1

The Advantages and Disadvantages of Telework to the Individual and the Organization

	Advantages	Disadvantages
Individual	Fewer distractions from co-workers More flexibility with organization of daily tasks (better personal time management) Savings in time, commuting, and other costs Higher job satisfaction	Isolation Lack of separation between home and work More distractions from family Potential for excessive working hours Less awareness of changes in company Fear of being under-managed or "out of sight, out of mind"
Company	Improved employee retention Often higher productivity Fewer lost hours because of traffic problems Reduced absenteeism Savings in energy, office space requirements, maintenance, and housekeeping Increased number of potential candidates for a job	Contacting the employee Maintaining adequate communication between other employees or with customers Possible delay in customer service

Canadian Centre on Occupational Health and Safety. http://www.ccohs.ca/oshanswers/hsprograms/telework.html Accessed June 2018.

In making a decision to work remotely, you should also consider your personality and work style. The Myers-Briggs Type Indicator, developed by Isabel Myers and Katharine Briggs and based on the work of noted psychologist Carl Jung, purports to classify individuals as **extroverts**—those who prefer to be energized by the outside world, or **introverts**—those who prefer to focus attention on the inner world.

If you are classified as an extrovert, you are more likely to be successful in telework that requires a high degree of communication with outside individuals—such as a consultant working from home but regularly visiting the customer's site. If you are classified as an introvert, you probably require little communication with others and may enjoy telework that involves the production of documents, such as setting up Web pages, writing reports, or transcribing medical or legal reports. Complete the personality tests located on the MindTap site to determine your personality type.

The disadvantages identified by CCOHS are particularly true for organizations just initiating telework; at the outset, they need to develop policies for managing and supporting teleworkers and procedures to minimize these disadvantages. It is important to identify the right people for telework and then ensure the proper support is provided, assuring that teleworkers remain and feel part of the total workforce team. Organizations can use video, telephone, and computer conferencing to link individuals from their remote locations to others within the organization. Biweekly or monthly staff meetings held onsite at the organization's office may help to provide a sense of belonging. Workplace collaboration tools can enable **virtual teams** to work together through telecommunications technology to accomplish a task.

To adequately support teleworkers, an organization must continually study and improve its support structures. Before commencing work on any task, both the manager and the teleworker must be clear about expectations and timelines. Since teleworkers receive less informal feedback than other employees, they must receive adequate information during their formal performance evaluation sessions. There are no easy answers, but many organizations are making the arrangement work effectively.

Societal Advantages

In addition to making a significant positive environmental contribution, with fewer cars on the road, thereby creating less pollution, telework provides for increased community stability. Teleworkers, who are generally more satisfied with their jobs and their personal or family lives, result in lower turnover for the company and thus greater community stability, as employees tend to stay with a company rather than move to a new area. Telework practices also provide more opportunities for employees who are also caregivers, since telework allows them to maintain a successful business operation while juggling family and home responsibilities.

Telework also encourages entrepreneurial activity. Technology and the Internet provide business opportunities for the virtual assistant since individuals can set up and maintain home offices at a relatively low cost.

Writing AT WORK

As an independent virtual assistant, you may be required to provide contracts and agreements to the organizations you work for in order to be paid for your services. It is important to ensure all contracts or agreements are clearly written and fully outline the services you will provide and the agreed payment structure. As contracts and agreements are legally binding, it may be beneficial to retain the services of a lawyer to ensure they have been properly written.

The Virtual Assistant

Virtual assistants have their own offices, often in their homes, equipped with the necessary technology for teleconferencing. Many who start their own virtual assistant service may have several years of office experience as an administrative assistant, sometimes with special expertise such as legal or medical administrative office experience. However, as this field of virtual assistants grows, it is no longer limited to former administrative assistants.

Many colleges and universities offer online training programs for the virtual assistant. Several professional organizations exist to support and promote virtual assistants and

teleworkers, and to advocate for professional certification. To learn more about these skills and professional standards, links to the websites of the following organizations are provided on the MindTap site for this textbook.

- CAVA—Canadian Association of Virtual Assistants
- TelCoa—The Telework Coalition
- IVAA—International Virtual Assistants Association
- Ontario College of Law

As a self-employed virtual assistant, you will enjoy the freedom and flexibility of choosing the type of work you do, the amount of time you spend at work, and the clients you serve. You are also responsible for determining the amount of remuneration (Figure 14-2).

FIGURE 14-2
Invoicing Options

Hourly	The virtual assistant and client will generally discuss the type and amount of work to be done before setting a mutually agreeable hourly rate.
Flat Rate	Virtual assistants who have an established client base may negotiate a fee that is based on a certain number of hours, days, or even weeks.
Per Project	In this method, it does not matter how long it takes to complete the project, the fee remains the same. When setting this type of fee, it is important that the virtual assistant and client have mutual trust in identifying the scope of the work.
On-Call	Rather than working specific days of the week or weeks of the month, the virtual assistant accepts work on an as-needed basis for a client with whom they have a long-standing relationship.

Personal Traits and Skills

To be an effective virtual assistant or teleworker, you must be productive. To accomplish the job tasks to the satisfaction of your clients or customers, you need to be certain you understand their expectations—when the job is to be completed and the timeline for completion. Repeat your understanding of the expectations. Then, if you have misunderstood something, the client or customer has an opportunity to correct you. To be productive, you need to be disciplined, a self-starter, organized, technologically proficient, and possess excellent oral and written communication skills.

Being Disciplined

Certainly a large part of your discipline is driven by external sources, such as your pay cheque or remuneration. As an independent worker, you understand the relationship between discipline and productivity. Those who are not disciplined enough to deliver the product or service the customer or client needs will soon find themselves with no customers or clients.

For the home-based worker, distractions are numerous—household chores, family members, and errands, to name a few. Do not let distractions interfere with your focus. Being disciplined means formulating a plan for dealing with distractions. Here are some suggestions:

- Establish specific times during the day to initiate communications with clients or customers.
- Tell both family and friends in a nice way that you cannot be interrupted—you have deadlines to meet; ask whether you or they can call back at a better time. Be pleasant but firm; they will soon understand the situation.
- If you have young children, you may need to hire some help during the day, or when your children are of school age, you will need to help them to understand when you can and cannot be disturbed.
- Be disciplined about when to quit work. High achievers may be tempted to work 14 hours a day. You might be able to keep up that schedule for a few days, but burnout and sleep deprivation will eventually occur.

A Self-Starter

Having the initiative to begin a project and follow it through to completion is the trademark of a self-starter. Working as a virtual assistant or teleworker means you must rely on your own sense of pride and satisfaction in the accomplishment of a job well done. No one but you are responsible for setting the goals and timelines. A self-starter is the opposite of a procrastinator. Self-starters do not wait to the last minute to begin a project or task but organize themselves early in the process, creating timelines and setting deadlines. It is a trait you must possess if you choose to join the virtual workforce.

Being Independent

In the traditional office setting, you generally have someone you can go to for help in solving problems. You are part of a team that can help you, and you soon learn each team member's strengths and weaknesses. You know which individual to go to for help. Not so in most remote working situations. You have to be independent and a creative problem solver. You need to figure out how a report should be written, the format that is most effective, and the appropriate graphs and charts to include. The old proverb "necessity is the mother of invention" is particularly true for the virtual assistant or teleworker. Whatever occurs, you must be creative enough to find a solution.

Being Well Organized

When working at home, it is important to establish a routine; each day, set objectives for yourself. Before you quit work each afternoon, record the objectives you need to accomplish the next day on your to-do list or computer notes program. It also helps to put timelines by each objective. Some projects will take more or less time than you had envisioned, but estimates help keep you focused the next day. You may wish to review the time management techniques covered in Chapter 2.

Technological Proficiency

Technology skills are essential for all administrative professionals. Using telecommunications to work from remote locations means that a teleworker performs his or her job in isolation, with no help readily available when problems with technology occur. Manufacturers of telecommunications equipment offer online services. Using these services demands more understanding of telecommunications on the part of the teleworker than is demanded of the worker in the traditional office. As a virtual assistant or teleworker, you need to be able to understand the problem well enough to describe it accurately and to follow instructions from the telephone or from an online or instant messaging assistant. You will need to be able to apply what you have read in manuals to prevent problems from occurring—in other words, you need to be your own troubleshooter.

As telecommunications equipment becomes more sophisticated, you, as a teleworker, must continue to upgrade your knowledge and skills. You can do so by reading computer periodicals, checking upgrades on equipment through the Internet, and talking with other teleworkers about what they are using.

Communicating AT WORK

As a virtual assistant, you may never see your clients or customers face to face. The importance of being a good communicator and continuing to develop your communication skills is crucial. Communicating by telephone means your verbal skills are just as important as the written ones you will use in email and when preparing reports and other documents for your clients. You may wish to review the chapters in Part 2 that focus on verbal and written communication skills.

Virtual Workplace Challenges

Being a successful teleworker demands that you conquer isolation, noise, and family issues. You also need to develop an appropriate balance between home and work responsibilities.

Isolation

To a great degree, the environment of a virtual assistant or teleworker is one of isolation. If you have been accustomed to working in a traditional office environment, you will understand the differences immediately. You are not able to get a cup of coffee and exchange small talk with a co-worker, nor do you have someone with whom you can discuss a work problem. You miss little things, such as taking a walk with a co-worker at lunchtime. The degree to which isolation bothers you depends to some extent on your personality traits, such as whether you are an introvert or an extrovert. If you are more extroverted, you can still enjoy being a successful virtual assistant or teleworker—you just need to be more proactive at connecting with others than someone who is introverted. You can follow these suggestions:

- Join a health club; exercise with people; sign up for an aerobics class or arrange to jog or walk with a neighbour.
- Go to a deli or coffeehouse where you can chat with people or occasionally have lunch with someone in a similar business.
- Take advantage of any professional development activities or events that are held in your area or even online webinars.

As a part-time teleworker, you will have other opportunities to connect with colleagues. You can follow these suggestions:

- Arrange for regular contact with your supervisor or other colleagues by phone, Skype, email, or instant messaging.
- Be available for phone or Skype calls. Email is not always the best medium when collaborating on projects.
- Participate in any company-sponsored professional development activities and social events.
- When visiting the office, be sure to make a personal connection with the colleagues with whom you collaborate.

Family Issues

If you have decided to become a virtual assistant or teleworker and you have a family, or live with other family members, you must talk with your family members about this arrangement. Many people have misconceptions about what it means to work from home. You need to talk with your family and explain that working from home does not mean you have time to take on additional responsibilities around the house, but that you are serious about your work and cannot be a full-time parent while maintaining a full-time work schedule. Everyone needs to understand their role and responsibilities in the new arrangement.

Ensure both family and friends know your working hours just as if you were going to the traditional office each day. You can help your family understand when you are working and should not be disturbed by posting your work schedule on a bulletin board in a place the family uses frequently, putting out a "do not disturb" sign, or closing your office door.

Work–Life Balance

Just as you cannot let family and friends interrupt your work to the point that you get nothing done, you also cannot ignore family and friends to the point that all you do is work. You must find a balance between family and work. What is that balance? You must answer that question for yourself. What is important is that you understand what a healthy balance is and maintain it. You may have heard the old saying "All work and no play makes Jack [or Jill] a dull person." The statement has great validity. If you allow work to become all-consuming, you can develop stress levels that make you physically and emotionally sick. If you never read a book, listen to a news program, read a magazine, or learn something new outside of your job, you may find that you have fewer good ideas and less creativity in your work projects.

People AT WORK

Depending on the type of work you choose to do as a virtual worker, you may come in contact with more than the clients and customers who have contracted your services. You may have a client who is planning an event—which may mean that the people in your work environment could include hotel and catering staff, representatives of multimedia rental agencies, and potential speakers. All of the skills you have acquired in this course of studies that qualify you to be an administrative professional will play a role. Working effectively with a wide variety of people in a variety of different and challenging situations can be very rewarding.

Creating an Effective Home Workspace

Deciding to become a virtual assistant or teleworker means that you will need to create a space in your home where you can work—a place you can call your office. Before considering the type and size of workspace you need, ask yourself these questions: What type of work will I be doing? How much space do I need to accomplish this work? What furniture and equipment do I need? What should I consider when selecting furniture and equipment so that I avoid ergonomic health-related problems? Will I be working on highly technical material that requires a distraction-free workspace? Will I be meeting clients or customers in my workspace? What environmental factors are important to me? For example, do I need to be close to a window?

Once you ask and answer these questions, you are ready to consider the location and size of your workspace.

Workspace Size and Location

If you need a distraction-free workspace, locate your office away from the family living area of your home—perhaps in a spare bedroom or a basement room. If clients, customers, and/or co-workers will be meeting with you occasionally, try to locate the space close to an outside entrance. If you have concerns about external noise, try to locate your workspace as far away as possible from the noise. How large the space needs to be depends on whether you are working from home full- or part-time. If you are a teleworker working at home only one or two days per week, you can be less concerned about workspace. Your space may be a small area in a corner of a room that can be set up with a minimum amount of equipment.

If you are working as a virtual assistant, you must consider the type and size of desk you need and the space required for all the necessary equipment and supplies. Your location needs to have space for file cabinets and bookshelves, and sufficient electrical outlets and telecommunications connections in proximity to your equipment—stringing extension and other cords across a room can be dangerous. Chapters 2 and 3 include several suggestions for setting up a workspace that is both safe and ergonomically sound. Some key points are repeated in Figure 14-3.

You may want to refer to these chapters and suggestions again. As a virtual assistant, you will have more control over creating your workspace than when working as an administrative professional in the traditional office.

FIGURE 14-3
Workstation Checklist

- Eliminate glare from your computer and your workstation.
- Be certain you have adequate light for reading without squinting.
- Adjust your chair height so that your feet are flat on the floor.
- Be certain your chair is sturdy—a base with five legs is more stable than four legs.
- Place your computer keyboard five centimetres below your desk surface.
- Eliminate loud noises from your workstation environment.
- If the colour of your workstation is depressive, change it.

Hardware and Software

Whether you are working from home or from some other remote/mobile location, you will need a computer. A desktop or laptop computer is a likely choice if working from a home office; a notebook, laptop, or tablet may be more suitable when working in a mobile environment. If you have ergonomic concerns about working exclusively with any of these mobile devices, remember that peripheral equipment such as a standard keyboard and mouse can be connected wirelessly to a notebook, laptop, or tablet. Your other equipment purchases should include a printer, copier, and scanner, or a multi-function machine that also includes a telephone. Identify your needs and then follow these suggestions to help you in your selection:

- Read or subscribe to digital versions of computer periodicals such as *Computer Shopper*, *PCWorld*, *Wired*, and *Maximum PC*.

- Conduct online research; equipment and software manufacturers advertise their products on the Web. Enter the search string "home office computing" to locate readings and other online resources.
- Shop your local computer stores and try the equipment.
- Talk with people who use the technology. For example, discuss the best buys with other teleworkers, computer technicians, or friends who are computer-literate.

The type of work you will be doing as a virtual assistant or teleworker will define the type of software you will need. Certainly you will need appropriate software to enable you to connect with clients, customers, or colleagues. Email, instant messaging, and teleconferencing software such as Skype, Google Hangouts, or FaceTime may all be necessities. Perch is another option which is a downloadable app that connects office spaces and facilitates natural unscheduled face-to-face communication among team members.

Some features such as Skype are built in to suite programs such as Microsoft Office, which can also include programs for word processing, spreadsheets, databases, presentations, and personal management. Virus protection, firewalls, spyware protection, and system maintenance software will also be necessary to protect your client's or employer's electronic data.

Technology AT WORK

In addition to determining and obtaining the software you need to complete projects for your clients, you may need to develop skills working with accounting software. Quicken, a popular personal and small business finance management software, may suit your needs. You can use it to customize estimates, track your income and expenses, create invoices, and process payments. It tracks federal and provincial or territorial taxes and identifies eligible tax deductions. A link to the Quicken website can be found on the MindTap site for this textbook. Take a look at the demos and videos to see what it can do for you and how easily you can develop the skill to manage your finances.

Workplace Safety

Be conscious of the need for security. Since you are often working home alone using computer technology and other expensive hardware, you want to do what you can to maintain a theft-proof environment. Here are several suggestions for keeping your workplace safe:

- Install simple locks on windows so they cannot be forced open from the outside.
- Install a security system that contacts the police if a break-in occurs.

- Install a deadbolt on the office door. Draw the shades when you are working at night.
- Be certain your office furniture and equipment is insured for the proper amount.

Health, Life Insurance, and Retirement Benefits

If you are a virtual assistant, you need to arrange for health and life insurance coverage and set up a program for retirement. Talk with several health and life insurance companies, and research the benefits available. If you have a friend who has a trusted insurance agent, you might start with that person. You must be concerned about providing adequately for you and your family during your retirement years. Options include **RRSPs** (registered retirement savings plans) and investments in **mutual funds** (funds that include a combination of stocks and bonds purchased through a mutual fund company) or individual **stocks** (ownership in a company) and **bonds** (a debt owed by an organization). Consult with a certified financial planner about your long-term plans and needs.

If you are a teleworker, ensure that you are covered by the organization's wellness plans. Check workers' compensation coverage in your province or territory. If you fall and injure yourself during established working hours while working in your home, will you be covered for the injury just the same as you would be as an employee in the traditional office?

Survival Strategies

Once you have created your office workspace and begin to work as a teleworker, you will find that creativity, self-management, productivity, and continual learning are essential skills for you to possess.

Certainly, these skills are many of the same skills demanded in the traditional workplace, but in that environment, you have the luxury of receiving input from your co-workers about your strengths and weaknesses and taking advantage of organization-sponsored staff development events. As a virtual assistant or teleworker, these opportunities are not as easily available to you; you must be sure to take care of yourself. You cannot keep up a pace of constant, effective work production if you do not also give yourself the opportunity for renewal. Review Chapter 2, which outlined strategies not only to minimize stress but to improve your overall well-being.

Soft Skills

SELF-MANAGEMENT

Self-management is the soft skill for this chapter. Self-management is the regulation of your feelings, behaviours, and actions as they relate to your work; it involves continually checking in with yourself to identify current priorities, goals, and challenges to achieving them. People with strong self-management skills are able to monitor and evaluate themselves so they can continue to work effectively. It means that you

- have self-knowledge—you know your personal and professional strengths and weaknesses
- manage your time effectively
- handle stress appropriately
- balance your work and your personal life
- understand your values
- can articulate your goals

Chapter Summary

The summary will help you remember the important points covered in this chapter.

- Advantages of telework for the individual include fewer distractions from co-workers; more flexibility with the organization of daily tasks; savings in time, commuting, and other costs; and higher job satisfaction.
- Disadvantages of telework for the individual are isolation, lack of separation between home and work, more distractions from family, potential for excessive working hours, less awareness of changes in the company, and a fear of being forgotten by colleagues and supervisors.
- Advantages of telework for the organization include improved employee retention; higher productivity; fewer hours lost to traffic problems; savings in costs of office space, maintenance, and housekeeping; an increased pool of candidates for positions; and reduced absenteeism.
- Disadvantages of telework for the organization include contacting the employee, maintaining adequate communication between other employees or with customers, and possible delays in customer service.
- To be successful in telework, the individual must be productive, disciplined, a self-starter, independent, well organized, and technologically proficient, and possess excellent oral and written communication skills.
- The teleworker must consider the home workspace and equipment, and workplace safety and health, life insurance, and retirement benefits.

Key Terms

bonds p. 272
extroverts p. 267
introverts p. 267
mutual funds p. 272

RRSPs p. 272
stocks p. 272
virtual teams p. 267
virtual assistants p. 266

Discussion Items

These discussion items provide an opportunity to test your understanding of the chapter through written responses and discussion with your classmates and your instructor.

1. Define telework. List three advantages and three disadvantages of telework for the individual. List three advantages of telework for the organization.
2. List and explain four qualities and skills necessary for success in telework.
3. Explain what is meant by self-management.
4. List the considerations when setting up a home office.
5. List and explain five survival strategies for the teleworker.

Critical-Thinking Activity

Ryan Stapleton has been working for A&I Telecommunications as an administrative professional for five years. His work involves researching and preparing reports, managing a website, providing computer and software training, and working on TQM teams. Recently, he was offered the opportunity to work two days per week from home, with the rationale that researching and preparing reports plus managing a website require a work environment free of interruptions. The company believes he can be more productive by working on these projects from a home office. A&I will provide him with the computer equipment he needs.

Ryan is married and has two children—one 10 years old and one 2 years old. Ryan's wife works full-time away from the home. Ryan has now finished his first two weeks of work as a teleworker. Although Ryan thought his wife understood that he has a full-time job the two days he is home, she began making additional demands of him. She suggested that he keep the 2-year-old on the two days he is home. She also expects him to cook on those two nights. He tried keeping the two-year-old at home, but he cannot get any of his work done. However, since his wife is insisting on the arrangement, he is going to give it more time.

Ryan considers himself an extrovert. Although he enjoys the freedom of working on his own the two days each week, he misses the hubbub of the workplace. He also is receiving a lot of email and telephone calls from his supervisor and co-workers about work issues. The report he prepared during his first two weeks took more of his time than usual. He had to work from 8 a.m. until 10 p.m. every day to finish the report; his childcare duties and meal preparation also interfered with his work time. He believes his productivity is decreasing rather than increasing. Ryan wants to continue telework but he is not sure the hassles he is facing are worth it.

What advice would you give Ryan? Using critical thinking, suggest how the issues Ryan is facing should be handled.

21st Century Skills

Life and Career Skills	Learning and Innovation Skills	Information, Media, and Technology Skills	Data

Building Workplace Skills

Project 14-1 (Learning Outcomes 1, 2, and 3)

Online Project

Research two online training programs offered for virtual assistants in Canada on either the federal or provincial or territorial level. Compare and contrast the findings to determine the pros and cons of each program and outline the employment opportunities that would be available to you upon completion of the program.

Summarize the information and present your findings to your instructor. Ensure you cite all of your references.

Project 14-2 (Learning Outcome 5)

Research two articles using periodicals such as *Computer Shopper, Wired,* and *PCWorld*; the website of the Canadian Centre for Occupational Health and Safety (www.ccohs.ca); or the ergonomics section of Chapter 2 to determine how to properly configure a workspace and how furniture and equipment should be used. Submit a short, keyed summary of the articles to your instructor, listing the resources you used, and place a copy in your e-portfolio.

Project 14-3 (Learning Outcomes 2 and 3)

Collaborative Project

With two or three of your classmates, search the Internet for information on the advantages and disadvantages and qualities and skills necessary for success as a virtual assistant or teleworker. If you know someone who is a virtual worker, talk to this person; however, an interview is not a requirement because you may not have access to such a person. If you are able to talk to a virtual worker in your area or on the Internet ask some of following questions:

- Why have you chosen to be a virtual assistant or teleworker?
- What education or experience prepared you for this job?
- What characteristics and skills do you feel are most important for a teleworker?
- Where is your workspace located? If it is at home, what challenges have you had to overcome?
- In what ways can virtual assistants be effectively utilized?
- What tips would you give a potential virtual assistant?

Prepare a presentation of your findings to share with the class. Place a copy in your e-portfolio.

Make the Grade with MindTap

Stay organized and efficient with **MindTap**—a single destination with all the course material and study aids you need to succeed. Built-in apps leverage social media and the latest learning technology. For example:
- ReadSpeaker will read the text to you.
- Flashcards are pre-populated to provide you with a jump-start for review—or you can create your own.
- You can highlight text and make notes in your MindTap Reader. Your notes will flow into Evernote, the electronic notebook app that you can access anywhere when it's time to study for the exam.
- Self-quizzing allows you to access your understanding.

Visit nelson.com/student to start using **MindTap**. Enter the Online Access Code from the card included with your text. If a code card is not provided, you can purchase instant access at NELSONbrain.com.

CHAPTER 15

Leading with Confidence

LEARNING OUTCOMES

After studying this chapter, you should be able to:

1. Describe the characteristics of effective leaders.
2. Describe common leadership styles.
3. Describe and develop skills and strategies for successfully leading.

Leading and Managing

Whatever form leadership takes, most of us find ourselves in leadership roles or have the opportunity to take on leadership roles at numerous times in our lives. If you assume positions of greater responsibility in the workplace, you may have one or more people reporting to you. While you may not choose to become a manager or a supervisor, you may still have opportunities to assume leadership roles by leading teams within the workplace, or becoming involved as an officer in a professional organization. Leading with confidence is an important ability to develop as you grow in your career. It will serve you well throughout life, regardless of the profession you choose.

Defining Leadership and Management

Leadership within an organization can be defined as the act of inspiring and motivating people to achieve organizational goals. The verb *to lead* is defined in *Merriam-Webster* as "to guide on a way especially by going in advance," "to direct on a course or in a direction," and "to direct the operations, activity, or performance of." The capacity to lead well is more than filling a position or an office—it is a philosophy, an attitude, and a practice in the workplace. An effective leader keeps the long run in mind, stimulating employees to do more than they thought they could.

Management in a business setting is the act of organizing and directing people to accomplish organizational goals. Chapter 1 identified the responsibilities of management as a subset of leadership. Often overlapping, these responsibilities are complementary but different in concept, purpose, and process. This chapter will help you understand some of the practical concepts of leadership and management.

Leadership and management are complementary but different in concept, purpose, and process. A manager organizes and coordinates, while a leader motivates and inspires.[1] An effective leader stimulates employees to do more than they thought they could. A manager provides purpose as he or she directs employees to a goal. Leaders keep the long run in mind, while managers practically consider the short term. While this chapter focuses on leadership, remember that the most effective managers are also effective leaders, and conversely, effective leaders are also effective managers.

Leadership Traits and Qualities

You probably have encountered people whom you consider to be good leaders. What makes you put someone into that category? Is it a person's effectiveness at getting things done? Is it the respect they show others, the ability to guide people, or the level of trust and rapport that person establishes with others? In addition to integrity and emotional maturity the following are several other important qualities of an effective leader.

People AT WORK

Project Specialist

A project specialist works for a project manager, assisting with multiple tasks. Duties include managing financial accounts, supervising bookkeepers and temporary workers, organizing reports, overseeing the payment of contract work, knowing and understanding regulations associated with the industry (such as tariffs for transportation), writing and submitting reports to government agencies, creating budgets, and providing general assistance with project-related tasks.

Proprietary software or spreadsheet and database software such as Microsoft Excel and Microsoft Access can be used to track expenditures and send reports. As an administrative professional, you may work with a project specialist to complete reports and do data entry related to ongoing projects.

Understands Self

Good leaders know themselves. They capitalize on their strengths, concentrate on developing those strengths, and try to make their weaknesses immaterial. We are all shaped by our background and experiences, learning through life how we should behave and what we should value. Individuals change as a result of new experiences and new knowledge. Making a mistake is not unique or even unforgivable. What is unforgivable is continuing to make the same mistake and refusing to learn from our mistake and accept responsibility for it. Acquiring

self-knowledge is a lifetime process. If we are to understand ourselves, we must continue to explore our own potential, to reflect on our experiences, and to seek new challenges.

Builds a Shared Vision

Visionary leaders work with and involve employees at all levels of the organization to create a shared vision of the organization. They do this by asking questions like the following:

- What values does the organization have? What values should it have?
- What contributions should the organization make to the community?
- What reputation does the organization have? What reputation should it have?
- Who are the clients and customers of the organization?
- How do people work together within the organization?
- Do the values of the individuals within the organization match the values of the organization?
- What contributions do individuals within the organization make to the community?

Effective leaders help employees understand the organization's vision and how their individual goals and objectives support that vision. Effective leaders publish the organization's vision statement so employees are aware of it. Many organizations publish their value or vision statement on their website to inform the general public about what is important to the organization.

Lives by a Set of Values

Ethical behaviour is the accepted practice in business. Leaders must work within the organization to identify and define the principles of ethical behaviour, and then ensure that they are carried out in the daily activities of the organization. Even though it can be difficult to determine what is and is not ethical in specific instances, few of us would disagree that our leaders must stand firmly on moral principles. When difficult decisions need to be made, leaders must follow a thoughtful decision-making process like the one outlined in Chapter 2. Effective leaders understand that establishing and living a set of values must begin with the top leaders and that living the organizational values must permeate every level of the organization.

Commits to Service

Effective leaders consider service to others as primary. More than just being concerned with their own career, effective leaders understand how they can serve the organization and its employees, as well as the external community. The values of effective leaders may include a commitment to helping people grow, a commitment to diversity, and a commitment to helping the world become a better place. Figure 15-1 provides Home Depot's statement about its commitment to supporting the work of its employee volunteers in the community.

FIGURE 15-1

About Home Depot of Canada Inc.

The Home Depot Canada Foundation—Building strong communities together. The Home Depot Canada Foundation was established to expand Home Depot of Canada Inc.'s commitment to the communities it serves. We bring together monetary grants and volunteerism to support affordable housing and community improvement projects that benefit Canadians in need.

Courtesy of Home Depot of Canada Inc.

Motivates Others

People are motivated to do work, and to do it well, by many different factors. Motivation can be *extrinsic* (from outside a person) or *intrinsic* (from within). For employees, an extrinsic motivation might be a salary increase or the opportunity for advancement. Examples of intrinsic motivators include the desire for personal recognition and the feeling of satisfaction from a job well done.

Good leaders find out what motivates (Figure 15-2) each employee and use that knowledge, as far as possible, to encourage employees to have a positive attitude about their jobs and to do their best work. For example, if you know that an employee likes getting frequent feedback on his performance so that he can improve, you might give him feedback more often than you would another employee. If an employee is interested in finding ways to improve her skills and abilities, you might arrange for her to attend an occasional workshop or class.

The effective leader has a commitment to the community.

FIGURE 15-2

What Motivates People at Work?

- Recognition of hard work
- Respect from leaders and co-workers
- Clear expectations from leaders
- Being a part of the company vision
- Opportunity for growth or advancement
- Appropriate compensation
- Opportunity to take responsibility

© Cengage Learning

Rewards Risk-Taking

Change is constant and the successful organization must be willing to seek new answers to problems, try new approaches, and be flexible. Successful leaders take risks themselves and encourage risk-taking in others. The following are some of the keys to successful risk-taking:

- **Trust your own abilities.** No matter what your age, do not put limits on your ability to learn and improve.
- **Be open-minded.** When analyzing situations that need solving, discard old assumptions; they can prevent us from seeing new possibilities.
- **Develop your intuitive powers.** Subconsciously, we take note of many things our conscious mind does not realize. These subconscious thoughts can be brought to the surface of our consciousness when we listen carefully to ourselves (our intuition).
- **Overcome the fear of making mistakes.** When trying something new, the possibility always exists that mistakes will occur. What is more important to consider, however, is the likelihood of success. For example, Sam Walton, in building Walmart, went through many failures and difficult times. Yet his vision was so clear and he had such a deep understanding of what he believed would be successful that he endured risks and temporary failures to achieve his dream.
- **Develop a support team.** Supportive colleagues can help determine what to do next by looking at a situation objectively. You can reciprocate and return that objectivity and support by helping them analyze their situations.

In an environment that encourages risk-taking, employees know they will not be punished but rather supported in their risk-taking ventures and rewarded for their successes.

Models Appropriate Conduct

An effective leader is someone who sets an example. Do you want your employees to have a good work ethic, not complain, and work toward the common goal of the team? Do you have a good worth ethic? Do you not complain? Do you work toward the common goal of the team? The power of modeling the conduct you expect from others is often underestimated. Effective leaders approach the task of directing other people by holding themselves accountable and avoiding double standards.

Young adults in leadership positions sometimes experience challenges due to their age and lack of experience, particularly when the group they are leading includes people who are older than they. In such a situation, leading by example can be especially helpful. What may be lacking in age can be compensated for in character. The successful leader practises the art of meeting individuals where they are and moving them forward, ultimately achieving the desired outcome.

Knows How to Follow

The effective leader knows the importance of stepping back and being a follower when the situation demands it. This person understands that leaders are sometimes followers, and followers are sometimes leaders. They understand the importance of not only following but also having the trust in others to know that, if they are given the appropriate opportunities and training, they too can be leaders.

Leadership Styles

Leaders have different leadership styles, or patterns of behaviour. You may be familiar with some of these styles from supervisors you have had at work, coaches on sports teams, and leaders you have had in other capacities in your life. The leadership style affects the performance of the people who are being led or supervised. Some people work better or more comfortably with one leadership style than with another.

Although effective leaders often prefer a particular leadership style, they use a variety of styles for different situations. For example, at times, a leader must make a decision with little or no input from those on his or her team, and at other times, a leader can trust the team to make a decision. The changing of leadership styles for different situations is called *situational leadership*.

Many leadership styles have been identified. The three most common styles are autocratic leadership, democratic leadership, and laissez-faire leadership.

Autocratic Leadership

The **autocratic leadership** style is one of control, where the leader directs and closely supervises the work that is done; employees have no input into the decisions that are made. While the leadership style may be appropriate for some situations when close control is very important, its use is declining. Most organizations and leaders tend to favour other styles that do not involve such close control and give employees more latitude to make decisions.

Democratic Leadership

The **democratic leadership** style is one in which employees share in authority, decisions, and plans. Popular in the workplace, it is a leadership style that both managers and employees often favour. This more flexible leadership style is commonly used in teams. It helps to improve the morale of the organization, and employees enjoy being able to work with less supervision. Attitudes are more positive and having a voice in plans and decisions makes employees feel more valued.

Laissez-Faire Leadership

Laissez-faire, according to *Merriam-Webster*, is French for "let people do as they choose." When a leader uses the **laissez-faire leadership** style, employees generally lead themselves. The leader is not involved in directing or controlling tasks. They may only monitor employees' progress in completing tasks and respond to requests for assistance. This leadership style is appropriate when employees are skilled and responsible, and their tasks are clearly defined.

Writing AT WORK

As you develop leadership skills, your vocabulary will also need to develop. This is part of growing professionally and of being perceived as a professional. Skills in expression are necessary for making your point and for people to see you as competent.

Develop a habit of being conscious of words. Are there words people use (in writing or conversation) that you have never heard or do not initially understand? Take the time to jot them down, discover the meaning, and then use them in your own writing so that you will remember them. Below are a few words to help get you started. Try using each word in a sentence.

adaptive (adj.)	having the capacity to adjust
attainable (adj.)	within one's capacity to achieve, gain, or obtain
contingent (adj.)	likely but not certain to happen; not logically necessary
inept (adj.)	lacking aptitude, fitness, sense, or reason; not suitable; generally incompetent
innovative (adj.)	new
static (adj.)	showing little change

Effective leadership relies on the leader bringing the appropriate set of values to the work environment. There is no real way to assess the values of the leader in isolation. The leader's values become apparent only as the leader guides an organization to accomplish its goals, which benefit not only the organization but also the external community and the individuals within the organization. Leadership has been discussed in several chapters in this textbook—in Chapter 8, where the responsibilities of team leaders were presented; in Chapter 11, where the leader's role in conducting meetings was described; and in Chapter 1, where the roles of organizational leaders were described. Leading people is an acquired ability that can be developed by observing leaders in your professional and personal life.

Management Responsibilities

The functions of management are relatively concrete and can be quantified, measured, and assessed. Although the traits of effective leaders and the responsibilities of effective managers are presented separately here, understand that the most effective leaders are also effective managers, and effective managers are also likely to be effective leaders.

The functions and responsibilities of management include planning, organizing, recruiting and employing, orienting, training, motivating, delegating, and evaluating. To be successful, an organization must ensure these responsibilities are understood and implemented. To be successful in a supervisory role, you need to perform these basic management functions effectively.

Planning

Planning is a crucial function of management. It sets the direction of the organization. A major part of planning is establishing goals and objectives. Defining goals in writing and establishing measurable results compose a process that was recommended by Peter F. Drucker. In *The Practice of Management*, Drucker outlined a process that came to be known as MBO (management by objectives).[2] Still used today in one form or another, MBO is implemented through the planning process described here.

When goals and objectives are established for a one-year period, it is known as **tactical planning**; when goals and objectives cover a three-to-five-year period, it is known as **strategic or long-range planning**. The company's overall goals may be established by top-level administrators—the board of directors, the president, and the executive vice-presidents. Once these goals have been determined, they are distributed to the managers in the organization. The managers along with their work groups then set objectives for their work units. Managers are held responsible by upper administration for achieving the objectives defined. In some organizations, bonuses are awarded on the basis of the accomplishment of objectives.

Consider your role in the planning process as the administrative assistant to Martin Albertson at CanAsian Airlines, where you supervise two support staff members. First you would review the strategic plan with the support staff and review the objectives. Then together you would set the objectives for your workgroup. With the objectives in place, the group would develop a tactical plan that specifies how the objectives will be accomplished—identifying the tasks to be done, who will carry out the tasks, when the tasks will be completed, and the financial resources, if any, required. It is important that the employees who report to you know what they, as part of the workgroup, are expected to accomplish and how the tasks will be evaluated. For example, assume that one of your objectives is to revise the document management system within your division. The objective might be written as follows:

Revise the document management system from a manual system to an electronic system by April 15. After two months of use, users will evaluate the system. The cost of the revision is in software, approximately $3000.

Organizing

Once the plans have been developed, the work is organized. Organization involves bringing together all resources—people, time, money, and equipment—to effectively accomplish the goals. Three factors that affect the organization of work are span of control, job analysis, and work periods.

Span of control refers to the number of employees directly supervised by one person. No formula rigidly defines the span of control. In an organization with a flattened hierarchical structure, a greater span of control may exist where a manager may supervise as many as 30 employees.

Job analysis is the second factor in the organization of work. When organizing work, a supervisor must determine the requirements of a job and the qualifications needed by personnel to get the job done. Once identified, a job description is created. Each chapter in this textbook begins with a job posting. You may want to review some of them now to see how they include a brief summary of the job duties and identify the skills, training, and education necessary for the job. They are helpful in the hiring process and for informing employees about the expectations of the job.

Work periods, or the time in which the work is to be performed, is the third factor to consider in organizing work. The workweek is traditionally from 8 a.m. or 9 a.m. to 5 p.m., five days per week. However, factors such as flextime, four-day weeks, job sharing, and telework may mean the work period differs from what has been previously established.

Recruiting and Employing

Human resources departments usually establish procedures that outline how the organization will recruit employees. Attention is needed to certain legal considerations so that the wording of any job posting does not conflict with laws regarding fair employment practices or antidiscrimination legislation. The Canadian Human Rights Act prohibits discrimination on a wide range of grounds, including sex, race, colour, language, religion, political or other opinion, national or social origin, association with a national minority, property, birth, or other status.

The case law relating to the Canadian Human Rights Act has shown that the term "other status" includes, among other things, sexual orientation, illegitimacy, marital status, trade union membership, transsexualism, and imprisonment. The Canadian Human Rights Act can also be used to challenge discrimination on the basis of age or disability. For example, an employer cannot advertise for a particular age group. Expressions such as *young person* or *retired person* cannot be used in advertisements. If you are recruiting employees, check with the appropriate individuals within your company to make sure you are observing the company rules and legal guidelines.

Organizations use three major screening and selection tools when employing people:

- résumés
- interviews
- testing

Before the job description is written and the job vacancy advertised, ask these questions:

- What type of person are we seeking?
- What qualifications does that person need to have?
- What education and experience does the person need?

The manager or a team of people may review the applications. If you are part of that team, you should be very clear about the knowledge, skills, abilities, education, and experience you are seeking in applicants. With these criteria in mind, screen the applications and select the most qualified individuals to interview, noting specifically the details in their résumés.

You may choose to conduct one-on-one interviews, team interviews, or a combination of the two. Before the interviewing process begins, compile a list of questions to ask each candidate. Such a list keeps you and the team on target as you begin the interviewing process and helps you treat all interviewees with fairness and consistency. Additionally, the list helps remind you that certain questions are not legal. The following questions are unlawful to ask during the interview:

- Are you married? Single? Divorced? Separated?
- What is the date of your birth?
- Where were you born?
- Is your spouse a Canadian citizen?
- To what clubs do you belong?
- What are the ages of your children?
- What church do you attend?
- Have you ever belonged to a union?

You must keep up with the latest laws concerning discrimination and interviewing procedures. Otherwise, you may inadvertently put your company in jeopardy of a discrimination suit.

Set aside enough time for a thorough interview. You will probably need to spend an hour or more with each applicant. Do not consider this time wasted. Hiring the right person for a job is one of the most important things you will do as a manager.

The third screening tool is the test. Here, too, legal considerations are important. The use of tests in selecting administrative professionals is not prohibited, but testing practices that have discriminatory effects are. Keep in mind that the test must measure the person's qualifications for the job, not the person as an individual. If you are employing an administrative professional, for example, and a requirement of the job is the ability to key at a certain rate with an established degree of accuracy, you can have all applicants do a keyboarding test. Applicants for an administrative professional job can be given grammar and spelling tests since the individual will be required to produce documents free of grammatical and spelling errors. You

cannot ask a person to take a math proficiency test unless the use of math is necessary in performing the job. You must treat all applicants equally—you cannot use different testing options with different applicants. Personality- or behaviour-based (psychometric) tests, such as the Predictive Index behavioural assessment, are very useful and can be implemented before, during, or after the interview. A link to PI Worldwide where you can find out more about Predictive Index assessment can be found on the MindTap site that accompanies this textbook.

Orientation

Once a person is employed, the next step is an orientation to provide that individual with the knowledge necessary to be successful on the job. The new employee will possess the skill set outlined in the job posting but know little about how your organization works. As a manager, you are responsible to inform new employees about the history of the organization, its policy and procedures (perhaps provide them with a policy and procedures manual), and its job evaluation procedures (frequency and criteria). Routine day-to-day procedures of the job (records management and technology) also need to be explained. Also include in your orientation any information on additional training, as a result of changes in technology, available through company-sponsored seminars, tuition-reimbursed courses at local colleges or universities, or job internships.

Assigning another experienced employee to mentor a new employee will help the new employee to learn the routine procedures that may be unique to the organization. A mentor can be the new employee's go-to person who will answer any initial questions, introduce the employee to other members of the organization, and generally help this person feel part of the team from the outset.

Communicating AT WORK

When leading others, it is very important to clearly communicate your expectations to them. Good written communication skills are important. Failing to communicate goals, deadlines, directions, and information so that they are understood can have serious consequences.

In addition, don't underestimate the power of face-to-face communication. Looking an individual or group of people in the eye helps you gauge their understanding and discern any resistance.

Team Training

If a team is to be successful, a manager working with teams must take on the following responsibilities:

- **Empower the team.** Give them the information needed to get the job done.
- **Trust the team.** Once the team has the information it needs, trust the team to produce the best possible solutions to problems.

- **Take a strong stand with the team when needed.** If the team is not accomplishing the task and is getting bogged down in personality issues, let them know that such behaviours are not acceptable.
- **Check on the team's development.** Are team members communicating with and trusting each other? Do they understand the goals of the team? Do they understand individual roles? Is every member involved in the process and product?
- **Do not micromanage.** To **micromanage** is to direct every small detail of another person's work.

Teams often cannot function effectively without acquiring some interpersonal skill development. As a result, managers may need to be involved in team training. The following skills are generally necessary for all team members as they work together:

- **Listening.** Summarizing, checking for understanding, and giving and receiving feedback

Ongoing training is essential.

Technology AT WORK

As a leader, you may need to gather and compute information for reports and meetings. Function formulas in Microsoft Excel are an efficient way to do this.

Scenario 1: You have a financial account with multiple subcodes to track expenditures in different areas (such as travel, salaries, and equipment). You create a spreadsheet and use the IF function so that Excel tracks finances in each subcode.

Scenario 2: Your supervisor owns a small food distribution service that distributes food to multiple restaurants in the metro area. She wants you to tell her which type of food brings in the most money. You have a spreadsheet that contains all the distributions. You use the SUMIF formula to have *Excel* consider all the food items distributed and sum the items that are coded "South-west," "Asian," and "Italian." With three new numbers, your supervisor has information that my help her expand or change her business.

- **Resolving conflicts.** Identifying and resolving conflicts within the team or with individuals outside the team
- **Influencing others.** Gaining respect as a team and as individuals
- **Developing solutions.** Creatively generating and sorting through alternative solutions to issues
- **Ensuring ongoing quality.** Determining how results will be measured

Delegating

Delegating means giving the responsibility for tasks to others and then empowering them to get the job done. Think carefully about the tasks you will delegate. Work out the details of what you want the person to do and write down your directions so the person can refer to them later. Provide the necessary information and let them do the planning and organizing. They might not do it the same way that you would, but who knows, they might find a better way, and everyone would learn something valuable in the process.

Arrange for the employee to check in with you periodically, and make yourself available for these exchanges. Try to anticipate questions but ensure the employee knows to approach you with any problems, questions, or requirements for additional support as they arise.

Delegating can be challenging. It requires you to relinquish control and allow others to make mistakes. Give them the authority they need and trust team members to complete their assignments responsibly.

Evaluating

Informal feedback can be invaluable to productivity, morale, and motivation. Taking the time to provide frequent, constructive feedback shows employees how you expect work to be done and helps them to improve. In Chapter 13, the topic of formal performance appraisal and evaluation was introduced. Formal appraisals assess long-term performance against a set of previously established goals. They are conducted as a method of identifying performance that is inadequate and recognizing performance that is exceptional. Most companies have formal evaluation periods in which personnel are evaluated every six months or every year. These evaluations may be individual evaluations, team evaluations, or work-group evaluations.

Individual evaluations are essential even if team evaluations occur. The human resources department may have developed forms and procedures for individual evaluations; the manager completes an evaluation and the employee completes a self-evaluation. At the evaluation conference, both evaluations are discussed and a final evaluation document is prepared. Once these processes have been developed, they should be implemented consistently with all employees throughout the organization. Figure 15-3 provides some techniques that will help you understand how to effectively evaluate employees.

FIGURE 15-3

Evaluation Techniques

- **Evaluate performance on a day-to-day basis.** Give employees immediate feedback on their performance. If a report or letter is not written or formatted correctly, inform the employee immediately. Praise a job well done; do not wait for a yearly evaluation session.
- **Allow adequate time for the evaluation.** Set aside enough time on your calendar to do a thorough evaluation. Hold it in an appropriate place where you are not likely to be interrupted.
- **Give credit where credit is due.** When work is done well, tell the responsible employees. Look at the total work of the employee; do not treat the evaluation as a time just for criticism. Express to employees the areas in which they are performing in an exemplary manner, in an average manner, and below expectations.
- **Be fair.** Analyze the employee's work objectively on the basis of established performance criteria not on how well you like or dislike the employee. When discussing errors, word your comments positively; suggest how the work could have been performed satisfactorily. Give the employee an opportunity to suggest possible alternatives. For example, you might say, "You are doing well in . . . but you need to improve in . . ." rather than, "Your performance is a problem."
- **Listen to what the employee is saying.** Too often we listen to others with only half an ear. By providing the employee with an opportunity to speak, they will be able to release much of their anxiety and thus be more receptive to constructive criticism. Let the person talk.
- **Avoid personal areas.** Do not try to counsel an employee about his or her personal problems that should be handled by a qualified professional.
- **Establish attainable objectives for improvement.** Help the employee develop a plan of action for improvement, which should include setting target dates for the accomplishment of each objective. Recognize any resulting improvement; this plan of action is meant to be a growth plan for improvement.

Team evaluations are used by some companies; employees who work together as a team are asked to evaluate each other. These evaluations may be administered by the team's supervisor or discussed among the team members only. Guidelines should be given to the team beforehand to ensure that the session does not become one of fault-finding or blaming others. The team leader should stress that the evaluation is meant to determine whether tasks have been successfully completed by the team and to acknowledge the contributions made by individual members.

Work-group evaluations should set measurable objectives that are related to the overall goals established by the organization. The manager and the work group might also use a total quality approach to identify ongoing improvements by asking:

- What needs to be improved?
- What actions should the work group take to improve the areas identified?
- Who does what and when is it done? Develop an **action plan** listing tasks to be achieved, identifying

who is responsible for them, and when each will be completed.

- How do we know the action is working? Monitor the action plan to determine whether the desired results have been achieved.
- How can we ensure that the problem will not recur? Implement training and other necessary measures to ensure that the problem does not happen again.
- What have we learned? Areas where difficulties occurred should be reviewed so performance can improve.

As a manager you may also be responsible for identifying and preparing employees for promotion. Promoting qualified personnel from within the organization can improve employee morale. You should watch for promising employees and use every opportunity to encourage them and further develop their skills. Using these evaluation techniques can help you to identify those employees who have potential for promotion.

Soft Skills — EARNING THE RIGHT TO LEAD

You have learned in this chapter that the effective leader has certain traits and is willing to follow a set of values to help the organization and its employees to learn and grow. You have learned that several management responsibilities are necessary in order for an organization to function efficiently. You have learned that a definite link exists between good leaders and good managers. Although management tasks are more concrete, effective

managers must have leadership characteristics—those traits that keep the organization focused on doing what is fair.

Needless to say, not all people have the leadership traits mentioned in this chapter, and not all are interested in developing them. The process of learning how to lead is ongoing. No one is born with the right to lead; leadership is earned. It is individuals who consistently demonstrate a commitment to the skills defined in this chapter who earn that right.

Chapter Summary

The summary will help you remember the important points covered in this chapter.

- Regardless of the profession you choose, the ability to lead with confidence will serve you well throughout life.
- Effective leaders have integrity and emotional maturity, understand themselves, work to build a shared vision, live by a set of values, commit to service, motivate others, reward risk-taking, model appropriate conduct, and know how to follow.
- Leadership styles include autocratic, democratic, and laissez-faire.
- Management responsibilities include planning, organizing, recruiting and employing, orienting, training, motivating, delegating, and evaluating.
- The process of learning how to lead is continual. No one is born with the right to lead. Only those who demonstrate a commitment to develop needed leadership characteristics earn that right.

Key Terms

action plan p. 282
autocratic leadership p. 278
delegating p. 281
democratic leadership p. 278
job analysis p. 279
laissez-faire leadership p. 278
leadership p. 275

management p. 275
micromanage p. 281
span of control p. 279
strategic or long-range planning p. 279
tactical planning p. 279
work periods p. 279

Discussion Items

These discussion items provide an opportunity to test your understanding of the chapter through written responses and discussion with your classmates and your instructor.

1. List the traits and qualities of an effective leader.
2. Explain the difference between leadership and management.
3. Define the essential responsibilities of management.
4. Describe the three most common leadership styles.
5. To work effectively and efficiently, teams must possess certain skills. Generally speaking, what are these skills?

Critical-Thinking Activity

Two months ago, CanAsian offered you a position as records manager. You accepted the offer since the position matches your skills and career goals. Five individuals report to you. During the two months, two staff members have committed what you believe to be serious ethical violations. The situations are as follows.

Situation 1

One of your first responsibilities was to develop an electronic document system for personnel records. You asked two of your staff (Nazira and Theodore) to work with you on the project. As your team started to work, you reminded them of the confidential nature of the project, stating that no information could be shared with anyone. Two weeks into the project, Nazira reported she overheard Theodore discussing project details with two administrative professionals in the accounting department. He gave them details of three executives in the company, including their ages, salaries, and employment history.

Situation 2

Kami, one of the five members of your staff, worked overtime one evening on a project you assigned. You left the office at 5 p.m., but returned at 8 p.m. Kami was not working when you returned. She provided the completed assignment the next morning. When Kami submitted her overtime hours for the week, she claimed overtime from 5 p.m. until 11 p.m. on that evening; overtime is paid at time and a half.

How should you handle each situation? As you respond, ask yourself whether you are living your values.

Building Workplace Skills

Project 15-1 (Learning Outcomes 1 and 2)

Collaborative Project

CAREER

Work as a team with four of your classmates on this assignment. Interview two top-level executives (presidents or vice-presidents, if possible). Ask them the following questions:

- What are the characteristics of an effective leader?
- How did you develop your leadership skills?
- How is planning conducted in your organization?
- Do you provide ongoing training for your employees? If so, what types of opportunities do you provide?
- What process do you use to evaluate employees? Summarize your findings and report them to the class.

Project 15-2 (Learning Outcome 3)

INNOVATION   DATA FILE

Locate the sound file Project 15-2 from the data files. Without pausing or stopping, play the file to hear Alberto telling his team leader, Ellen, about a problem. Play the file once more. What is the problem that Alberto is describing? If you were the team leader, what steps would you take to resolve it? Discuss this in pairs or submit an interpretation and proposed resolution to your instructor.

Make the Grade with MindTap

Stay organized and efficient with **MindTap**—a single destination with all the course material and study aids you need to succeed. Built-in apps leverage social media and the latest learning technology. For example:

- ReadSpeaker will read the text to you.
- Flashcards are pre-populated to provide you with a jump-start for review—or you can create your own.
- You can highlight text and make notes in your MindTap Reader. Your notes will flow into Evernote, the electronic

Project 15-3 (Learning Outcome 3)

CAREER   TECHNOLOGY

Assuming you are in a leadership position, identify and record the leadership values you would uphold and demonstrate to your employees. Save this document in your e-portfolio folder.

Your e-portfolio should now be nearing completion. Review the *Employability Skills 2000+* chart you created in Chapter 1. Did you successfully acquire all these skills? Write a summary of what you intended to accomplish. Include an evaluation of your actual accomplishments and your future plans. Submit this summary to your instructor or arrange a meeting to review your e-portfolio.

Project 15-4 (Learning Outcomes 1, 2, and 3)

CAREER   TECHNOLOGY

Your supervisor will be giving a presentation on leadership to a local civic group. He has asked you to create a visual outline of topics related to leadership that he can use to stimulate ideas. Use the chapter and other sources for topics. Use the Shapes or SmartArt feature of Microsoft Word or an online mapping tool to create your visual outline. Links to some of these tools are provided on the website for this text.

notebook app that you can access anywhere when it's time to study for the exam.
- Self-quizzing allows you to access your understanding.

Visit nelson.com/student to start using **MindTap**. Enter the Online Access Code from the card included with your text. If a code card is not provided, you can purchase instant access at NELSONbrain.com.

Endnotes

1. Alan Murray, "What Is the Difference Between Management and Leadership?" *The Wall Street Journal*, http://guides.wsj.com/management/developing-a-leadership-style/ what-is-the-difference-between-management-and-leadership/ accessed February 5, 2015.
2. Peter F. Drucker, *The Practice of Management* (New York: HarperBusiness, 1993).

Glossary

A

accession log A document that records the numbers that have been assigned. p. 178

accountable items Express items; for example, items sent via FedEx, UPS, Purolator, and registered mail. p. 135

accounts payable The amount owed to a supplier or vendor for goods or services purchased on credit. p. 164

action plan A plan that includes specific tasks to be achieved, who is responsible for each task identified, and when the task will be completed. p. 282

active listening Listening for the meaning as well as to the words of the speaker. p. 74

ad hoc committee A special committee that is formed to deal with a specific issue or problem; also known as a *taskforce* or a *project team*. p. 199

administrative assistant See *administrative professional*. p. 9

administrative professional Workplace support person. This occupation was formerly referred to as *secretary* or *receptionist*, and by such specialized titles as *legal secretary* and *medical secretary*. Although these titles are still in use, shifting roles have led to the more common use of *administrative assistant*, *executive assistant*, *marketing assistant*, *payroll assistant*, *human resources assistant*, and *office manager*. p. 9

agenda An outline of what will occur at a meeting. p. 204

alphabetizing Comparison of units in a *caption*, unit by unit and letter by letter, to determine a difference. p. 180

amendment Used to change the wording of a *motion* that has been made. p. 211

annotate To make notations on a piece of mail concerning a previous action taken or facts that will assist the reader. p. 133

APA style Documentation guidelines established by the American Psychological Association. p. 85

application software Programs that work with operating software to perform specific tasks, such as a word processing program. p. 93

appointment A time set aside for people to discuss an issue. p. 99

assets A list of what a company owns. p. 164

ATMs Automated teller machines. p. 230

attitude The position, disposition, or manner you have about a person or thing. pp. 71, 237

autocratic leadership A controlling leadership style in which the leader directs and closely supervises the work that is done; employees have no input into the decisions. p. 278

B

balance sheet A financial statement showing a company's *assets*, *liabilities*, and net worth. p. 163

BCS Bar code sorter. p. 136

bill of lading A document that itemizes a shipment's contents, the quantity, and the delivery destination. It accompanies items such as parcels or packages being shipped from a supplier to a customer. p. 141

blank endorsement The signature of the *payee* of a financial instrument. p. 153

blog Also called a *weblog*; a Web-based journal in which participants express their opinions, thoughts, and feelings. p. 98

body language Various meaningful body motions or gestures. p. 76

bonds Debt owed by an organization. p. 272

Boolean operators Words or symbols that identify a relationship between the keywords. p. 95

business-class accommodations A mode of air travel slightly more expensive than *economy class*, but less expensive than *first class*; located in front of economy class or directly behind first class. p. 224

bylaws The rules and procedures that govern the operation of an organization. p. 199

C

Canada Post Corporation (CPC) Canada's postal service. p. 130

cancelled cheques Written *cheques* that have been cleared by the bank. p. 157

caption One or more *filing units*, such as the entire name or a part of the name by which the *record* will be stored. p. 173

carpal tunnel syndrome A major occupational illness that occurs because of the compression of a large nerve, the median nerve, as it passes through a tunnel composed of bone and ligaments in the wrist. p. 31

CARS checklist A way to evaluate online sources by checking for credibility, accuracy, reasonableness, and support (or sources). p. 96

casual listening Hearing and trying to understand what is being said with the objective of relating to others. p. 74

CEO (chief executive officer) The top executive responsible for implementing the policies and goals established by a company's board of directors. p. 7

CFO (chief financial officer) The senior executive responsible for the financial direction of a company. p. 8

channel A means by which a message is sent, such as a letter or an email, or speaking in person or by telephone. p. 72

cheque register A log used to record the details of all *cheques* written and deposits made. p. 156

cheques Legal documents authorizing the bank to pay a specific sum to a designated *payee*. p. 152

chronic stress Occurs when a distressful situation is prolonged, allowing no rest or recuperation for the body; it can cause physical and emotional problems. p. 32

chronological résumé A *résumé* that lists a person's credentials in reverse chronological order, with the most recent entries listed first. p. 250

CIO (chief information officer) The senior executive responsible for overseeing information technology and computer systems in a company. p. 8

circular and oval arrangements Two effective seating arrangements for minimizing status positions. Works well for small groups of six to eight people. p. 207

cloud A remote network of servers that provide a service or run applications; another term for the Internet. p. 93

cloud computing The storing and accessing of applications and computer data through a Web browser that provides computer services to computers and mobile devices on demand. p. 93

cloud storage Computer data are stored on remote servers accessed by using the Internet (the cloud), which allows the user to obtain files or programs from any computer, tablet, or smart device with Internet access. p. 93

coding Marking a *record* by the name, subject, location, or number determined in the *indexing* process. p. 180

cold call See *direct contact*. p. 246

collating Assembling, in chronological order, the pages in a multiple-page document. p. 144

combination-style résumé A *résumé* that presents experiences in reverse chronological skill set order. p. 252

communication barrier Anything that interferes with successful *communication*; can be internal or external. p. 73

communication The process that occurs when a message is sent by one person and received and understood by another person. p. 72

compressed workweek Employees work the usual number of hours; however, the hours are compressed into four days. p. 7

computer vision syndrome A health problem that develops from screen glare. p. 31

conference call A meeting in which more than two individuals at different locations attend and communicate with each other via a telecommunications network; also known as a *teleconference*. p. 201

confidentiality Secrecy of the information received or the confidences shared. Many firms require employees to sign a confidentiality agreement to highlight the importance of this aspect to new employees. p. 12

conflict of interest When private interests of a member of the board of directors conflict with the duties they owe the company. p. 8

conflict resolution Addressing and dealing with conflicts in a positive manner. p. 33

consulate An office of a government in a foreign city that acts to assist and protect citizens of the consul's country. p. 230

COO (chief operating officer) The senior executive responsible for the day-to-day operations of a company. p. 8

copyright The exclusive right granted to the author or creator of an original body of work to reproduce or authorize someone else to reproduce the material. p. 144

corporations Legal entities formed by following a formal process of federal or provincial incorporation; may be publicly or privately owned. p. 7

cover letter A letter that is used when applying for a job, with the *goal* of arousing the prospective employer's interest, describing the abilities of the person writing the letter, and requesting an interview. p. 247

creativity Having the ability or the power to cause to exist. p. 115

credible Believable or trustworthy. p. 122

critical thinking Conscious and deliberate inquiry. *Critical* comes from the Greek word *krinein,* which means "to separate, to choose." p. 17

cross-referencing A method of identifying an alternate name that could be used when a record is requested. p. 180

culture The ideas, customs, values, skills, and arts of a specific group of people. p. 5

current assets Cash, or *assets* such as accounts receivable or inventory, that can readily be converted into cash in a short time. p. 164

customer Also known as a *client* or *buyer,* someone who buys or uses the products or services of a company or organization. p. 56

customer focus A commitment to providing high-quality *customer service* to all customers. p. 56

customer service The ability of an organization to consistently give customers what they need and want. p. 56

cuts Tabs of various widths on folders. p. 173

D

delegating Assigning tasks to others and then *empowering* them by providing the necessary information to get the job done. p. 281

democratic leadership A leadership style in which employees share in authority, decisions, and plans. p. 278

demographics Characteristics such as age, gender, race, education, and income level. p. 116

dependability Trustworthiness. Examples are being at work on *time* if you are working at an established location; being productive when engaged in *telework*; being willing to put in additional time on important assignments; doing what you say you will do, when you say you will do it. p. 12

deposit slip A form that accompanies a deposit and itemizes the amount of cash and the value of cheques being deposited. p. 152

die An engraved metal stamp used for impressing postage on a meter; may include business logos or other messages that are printed concurrently and in addition to the postage. p. 138

direct access A system that does not require referring to anything but the file to find the name. p. 175

direct approach Used when the *message* is favourable or neutral; it begins with the reason for the correspondence, continues with any needed explanation, and closes with a thank you for the action that has been taken or with a request that action be taken by a specific date. p. 77

direct contact or cold call Going directly to an organization without having an *appointment* or without knowing whether a job is available. p. 246

discrimination Treatment or consideration based on class or category rather than individual merit. p. 41

downsize To reduce the number of employees within a business. p. 32

drawer The organization or person who has written the *cheques*. p. 153

due process The requirement of managers to impose sanctions on employees only after offering them a chance to correct the organizational grievance. p. 44

duplexing In *reprographics*, copying on both sides of a sheet of paper. p. 143

E

e-cheques Also known as email money transfers, these electronic payments are used to send money directly from a personal bank account to anyone with an email address and a personal bank account at one of many Canadian financial institutions. p. 158

ecologically Important to the relationships between human groups and their physical and social environments. p. 144

economy-class accommodations The least expensive of the three classes of flight; seats are closer together, there is less legroom, and service is not as good as in first class or business class. p. 224

e-deposit or remote capture deposit An image of a cheque is captured by scanning (or taking a picture) and is then electronically delivered to a financial institution for deposit to an account. p. 153

editing Reviewing and revising a message to improve its form and content. p. 79

EFT See *electronic funds transfer*. p. 157

electronic funds transfer (EFT) A method whereby a bank uses computer technology to effect a transfer of funds. p. 157

electronic résumé An online statement of one's background and experiences. p. 253

emoticons Short for *emotion icons*; they mimic facial expressions using punctuation marks, numbers, and letters. Can be perceived as too casual in business interactions. p. 81

emotional intelligence The capacity to develop self-awareness, self-discipline, and empathy in ways that affect relationships with others. p. 12

empathy statement A statement that acknowledges how someone is feeling. p. 61

empathy The ability to feel or think the same way another person is thinking or feeling. pp. 34, 61

emphatic listening *Listening* used to hear, understand, and offer *feedback* that shows the *message* was understood. p. 74

Employability Skills 2000+ A profile developed by the Conference Board of Canada and updated regularly that identifies critical skills needed in the workplace. p. 9

Employment and Social Development Canada The national public employment agency whose services are provided free to Canadian job seekers. p. 246

employment application A form used by companies to obtain information about prospective employees' education, background, and experience. p. 253

employment at will The doctrine that allows employees to be fired for no valid cause if the employer wishes to do so. p. 44

endorsing a cheque Signing a *cheque* on the back. p. 153

epost A free, secure, online personal digital mailbox that allows individuals and businesses to access, view, and pay bills online. p. 130

epost Connect A secure service linked to an *epost* account that provides private and confidential online secure communications services for business customers through bulk and collaboration options. p. 131

ergonomics The study of the fit between people, the tools they use, and the physical setting in which they work. For example, ergonomics can help in the design of office furniture and equipment that is physiologically sound so that the user remains healthy while using it. The Greek words *ergoes* and *nomos* were combined to coin the word. p. 30

e-stamps Electronic postage purchased via the Internet and downloaded to a PC. Also known as *PC postage*. p. 138

ethics The systematic study of moral conduct, duty, and judgment. p. 52

evaluative listening *Listening* used to hear, understand, and judge what is being said. p. 74

executive summary A one or two-page summary of a report. p. 85

exit interview An interview done by the employer when an employee leaves the company. p. 261

external customers The people or other organizations that buy or use the products and services provided by the organization. p. 57

extranet A private network that belongs to an organization, such as a bank, and requires authorization to use. p. 94

extrinsic motivation An impulse to action that comes from outside a person, such as a possible salary increase or a promotion. p. 13

extroverts People who prefer to be energized by the outside world. p. 267

F

feedback A return *message* sent by the *receiver* that helps the sender know whether the message was understood correctly. p. 73

file transfer protocol (FTP) A method of transferring data from one computer to another. p. 98

firewall Software that prevents unauthorized individuals from using an *intranet* or an *extranet*. p. 109

first-class accommodations The most expensive of the three classes of airline flights and the most luxurious. p. 224

fiscal year A 12-month period used for accounting purposes; might be from January 1 through December 31, from July 1 through June 30, or any other continuous 12-month period. p. 164

fixed assets Land, buildings, or equipment that will be used over the life of the organization. p. 164

flash memory Computer memory that stores basic start-up instructions. p. 92

flattened organizational structure Fewer management levels than the traditional structures of the past. p. 8

flextime The staggering of working hours to enable an employee to work the full quota of time but at periods defined by the company and the individual; helps to reduce traffic congestion at the traditional peak hours and allows employees needed flexibility in their schedules. p. 7

flipcharts Pads of large paper for drawing pictures or recording notes during a presentation or meeting; pages can be removed from the pad and displayed on meeting room walls as reminders of the discussion as the meeting progresses. p. 119

follow-up letter A letter thanking the prospective employer for an interview and reviewing points of special interest. p. 258

franking A stamped impression affixed or applied to mail to qualify it to be posted. p. 139

frequent flyer program An incentive program offered by most airlines that provides a variety of awards after the accumulation of a certain number of mileage points. p. 231

full endorsement Permits *cheques* to be transferred from the original *payee* to another payee. p. 153

functional résumé A *résumé* that highlights and emphasizes skills; chronological order is not a consideration. p. 250

G

geographic storage method Arrangement of *records* by their geographic location. p. 176

girth A measurement around the thickest part of a package used in determining postage. p. 140

goal An objective, a purpose, or an end to be achieved. p. 23

government entity An organization that carries out the functions of a provincial, territorial, municipal, or federal government, such as government agencies, public schools and universities, municipal departments, and numerous other departments, commissions, bureaus, and boards. p. 7

groupware Software that assists workplace collaboration. p. 97

H

heterogeneous group A group having dissimilar backgrounds and experiences. p. 205

hits A list returned by a search engine of links to webpages that match your keywords or search phrase. p. 95

homogeneous group A group of people with similar backgrounds and experiences. p. 205

hot keys User-defined combinations of keystrokes that provide quick access to a command or menu. p. 101

human relation skills Abilities that allow people to interact with others effectively. p. 61

I

important records *Records* that are necessary for an orderly continuation of a business and are replaceable only with considerable expenditure of *time* and money. p. 187

income statement A summary of an organization's income, expenses, and profit or loss over a specified period. p. 163

index A listing of the names or titles used in a filing system. p. 176

indexing Determining how a *record* is to be filed: by name, subject, number, or geographic location. p. 180

indexing units The individual words that make up a *caption*. p. 180

indirect approach Used when one is delivering a *message* that is unfavourable. This approach begins with an opening statement that is pleasant but neutral, reviews the circumstances, gives the information, and then closes on a pleasant and positive note. p. 78

informative listening Listening used when you want to hear, understand, and remember the information being presented. p. 74

initiative The ability to, on your own, start a plan or task and ensure its completion. It means having the ability to set your own work goals p. 13

inspecting Checking to see that correspondence is ready to be filed. p. 179

instant message An electronic *message* sent and received by two or more people who are connected to a network at the same time. p. 97

integrity Adherence to a code of behaviour. pp. 13, 52

intelligent mobile hotspot A portable Internet connection that makes Internet access possible through a cellular network; can come in the form of a small portable device or as a feature available on a smartphone. p. 92

interactive electronic whiteboard (IWB) A large interactive display board that can be connected wirelessly to a computer using Bluetooth technology or physically through a USB cable. A projected image of the computer desktop is displayed on the whiteboard. The IWB also has the ability to electronically scan images drawn or written on it and to then transfer the data to a computer where it can be edited, printed, or emailed. p. 119

internal customers Departments or employees within an organization who use the products or services provided by others within the organization. p. 57

intranet A private network that belongs to an organization and is accessible only by the organization's employees. pp. 9, 114

intrinsic motivation An impulse to action that comes from within a person, such as a desire to excel. p. 13

introverts People who prefer to focus attention on the inner world. p. 267

invoice A notice prepared by a vendor or seller of money the recipient owes to it in exchange for goods or services. p. 154

IP technology Transmits voice over a private network or a public IP network such as the Internet. p. 101

itinerary A detailed outline of a trip showing all the arrangements, including flight numbers, airports, departure and arrival times, hotels, car rental information, *appointments*, and so on. p. 232

J

jet lag The feeling of exhaustion following a flight through several time zones. p. 224

job analysis The second factor in the organization of work; determining the requirements of a job and the qualifications needed by personnel to get the job done. p. 279

job interview A meeting between a job applicant and a potential employer to discuss a job and the applicant's qualifications. p. 254

job search agents Programs that automatically search job listings and retrieve job postings that match chosen criteria, such as a geographic area; results are sent by email at an interval selected. p. 246

job sharing A work arrangement in which two part-time employees perform a job that otherwise would be held by one full-time employee. p. 7

K

key unit The primary or first unit used in *alphabetizing*. p. 180

keywords Words that uniquely identify a file in an electronic system so it can be found by querying the system in a variety of ways. pp. 95, 177

L

laissez-faire leadership A *leadership* style in which employees lead themselves. The leader is not involved in directing or controlling tasks. p. 278

leadership The act of inspiring and motivating people to achieve organizational goals. p. 275

liabilities A list of what a company owes. p. 164

limited liability partnership (LLP) A form of company ownership that combines the tax advantages of a partnership with the limited liability of a corporation. Professionals such as medical doctors, accountants, and lawyers often operate as LLPs. p. 7

liquidity order The order of listing current assets before fixed assets. p. 164

listening Hearing and trying to understand the message. p. 74

M

management In a business setting, the act of organizing and directing people to accomplish organizational goals. p. 275

message The idea being presented by the sender of a communication; a symbol or group of symbols that conveys meaning, such as a thought or an idea. p. 72

metadata Information about data p. 190

micromanage To direct every small detail of another's work. p. 281

minutes A written *record* of a meeting. p. 211

mission statement A statement that defines an organization's purpose and can include its customer or market base as well as its territory. p. 7

MLA style Documentation guidelines established by the Modern Language Association. p. 85

mobile application (app) Software that is designed to run on a portable device, such as a tablet or smartphone. p. 92

monthly statement A document prepared by a vendor or seller listing purchases and payments made during the month. p. 154

morality A set of ideas of right and wrong. p. 52

motion A formal expression during a meeting of a proposal or an action to be undertaken. It requires a mover (someone who makes the motion) and a seconder (someone who is in favour of discussing the motion). After debate, a motion is voted upon by the meeting participants. It must be recorded *verbatim* in the *minutes* of the meeting. p. 211

multicultural Relating to or including various cultural differences and backgrounds. p. 5

mutual funds Investment funds that include a combination of *stocks* and *bonds*, purchased through a mutual fund company. p. 272

N

net pay Gross pay less compulsory and voluntary deductions. p. 161

net worth The difference between *assets* and *liabilities*. p. 163

networking The process of identifying and maintaining contact with acquaintances, friends, and relatives who can assist you in the job search process. p. 245

nonessential records *Records* that have no future value to an organization. p. 187

nonprofit corporation An organization formed to engage in civic, charitable, educational, or artistic endeavours, such as hospitals, schools, charities, and arts organizations. p. 7

nonverbal communication Sending a *message* without spoken or written words. p. 76

O

offset Not folded to the edge of the paper. p. 144

online appointment software Web-based software that provides clients and customers with 24/7 access to schedule their own appointments online. p. 100

operating system software Software that translates a user's instructions—entered by keyboard, mouse, or touch—into a form that can be understood by the computer. p. 93

operating system The software that supports a computer's basic functions and manages hardware and software. p. 93

outsourcing One company hiring another to take over an existing internal activity, such as mail services or payroll. p. 135

P

parliamentary procedures The procedural rules that ensure all participants have a voice and vote in the decision-making process. p. 211

partnership An association of two or more people as co-owners of a business. p. 7

passport An official government document that certifies the identity and citizenship of an individual and grants the person permission to travel abroad. p. 228

payee The organization or person to whom a *cheque* is written. p. 153

per diem Latin for "per day"; the expression is used in conjunction with how much a company is willing to reimburse an individual for travel. p. 231

performance appraisals *Evaluations* of employees done by the employer. p. 260

periodic transfer The transfer of active *records* to inactive status at the end of a stated period of time. See also *perpetual transfer*. p. 188

perpetual transfer The continuous transfer of active *records* to inactive status. See also *periodic transfer*. p. 188

persuasive approach A method of writing used to convince the reader to take a specific action or change an indifferent or negative reader reaction. p. 78

petty cash fund A cash fund established to handle the purchases of small incidental business office items. p. 160

phishing A type of scam whereby online criminals send an email or *instant message* that looks as though it is from a legitimate financial institution or business, such as a bank, and requests your credit card number, social insurance number, or other personal information. p. 107

PIM (personal information management) A software application that serves as a planner, notebook, and contact manager. p. 26

pitch An attribute of sound and voice that can be described as high or low. p. 75

platen cover In copiers and scanners, the protective panel that fits over the platen, the flat glass surface on which an original document is placed faced down before the cover is lowered. p. 143

postdated Dated for some time in the future, not today; said of *cheques*. p. 152

posters Effective visual aids that are used in meetings and presentations to small groups; may show an image related to the discussion or list the key point for the audience to remember. p. 118

pragmatic Relating to actual practice in day-to-day activities, as opposed to theory. p. 39

preauthorized automated transfer A method for making regular payments on accounts where the amount *invoiced* each month is constant. p. 158

predictive search feature The use by search engines of an algorithm based on the most popular searches to predict what you are looking for. p. 95

prejudice A system of negative beliefs, feelings, and actions. p. 41

presentation A speech, lecture, or seminar that may be delivered in person or via the Internet or another network. p. 114

primary research The collecting of original data through surveys, observations, or experiments. p. 84

priority Something that merits your attention ahead of other tasks. p. 25

private employment agencies Privately owned employment agencies that charge a fee (either of the employer or the client) when providing services. p. 246

procrastination The postponement or needless delay of a project or task that must be done. p. 28

professional A person who looks, speaks, writes, and behaves in a manner that reflects well on both the employer and employee. p. 13

Q

quorum The minimum number of participants required to be present at a meeting before decisions can officially be made. p. 211

R

random access memory (RAM) A type of computer storage that works very fast and is used to temporarily store and run software program instructions and to store data currently in use. The contents are lost when the computer is turned off. p. 92

read-only memory (ROM) A type of computer storage that holds basic operating instructions needed when a computer is turned on. The contents are not lost when the computer is turned off. p. 92

real time A way of collaborating online in which individuals can simultaneously work on electronically produced documents, such as *presentations*, spreadsheets, reports, and proposals. p. 202

receiver The person for whom a *message* is intended; the person who receives the message, such as the recipient of a letter or an email message. p. 73

record Any type of recorded information. p. 171

records management The systematic control of *records* from their creation to their final disposition. p. 171

rectangular arrangement A seating arrangement that allows the leader to maintain control. p. 207

reflective listening *Listening* used to hear, understand, and offer *feedback* that helps the speaker think about her or his feelings or objectives. p. 74

remote employment Any working arrangement in which the worker performs a significant portion of work at some fixed location other than the traditional workplace. p. 6

reprographics An inclusive term used to refer to the copying process. p. 143

resolution (1) A formal expression of opinion or direction of an organization. (2) The quality of a digital picture. (3) The act of addressing and dealing with a problem. p. 211

restrictive endorsement The highest level of protection; limits what actions can be done with a *cheque*. p. 153

résumé A concise statement of a person's background, education, skills, and experience that accompanies a *letter of application* when seeking a job. p. 248

retrieving Removing a document or a complete folder from storage. p. 180

rightsize To determine the most efficient and effective number of employees and organizational structure. p. 32

Robert's Rules of Order A set of guidelines for *parliamentary procedure* covering the conduct of participants. p. 210

RRSPs Registered retirement savings plans. p. 272

RSI Repetitive *stress* injury, a generic name given to injuries that occur over a period of time. Also known as *overuse disorders*. p. 31

S

search phrase Multiple keywords used together to carry out a Web search. p. 95

secondary research Data or material other people have discovered and reported via the Internet, books, periodicals, and various other publications. p. 84

self-confidence Believing in yourself and your abilities. which improves over time through learning, growing, and refining new skills. p. 13

semicircular or U-shaped arrangement Seating arrangements that work well for small groups of six to eight people. p. 207

sender The person who creates the *message* and transmits it via a *channel*, such as the person who writes a letter. p. 72

sexual harassment Persistent torment arising from sexual conduct that is unwelcome by the recipient; may be physical or verbal. p. 42

shareholders (stockholders) Investors in a company who have purchased *stock* representing a portion or share of the company. p. 7

shredder A machine that cuts paper into strips or confetti-like material. p. 145

smartphone A full-featured mobile phone that includes many of the functions of a handheld computer. p. 92

social networking The use of a particular website or application to find others with similar interests and build social relationships. p. 99

sole proprietorship A business organization that is owned and controlled by an individual. p. 7

sorting Placing *records* in order for storage. p. 180

space A certain amount of distance maintained between people in a conversation. p. 71

span of control The number of employees directly supervised by one person. p. 279

speaker's list A list of meeting participants wanting to comment on a discussion item—the chair makes a note of the names of participants in the order in which they indicate a desire to comment and then calls upon them in that order. p. 210

spear phishing A specific scam that involves personalized email sent to only a few people. p. 108

specialized software Programs and application used only within specific settings such as health services or legal industries. p. 93

staledated Said of *cheques* that are dated more than six months earlier. Such cheques are not honoured by the bank. p. 152

standing committee A committee established for an ongoing purpose. p. 199

stereotype To evaluate an entire group of people or things according to a perception or an image held, which may be favourable or unfavourable. p. 5

stocks Certificates or book entries representing ownership in a company. p. 272

storing Placing a *record* into storage containers—file folders, drawers, or shelves. p. 180

strategic planning Setting *goals* and objectives for a three- to five-year period; also known as long-range planning. p. 279

stress The body's response to a demand placed upon it. p. 32

subject storage method Arrangement of *records* by their subject. p. 176

substance abuse The use of alcohol or drugs to an extent that is debilitating. p. 46

synergy The ideas and products of a group of people developed through interaction with one another. p. 205

T

tablet computer Commonly shortened to "tablet," a wireless mobile device with a touch screen panel that operates by touch or stylus and keyboard. p. 92

tactical planning Setting *goals* and objectives for a one-year period. p. 279

targeted résumé A *résumé* created specifically for the job that is being applied for. p. 253

team Groups of people who work together and need one another to accomplish a given task. p. 11

telecommunications The electronic transmission of text, data, voice, video, and images (graphics and pictures) from one location to another. p. 91

teleconference A meeting in which more than two individuals at different locations attend and communicate with each other via a telecommunications network; also known as a *conference call*. p. 201

telework The use of *telecommunications* to work from home. p. 6

temporary agency A company that supplies temporary workers to employers. p. 246

time An attribute that cannot be bought, sold, borrowed, rented, saved, or manufactured; it is the only resource that must be spent the minute it is received. p. 23

time management Directing ourselves and our tasks in relation to the *time* we have available in a day, a week, or a year. p. 23

tone An attribute of voice that conveys the attitude or emotional state of the speaker. p. 76

two-factor authentication The use of more than a password to log in, such as a password and a code texted to a smartphone; also known as *two-step verification*. p. 108

U

USB An external port on a computer for connecting peripheral devices. p. 93

useful records *Records* that are useful for the smooth, effective operation of an organization. p. 187

V

values statement An outline of the behaviours and attitudes the organization will abide by when making decisions. p. 7

values The ideas or qualities that people view as important and that determine how they live on a day-to-day basis; for example, knowledge is a value. p. 218

verbal communication The process of exchanging ideas and feelings through the use of words. p. 75

verbatim A word-for-word record of what has been said. p. 212

video conference A meeting in which two or more people at different locations use *telecommunication* technology—computers, video/web cameras, and/or microphones—to participate in a virtual meeting in *real time*. p. 201

virtual assistants Entrepreneurial self-employed freelance *administrative professionals*. pp. 6, 266

virtual office The operational domain of any organization that includes remote workers. p. 6

virtual private network (VPN) A private computer network that is extended across a public network and allows users to work online more securely by using encryption. p. 109

virtual teams Dispersed workers who come together through *telecommunications* technology to accomplish a task. p. 267

visa A document granted by a government abroad that permits a traveller to enter and travel within a country. p. 229

vision statement An organization's roadmap that identifies what the organization wants to become. p. 7

visual aid An object or image that listeners can see and that will help them understand a message. p. 118

vital records *Records* that cannot be replaced and should never be destroyed. p. 187

voice mail or voice messaging An efficient method of managing incoming calls when call recipients are unavailable and when broadcasting messages (sending the same message) to multiple voice mail boxes. p. 107

VoIP (voice over Internet protocol) Software and hardware that allow voice signals to be carried over an IP-based network; also known as *IP telephony*. p. 101

voucher cheque A *cheque* that includes a form for recording the details of the payment. p. 155

W

Web browser Software that provides a way to look at and interact with all the information on the World Wide Web in a single unified interface. p. 94

Web meeting A meeting that uses technology to enable groups of people anywhere in the world to exchange ideas and information via computers and an Internet or LAN connection. p. 202

webcast A type of broadcast that is similar in nature to a television broadcast, except it takes place over the Internet. p. 202

webinar A seminar presented over the Internet. pp. 114, 202

Wiki A website or group of Web pages on which anyone can add, edit, or delete content. p. 98

work ethic An inner drive to work hard and well. p. 13

work periods The time in which work is to be performed, such as a traditional workweek or a schedule involving *flextime*, four-day weeks, job sharing, and *telework*. p. 279

X

Xpresspost A *Canada Post* service that offers next-business-day mail delivery to local or regional destinations and two-day service between most major Canadian locations. p. 140

Index